The Ivory Tower
and Harry Potter

The Ivory Tower
and Harry Potter

Perspectives on a
Literary Phenomenon

Lana A. Whited, Editor

University of Missouri Press

Columbia and London

Copyright © 2002 by
The Curators of the University of Missouri
University of Missouri Press, Columbia, Missouri 65201
Printed and bound in the United States of America
All rights reserved
5   4   3   2   06   05   04   03

Library of Congress Cataloging-in-Publication Data

The ivory tower and Harry Potter : perspectives on a literary phenomenon
  / Lana A. Whited, editor.
        p.   cm.
    Includes bibliographical references and index
    ISBN 0-8262-1443-6
    1. Rowling, J. K.—Characters—Harry Potter.   2. Children's stories,
English—History and criticism.   3. Fantasy fiction, English—History
and criticism.   4. Potter, Harry (Fictitious character)   5. Wizards in literature.   6. Magic in literature.   I. Whited, Lana A., 1958–
    PR6068.093 Z734   2003
    823'.914—dc21   2002012923

♾ ™ This paper meets the requirements of the
American National Standard for Permanence of Paper
for Printed Library Materials, Z39.48, 1984.

Text designer: Elizabeth Young
Jacket designer: Jennifer Cropp
Typesetter: Bookcomp, Inc.
Printer and binder: The Maple-Vail Book Manufacturing Group
Typefaces: Eras, Galliard, Pepita

For all those who help children become readers

Contents

Acknowledgments

Like a Quidditch match, a book requires a good team of people working together in order to achieve a successful result. The most valuable players of my team have been the scholars I am fortunate to have as my teammates and contributors; their work is my Golden Snitch.

Very early in the game, I was lucky to have Julia Grimes Hayes of Catawba College and Karin Westman, then at the College of Charleston, now at Kansas State University, to help me draw up the playbook and select the players for the roster.

I have been fortunate to have a number of Beaters and Chasers who were willing to chase down details and beat inconsistencies out of the manuscript. These players include Denna Austin, George Loveland, Betsy Smith, and Kristina Stump, all of Ferrum College. For sound advice on dodging the legal Bludgers, I am grateful to Cy Dillon of Ferrum College and Sally Wiant of Washington and Lee University, as well as the list members of ChildLit. And I am grateful for the work of Ray East of Charlottesville, Va., the official team photographer.

I am deeply indebted to my colleague Tina Hanlon, my first children's literature coach, who showed me the way to the field when I was an amateur. I was also expertly coached by Clair Willcox, Jane Lago, and John Brenner of the University of Missouri Press. This was my first start in the professional Book Leagues, and Clair, Jane, and John were instrumental in helping me through my rookie season.

Many years ago, my mother, Joan McDavid Whited, took me to the library where my flying lessons began, and she and my father, Paul Whited, and the rest of my family were my constant cheerleaders through all the years of "practice" it took for me to turn professional.

Katherine Grimes simultaneously rode a contributor's broomstick and toiled away back at the castle, allowing me time and space to stay on the field until the match was finished. I am grateful to her for helping me dodge the Bludgers and keep my eyes on the Snitch.

· · ·

"Harry Potter and the Tower of Babel: Translating the Magic" by Nancy K. Jentsch is reprinted with permission from the *Kentucky Philological Review*, where it appeared as "Harry Potter Speaks in Tongues: Translating J. K. Rowling's Magical World" in volume 16.

"Crowning the King: Harry Potter and the Construction of Authority" by Farah Mendlesohn is reprinted with permission from the *Journal of the Fantastic in the Arts*, volume 12, number 3 (fall 2001).

"Harry Potter and the Extraordinariness of the Ordinary" by Roni Natov is reprinted with permission from *The Lion and the Unicorn*, volume 25, number 2 (April 2001).

The Ivory Tower
and Harry Potter

Introduction

Harry Potter

From Craze to Classic?

Lana A. Whited

In June 2000, I was on a Harry Potter panel at the Children's Literature Association (ChLA) conference in Roanoke, Virginia. It was the first such session I'd heard of at a professional conference. I was delivering a paper cowritten with M. Katherine Grimes, and the other presenters were Amanda Cockrell, Roberta Seelinger Trites, and Karin Westman. There must have been a hundred people at the session, and we had to open the doors of our small salon to allow additional chairs to spill out into the lobby. The quality of the other presenters' papers was superb, and the discussion, stimulating. Driving home from the conference, I realized it was time for a collection of critical essays on Harry Potter. This is the book I envisioned that day.

After the conference, I ran the idea by my colleague Tina Hanlon, our moderator in the Harry Potter session, who had pointed me down the path of scholarly approaches to children's literature a few years earlier when I audited her class at Ferrum College. Tina agreed that the book was a good idea and added that I was a lunatic for taking on such a big project. Immediately, I sent out calls for proposals on several listservs, and the response confirmed both my hunch and Tina's. It was clear to me, by August 2000, with only three books by J. K. Rowling on the market, that there was a wealth of serious scholarly interest in Harry Potter.

In the two years that have passed since the ChLA conference, the interest of literature professionals in Harry Potter has only accelerated. Other professional organizations, including the Modern Language Association, have devoted whole sessions to the books at their annual meetings. Despite the fact that J. K. Rowling's agent discourages books about the series, several readers' guides have been published, along with a couple of unauthorized biographies of Rowling herself and collections of children's writing in response to the series.[1] Critical essays on the books are beginning to show

1. In an e-mail to me dated March 6, 2002, a representative of the Christopher Little Agency wrote, "For your information we do not approve companion books based on

1

up in scholarly journals. So the answer to the question of whether Harry will be taken seriously by those within the "Ivory Tower" appears to be a resounding "yes."

Of course, Harry Potter has also captivated the general public. He has become a regular fixture in the popular press, even serving as an occasional muse for the columnists of the *New York Times,* as Philip Nel, author of *J. K. Rowling's Harry Potter Novels,* points out in his essay in this volume. The hoopla about Harry seems to have picked up steam following the publication of *Harry Potter and the Prisoner of Azkaban* in September 1999, with an afternoon release in Great Britain reportedly timed to prevent children from skipping school to buy it. The fanfare surrounding that book's appearance paled in comparison to the appearance of *Harry Potter and the Goblet of Fire,* with an internationally coordinated release on July 8, 2000. Children dressed as Harry and his chums lined up outside bookstores that remained open until the early morning hours to capitalize on the event with Harry Potter parties and healthy sales. In the United States, Scholastic initially printed 3.8 million copies of the book, and 5.3 million copies in the Bloomsbury edition had been sold prior to publication in the United Kingdom. In its first week, *Goblet* sold nearly 3 million copies, breaking all previous publishing records. For the year 2000, Rowling was nineteenth in celebrity earnings in *Forbes* magazine's Celebrity 100 list, two places behind Michael Jordan and just ahead of the Backstreet Boys. She also moved to the top of Great Britain's list of wealthiest women (she was ranked third in 1999). *Forbes* estimates that Rowling earned $36 million in 2000 alone.[2] It is difficult to recall another occasion when the public was so enraptured by an author's work since Americans stood on the wharves of Boston Harbor awaiting the latest installment of Charles Dickens' *The Olde Curiosity Shop.*

Nor did this furor die down quickly. According to *Publisher's Weekly,* nearly 10 million copies of *Harry Potter and the Goblet of Fire* were in print by the time the film version of *Harry Potter and the Sorcerer's Stone* was released in November 2001. Some theatres sold tickets for the film weeks in advance. The same month, Scholastic, Rowling's American publisher, estimated that there were 55 million copies of the first four novels in print in the United States alone. By March 2002, when the VHS and DVD versions of *Harry Potter and the Sorcerer's Stone* were offered for "presale," it shot to the top of Amazon.com's and Barnes&Noble.com's video bestsellers list—nearly three months before copies would actually be available. At the time of

---

the series." Books that have appeared so far are included in the bibliography; see listings for Bill Adler, Ben Buchanan, David Colbert, Lindsey Fraser, Allan Zola Kronzek and Elizabeth Kronzek, Sharon Moore, Philip Nel, Elizabeth D. Schafer, Marc Shapiro, and Sean Smith.

2. "Forbes Celebrity 100"; Nel, *J. K. Rowling's Harry Potter Novels,* 71.

this writing, both booksellers also maintained lists of customers to e-mail when the fifth book in the series, tentatively titled *Harry Potter and the Order of the Phoenix,* appears.

With no new Harry Potter book released in the previous twenty months, by March 2002, Rowling's works were still faring extremely well on bestseller lists. The first three books were among the top five on the *New York Times*'s Children's Bestsellers List—a list created in January 2000 largely to clear the spaces the books had hogged for months on the regular Bestsellers list. *Prisoner of Azkaban* had been on the list for six months, *Chamber of Secrets* for a year and a half, and *Sorcerer's Stone* for a whopping two and a half years. All four books were still in *USA Today*'s top thirty fiction bestsellers, at numbers thirteen (*Chamber of Secrets*), fourteen (*Prisoner of Azkaban*), twenty-one (*Goblet of Fire*), and twenty-nine (*Sorcerer's Stone*). *Chamber, Prisoner,* and *Goblet* were still the top one, two, and three children's selections for Barnes&Noble.com and in the top fifty in general. In addition, *Publisher's Weekly* was listing at number two and number three on its Children's Bestsellers list the companion books *Fantastic Beasts and Where to Find Them* and *Quidditch Through the Ages,* both published by Scholastic in 2001 to benefit the British charity Comic Relief. That even books marketed as footnotes to the Harry Potter series were enjoying a wide audience testifies to the series' phenomenal success.

Several controversies surrounding Harry Potter have helped keep the books in the media. The most prominent of these is the claim of conservative Christians that the books are inappropriate for children. By the time *Harry Potter and the Goblet of Fire* appeared on July 8, 2000, *Newsweek* reported that the series had been "challenged in 25 school districts in at least 17 states." Although the southeastern United States is often stereotyped as its most conservative region, conservative Christians' attacks have not been confined to those states. For example, the books' appropriateness for the classroom was contested before school boards in California, Colorado, Oregon, Nebraska, and other states. Nor have challenges occurred exclusively within the United States. In September 2000, the superintendent of the Durham Regional School Board in Ontario sent to all one hundred elementary schools in his district a memo with strict guidelines about reading Rowling's books in classrooms. Furthermore, Harry is not even safe in his native land; in April 2000, the London *Sunday Times* reported that the books had been banished from the library at St. Mary's Island Church of England primary school in Chatham, Kent. The school's head teacher, Carol Rookwood, said she believes that "devils, demons, and witches are real and pose the same threat as, say, a child molester." Conservative Christians' objections to the Harry Potter books are perhaps best described in specific, unimpassioned terms by Kimbra Wilder Gish in the

May/June 2000 issue of *Horn Book*. Gish, a fifth-generation member of a conservative Christian church, explains that the argument against Harry Potter is based on a literalist interpretation of the Bible and what conservative Christians perceive as Rowling's unflattering depiction of nonmagical people, or "Muggles." It is interesting to note that while Gish articulates the conservative Christian argument, she does not appear to subscribe to it, as she told a Banned Book Week audience in September 2000 that she personally finds Harry Potter "one of the most admirable characters to grace children's literature."[3]

In response to challenges mounted so far, most school boards have reacted less drastically than the St. Mary's School. Some, like administrators in Moorpark, California, have considered complaints, read the book under attack (*Prisoner of Azkaban*) and "decided to allow . . . teachers to use their own discretion when choosing books to read." The more common response is a compromise, with schools providing that pupils whose parents object to Harry can avoid him while other students can read the books or use them for projects. The Ontario school board, for example, instituted a policy that any teacher reading from a Harry Potter book in class must have the written permission of all students' parents. A similar policy in the Douglas County School District near Denver mandates that parents be notified before Rowling's books are read as a part of the curriculum. In the case of the Oregon complaint, one child was allowed to go to the library while his teacher read Harry Potter to the class.[4] These discussions among parents, teachers, and administrators have been very public, and it is reasonable to assume that the controversy itself has probably drawn Rowling some readers eager to see what all the fuss is about.

A second controversy that kept Harry Potter and his creator in the spotlight is the legal battle that ensued when writer Nancy Stouffer brought charges against Rowling in fall 1999. According to a document drafted by her former attorney, Stouffer contacted Scholastic in late summer 1999 about resemblances between J. K. Rowling's work and her own, including *Rah* (1987) and other works involving characters named Larry Potter, his friend Lilly, and creatures called "muggles." Representatives for both authors met in New York that fall to discuss Stouffer's claims. Just before Thanksgiving that year, Rowling, Scholastic, and Time-Warner Entertainment (holder of film rights) asked a judge to dismiss Stouffer's claim, arguing that she had misrepresented her own intellectual property. Stouffer's

3. Malcolm Jones, "Why Harry's Hot"; Peter Kuitenbrouwer and Shannon Black, "School Board Puts Limits on Harry Potter Books Due to 'Magic' "; India Knight, "The Trouble with Harry"; Kimbra Wilder Gish, "Hunting Down Harry Potter"; Associated Press, "Harry Potter Banned."
4. Sylvia L. Oliande, "Harry Potter Books OK'd for Simi Schools"; Kuitenbrouwer and Black, "School Board"; Bruce H. Caughey, Letter to the Editor; Associated Press, "Harry Potter Banned."

attorney answered with several counterclaims against Rowling et al., including federal trademark and copyright infringement and "injury to business reputation." On December 5, 2000, Judge Allen G. Schwartz dismissed all charges except copyright and trademark infringement, and Stouffer dropped similar charges in Pennsylvania.[5]

After Schwartz's ruling, the case virtually disappeared from U.S. media, and Stouffer told me on March 17, 2002, that the public probably assumed the dispute was resolved. She also alleged that her scheduled television interviews regarding the lawsuit were canceled due to pressure from Rowling's attorneys or Time-Warner. Stouffer said the case was nearing the end of the discovery phase, with Arthur Levine and J. K. Rowling to be deposed that month. She expected a trial date to be set. Stouffer said she regarded her legal battle as a referendum on intellectual property law and vowed to see the case through, despite claiming to have received death threats.[6]

Rowling and her representatives refused to comment publicly on Stouffer's charges but continued to fight them. In mid-June, Rowling's attorneys requested dismissal of the copyright infringement claim, arguing that Stouffer fabricated evidence. For example, "an expert on printing technology" found that a copy of the *Rah* book dated 1987 and bearing the title *The Legend of Rah and the Muggles* used fonts not available until the early 1990s. Intending to demonstrate her books' circulation, Stouffer also introduced shipping invoices later determined to be invalid. As a direct result of problems with Stouffer's evidence, Judge Schwartz granted Rowling's motion for summary judgment on September 17, 2002, and the matter was formally resolved. He fined Stouffer fifty thousand dollars for fraud and ordered her to reimburse Rowling for attorneys' fees incurred in defending herself against the original claim. In this decision, Schwartz, said, "Stouffer has engaged in a pattern of intentional bad faith conduct and failed to correct her fraudulent submissions, even when confronted with evidence undermining the validity of those submissions."[7]

A flurry of news from Rowling followed the verdict. More than two years had passed without the appearance of book five, reportedly titled *Harry Potter and the Order of the Phoenix,* spurring rumors that Rowling suffered from writer's block. Online booksellers began offering the book for pre-sale in spring 2002, but in September, no publication date had been announced. The week of the verdict, Rowling gave several interviews. On September 20, the *Evening Standard* of London reported that Rowling was pregnant

5. *Scholastic, Inc., et al. v. Nancy Stouffer* (August and December 2000); Kevin R. Casey, "Case Summary: Perseverance Pays?"; David Kirkpatrick, "Of Muggles and Lawyers."

6. Nancy K. Stouffer, telephone interview with the editor.

7. "Muggle Court to Decide: Who Conjured Boy Wizard?"; *Scholastic, Inc. v. Nancy Stouffer* (September 2002).

and that book five "may well be on sale in time for Christmas after all."
Rowling said she is simply a perfectionist who pores over her manuscripts.
While Stouffer's claims were pending, Rowling and her advisers never indicated that they felt seriously threatened; however, it seems reasonable that
an attorney might counsel an author facing copyright infringement claims
over four books not to publish a fifth that might also be subject to legal
action. Whether or not her attorneys counseled her to delay the fifth book,
the litigation apparently distracted Rowling, who, after the verdict, told a
reporter, "There have been times when I've been writing and [the case has]
been uppermost in my mind, whereas what should have been uppermost in
my mind is what's going on with Harry and Co."[8]

In addition to these very prominent controversies, considerable space in
the mainstream media and in forums for literature professionals has been
devoted to questions of the Harry Potter books' literary merit. The publication of *Harry Potter and the Prisoner of Azkaban* accelerated the status of
the Harry Potter series as public craze, and *Prisoner of Azkaban*'s reception
also signaled an increase in Rowling's stock with some literary critics. This
is not to suggest that *Harry Potter and the Philosopher's/Sorcerer's Stone* and
Harry Potter and the Chamber of Secrets had arrived without notice. The former received several awards, including the British Book Awards' Children's
Book of the Year. *Harry Potter and the Sorcerer's Stone* was recognized with
an ABBY award from the American Booksellers Association, and the recording, narrated by Jim Dale, was nominated for a Grammy (in 2001, Dale won
a Grammy for his reading of *Harry Potter and the Goblet of Fire*). *Harry Potter and the Chamber of Secrets* won many of the same awards, including BBA
Book of the Year.[9] But *Harry Potter and the Prisoner of Azkaban* took the
argument about Rowling's literary merit to another level when it was nominated for the Whitbread Book of the Year prize in Great Britain, competing
with Nobel laureate Seamus Heaney's new translation of *Beowulf.* Heaney
won, and *Prisoner* was, instead, named Whitbread Children's Book of the
Year (Rowling received £10,000 to Heaney's £21,000). The Whitbread
committee's decision was controversial for the same reason as the *New York
Times*'s establishment of a separate Children's Best Sellers list around the
same time (January 2000). It raised the question of whether a book marketed primarily for young readers but also successful with adults is a less
laudable achievement than a successful book targeted primarily at adults.
Children's literature scholars sensed the recurrence of a long-standing prejudice, the notion that even a highly regarded and phenomenally successful
children's book could not be measured against critically acclaimed books
for adults.

8. Rob McNeil, "Baby on way for J. K. Rowling"; David Lee, "Slow Spell the Work
of Legal Muggles and Not Writer's Block, Claims Potter Author."
9. Nel, *J. K. Rowling's Harry Potter Novels,* 72–73.

This prejudice is clearly stated by William Safire of the *New York Times,* in a January 2000 column expressing relief at the Whitbread committee's selection and conceding that Rowling "deserves the lesser award she received for best children's book." Safire endorses another critic's remark that awarding the prize to *Harry Potter and the Prisoner of Azkaban* would have constituted "the infantilization of adult culture, the loss of a sense of what a classic really is." "Prizeworthy culture [Harry Potter] ain't," Safire declares, "and more than a little is a waste of adult time." Oddly, Safire seems to have considered it a waste of his time to read the book actually under consideration by the Whitbread committee; instead, he admits, he read only *Harry Potter and the Sorcerer's Stone.*[10] This is tantamount to offering an opinion about *Adventures of Huckleberry Finn* on the basis of having read *Tom Sawyer.*

What might provoke a writer of Safire's stature to take such an unfortunate stance? I suspect that the Harry Potter books' unprecedented success has been both a blessing and a curse. A fairly common critical stereotype is the notion that works of great literary or artistic value do not enjoy commercial success. This is a stereotype, not a prejudice, because it has some basis in fact. Books by John Grisham, Stephen King, and Jan Karon do very well on bestseller lists, but they do not win major literary awards. However, some critics extrapolate from this stereotype the notion that commercial success and literary value are mutually exclusive at worst or inversely proportional at best. James M. Cain's fine novel *The Postman Always Rings Twice* was undervalued as an expression of naturalism during Cain's lifetime, largely because the success of the Hollywood film version led some to believe Cain was just out for profit. The recent controversy stemming from Jonathan Franzen's refusal to let Oprah Winfrey name his novel *The Corrections* a book club selection probably resulted from the same flawed assumption. After all, Winfrey chose Nobel laureate Toni Morrison's *Song of Solomon* for her first book club selection. Of course, enduring literary value cannot be assigned by referendum, but occasionally, the general reading public does recognize a book of quality. In fact, in its "Books of 2001" round-up, *Time* noted that Franzen's book was a "rare . . . mix of high literary ambitions with reader friendliness." Certainly commercial success or commodification can interfere with the process of assessing a work's true merit, as Jack Zipes has pointed out in relation to the Harry Potter books: "I am certain that the phenomenal aspect of the reception of the Harry Potter books has blurred the focus for anyone who wants to take literature for young people seriously and who may be concerned about standards and taste that adults create for youth culture in the West. How is it possible to evaluate a work of literature

---

10. William Safire, "Besotted with Potter."

like a Harry Potter novel when it is so dependent on the market conditions of the culture industry?"[11]

The Harry Potter books fail the test of what constitutes a classic, Safire argues, because they are "not written on two levels, entertaining one generation while instructing another." He cites as examples of such dual-level narratives *Adventures of Huckleberry Finn* ("it uses the device of a boy's coming of age to illuminate a nation's painful transformation"), *Alice in Wonderland* (Lewis Carroll "dealt with madness and injustice in this world by mocking a parallel world") and *The Wonderful Wizard of Oz* (a "children's fantasy, complete with a Wicked Witch of the West, [which] dealt deftly with heartlessness, mindlessness, and cowardice").[12] It is a shame that Safire did not make it to the third Harry Potter book, for it satisfies the columnist's criteria far better than either book one or book two. In *Harry Potter and the Prisoner of Azkaban,* our young hero is confronted with choices that average children do not have to contemplate, foremost among them the opportunity to exact revenge on the person who betrayed his parents and thereby precipitated their deaths. Harry passes on this opportunity, reasoning that James Potter would not want his son and his old friends to become killers for his sake. The decisive scene of *Prisoner of Azkaban* is very similar in substance and tone to Huck Finn's famous "crisis of conscience," when, faced with the dilemma of turning in the runaway slave Jim or protecting Jim and going to hell, he declares, "All right then, I'll go to hell." Harry does not face the same risk Huck perceives, but his decision, like Huck's, is one of high moral seriousness; a child reader will not fully appreciate the moral reasoning Harry exhibits, nor would some adult readers. In addition, in a culture with stigmatizing diseases such as AIDS, the subplot in *Prisoner of Azkaban* involving Remus Lupin, a professor ostracized by the wizarding society due to his condition as a werewolf, has resonances that a juvenile reader may miss. (Philip Nel, author of *J. K. Rowling's Harry Potter Novels* and a contributor to this volume, argues that Rowling's characterization of Lupin was heavily influenced by her mother's bout with multiple sclerosis.)[13] In the staging of the Quidditch World Cup and the International Triwizard Tournament in *Harry Potter and the Goblet of Fire,* Rowling introduces questions of nationalism and cultural stereotyping that are universal and now, in the wake of recent terrorist activities and the U.S. military response, more timely than ever. These themes in the third and fourth books are meaningful to adult readers, while children may be more preoccupied with Harry's use of the top-secret Marauder's Map to sneak into Hogsmeade, Hermione's use of the Time-Turner to rescue the

11. "Books: Best of 2001"; Jack Zipes, "The Phenomenon of Harry Potter, or Why All the Talk?" 171–72.

12. Safire, "Adult Fare."

13. Nel, *J. K. Rowling's Harry Potter Novels,* 15.

Hippogriff Buckbeak, the details of the various tests Harry faces as Hogwarts champion, and (for teen readers) Harry's and his friends' preliminary interest in members of the opposite sex. Clearly, as M. Katherine Grimes argues, the books function on more than one level. Even in the book Safire read, *Harry Potter and the Sorcerer's Stone,* the desirability of immortality is questioned—clearly an issue more meaningful to adults than to children.

Perhaps William Safire found the merit of the Harry Potter books "blurred" by their commercial success, as Jack Zipes warns. I am convinced, however, that literary scholars can see past the distraction of the books' commodification to accomplish the sort of thorough analysis the series begs. An assessment of the lasting literary value of Rowling's books involves more than Safire's question of multilevel themes. Surely any books that will be deemed "classics" must reflect something about the values of the age and society that produce them. They must conjure a real world or one that parallels the real world in intriguing ways. They must use language in a way that calls readers' attention to language itself and to how language reflects culture and cultural values. They must have some roots or branches in familiar forms, genres, or subgenres of literature and folklore and yet not be purely derivative. I hope the essays contained in this volume will lay the groundwork for a discussion of how all these criteria apply to J. K. Rowling's Harry Potter novels past and future.

A significant portion of the book is devoted to examination of Harry's literary ancestors. Among these are other works about the British boarding school, the best-known of which is *Tom Brown's School Days.* Several contributors to the volume attempt to locate the Potter series within the subgenre of magic and fantasy. In particular, Harry Potter is descended from a tradition of books about the education of young wizards, including Ursula K. Le Guin's *Earthsea* trilogy, Monica Furlong's *Wise Child,* Jill Murphy's *Worst Witch* books, and Anthony Horowitz's *Groosham Grange;* the Murphy and Horowitz works are also set in boarding schools. In addition, the Potter series shares similarities with Diana Wynne Jones's *Chrestomanci* books, recently reissued with the words "Hotter than Potter" stamped on their covers. Contributors also discuss Rowling's employment of epic conventions for the series' plot and themes, as well as the author's characterization of Harry as epic hero. In addition, Rowling's use of folkloric elements and devices, such as taboo themes and reversals, is explored in detail, particularly in the context of how these aspects increase the series' appeal for children.

Even before Rowling's *Harry Potter and the Goblet of Fire* made its much-heralded appearance in July 2000, the first three books in the series had been translated into nearly three dozen languages. In addition, the books have been issued in several English-language editions, including U.S. editions responsible for about 70 percent of worldwide sales and two British editions, one for children and one for adults.[14] As one of the books' most striking features is Rowling's linguistic inventiveness, a number of issues involving language have been raised by the books' global popularity. One of those issues is the translation into other languages of names invented by Rowling and terminology she coined specifically for the books, as well as translators' handling of problems raised by formal and informal forms of address not present in English. Another issue involves Scholastic's transformation of expressions common in British English into American English vocabulary in U.S. versions, particularly in the case of *Harry Potter and the Philosopher's/Sorcerer's Stone*. These knotty linguistic matters are examined in the volume, in the context of whether translations from one language to another and substitutions within English versions render the books more accessible for a broad range of readers or constitute acts of cultural bias.

At least two essays deal with the issue of how the books engage readers, including readers of differing ages and reading experience. One of the most remarkable aspects of the Harry Potter phenomenon is the books' appropriation by adolescent boys, not traditionally a large presence in the reading market. One contributor examines this phenomenon in the context of the "boys' book" market. Another contributor analyzes gender dynamics within the books from the standpoint of contemporary feminist literary theory, focusing on the character of Hermione Granger. This essay includes discussion of Hermione's literary predecessors, including characters in *Andromache* and D. H. Lawrence's *Women in Love,* as well as the Christian Bible's St. Hermione.

Several other studies of the books' cultural impact and their reflection of societal values are included. One examines the fan communities that have developed as a result of the books' popularity, with special emphasis on Harry Potter web sites, including the very recent controversy over Warner Brothers' stern reprobation of children and teens who maintain these sites. Other essays examine the series' commodification, including the extent to which the books themselves have become commodities, and the commercialization of Harry Potter, including the film version of *Harry Potter and the Sorcerer's Stone* released in November 2001. In spite of Rowling's fabulous financial success, one contributor argues that the Harry Potter books have a distinctly antimaterialistic theme. Another essay examines the moral order presented in Rowling's books, with the author arguing that Harry's decisions reflect liberal intent and morality, despite the essentially conservative and autocratic structure of his environment.

The jury is still out on whether the Harry Potter books will, in the long run, be regarded as classics, occupying a permanent place in the literary canon, or be viewed as merely a phenomenal publishing success. In

14. Helen M. Jerome, "Welcome Back, Potter," 41, 44.

other words, it remains to be seen whether history regards the chief distinction of the Harry Potter books as cultural or commercial. Rowling herself appears to be very seriously attempting a literary achievement, but recent actions by her promoters could actually undermine her efforts. To date, those involved in marketing Harry Potter have discouraged endeavors by both fans and scholars. For example, in December 2000, a fifteen-year-old British girl named Claire Field who maintained a fan site called *The Boy Who Lived* received what a *Boston Globe* editorial termed "a terse, pro-forma copyright protection letter" from attorneys at Warner Brothers, which owns, according to the *Globe,* "all things Potter." Warner Brothers' letter, according to the Globe, asked Field to turn over her domain name (www.harrypotterguide.co.uk) because it could "cause consumer confusion or dilution of the intellectual property." Youngsters with similar sites and similar letters were said by the *Globe* to be "scared to death."[15]

Quickly, an online community emerged for the support of young webmasters who received similar letters. This effort, called "The Defense Against the Dark Arts Project" (DADA), was jointly spearheaded by two webmasters who did not receive Warner Brothers' letters: sixteen-year-old Heather Lawver of Reston, Virginia, and Alastair Alexander, thirty-three, of London. According to the DADA web sites (www.dprophet.com/dada), Lawver and Alexander called for a complete boycott of Warner Brothers, including Harry Potter tie-in merchandise and the film *Harry Potter and the Sorcerer's Stone.* In February 2001, Lawver sent press releases about the DADA project to national media organizations in the United States and the United Kingdom. According to Alexander's web site (www.PotterWar.org.uk), by mid-March, Warner Brothers announced that it would take no further action against Claire Field or anyone else who had received a letter. Alexander says that Warner Brothers did not expediently clarify this position to all the young webmasters they had previously targeted and that one young man permanently lost his domain name. In his book on Rowling's novels, Philip Nel reports that "Following an exchange of correspondence," the matter was "resolved to the satisfaction of both parties." (This characterization of the resolution was suggested to Nel by Warner Brothers prior to the publication of his book.)[16]

Then, just a few weeks before I handed over the final manuscript of this book to my publisher and in response to a general request for permissions, I received an e-mail message from Neil Blair at the Christopher Little Agency, the firm that represents J. K. Rowling, cautioning me that I should reconsider my proposed title, "Harry Potter and the Ivory Tower," and provide

15. "Harry and the Web Wars," E6.
16. Heather Lawver and Alastair Alexander, *Defense against the Dark Arts;* Alexander, "A Brief History of PotterWar"; Nel, *J. K. Rowling's Harry Potter Novels,* 79; Nel, e-mail to the editor.

"an appropriate disclaimer." Otherwise, Blair wrote, "an unsuspecting 7 or 8 year old could easily see the title and believe it to be another book in the series (or at the very least a book approved by JK Rowling)."[17] I liked the way my title mimicked the names of the Harry Potter novels, and I felt that, as "ivory tower" was a common phrase used to describe the academic community, as the book would be listed by booksellers under my name, not J. K. Rowling's, and as I had furthermore appended a subtitle in a conscious effort to distinguish the book from one of Rowling's, confusion could be averted. The entirety of Mr. Blair's correspondence with me was courteous and professional. I never felt I was being threatened, merely advised. Although I think that only someone who isn't reading very closely could take this volume for a Harry Potter novel, and I don't think the seven- or eight-year-olds Mr. Blair fears for should be purchasing books without their parents' involvement, I do believe that Mr. Blair's central concern has validity. So after a few days' deliberation and consultation with experts in copyright and trademark law, I elected to change my title from *Harry Potter and the Ivory Tower* to *The Ivory Tower and Harry Potter.* I was neither completely satisfied nor devastated by this turn of events. For a few days, I joked about calling it "the book which must not be named." Ultimately, what seems more significant to me than the issue of my own title is the commodification of the Harry Potter property that my correspondence with Neil Blair represents.

Culture and commerce are strange bedfellows. The credo of "art for art's sake" is as distant as any I can imagine from the modern media conglomerate with which J. K. Rowling now must deal. Books that become classics may inspire film versions, but they do not usually engender hordes of plastic tie-in merchandise or miniature "character collectibles" distributed by fast-food restaurants. Imagine Huckleberry Finn's face on a soft drink can, Moby Dick as an action figure sold in discount stores, a computer game based on *Romeo and Juliet* that invites players to designate themselves "Capulets" or "Montagues." The point is that the serious discussion we ought to be having about the literary merits of J. K. Rowling's Harry Potter novels is threatened by the cloud of commercialism encircling the books. And the Potter-pushers, those who promote the commodification of Harry Potter, in their attempt to micromanage Harry's every appearance on a web site, on film, in paint, on plastic, or in a scholarly book, impose an impediment over which their client, J. K. Rowling, will have to leap on her way to the permanent canon of literature.

17. Neil Blair, e-mail to the editor.

1

Harry's Cousins in the Magical Realm

Harry Potter and the Secret Password

Finding Our Way in the Magical Genre

Amanda Cockrell

Since the publication of his first adventure, Harry Potter has caused more disagreement both among parents and others who decide what children ought to be reading, and among the scholars I have talked to, than any other children's book in recent memory. This may be because J. K. Rowling has done something new and bent a number of the "rules" of the fantastic.

To begin with, she has departed from the imaginary into the real. She has abandoned the realm of high fantasy and laid her story in contemporary England, rather than in the imaginary and medievally flavored otherworlds of Middle Earth or Earthsea, or even the world of Alan Garner's *The Owl Service* where the magic is a remnant, a revenant, of ancient and powerful myth. There are no swords in this sorcery. Rowling suggests the existence of witches and wizards in the world we inhabit here and now in a way that is disturbing to those who like their world to stay still.

In Harry's world, very little stays still. The subjects in photographs and oil paintings move about, the latter occasionally leaving their frames entirely to visit other artwork. The setting for most of the books' action, Hogwarts School of Witchcraft and Wizardry, is enchanted so that it cannot be plotted on a map, and its architecture is unstable: "There were a hundred and forty-two staircases at Hogwarts: wide, sweeping ones; narrow, rickety ones; some that led somewhere different on a Friday; some with a vanishing step halfway up that you had to remember to jump" (*Sorcerer's Stone,* 131). It is as if Rowling is saying to her reader from the start: Don't count on anything staying still. Don't count on things being what you're used to, or even what you might approve of.

In this world, magic is part of everyday life, unseen by the Muggles, but practiced with casual cheerfulness by all those who understand it. There are no quests for magic rings or dragon feathers. This is contemporary England, and instead we find bankers and government bureaucracy. People, even magical ones, have to get jobs. But across everything is the veil of magic, the overlay that skews the world we know and brings us up, surprised, on startling perspectives. Ron Weasley's older brother Charlie is studying dragons in Romania, and his stuffy brother Percy lands a job with the Ministry of Magic, where he worries about standardizing the thickness of cauldron bottoms. Their brother Bill works for a goblin bank. The goblins who manage Gringotts Bank are among Rowling's best inventions:

> A pair of goblins bowed them through the silver doors and they were in a vast marble hall. About a hundred more goblins were sitting on high stools behind a long counter, scribbling in large ledgers, weighing coins in brass scales, examining precious stones through eyeglasses. . . . Griphook held the door open for them. . . . They were in a narrow stone passageway lit with flaming torches. It sloped steeply downward and there were little railway tracks on the floor. Griphook whistled and a small cart came hurtling up the tracks toward them. They climbed in . . . and were off.
> . . . [they] . . . hurtled through a maze of twisting passages. . . . The rattling cart seemed to know its own way, because Griphook wasn't steering. (*Sorcerer's Stone*, 73–74)

Even small things are told again and told slant-appropriately: the wizards' shopping district where Harry buys his wand and robes is called Diagon Alley. Messages are delivered by owls. Letters from home may contain a Howler, an audible missive that permits a hapless student's mother to yell at him or her from a sheet of paper that cannot be suppressed until it is quite finished.

To catch a train to Hogwarts School, one goes to platform number nine and three-quarters, which, like Brigadoon, exists only at certain times and is reached by walking straight through the wall between platforms nine and ten. On the train Harry buys food for the journey—chocolate frogs and Bertie Bott's Every Flavor Beans, a chancy confection that means what it says: along with the lime and grape, you are just as likely to get spinach and tripe.

Good does not always win in Harry Potter's world, and indeed the ending of the fourth book, *Harry Potter and the Goblet of Fire,* which Rowling has called pivotal to the series, leaves us with one character dead and the reader uncertain that good will win even in the end. But against this sometimes queasy shifting of the ground, Rowling manages something else unusual in a tale with as dark a theme as hers: she is funny.

At Hogwarts School, History of Magic, a required course, is taught by a ghost, and other ghosts stroll the halls, including Nearly Headless Nick, whose fifteenth-century execution was slightly botched. Harry Potter's fight against the evil unleashed by Lord Voldemort is every bit as serious as Ged's battles with the dark side of magic in Ursula K. Le Guin's *Earthsea* series, but the Harry Potter books' goofily skewed reality is sometimes so funny that we forget that, and then we are brought up short, heart pounding, on the precipice again.

The juxtaposition of schoolboy humor with the battle against the darkness is a disturbing notion in itself, arguing an ambiguity that is rare in children's fantasy. It is only in part the belonging of the hero to the world of magic that has upset those who find Harry a dangerous advertisement for tinkering with the occult. Conservative parents may also view with suspicion a fight against evil that employs humor as well as a few characters who are neither wholly bad nor wholly good and don't seem to know which side they are on. Given the magical element as well, a charge of Satanism is probably to be expected in our current state of hysteria. (A Roanoke, Virginia, policeman recently told my son that his Frisbee, which bore a peace sign, was satanic. It looked like horns, he said, holding it upside down.)

Other more educated adults, such as William Safire, are outraged at the number of adults who are reading Harry Potter for their own enjoyment and possible enlightenment.[1] Safire devoted a whole column in January 2000 to fuming that grown people are reading a children's book. His rather circular argument was that children's books, as everyone knows, are without the depth and texture and serious messages of good adult fiction—except, of course, for his favorites, *Huckleberry Finn, The Wizard of Oz,* and *Alice in Wonderland,* which aren't really children's books at all, because he likes them and they have depth and texture.

Despite such disapproval, Harry has been on the bestseller list, has been the subject of intense media hype, has been licensed for screen adaptation and action figures. There is a reason for that: children love him. Rowling's books are consistently outselling everything else on the horizon, and parent after parent reports that nine-year-old boys (and girls) who "didn't read" are reading. From the child's-eye view, then, Rowling is doing something right, and children do, in the lump, tend to know what is good. As Le Guin points out in her essay "Dreams Must Explain Themselves" in *The Language of the Night,* of *course* it's simple to write for children:

> All you do is take the sex out, and use little short words, and little dumb ideas, and don't be too scary, and be sure there's a happy ending. Right? Nothing to it. . . .
> If you do all that, you might even write *Jonathan Livingston Seagull* and make twenty billion dollars and have every adult in America reading your book.
> But you won't have every kid in America reading your book. They will look at it, and they will see straight through it, with their clear, cold, beady little eyes, and they will put it down, and they will go away. Kids will devour vast

---

1. William Safire, "Adult Fare Harry Potter Is Not."

amounts of garbage (and it is good for them) but they are not like adults: they have not yet learned to eat plastic.[2]

R. H. W. Dillard once told a Hollins College class in children's literature that *"Peter Rabbit* is a book that grows in richness with every reading, but *War and Peace* is only good the first time through." There is actually a lot in that. *Peter Rabbit* is about as mythic as you can get. He misbehaves in the garden, is pursued by the avenging angel in the form of Mr. MacGregor with a rake, loses his shoes, begins to run on four legs the way he was intended, and is again caught by the buttons on his jacket. (Rabbits don't need jackets any more than people need giant-screen televisions and cell phones.) At the urging of benevolent winged creatures, he sheds the jacket, only to experience flood next, in the form of the watering can. He avoids predatory beasts and makes a final run to freedom. Then he pays for the error of his ways with a stomachache and camomile tea.

Far from being simple, *Peter Rabbit* is about life and death, about the monster in the beautiful garden and the possibility of ending up as stew. *Harry Potter* is about the monsters within and without the self. Like Peter, Harry strays from the normal world into a frightening place that his family has warned him away from. In Harry's case, however, he proves to belong to that place despite its dangers, to be its natural child.

A few scholars of children's literature, on the other hand, while they would most certainly argue with Safire's contentions, have been conditioned to view what is immensely (and recently) popular as shallow and dreadful—a not surprising result of the commercial popularity of series such as *Goosebumps* and *Sweet Valley High* (although I might argue that those have their cultural significance, and one day we will study them as we now study Nancy Drew).

In any case, we are all preconditioned to see anything vastly popular as probably not much good. Since Harry Potter is considerably harder to read and requires more taxing thought than these popular series (the fourth book is 734 pages long) and children devour him anyway, we could make an argument that they are finding more than easy escapism in his doings. I think we need to take a deeper look into Harry Potter, who is deeper than we think.

To begin with, Harry Potter is not the lightweight imitation of such serious high fantasy as *A Wizard of Earthsea* or *The Lord of the Rings,* but a legitimate descendant of the darker and more complicated form of the school story, such as Rudyard Kipling's *Stalky and Co.*

Stalky and his classmates are bound for careers in the British Army, Harry and his for careers in the world of wizardry. On their way they indulge in

2. Ursula K. Le Guin, *The Language of the Night,* 49.

similar rivalries between houses (dormitories), and illicit excursions about the school at night. Where Stalky and his companions Beetle and M'Turk spend their time outwitting Foxy, the school Sergeant whose "business was to wear tennis-shoes, carry binoculars, and swoop hawk-like upon evil boys," Harry and his friends Hermione Granger and Ron Weasley, on similar illegal outings, must evade Argus Filch, the Hogwarts caretaker, and his possibly telepathic cat Mrs. Norris.[3] Stalky and his study-mates revenge themselves for unfair treatment by a master, King, with the weapons they find at hand—a dead cat surreptitiously placed under the floorboards of his house—and are ultimately set on the path to adulthood by a benevolent headmaster. Harry is regarded with suspicion and outright dislike by Professor Snape, head of the rival Slytherin House, for reasons outside Harry's understanding, but is able to evade him with a cloak of invisibility, given him by his own headmaster, and a magical map.

Like Stalky, Harry is outside, and at times almost outcast from, the main body of the school, because he is—and masters as well as students know this—different. Neither abides by any but the most important of the rules of the school, and by their very rebellion prove their mettle. Both are chastised by headmasters who are secretly grooming them for a future success that they do not expect of their other pupils. Both are regarded with wary respect or jealousy by their peers for their very capacity for rule-breaking. They are those rule-breakers, crafty and dangerous in their own right, that Joseph Campbell maintains dance on the hero's edge of neuroticism because they must travel over new ground with no public mythology to guide them:

> They've moved out of the society that would have protected them, and into the dark forest, into the world of fire, of original experience. Original experience has not been interpreted for you, and so you've got to work out your life for yourself. Either you can take it or you can't. You don't have to go far off the interpreted path to find yourself in very difficult situations. The courage to face the trials and to bring a whole new body of possibilities into the field of interpreted experience for other people to experience—that is the hero's deed.[4]

Harry, orphaned when his parents were killed by Voldemort, an evil wizard whose name most legitimate witches and wizards are afraid even to speak, is famous for having survived the attack. By rights, Voldemort should have killed him too, but did not—and furthermore, Voldemort hasn't been heard from since, and general opinion holds that the infant Harry was somehow able to contain or destroy him, although Harry does not remember it

---

3. Rudyard Kipling, *Stalky and Co.,* 1.
4. Joseph Campbell, *The Power of Myth,* 41.

and has no idea how. Nevertheless, Harry retains the mark of the experience, a lightning-shaped scar on his forehead, and an unconscious facility with magic that is beyond his years and may somehow have actually been imparted by Voldemort. He proves, for instance, to be a Parselmouth, one who can speak to snakes, a talent regarded as rather sinister by most wizards.

Early in the first book, Harry learns that his magical wand and Voldemort's are twins, each containing a feather from the tail of the same phoenix. "The wand chooses the wizard," Mr. Ollivander (Maker of Fine Wands since 382 B.C.) tells him. "I think we must expect great things from you, Mr. Potter. . . . After all, He-Who-Must-Not-Be-Named did great things—terrible, yes, but great" (*Sorcerer's Stone*, 85).

Harry remains paired with Voldemort for reasons that Voldemort understands better than Harry. "There are strange likenesses between us, after all," he tells Harry. "Even you must have noticed. Both half-bloods, orphans, raised by Muggles [nonmagical folk]. Probably the only two Parselmouths to come to Hogwarts since the great Slytherin himself. We even look something alike . . ." (*Chamber of Secrets*, 317).

Voldemort is Harry's shadow side, his dark twin, and Harry must meet and defeat him as Le Guin's Ged must meet and acknowledge his shadow. In "The Child and the Shadow" in *The Language of the Night*, Le Guin talks about that idea:

> The shadow is the other side of our psyche, the dark brother of the conscious mind. It is Cain, Caliban, Frankenstein's monster, Mr. Hyde. It is Vergil, who guided Dante through hell, Gilgamesh's friend Enkidu, Frodo's enemy Gollum. . . . The shadow stands on the threshold between the conscious and the unconscious mind, and we meet it in our dreams, as sister, brother, friend, beast, monster, enemy, guide. It is all we don't want to, can't, admit into our conscious self, all the qualities and tendencies within us which have been repressed, denied, or not used. . . . Jung himself said, "Everyone carries a shadow, and the less it is embodied in the individual's conscious life, the blacker and denser it is." The less you look at it, in other words, the stronger it grows, until it can become a menace, an intolerable load, a threat within the soul.[5]

And it is in adolescence, argues Le Guin, that the child begins to see his or her own shadow and to

> take responsibility for his or her acts and feelings. And with that responsibility may come a terrible load of guilt. The adolescent shadow often appears as much blacker, more wholly evil, than it is. The only way for the youngster to get past the paralyzing self-blame and self-disgust of this stage is to really look at that shadow, to face it, warts and fangs and pimples and claws and all—to accept it as the self—as *part* of the self. The ugliest part, but not the weakest.

5. Le Guin, *Language*, 59.

For the shadow is the guide. The guide inward and out again; downward and up again; there, as Bilbo the Hobbit said, and back again. The guide of the journey of self-knowledge, to adulthood, to the light.[6]

As Harry progresses through adolescence, with Voldemort for his shadow guide, he tackles the things that most adolescents, his readers, are confronting on their own: the jealousy of friends, emerging sexuality, the desire to belong to the tribe of his peers, to separate himself from the adult authorities of his childhood. All these things become tied to his need to confront and subdue Voldemort.

Similarly, Voldemort must defeat Harry if he is to regain his powers, if the shadow is to subdue the Self. In the fourth book Voldemort uses Harry's blood to regain a human (or semi-human) body. As a result, just as Voldemort is in some sense Harry's father, having inadvertently bestowed on him his extraordinary powers, Harry is Voldemort's in the unwilling gift of blood. It is this kinship with Voldemort that Harry strives throughout the series to break, and to find his own true family. Thus, while *Harry Potter* is a hero tale of the adolescent's journey to selfhood, it is also a tale of the search for family and belonging.

When his parents are killed, Harry is sent to live with his aunt and uncle, who are Muggles. The Dursleys are wonderful parodies of every child's most awful relatives: the brother-in-law who thinks you ought to go to military school, the aunt who disapproves loudly of your hair and skirt length. Imagine being sent to *live* with these people. They make Harry sleep in a closet under the stairs.

To the reader, the Dursleys represent not only every child's dreadful kin, his or her own potential wicked stepmother, but also the child's own real parents when those parents are being "unfair." The Dursleys dislike, and are afraid of, everything magical. (Terrified that their relatives will find out Harry is a wizard, they tell them that he attends a reform school instead.) In this they echo readers' parents, disapproving of adolescent friends, music, or clothes. For Harry, the average child's resentful wish for super powers like those of his favorite cartoon heroes is granted. But there is a catch. It is not all as easy as it might have looked. He is sent to Hogwarts School of Witchcraft and Wizardry, where he indeed finds people like himself, but also discovers that magic is not super powers but a science to be learned. It is dangerous in the wrong or inexperienced hands.

At Hogwarts, Harry finds his friends, a world of school cliques and secret passwords automatically familiar to any but the home-schooled, and even temporary surrogate parents in the Weasleys, a cheerful household of wizards whose large, affectionate family represents what Harry has longed

6. Ibid., 61.

for and been denied. He studies Charms, Herbology, Defense Against the Dark Arts, and Care of Magical Creatures. Entrance to the student common room in Gryffindor Tower is gained by giving the current password to a portrait of a fat lady in a pink silk dress. She talks back and won't let in anyone who has forgotten it. Occasionally they can't get in at all because she is visiting another portrait.

Details like this keep the reader reading, in delight at Rowling's invention. But the humor and the tale have a darker edge. In his first year at school, Harry must come to terms with the fact that his efforts to destroy a dangerous talisman have indirectly caused a dear old man to die. In his second he learns of a beloved friend's foolishness. In his third he must face his own deepest fears in living form. And in his fourth year he meets Voldemort face to face, escaping from him only after the death of a fellow student and Harry's unwilling contribution of his blood to Voldemort's resurrection.

Hogwarts students are divided by a telepathic Sorting Hat into four "houses" or dormitories, whose house personalities reflect the balance of forces necessary in the world: Slytherin for the politicians, from whose ranks the power-mad Voldemort and his disciples came; Ravenclaw for the intellectuals; Hufflepuff for the workers, the ones who get things done; and Gryffindor for the potential heroes, the warriors. Harry begs the hat for Gryffindor, and it grants his wish, but it also tells him that he would have done very well indeed in Slytherin. Harry has the potential for both.

Harry is the wounded hero whose wound gives him a power he wouldn't otherwise have, a power that may have come indeed from the brush with the dark force that wounded him. It is duality that gives the Harry Potter books their power: a duality both of Voldemort and Harry, of dark and light forces, and of tone, of dark and light storytelling alternating, ranging from the dark retelling of the Lucifer legend with Voldemort as the fallen sorcerer angel to the whimsical inventions of Rowling's magical world.

At school Harry finds the usual house rivalries, similar to those experienced by Stalky and his friends, but with Rowling's magical overlay: the sport of Hogwarts and the rest of the magical world is Quidditch, a game played on flying broomsticks. Quidditch relies more on skill than brute strength, and consequently includes girls among its best players, a refreshing change from the usual school sports rivalries.

The female characters at Hogwarts are more likely to play a major role than a mere love interest, even in the fourth volume in which Harry and Ron discover girls, in the sense that, as Ron says to Hermione, "Neville's right—you *are* a girl . . ." (*Goblet of Fire,* 400). Hermione is the smartest of the three, the one most likely to get Harry out of trouble, as well as to warn him bossily of it in the first place. Professor McGonagall, head of

Harry's Gryffindor House, is a witch to be reckoned with. She is among the few magical folk who can transform themselves into animals, and she is not above giving Harry his own broom, a thing normally forbidden to first-year students, as soon as she discovers that he has the makings of a Gryffindor House Quidditch champion. Her first name is Minerva, Roman variant of the all-wise goddess Athena.

Rowling has a good deal of fun with her names. The caretaker Filch's first name is Argus, for the hundred-eyed guardian of Greek mythology. The headmaster's phoenix, a bird that bursts into flame every five hundred years, to be reborn from its own ashes, is named Fawkes, as in Guy. Draco Malfoy, Harry's school rival and nemesis, translates roughly as "bad-acting dragon" or "dragon of bad faith." Draco's father Lucius, a follower of Voldemort, shares his name's origins with Lucifer, the fallen light-bringer. Draco's toadies, Crabbe and Goyle, suggest crabs and gargoyles and have personalities to match. A rival school of wizardry, Durmstrang, is a flip of the German *Sturm und Drang,* "storm and stress." The ineffective Minister of Magic is named Cornelius Fudge. Remus Lupin, who turns out to be a werewolf, is doubly wolf-named: Lupin/lupine and Remus, brother of Romulus, suckled by the she-wolf. Harry's godfather, Sirius Black, is another double pun: named for the brightest star in the constellation Canis Major, the Great Dog, Sirius can also transform himself into a black dog.

The headmaster of Hogwarts, Albus Dumbledore, bears a name which means literally "white bumblebee." I suspect that some clearer meaning may attach itself to that name as the series progresses. Certainly white stands for the light against the darkness of Lord Voldemort, whose name itself contains the word death. And Voldemort's true name, his human name when he was human (he is now something both more and less) was Tom Riddle. Clearly he is the heart of the riddle Harry must solve on both his journey to adulthood and his journey as hero, which, mythologically speaking, may be one and the same.

In counterpoint to Harry's ties to Voldemort, part of Harry's search through all the books is for his true father, or father figure. He first tries to make a father of Hagrid, the school gamekeeper, but slowly learns that Hagrid is unreliable, with a penchant for dangerous pets: huge spiders, dragons, hippogriffs, and a kind of combination of scorpion and jet engine called Blast-Ended Skrewts, which Hagrid introduces to the Care of Magical Creatures class. Hagrid's first name is Rubeus, Latin for a bramble, which he resembles: a giant of a man (he proves indeed to be half-giant in parentage) with a shaggy mane of hair and a wild, tangled beard. He conceals his wand in a pink umbrella, as he isn't supposed to use it, having been expelled years ago from Hogwarts after one of his monsters imperiled the entire school. Knowing this, Harry must learn to love Hagrid anyway, a difficult and unusually complex acknowledgment that we have no perfect parents, no true fairy godmothers.

Instead we have a literary descendant of James Thurber's Golux in *The Thirteen Clocks,* who tells the Prince, "Half the places I have been to, never were. I make things up. Half the things I say are there cannot be found. . . . I make mistakes, but I am on the side of Good." Then he adds, significantly, "by accident and happenstance."[7]

In the third book, *Harry Potter and the Prisoner of Azkaban,* Harry finds not a godmother but a godfather in Sirius Black, who has been imprisoned in Azkaban for a grisly murder he convinces Harry he did not commit. Hardly anyone else trusts Sirius, except Albus Dumbledore, the headmaster of the school, who, as Kipling says elsewhere, "can see farther into a millstone than most." And even the powerful Dumbledore cannot circumvent the verdict of the wizards' court that has condemned him. Black is sentenced to destruction at the hands of the Dementors and escapes only with Harry's help. Harry does indeed find a father, but one who is himself an outcast and fugitive.

The sense of ambiguity, of no clear answers, grows with each book, as Harry grows and sees more and farther. The schoolmasters, well-meaning as well as malevolent ones, are marked by this duality. Professor Snape is a thoroughly unpleasant, mean-spirited man driven by jealousy of Harry, and yet he is willing to protect him when he must. In *The Prisoner of Azkaban,* we meet the Dementors, hideously telepathic creatures able to suck a victim's sanity away by draining him of all hope and happy memory, leaving only despair. They are used by the "good" side as guards at Azkaban, the prison where rogue wizards are incarcerated, although they are plainly evil in their nature.

The nonhuman creatures who inhabit Rowling's world have their own duality. Mythological creatures from all traditions abound, living unseen by Muggles, in our midst like the goblins, or inhabiting the classrooms and hallways of Hogwarts or the sinister depths of Hagrid's charmed wood. There are merpeople in the lake and hags in the village. Professor Lupin, instructor in Defense Against the Dark Arts, introduces his students to a boggart, a shape-shifting creature of Irish legend that takes on the form of its victim's deepest fears. Characteristically, it is defeated by laughter, reminiscent of the Golux's charge, "Remember laughter. You'll need it even in the blessed isles of Ever After."[8]

The Forbidden Forest contains centaurs and unicorns, as well as more sinister and dangerous creatures. The unicorns represent the innocent among

---

7. James Thurber, *The Thirteen Clocks,* 34.
8. Ibid., 120.

the creatures; the centaurs are the learned ones, more interested in studying the predictions of the stars than in interfering in events happening in
the present. It is also home to Hagrid's huge spider, Aragog, whom Harry
makes the mistake of trusting because the spider is tame with Hagrid. As
a result, he is nearly eaten. Aragog tells him, "My sons and daughters do
not harm Hagrid, on my command. But I cannot deny them fresh meat,
when it wanders so willingly into our midst. Good-bye, friend of Hagrid"
(*Chamber of Secrets,* 279).

There are no sure things, even with magic to aid you. That may be the
heart of the Harry Potter books. When Harry, pleading desperately for
the life of Sirius Black, says to the headmaster, Dumbledore, that Dumbledore must believe him, Dumbledore responds that indeed he does, but
has no power to make others see truth. Instead Dumbledore tells him, after
Harry has rescued Sirius Black himself with Dumbledore's connivance, that
in essence, there is no sure thing and that that knowledge is the heart of
magic. Harry is bemoaning the fact that he has spared the life of a rogue
wizard and by doing so may have helped the evil Voldemort back to power.
Dumbledore tells Harry that the wizard, Pettigrew, now owes his life to
Harry, a development that creates a certain bond between them, and that
Voldemort is not likely to be happy to have a servant who is in Harry's debt.
When Harry, repulsed, says he doesn't want any connection with Pettigrew,
who helped kill his parents, Dumbledore replies, "This is magic at its deep-
est, its most impenetrable, Harry" (*Prisoner of Azkaban,* 427).

It is this sense of uncertainty, of the mystery and interconnectedness of all
actions, that gives Rowling's books the depth that Safire confidently claims
a true children's book cannot possess and the complexity that may well
sustain them through three more volumes as Harry works his way from
first year to seventh at Hogwarts.

And here Rowling has done something else unusual in children's fantasy.
Her series is growing up with its initial audience. The first volume, *Harry
Potter and the Sorcerer's Stone,* featured Harry at age eleven, in a novel suit-
able for eleven-year-olds. The second, *Harry Potter and the Chamber of
Secrets,* dealt with a basilisk—a slightly scarier menace than the trials of the
first book—and the near death of little Ginny Weasley, Ron's young sister,
at the hands of Voldemort. In addition, we saw more clearly the frightening parts of the action. In the third book, *Harry Potter and the Prisoner
of Azkaban,* as Harry and his first readers reached thirteen, the Dementors
appeared, and a beloved pet was executed on trumped-up charges of vicious
behavior, albeit rescued at the very end of the book by the judicious use of
a Time-Turner.

Finally, the fourth volume, *Harry Potter and the Goblet of Fire,* brings us
Harry at fourteen, in a book considerably darker in tone, more complex,

and very much longer, than the first three. It is considerably more "contemporary," from Mrs. Weasley's complaints about Bill's ponytail and earring, to the explanation that computers and other electronic Muggle gadgetry do not work at Hogwarts (the magic is too thick in the air). And it focuses on Harry's growing interest in sex and girls, and his resulting confusion.

Rowling is still dealing with the same theme of good versus evil, and the inevitable intertwining and mirroring of the two, but in an increasingly more adult fashion. This book opens not with Harry, as the previous ones do, but with Voldemort, in a particularly grisly scene, committing a grisly murder. Later, Voldemort's followers, the Death Eaters, amuse themselves after a Quidditch match by brutally tormenting Muggles. At the end of the book, Harry sees his parents as ghosts in a heart-wrenching scene and, most disturbing to the reader, Cedric Diggory, a character we have come to know and care about in the course of the book, is killed by Voldemort. Death here is sudden, tragic, and irreversible, and the true mark of Voldemort's evil is his willingness to casually dispose of Cedric Diggory. In the process Harry begins to see the grown-up world with grown-up, increasingly cynical eyes, as he encounters an incompetent (and powerful and stupid) government official, is the victim of a self-serving and mendacious newspaper reporter, witnesses a rigged trial, and is thrust into the chancy winds of international relations.

Will this progression book by book from middle-grade chapter book to young adult novel slow down the child who at nine or ten comes upon the first of the series, and plunges headlong through all the rest? Perhaps.

Or perhaps not. In the final chapter of *Stalky & Co.*, the reader meets the characters again, as men somewhat the worse for wear and with some horrible stories of the frontier to tell. Stalky is not there. We see him again only offstage, in the voices of the rest, as they recount his adult exploits. He has become larger than life, moved from school legend into Border myth.

Harry began his life as myth, as magic infant, the force that alone could hold evil at bay. Throughout the first four books, he has struggled to become a human boy instead, against the tide of others' preconceived ideas of him. It will be interesting to see, in five years or so, how that works out. In the meantime, I think Rowling will keep her original audience by letting her writing and her storytelling voice grow up as they do.

The Education of a Wizard

Harry Potter and His Predecessors

Pat Pinsent

Joanne Rowling's Harry Potter books follow earlier children's novels that have depicted one or more characters learning how to use magic. Sometimes mentioned are Ursula Le Guin's Earthsea saga, in the first volume of which the leading character, Ged, becomes an apprentice to a senior magician and then goes on to attend a school for wizards, and Monica Furlong's book about a young girl, "Wise Child," learning in eighth-century Mull to be a "doran," a kind of witch who works closely with the powers of nature. More directly similar, however, to Rowling's work are Jill Murphy's Worst Witch books and Anthony Horowitz's *Groosham Grange*, both of which are set in boarding schools. It is interesting also to relate the Harry Potter series to the work of Diana Wynne Jones, whose Chrestomanci books, written in the 1970s and 1980s, have recently been reissued, with striking new covers bearing the words, "Hotter than Potter"; Jones's new publishers clearly hope to lure some of Rowling's immense reading public.[1]

I contend that Rowling's originality is in no way diminished by not being the first in the field, or by the fact that elements of her books recall those of earlier writers, especially Murphy and Horowitz. Whether or not Rowling was familiar with these prototypes before she began the Harry Potter saga, she supplements her use of the vocabulary of magic and the common themes of the boarding school genre with additional levels of meaning that render the books more attractive to adult readers than those of Murphy and Horowitz. Diana Wynne Jones's complex vision of the worlds of Chrestomanci, however, is as multi-layered as Rowling's universe, and her books have much to offer adults, though they have not been so popular with children as Rowling's work.

1. Ursula Le Guin, *A Wizard of Earthsea, The Tombs of Atuan,* and *The Farthest Shore;* Monica Furlong, *Wise Child;* Jill Murphy, *Adventures of the Worst Witch;* Anthony Horowitz, *Groosham Grange;* Diana Wynne Jones, *Charmed Life; The Lives of Christopher Chant; Witch Week.*

Magic Boarding Schools

Denigrators of J. K. Rowling's Harry Potter series often claim that her work is not truly original—ignoring the fact that the same could be said of Shakespeare! Her comedy is described as resembling Roald Dahl's ostensibly subversive iconoclastic tales, while C. S. Lewis's Narnia series is cited as providing a precedent for embodying the conflict between good and evil in a fantasy framework. Rowling herself, while admiring Lewis, disclaims any affinity with Dahl. The boarding school tradition, most famously exemplified in the past by Thomas Hughes's *Tom Brown's School Days* (1857), is also frequently cited as an influence on Rowling, though, as Robert J. Kirkpatrick remarks of the Harry Potter books, "As school stories, they take the genre to its extreme edge."[2]

Hogwarts, despite its similarities to boarding schools in other literature, is distinguished by being a "School of Witchcraft and Wizardry," and the subjects taught there differ as much from the Latin and Greek at Hughes's Rugby as they do from the more contemporary curricula of day schools as portrayed in Gene Kemp's *The Turbulent Term of Tyke Tiler* (1977) and other more recent books.[3] There are, however, precedents for Rowling's portrayal of Harry's schooling; I will examine some similarities between her work and earlier texts that have depicted education in magic. Why is Hogwarts already so much better known than "Miss Cackle's Academy for Witches" in Jill Murphy's Worst Witch series or the Roke Island School for Wizards in Ursula Le Guin's Earthsea? Does Rowling owe anything to her predecessors in this mode? How far, if at all, is the work of the creators of such magic institutions driven by similar preconceptions and intentions?

Apprenticeship in Magic

While several fairly recent books have depicted magic education taking place in a school, an earlier tradition is that of the apprentice in magic who worked with an accomplished master in what we might today describe as an individual tutorial situation. The most familiar story of this kind is *The Sorcerer's Apprentice;* Carpenter and Prichard describe its origin: "The symphonic poem *L'Apprenti Sorcier* (1897) by Dukas . . . was based on a poem by Goethe; this in turn is based on a dialogue by the 2nd-cent. AD Latin poet Lucian."[4] The story and the music owe much of their familiarity to their use by Disney in *Fantasia* (1940), in which Mickey Mouse is portrayed

2. A good example of the charge of derivation is Matthew Fort's article in *The Guardian;* Robert J. Kirkpatrick, *The Encyclopaedia of Boys' School Stories*, 286.

3. Gene Kemp, *The Turbulent Term of Tyke Tiler.*

4. Humphrey Carpenter and Mari Prichard, *The Oxford Companion to Children's Literature*, 491.

as the apprentice who casts a spell on a broom, forcing it to continue fetching buckets of water; unfortunately he does not know how to make it stop. The moral of this story is simple, and in accord with the official ideology of most periods up to the present day: if children meddle with knowledge beyond their years, they may regret it.

The same theme also appears to lie behind an incident early in *A Wizard of Earthsea*, before the eponymous Ged reaches Roke, but Le Guin adds greater psychological complexity. At this stage Ged, as an apprentice to the Mage Ogion, is bored by what he feels is the slowness of his initiation into magic; when he is taunted with his immaturity by a disdainful girl, he inadvertently summons the spirits of the dead and is only saved from horror by the return of his master. The incident liberates a dark force, which we later learn is, in Jungian terms, Ged's shadow self. (Later the shadow is given power when Ged responds to the taunts of another boy at the Wizardry School, Jasper, and harmony is only restored at the end of the novel when Ged acknowledges this aspect of his being.)[5] In the initial incident, Le Guin would seem to have a slightly different stance from that in the classical story; her intertextuality, like a good many instances in which folktale themes are employed, has a psychoanalytic function in relation to Ged's character, while his subsequent more formal education at the School for Wizards places more emphasis on what is external to him, the nature of the right kind of knowledge about the universe.

Another book that portrays the aspirant magician as an apprentice is Monica Furlong's *Wise Child* (1987), set in the Scottish island of Mull during the eighth century. The title character, disowned by her family, is being brought up by Juniper, who has the reputation of being a witch. One of Wise Child's "friends" says: "I bet she'll make you her apprentice . . . Witches choose little girls to be their apprentices. Then you'll be a witch too." The lessons in magic are not immediately forthcoming, however; Juniper says, "I thought we'd begin with reading, writing, astronomy, fairy stories—that kind of thing. Later on we'll do a bit of Latin." Wise Child's education also includes learning herbal remedies, and it isn't until she has proved that she holds the potential to become a "doran," by a trance in which she experiences "flying," that she begins her education in the language of magic. Despite her many complaints, she is made to repeat strings of apparently meaningless words, until at last they begin to make sense: "I had the sensation that the words were uttering *me*, that sometimes I was the speaker and sometimes I was the hearer, that sometimes Wise Child disappeared altogether and sometimes I was more Wise Child than I had ever been before in my life."[6] Furlong, a Christian feminist who has devoted

---

5. Le Guin, *Wizard*, 33–35, 74, 198.
6. Furlong, *Wise Child*, 26, 44, 174.

herself to the campaign for the ordination of women to the Anglican priest-hood, would seem to have a rather different agenda from Le Guin's; the character she creates is not only learning about the true nature of things but also receiving the potential for mystical experience and the realization of female power in the universe.

A slightly different version of a one-to-one education in magic appears in Diana Wynne Jones's *The Lives of Christopher Chant* (1988), the "pre-quel" to her better-known *Charmed Life* (1977); the later book shows the youth of her powerful magician, whose name literally means "useful div-ination," while the earlier text is concerned with the education of several trainee sorcerers. Because of the complexity of Jones's work, it is convenient to consider both the individual and the group situation together at a later point in this chapter.

Texts concerned with education in magic by means of a pupil's appren-ticeship to a competent magician inevitably reflect the conscious or implicit ideology of the writer. The nearest parallels to the apprenticeship situation within the Harry Potter books are the occasions when Harry receives in-dividual tuition from one of the teachers. An important instance of this is when Professor Lupin, the Defense against the Dark Arts Master, instructs Harry in how to conjure up a Patronus in order to defeat a Dementor. Lupin says, "The Patronus is a kind of positive force, a projection of the very things that the Dementor feeds upon—hope, happiness, the desire to survive—but it cannot feel despair as real humans can, so the Dementors can't hurt it" (*Prisoner of Azkaban,* 176). This one-to-one conversation between Harry and Lupin has the twofold function of allowing Lupin to reveal himself as a trustworthy character (even though we later learn that at certain times he becomes a werewolf) and giving Harry the kind of access to power that would not be possible in a class situation. Like Le Guin and Furlong, Rowling appears to reveal something of her own values through this situation: the belief that despair is a part of being human, but also that it can be countered by what might be termed as an act of faith and hope, seems to be important to her, as a reinforcement of the conviction that there is a meaning to life. In religious literature of the nineteenth century the equivalent of this would be an act of faith in God, but this kind of direct reference to the divine would be out of place here. Harry at first identifies his Patronus with his dead father, but later comes to realize that it is derived from his own inner strength (*Prisoner of Azkaban,* 282, 301).

The Earthsea School for Wizards
The curriculum that Le Guin's wizard, Ged, follows at the school on Roke includes "the Deeds of heroes and the Lays of wisdom," learning

from the Master Windkey how to control wind and water, from the Master Herbal "the ways and properties of things that grow," and from the Master Hand "sleight and jugglery and the lesser Arts of Changing." Something more central to Le Guin's Taoist philosophy, however, is taught to Ged when he asks how he can get beyond mere illusion and permanently change a stone into a diamond. The Master Hand tells him he will learn this from the Master Changer, but "You must not change one thing, one pebble, one grain of sand, until you know what good and evil will follow on the act. The world is in balance, in Equilibrium. A wizard's power of Changing and of Summoning can shake the balance of the world. It is dangerous, that power." He also learns that "magic consists in this, the true naming of a thing" and "is worked only by those beings who speak . . . the Old Speech." However, there are limits to the power of a Mage; the Master Namer tells the pupils that a Mage "can control only what is near him, what he can name exactly and wholly. And this is well. If it were not so, the wickedness of the powerful or the folly of the wise would long ago have sought to change what cannot be changed and Equilibrium would fail."[7]

In Rowling's books, too, the idea of transformation is handled with care, even though there is no evidence of a concern with the question of balance in the universe. Spells inevitably occur, though unlike Le Guin and Furlong, Rowling does not suggest a totally private language for them. The origin of the words Rowling chooses to introduce spells generally seems to be Latinate (we may recall that Juniper planned to teach Wise Child Latin as well as the esoteric language of the "dorans"); a common example is "Accio," presumably from the Latin "accessus," "approach," which Harry uses frequently, such as when summoning his broomstick against the Hungarian Horntail: "Accio Firebolt" (*Goblet of Fire*, 309). Among many other instances are "Imperio" (from "Imperare," to command) and "Crucio" (from "crux," a cross) (*Goblet of Fire*, 188–89).

Le Guin's moral didacticism is evident also in her emphasis on Ged's hostility to another student at the school, Jasper. Unlike Harry Potter's attitude toward Draco Malfoy, however, Ged's negative feelings about the older boy are subjected to critical scrutiny—the evil is not seen as only residing in Jasper, who is undoubtedly arrogant about his aristocratic ancestry, but also in Ged, who is hypersensitive about his more lowly origins and harbors a grudge against Jasper before he has had any real grounds for having one. Altogether, we are much more conscious both of Ged's moral failings and of his development as a person; *A Wizard of Earthsea* thus seems more evidently a bildungsroman than is the case for any single Harry Potter book,

7. Le Guin, *Wizard,* 55–56, 59, 60.

though the much larger scale of Rowling's portrayal of growing up, seven projected volumes against the initial three, rather shorter, ones about Ged's youth, needs to be borne in mind.

While there are certainly affinities between the descriptions of Ged's education and that of Harry, the differences are perhaps more noticeable, and not all of these result from the difference of scale. Humor is not much in evidence in Le Guin's books, and although her earnestness befits her exposition of her philosophy, it may well have deterred some younger readers from approaching her work, since surveys reveal that humor is one of the factors most appealing to children, particularly to those under eleven.[8]

The Earthsea books were very popular when first published but never won readers on the scale of the Harry Potter books; they are probably less familiar today than they deserve to be, though still popular with Le Guin devotees, including those who have encountered her science fiction for older readers. A resurgence in their popularity is possible since the recent publication of further books in the series. The events in *Earthsea,* presented in epic mode, occur entirely in their own universe and there is no reference to "our" world. It is noticeable that this kind of "high" fantasy often presupposes an audience of adolescents or young adults; the contrast between J. R. R. Tolkien's *The Lord of the Rings* (1954–1955), once a cult series read among university students, and C. S. Lewis's Narnia series (1950–1956), accessible to children as young as eight, highlights this distinction. Even *The Hobbit* (1937) presupposes a more mature reader than *The Lion, the Witch and the Wardrobe* (1950). Interplay with "our" world seems to mediate the entry of the younger reader into the secondary world and also allows for occasional interaction with the primary world; the White Witch's incursion into London in Lewis's *The Magician's Nephew* (1955) bears some resemblance to the transitional elements at the beginning and end of each of the first four Harry Potter books. Such interactional elements allow Rowling's message about not using magic wrongly against Muggles to be expressed more directly, whereas a similar message has to come out through plot and character in *Earthsea*. While Rowling's moral purpose appears to be as strong as Le Guin's, there is less evidence of it being associated with a holistic view of the universe, and it is therefore easier for her to rely on already existing latent responses in her readers to what is expected to be good or evil, as indeed is also the case with Lewis.

8. A survey of young people between four and sixteen, carried out by the National Centre for Research in Children's Literature at Roehampton, revealed that "funny stories" were the top choice of 60 to 70 percent of readers under eleven, their attraction gradually becoming superseded by horror among the older readers. It would appear from the rather more horrific situations in which Harry finds himself in the later books that Rowling is well aware of these preferences (Kimberley Reynolds, ed., *Young People's Reading at the End of the Century,* 70–72).

Miss Cackle's Academy for Witches

Jill Murphy's stories about Mildred Hubble center to a much greater degree than Le Guin's Earthsea saga on the school that her main protagonist attends. The link with the boarding school genre is very marked in this series, and the elements in which Rowling's books resemble Murphy's are those which are most dependent on this tradition, particularly some of the stock humor that relies on the mischievous behavior of the pupils and their virtual war against the authority of the staff. This creates a superficially subversive atmosphere, not uncommon in the school story; readers are likely to find themselves sympathizing with naughty pupils but are placed in an ambivalent position once the more congenial character of the head teacher is encountered. Earlier examples of these divided sympathies include Thomas Hughes' Rugby in *Tom Brown's School Days* (1857) and the school in Kipling's *Stalky & Co.* (1899), and this aspect is also very apparent in Hogwarts. The effect often reveals something significant about the value systems of the writers concerned.

Murphy's transmutation of routine school themes by the addition of magic is very similar to Rowling's, but there are some significant differences.

Location

The Worst Witch begins,

> Miss Cackle's Academy for Witches stood at the top of a high mountain surrounded by a pine forest. It looked more like a prison than a school, with its gloomy grey walls and turrets. Sometimes you could see the pupils on their broomsticks flitting like bats above the playground wall, but usually the place was half hidden in mist, so that if you glanced up at the mountain you would probably not notice the building was there at all.
>   Everything about the school was dark and shadowy: long, narrow corridors and winding staircases . . . [9]

The initial description of Hogwarts in *Harry Potter and the Sorcerer's Stone* (1997) has a good deal in common with this. The new pupils, led by Hagrid, approach by a steep narrow path, from which they see the building over a dark lake: "Perched atop a high mountain on the other side, its windows sparkling in the starry sky, was a vast castle with many turrets and towers" (*Sorcerer's Stone*, 83). Like the Academy, Hogwarts is in effect hidden: as Hermione points out, "It's bewitched . . . If a Muggle looks at it, all they see is a mouldering old ruin with a sign over the entrance saying DANGER, DO NOT ENTER, UNSAFE" (*Goblet of Fire*, 148). Despite its many ghosts restricting entrance to parts of the building, its underground passages and dungeons, and its nearly inaccessible turrets, the atmosphere

9. Murphy, *Worst Witch*, 7.

at Hogwarts is in fact rather more welcoming than that of the Academy; emphasis is often placed on splendor and light. Pupils enter through "a pair of magnificent wrought-iron gates, flanked with stone columns topped with winged boars" (*Prisoner of Azkaban*, 68) into "the vast echoing entrance hall, which was lit with flaming torches" (*Chamber of Secrets*, 62). Miss Cackle's Academy also has a Great Hall, "a huge stone room with rows of wooden benches, a raised platform at one end and shields and portraits all round the walls." In general, however, Murphy's style is appropriate to its appeal to somewhat younger children who are wary of extended descriptive passages; J. Appleyard's generalization that books for later childhood "have uncomplicated sentences, short paragraphs, and little description of people and settings" is very valid of *The Worst Witch* and its successors.[10] The books instead rely on the illustrations (by the author herself) and occasional references to long corridors to remind the reader of the atmosphere.

Hogwarts is more three-dimensional than Murphy's Academy; it is *there* in the reader's consciousness even when the characters are elsewhere. By contrast, Mildred and her companions, at least in the first three books, never leave the school and its surroundings, the solidity of which entirely depends on the pupils' presence. Rowling's setting is portrayed in far more detail—scarcely surprisingly given the greater length of her books—and has some affinities with the complex world of Mervyn Peake's Gormenghast trilogy (1946–1959).

Despite the ghostly elements of Hogwarts, on the whole its interior is more attractive than that of Miss Cackle's Academy. Murphy makes surprisingly few references to food, although we learn that it is substantial: Mildred's friend Maud looks forward to "good old school dinners . . . date-pudding and custard." By contrast, there are many references to the appetizing food at Hogwarts, starting with Harry's delight on his arrival after being half-starved at the Dursleys: "He had never seen so many things he liked to eat on one table: roast beef, roast chicken, pork chops and lamb chops, sausages, bacon and steak, boiled potatoes, roast potatoes, chips, Yorkshire pudding, peas, carrots, gravy, ketchup and, for some strange reason, mint humbugs" (*Sorcerer's Stone*, 92). The bedrooms at Hogwarts also share this opulence—"Five four-posters hung with deep-red velvet curtains (*Sorcerer's Stone*, 97)—while Mildred has to make do with a "wardrobe, an iron bedstead, table and chair, and a slit window."[11]

Hogwarts may be hidden from Muggles, but even its wizard inhabitants find that getting round the building presents a considerable challenge; they are quite likely to be kept out of some areas because of ignorance of the

10. Ibid., 19; J. A. Appleyard, *Becoming a Reader*, 61.
11. Murphy, *Worst Witch*, 206, 12.

current password. Harry, however, eventually acquires the Marauder's Map (*Prisoner of Azkaban,* 144), which not only proves to be an invaluable aid to detecting the movements of evil-doers but also serves as a symbol of his abilities and private knowledge of this world; Harry's competence here provides an attractive image to young people who crave a place of their own, both physically and metaphorically.

School Song

As befits boarding schools with long traditions, both Hogwarts and the Academy have their school songs. Murphy's begins: "Onward, ever striving onward,/Proudly on our brooms we fly . . ." and concludes: "Full of joy we mix our potions,/Working by each other's side./When our days at school are over/Let us think of them with pride." This is immediately followed by the deflating sentiment: "It was the usual type of school song, full of pride, joy and striving. Mildred had never yet mixed a potion with joy, nor flown her broomstick with pride—she was usually too busy trying to keep upright!"[12] It is as if Murphy is anxious that the reader should not take the sentiments overseriously.

The deflationary effect of the Hogwarts school song is more overt, beginning "Hogwarts, Hogwarts, Hoggy Warty Hogwarts,/Teach us something please" and concluding, "So teach us things worth knowing,/Bring back what we've forgot,/Just do your best, we'll do the rest,/And learn until our brains all rot" (*Sorcerer's Stone,* 95). All the students choose their own tunes so that they finish at different times, but Dumbledore is nevertheless moved to describe the effect as "A magic beyond all we do here!" (*Sorcerer's Stone,* 95). The simplistic language, internal rhyme, and anarchic rendering mean that there is no need for a narratorial voice to alert the reader against taking the sentiments too seriously; rather the effect is to cast an unusual shadow on Dumbledore's judgment.

It would appear that both Murphy and Rowling have set out to expose the triteness of many traditional school songs, from "Forty Years On" at Harrow to the more recently evolved lyrics of state schools, but whereas Murphy produces her own version in this mode, merely altering details to fit a witchly curriculum, Rowling intensifies the explicit parodic effect by emphasis on the potentially ludicrous title of her establishment. There is little to choose between the songs as verse!

Relationships and Spells

Mildred Hubble quite soon makes a friend in Maud, and a little later the arrival of a new girl, Enid, makes this a trio. Mildred's enmity against

---

12. Ibid., 19–21.

the always word-perfect Ethel is also established early on, but despite the mention of there being many other pupils in the school, only a few names are ever given, and the role in the stories of anyone other than Mildred and her immediate friends or enemies is relatively slight. The staff too seem somewhat few in number; other than the headmistress Miss Cackle, Miss Hardbroom is almost the only member of the staff to merit a name, although others are mentioned in more general terms. The effect is to focus on the named characters against a rather ill-defined background, sketched in by Murphy's illustrations of countless witch stereotypes of various sizes, in pointed hats, or of schoolgirls with brooms instead of hockey sticks.

The typical schoolgirl scrapes in which Mildred gets involved are inevitably adapted to this environment; the first of these occurs early on when she responds to the taunts of her archenemy Ethel: "Mildred muttered the spell under her breath—and Ethel vanished. In her place stood a small pink and grey pig." Ethel retains her power of speech, so the authorities soon discover Mildred's prank; Mildred is ordered to learn how to turn Ethel back to human shape, but the incident does not seem to be taken too seriously by the school authorities. A less frivolous situation arises a little later when Mildred discovers a large group of hostile witches who are planning to take over the school and to turn everyone there into frogs; Mildred rushes off for her book of spells and finds how to transform the enemies into snails before they can act against the school: "I know it's against the Witches' Code . . . but *they* don't seem to follow any rules."[13] On this occasion, Mildred is honored by the whole school.

Harry Potter's casting of spells is generally performed either in situations that have a function in the overall plot, such as the Triwizard Tournament, or for his own self-preservation or the rescue of other characters; additionally, as part of his continual struggle against the Dursleys, he sometimes defies the strict prohibitions that magic should not be used against Muggles. The obnoxious Aunt Marge, for instance, is blown up like a balloon when she insults Harry's parents: "Aunt Marge . . . was entirely round, now, like a vast life buoy with piggy eyes, and her hands and feet stuck out weirdly as she drifted up into the air, making apoplectic popping noises" (*Prisoner of Azkaban*, 27). Harry knows he has broken wizard law by doing this, but to his relief he is told by Cornelius Fudge, the Minister for Magic, "We don't send people to Azkaban just for blowing up their aunts!" (*Prisoner of Azkaban*, 39). Nevertheless the potential threat of a serious, possibly fatal, punishment for such behavior remains.

Another incident involving transformation occurs later in Rowling's work, when, in a scene superficially resembling Murphy's Mildred turning Ethel

13. Ibid., 31, 82.

into a pig, Mad-Eye Moody transforms the unpleasant Draco Malfoy into a ferret. While Professor McGonagall points out that transformation should never be used by teachers as a punishment, it is evident that Moody has acted in defense of Harry, who was about to be attacked by Malfoy. It is later revealed, however, that the character who appeared to be Moody was really Barty Crouch Jr., a servant of Voldemort, anxious for his own purposes to ensure that Harry wins the Triwizard contest, so the transformation situation provokes renewed questioning. The message of these and other incidents seems to be that power should always be used with responsibility, in defense against evil; rules may on occasion be flouted, but only for a good reason. Both Murphy and Rowling here, as elsewhere, seem to present a clear distinction between good and evil, so that if characters are basically good and have learned that the rules should normally be obeyed, there is little danger that they will use power wrongly.

Both schools have at least one unpleasant teacher; Mildred and her friends at the Academy suffer from the near omnipresence of Miss Hardbroom, "a tall terrifying lady with a sharp bony face and black hair scragged back into such a tight knot that her forehead looked quite stretched." Her attitude is portrayed in stereotypical terms associated with coldness and an incisive gaze; she is described as smiling nastily, asking coldly, saying sourly, looking round piercingly, having a "frosty glare," "fixing Ethel with one of her nastiest looks" and speaking in "icy tones," and "narrowing her eyes and glaring."[14]

Similar attributes to those of Miss Hardbroom occur in Severus Snape, the stereotypically unpleasant teacher at Hogwarts, who is initially encountered by Harry at the first "Sorting," being described as "A teacher with greasy black hair, a hooked nose and sallow skin." The impression is given that he is associated with Harry's enemy, Voldemort: "The hook-nosed teacher looked past Quirrell's turban straight into Harry's eyes—and a sharp, hot pain shot across the scar on Harry's forehead" (*Sorcerer's Stone,* 94). Harry's scar always alerts him to the presence of evil. Suspicion later falls on Snape, who appears to have been cursing Harry's broomstick and attempting to win a Quidditch victory for his own house, Slytherin, over Harry's house, Gryffindor. It eventually becomes evident, however, that the real villain is Quirrell, whose evil probably activated Harry's scar; at the Quidditch match, Snape has been reluctantly protecting Harry from Quirrell. The need for a stereotyped enemy among the professors is such that the reader anticipates and even welcomes Snape's presence in every book. His physical actions and features are not dissimilar to those of Miss Hardbroom; for instance, when he accuses Harry of being in Hogsmeade,

14. Ibid., 15, 21, 33, 43, 55, 57, 59, 115.

the local village, illicitly, "Snape's eyes were boring into Harry's . . . [he] snarled . . . Snape's thin mouth curled into a horrible smile," his eyes glint, and "his thin face [was] full of malice" (*Prisoner of Azkaban*, 208–9). Mildred says of Miss Hardbroom, "Sometimes I think . . . she probably isn't as mean as we think she is."[15] Whether this is also true of Snape remains to be seen.

Broomsticks

As has been noted, flying on broomsticks is very important to the pupils at Murphy's Academy. On one occasion, formation flying is arranged for the school celebration of Halloween in the presence of the Chief Magician, and Ethel is forced to lend her spare broomstick to Mildred; in revenge for the pig incident, Ethel casts a spell on it and Mildred's already uncertain flying is fated, with implications for the rest of the formation team: "The broomstick gave a violent kick like a bucking bronco and she fell off, grabbing at Maud as she fell. There was chaos in the air. All the girls were screaming and clutching at each other, and soon there was a tangled mass of broomsticks and witches on the ground. The only girl who flew serenely back to earth was Ethel." In punishment for this incident (even though it was not directly Mildred's fault), she and Ethel are banned from the flying display the following year, but Mildred knows that she needs to be there in order to be in contact with the Chief Magician so that he may liberate an elderly magician from a spell that has turned him into a frog. (Mildred discovered his secret when she herself was temporarily transformed into a frog by Ethel). Mildred kidnaps another girl, Geraldine, in order to replace her on the flying formation; her eventual triumph, as well as her more accomplished flying when she is partnered by Geraldine's sleek black cat rather than her own tabby, perhaps reflects her development during her time at the school.[16]

The contrast between Mildred's initial ineptitude, even when her broomstick has no spell on it, and Harry's brilliance as a flyer suggests something about the extent to which each is able to take control over life, while the contrast between their "familiars," Mildred's tabby kitten and Harry's messenger owl, Hedwig, also suggests that however unfamiliar Harry may be with the world of magic at the beginning of the series, he has special qualities, something attested to by the recognition he is given by both good and bad characters, without his having to perform any action. Keeping the balance between Harry's distinction and his otherwise "ordinariness" is a task that Rowling seems so far to have achieved successfully.

15. Ibid., 106.
16. Ibid., 68, 307.

Other Elements

Rowling seems occasionally to have developed aspects sketched in by Murphy and made them far more extensive. The girls at the Academy have a textbook for their magic, *The Book of Spells,* while the pupils at Hogwarts have a much larger range of required reading. There is a potions lesson at which Mildred and Maud, by adding "pondweed-gathered-at-midnight," turn their laughter potion from the desired red to green; when they sample it, they accidentally disappear. The similarity between this and the many instances of Harry and Ron (not to mention Neville) making the wrong concoction in Snape's potions lessons seems almost beyond coincidence; an instance is where Neville adds porcupine quills at the wrong time and breaks out in boils (*Sorcerer's Stone,* 103). Rowling, however, develops the curriculum to a much fuller extent than Murphy's more limited scope allows.

The many instances of similarity in material between Murphy and Rowling inevitably raise the question of influence, an issue that I will soon explore more fully. I would, however, suggest that there are some very significant differences between the work of the two writers. Perhaps the most important of these, and the one which subsumes other lesser differences, lies in the episodic nature of Murphy's books. Insofar as there is any overall theme, it is that of Mildred's lack of competence, and her mistakes are the material for comedy. Apart from the one scene where she defeats the invading witches, something achieved fairly easily by the snail spell, there is little sense of the outside world impinging on the closed community of the Academy, nor that anything done there has any wider repercussions. Although the Chief Magician comes to visit, we have no hint as to his wider responsibilities, nor indeed any idea of what the pupils do during the holidays or their occupations when they leave school. Whether they are good citizens of that outside world by being witches is not examined; the only mention of relationships with their parents relates to the relatively trivial matter of Maud being put on a diet by her parents.[17] The overarching plot of the Harry Potter series, which relates to the whole question of the struggle between good and evil, has no parallel in Murphy's work. Equally, there is little evidence of Murphy displaying an interest in the power of language over nature comparable to that of Le Guin, Furlong, and Rowling.

Intrinsic to the fact that Murphy's implied audience is younger than Rowling's is the way in which the narrator sometimes addresses the reader directly in a kindly avuncular way. Chapter 3 of the first volume begins: "Do you remember I told you about a certain young witch named Ethel . . . ?" while the experience of invisibility is also described in terms of direct address: "Imagine holding out your leg and feeling it with your invisible hand

17. Ibid., 206.

while being unable actually to see it. For this reason, walking becomes rather a difficult experience as you can feel your feet moving along but cannot see where they are going. This means that you often find yourself moving in the opposite direction to the one intended, which, of course, is extremely annoying."[18] While most of the time we share Mildred's consciousness, at times we are allowed to know what other characters are thinking, which is not normally the case in the *Harry Potter* books.

It would be difficult to imagine many boys reading *The Worst Witch;* Rowling's choice of a mixed school and a male hero, and her initial concealment of her gender by using initials only, may occasion some feminist sighs but it does seem justified by the limitations imposed by the single-sex environment, especially, for the adolescent reader, once the focal character reaches the stage of interest in the opposite sex.

Groosham Grange

The cover of the 1995 edition of Anthony Horowitz's book bears the words from the *Young Telegraph:* "Move over Roald Dahl, here comes Anthony Horowitz," and unquestionably Dahl's irreverential delight in wordplay is recalled in this book, though some readers may also find themselves comparing Horowitz's work to that of Terry Pratchett. The book and its radio adaptation won several awards. Whereas Murphy's Worst Witch series appeals largely to female readers, *Groosham Grange* (1988) seems to imply a predominantly male readership, old enough to have some knowledge of, among other things, the names and characteristics of prominent public schools, and delighting in tricks and "over-the-top" macabre elements. The plot concerns David, a seventh son of a seventh son, who is expelled from his public school, Beton [presumably "Eton"], "for constant and wilful socialism," and is sent by his supremely unpleasant father to Groosham Grange, situated on an island off the Norfolk coast that cannot be located on a map (recalling the invisibility of Hogwarts to "Muggles").[19] On the journey there he meets Jeffrey, expelled from Godlesston, a toughening-up establishment in Scotland [remember "Gordonstoun," which toughened up Prince Philip, the Duke of Edinburgh, and tried to do the same for Prince Charles, the Prince of Wales], and Jill, rejected by her finishing school in Switzerland. This trio, inevitably foreshadowing Harry, Hermione, and Ron, and all approaching their thirteenth birthdays, discover to their dismay that the teachers at their new school are all in some way supernatural, while the pupils all go under the assumed names of wizards of the past. What happens to an unfortunate schools inspector as a result of the teaching staff

18. Ibid., 29, 259–60.
19. Horowitz, *Groosham Grange,* 13.

sticking pins into his effigy is too horrible to be wished on this scorned profession by even the most long-suffering real teacher!

There are many affinities between *Groosham Grange* and the Harry Potter series. Perhaps the most striking is the structural similarity. The earlier book begins and ends with David's unattractive family; on reading his bad school report from Beton, his father tells David that he has canceled Christmas for him, and threatens him with a sound beating:

> "If you ask me, there's not enough caning in this house. I was caned every day when I was a child and it never did me any harm."
>
> "It did do you a bit of harm," Mrs. Eliot muttered in a low voice.
>
> "Nonsense!" Mr. Eliot pushed himself away from the table in his electric wheelchair. "It made me the man I am!"
>
> "But, darling. You can't walk . . ."
>
> "A small price to pay for perfect manners!"[20]

Even the Dursleys are less unpleasant than this sadist! This passage also reveals the extravagant, very deliberately politically incorrect tone of the book, its caricatures designed to appeal to a comic-paper-reading clientele. Still, there are many other points of similarity between this school and Hogwarts.

Location and Transport

Skrull Island, on which Groosham Grange stands, is normally approached, after a journey in an undertaker's hearse from the mainland station, by means of an old fishing boat "held together by rust and lichen." When Jeffrey mutters, "I'm not much of a sailor," the captain "chortles": "Don't worry! This ain't much of a boat." The children at last see the school: "It was a huge building, taller than it was wide; a crazy mixture of battlements, barred windows, soaring towers, slanting grey slate roofs, grinning gargoyles and ugly brick chimneys. It was as if the architects of Westminster Abbey, Victoria Station and the Brixton gasworks had jumbled all their plans together and accidentally built the result. As the Jeep pulled up outside the front door (solid wood, studded with nails and sixteen inches thick) there was a rumble overhead and a fork of lightning crackled across the sky. Somewhere a wolf howled. Then the door creaked slowly open."[21] This description reveals the way in which Horowitz blends the signifiers of horror with deflationary touches that succeed in creating an element of absurdity. The first sentence generates a similar feeling to that created by both Murphy and Rowling in the first vision of their respective schools, but the incorporation of references to famous London landmarks with very

20. Ibid., 10–11.
21. Ibid., 37, 39, 41.

different associations, solemnity, railway travel, and rotundity, means that the reader is swiftly aware that laughter rather than terror is the response demanded. It is difficult, too, to regard a jeep as an appropriate carrier to a huge castle, while the lightning and the wolf are the finishing touches to what seems to be a kind of stage set. At a later point, David has escaped to the mainland but finds himself pursued by Gregor, the chauffeur of the hearse, and tries to evade him by taking refuge on the ghost train at an amusement park; this, however, swiftly takes him back to Skrull Island and the school.

Staff

The teachers at Groosham Grange are as supernatural in their attributes as those at Hogwarts. Both establishments have ghost teachers, Professor Binns who teaches History of Magic at Hogwarts (*Sorcerer's Stone,* 99) and Mr. Creer, the Groosham teacher of religious studies. He is described as "the only normal-looking teacher in the whole school . . . David had been a little unsettled to see the same name on a tombstone in the school cemetery—'Drowned off Skrull Island: 1955–1985'—but he had assumed it was a relative. Nevertheless Mr. Creer did smell very strongly of seaweed."[22]

No establishment of this kind would be complete without a werewolf. Professor Lupin is Rowling's representative of this group; the dependence of the names of both Lupin and Horowitz's character, Leloup, on the French word for wolf can surely be no coincidence. Lupin's year at Hogwarts, as teacher of Defence against the Dark Arts, is marked by his occasional absences and his drinking of a potion brewed by Snape to help him. At Groosham, further evidence of Leloup's nature is supplied by this dialogue:

> WILLIAM: Monsieur Leloup never teaches when there is going to be a full moon.
> ME [David]: Is he ill?
> WILLIAM: Well, he isn't quite himself.

Later the reader is given a very full description of the process of Leloup's monthly metamorphosis.[23] Incidentally, his stereotypically extreme French accent could have provided a model for that of Rowling's Madam Maxime (*Goblet of Fire,* 215), though many other parallels exist, for instance in the work of Enid Blyton.

Among the other strange employees at Groosham Grange are Mr. Teagle and Mr. Fitch, the "Heads," who share a single body, the assistant head,

22. Ibid., 71–72.
23. Ibid., 54, 100.

Mr. Kilgraw, who is a vampire, and the history teacher, Miss Pedicure, who is six hundred years old.[24] It is evident that the Hogwarts professors are not a whit stranger than those at Groosham Grange.

Curriculum

At the end of the book we learn that David and Jill "would both be taking their first 'O' levels in the summer: Telepathy, Weather Control, Wax Modelling and (the trickiest of the four) Advanced Blood Sacrifice," while Latin, reminding us of its importance in Hogwarts spells (based, presumably, on the actual history of witchcraft), figures prominently on the curriculum.[25] We recall both the Hogwarts curriculum (Divination, Potions, History of Magic, and the rest) and the importance attached to O.W.L.s (Ordinary Wizarding Levels); both authors seem to be making use of the examination, O or Ordinary Levels, which for many years marked the end of British pupils' compulsory schooling.

The Appeal of Groosham Grange

I have suggested that despite the occasional references to a wider world, such as those to Beton and Godlesston, Horowitz's book is primarily addressed to young male readers. This passage from near the beginning, when David's parents are discussing his report, reflects this kind of appeal:

> "Eliot has not made progress," the maths teacher had written. "He can't divide or multiply and will, I fear, add up to very little."
> "Woodwork?" the carpentry teacher had written. "I wish he would work!"
> "If he stayed awake in class it would be a miracle," the religion teacher had complained.
> "Very poor form," the form master had concluded.
> "He'll never get ahead," the headmaster had agreed.

This kind of play on words is directly from the "joke-book" genre, beloved of schoolboys, while the description of the chauffeur, Gregor, is deliberately offensive in its language:

> He was horribly deformed. If he had been involved in a dreadful car crash and then fallen into an industrial mangle it could only have improved him. He was about five foot tall—or five foot short rather, for his head was closer to the ground than to his shoulders. This was partly due to the fact that his

24. Another fairly recent book with a teacher who is a vampire is Virginia Ironside's *Vampire Master of Burlap Hall* (1987), the title establishment of which has much in common with Groosham Grange, though relatively little with Hogwarts. A trio of pupils, Tom, Susan, and Miles, discover that the new biology teacher, Mr. A. Culard, is really Dracula (note the anagram). The book differs from Horowitz's, however, in the fact that Culard's behavior is contrary to the ethos of the school, and he is ultimately defeated.

25. Horowitz, *Groosham Grange*, 152.

neck seemed to be broken, partly due to his hunched back. He had only one eye, several inches lower than it should have been, a swollen cheek and thin straggly hair . . . People walking along the station were trying so hard not to look at him that one unfortunate woman accidentally fell off the platform.[26]

By comparison, "Mad-Eye" Moody is positively attractive and Rowling's occasional stereotyping of characters by their obesity seems relatively harmless! *Groosham Grange* was originally published in 1988, at a time when potentially offensive material by Blyton, Dahl, and Lofting was being edited out of their much older texts, so it seems likely that Horowitz is being deliberately provocative, as well as using the kinds of insulting language beloved of generations of schoolboys.

A more significant difference between this book and the work of Rowling seems to lie in its ideological stance. This includes a very blatant attack on a clergyman whom David, Jill, and Jeffrey meet on their journey: "The young man came into the compartment, beaming at them in that horrible way that very religious people sometimes do . . . 'I'm Father Percival,' he announced . . . 'But you can call me Jimbo.' " When he discovers that they are unhappy about going to school he tells them: "Life's a great journey and it's first-class all the way when you're travelling with Jesus," at which Jill mutters, "I thought you said your name was Jimbo."[27] Again we can see how Horowitz is playing with potentially offensive material, while satirizing Christian evangelism, but there is little in the book to suggest an alternative, positive standard. Unlike Rowling, who offers an ideal of courage and fidelity in Harry himself and in his parents' self-sacrifice, Horowitz's satire, whether of religion or of school, seems intended purely as destructive.

This subversiveness is most apparent in the ambivalence of the ending. Throughout the first three quarters of the book, readers are encouraged to share the fears that the trio of children have of their enforced environment; as outsiders faced with other pupils who do not seem to bear their own names and who vanish for mysterious rites in the middle of the night, they are in a position somewhat similar to the children who are outside the hypnotic spell in Gillian Cross's *The Demon Headmaster* (1982); as a result, our expectation may well be that David and his friends ultimately will escape from this threatening environment, in which the killing of innocents such as an inspector and earlier a historian of magic are described without any apparent moral censure. But near the end, David is faced with Mr. Kilgraw's alternatives, death or joining the school community: "David felt himself being forced down on to the granite block. The circle of faces

---

26. Ibid., 7–8, 34–35.
27. Ibid., 31–32.

spun round him. There was the ring. And there was the knife. 'Now, David,' Mr. Kilgraw asked, 'What do you say?' "[28]

David's decision is clear from the final chapter, when he visits his parents again: "When he looked at them, it was with soft, almost merciless, eyes." By the end of the book, David has started to take revenge on his parents, locking them into a ridiculous posture: "Mrs. Eliot was halfway out of her chair, slumping towards the carpet. Mr. Eliot was about to speak, his mouth open, his tongue hovering over his teeth. It was a simple spell. But they would remain that way for the next three weeks."[29]

The description of David's relatively mild revenge reveals that, despite his initial misgivings, he has decided to accept his magic heritage and continue his education at Groosham Grange. We know that his father in particular deserves anything David can do to him, but David himself can scarcely now be seen in an entirely positive way. Where do our sympathies lie? Magic power, which in this book has not in some respects been seen as moral, has triumphed over human sadism. The trick that Horowitz seems to be playing on the reader may have been performed for a quick and easy effect, perhaps offering a warning that no one is to be trusted, but it does not reflect any coherent set of ideals. Alternatively, however, this book could be seen as "endemically subversive of such things as social authority, received paradigms of behaviour and morality," qualities that Stephens regards as characteristic of those texts which not only depict a carnivalesque reversal of values but also interrogate the status quo.[30]

There are sufficient similarities between Groosham Grange and Hogwarts to make it more than likely that Rowling was familiar with the earlier work, as either a book or a TV adaptation, but both in the extension of the theme and in the underlying ideology, the differences appear more important than the similarities.

The Work of Diana Wynne Jones

Charmed Life (1977) introduces the character of Chrestomanci, the magician whose role, we learn in a later book, is to "watch over all the magic in the world and prevent any harm being done with it."[31] The earlier book gives an account of the education of Eric (Cat) Chant and his sister Gwendolen at Chrestomanci Castle, together with Julia and Roger, the children of their uncle Christopher and his wife, Millie. Some years after producing this book, Jones felt it necessary to supply the details of how Christopher himself was educated into his important role. He is shown initially having

28. Ibid., 148.
29. Ibid., 150, 151.
30. John Stephens, *Language and Ideology in Children's Fiction*, 121–24.
31. Jones, *Christopher Chant*, 140.

home lessons from a series of governesses, the last of whom combines in her curriculum such traditional subjects as arithmetic and French with the more unusual item of levitation, at which Christopher is not particularly adept. The reader is led to distrust the governess because of the totally unemotional image she presents to the young boy. She differs considerably from the tutoring magicians of Le Guin and Furlong; as we later learn, instead of being autonomous, she is the tool of Uncle Ralph, whose villainy in smuggling dragon's blood, weapons, and portions of murdered mermaids between universes is eventually unmasked.

This tutorial situation is soon replaced by Christopher's attendance at school, but although his stay there is brief, the notion of school education has some significance in the book, in so far as it serves to suggest something about Jones's views about education. It is only at school that Christopher feels truly happy, enjoying the companionship of his friends Oneir and Fenning and the chance to take part in cricket matches. His stay there takes place early in the book, before it has been discovered that the possession of any silver object prevents the exercise of his magic powers: "The one lesson he did not enjoy was magic . . . the elementary spells he had to learn bored him nearly to tears." In the time-honored way of school, in both fact and fiction, he gets Oneir to do his magic homework while he does his friend's algebra. That magic lessons should be boring reminds us of similar situations in the books by Furlong, Le Guin, and Rowling, and suggests to the child reader that all in the world of magic is not automatically glamorous. He then becomes the pupil of the learned Dr. Pawson, with whom he learns not only powerful spells but also the equally important aspect of how to control them. Once Dr. Pawson has discovered Christopher's considerable magic potential, the current Chrestomanci, Gabriel de Witt, recognizes Christopher as his eventual successor in the post. The boy is reluctant: "His visions of himself as a famous cricketer faded and fell and turned to ashes . . . Papa thought Christopher did not understand. 'You will become a very important man,' he said," and goes on to inform him of the responsibility of the position.[32] The initially negative aspects of Christopher's education at the hands of the last governess, who is an associate of his uncle, "The Wraith," together with the uncle's wicked plots, reinforce the message that magical powers (which here perhaps serve as an image for knowledge in general) need to be treated with caution and responsibility.

The latter section of the book, showing Christopher's growth both in the control and use of his powers, and his realization that he cannot expect to be liked if he does not react in a friendly manner to other people, could

32. Ibid., 81, 140.

be seen as a form of bildungsroman. Once all crises have been resolved, Christopher's need for companionship is recognized, and Gabriel arranges for a number of young enchanters to be brought to the castle to be trained.

School as an idealized environment is also significant in this book through the character of "the Goddess," the girl who is the "living Asheth" and escapes from her world once she realizes that as she grows up, she will be unlikely to be allowed to survive her replacement by another young girl. When Christopher takes her a collection of school fiction, starting with *Millie Goes to School* and culminating in *Head Girl Millie*, she develops a burning ambition to follow her heroine to boarding school: "I want to do Prep and eat stodge and learn French and play hockey and write lines . . . I want to cheek the Prefects and cheat in Geography test and sneak on my friends."[33] At the end, her sense of schoolgirl honor means that she has to own up to having used up one of Christopher's lives, but nevertheless she has her wish and is sent to the school of her desires. In *Charmed Life*, we discover that the childhood attachment between Christopher and the Goddess, now named Millie after her heroine, has been consolidated into marriage.

Jones seems to be using school in this book as a metonym for ordinariness; the companionship it permits is set against the powerful positions of both Christopher and the Goddess; their wish to be ordinary and have the friendship of other pupils indicates that they do not relish having been singled out. Jones may be suggesting that it is undesirable to have power and adulation until one is ready for it, something which recalls Harry Potter's embarrassment at always being swooned over by Ginny Weasley (*Chamber of Secrets*) or followed worshipfully around by Colin and Dennis Creevey (*Goblet of Fire*). Harry seems to need none of the correctives against being unlikable that Christopher requires, and Rowling tends to imply that to some extent Harry's unpleasant upbringing has prevented him suffering from the kind of swollen-headedness to which he might otherwise be prone. Jones too seems to see education, whether at school or with a tutor, as an important agent of character development.

The education that the children of Christopher and Millie share with their cousins Gwendolen and "Cat" is a cross between the individual tutorial situation and school proper; it inevitably results in a good deal of attention being given to unsatisfactory behavior, notably that of Gwendolen, who, we later learn, owes her powers as a witch to having abstracted Cat's magic without his being aware of it. Thus he regards himself as magically inert, and does not realize that as an individual with nine lives (until he lost some) he will be the successor to his uncle as Chrestomanci.

33. Ibid., 178.

As in the books by Murphy and Horowitz discussed earlier, as well as the Harry Potter series, some attention is given in this book to the nature of the magic curriculum. Before going to the castle, Gwendolen is a pupil of Mr. Nostrum, whose "charges for teaching magic turned out to be £1 an hour for the Elementary Grades, and a guinea [£1.05] for the Advanced Grades beyond." In the classroom at the castle, however, Gwendolen is speedily put in her place. Unable to answer the simple question, "What part did witchcraft play in the Wars of the Roses?" she is forbidden to study witchcraft again until she has learned other subjects, such as arithmetic. Gwendolen is not to be thwarted, however; she borrows *Other-World Studies III* from the castle library (we may recall Hermione's love of the Hogwarts Library), and performs unpleasant tricks on everyone until she sends herself into another world where she considers she will be properly valued, and is replaced by a much more pleasant look-alike, Janet. The incidents that ensue before Cat discovers his true magic potential are complex, and at one point involve Janet and him distrusting Chrestomanci, whose habit of appearing whenever his name is mentioned leads Janet to refer to him as "You know Who," somewhat recalling the way in which characters in the Harry Potter books are fearful of referring to Voldemort by name.[34]

Jones's direct moral teaching in these books, and in *Witch Week* (1982), is evident; what Christopher, Gwendolen, and the other characters are taught involves not thinking too much of oneself, behaving properly to other pupils, being honorable, being able to recognize one's own abilities. It seems unlikely that the inevitable similarities in moral codes between the books of Jones and of Rowling reflect anything more than their mutual dependence on the boarding school genre; unlike Horowitz, neither of these writers seem to make any attempt to question or disrupt these values.

Conclusion

Whether or not Rowling read *The Worst Witch, Groosham Grange,* or books on a similar theme by Monica Furlong, Ursula Le Guin, and Diana Wynne Jones before beginning to write the Harry Potter books, and whether such books inspired her to make use of some of their motifs, does not seem to me, despite their many similarities, to be a vital question. The combination of some of the impedimenta of witchcraft and magic, plus the affinity between the portrayal of teachers and the staples of the boarding school genre, is not in itself proof of influence, nor are similarities such as that of the unpleasant home situations. What is at issue here is the nature of intertextuality; all these writers, and others, are using the same kind of

34. Ibid., 10, 54–55, 180.

"vocabulary," but Rowling is using it with a wider range of levels of meaning and thus appealing to audiences of all ages; by comparison with Murphy and Horowitz, at least, she is also employing a larger moral framework.

By combining stock material from the genre of magic fantasy such as the enchanted castle and the casting of spells, all ultimately emanating from the fairy tale tradition, with equally stereotypical elements from the boarding school story such as the trio of friends foiling the unpleasant teacher, Rowling is making use of several varieties of intertextuality; from the list given by Stephens we might select: specific earlier texts; well-known stories existing in several versions; archetypes; genres and conventions; and occasionally other discourses.[35] Equally, since her own work is clearly going to be encountered by many readers before they meet some of these earlier texts, it will serve as a pre-text to them.

Altick and Fenstermaker suggest that the significance of intertextuality lies not so much in identifying sources in the works of earlier writers as in detecting how "the original meaning changed as it resonated in the work of a later one, where it appeared in a new context and with some—perhaps major—difference of purpose and effect."[36] I would suggest that Rowling's use of similar elements, whether or not she has, accidentally or deliberately, adapted them from other writers in a similar tradition, reveals how different their effects can be. Unlike Murphy or Horowitz, whose books seem primarily to be addressed respectively to preadolescent girls or young adolescent boys, Rowling's books work at more than one level, so that adult readers are able to detect allegorical elements, or may sometimes feel that the complex structures and development of suspense resemble examples of the detective or thriller genre. I am not disparaging Murphy or Horowitz; their intentions and implied audiences are different and their books have been very popular, being awarded prizes, being adapted for film and television, and attracting relatively large sales. Nevertheless, they have not been so popular with adult readers as Rowling's, and must rank as largely entertainment for the young.

Comparison between Rowling's work and the more thought-provoking novels of Ursula Le Guin and Diana Wynne Jones does not yield so many close correspondences, and it would be difficult to claim that Rowling was directly influenced by the work of either of these authors. Both Le Guin and Jones have received a fair amount of critical acclaim, and even attracted cult followings. Conversely, however, both they and Furlong have probably less appeal to many younger readers, though they are capable of attracting considerable enthusiasm among their more restricted readership.

35. Stephens, *Language and Ideology in Children's Fiction*, 84–85.
36. Richard D. Altick and John J. Fenstermaker, *The Art of Literary Research*, 109.

I would suggest too that differences in the ideologies of all these writers are reflected in the way in which they make use of elements that have some similarity. Le Guin undoubtedly exploits her fantasy about Ged's development in a way consonant with her own philosophy, recognizing balance in the universe, while Furlong clearly has a feminist agenda. Murphy perhaps sees the function of her fantasy as empowering young readers, who, like Mildred, lack confidence in their abilities. If they, with Murphy's protagonist, are encouraged to feel sure of triumphing in the end, this has much in common with the ideology to be detected in a large range of other school stories. Horowitz's main intention would appear to be entertainment, with perhaps a hint of the inverted values of the carnivalesque. His books could be put in the category that Stephens describes as "endemically subversive," for there seems to be little evidence of any kind of positive alternative set of values.[37]

While Jones, like Rowling, certainly offers a number of positives, such as the companionship of friends, the danger of being deceived by appearances, and the importance of being true to one's own nature, the complexity of her books defies any easy categorization. Rowling, however, presents a somewhat broader canvas; the greater quantity of material focusing on Harry enables a fuller development of his character over a longer period, and allows Rowling to touch on a range of issues, such as the need to be reliant on one's own integrity even if mistrusted by friends, the danger of depression and even betrayal, and the possibility that a variety of qualities, as exemplified by the four different houses at Hogwarts, are needed for sound psychological development. Over the projected volumes of her series, she is offering a bildungsroman, not only of Harry himself but also of Ron and Hermione. Not all school books have this element, as some writers (such as Anthony Buckeridge in his "Jennings" series) prefer to create characters who remain virtually identical throughout many volumes. The nature of the school story genre does, however, allow for this possibility.

That Rowling has succeeded in attracting so huge a following of both adults and children of a range of age groups is a testimony to the freshness of much of her writing. She has cleverly made use of the features of the school story genre, and if in this she has not always been totally original, she has recombined these elements in a nontraditional way. The potential for her books lasting as classics of children's literature lies not only in her large sales but also in the amount of critical analysis that they have the potential to stimulate.

37. Stephens, *Language and Ideology in Children's Fiction,* 121.

II

Harry's Roots in Epic, Myth, and Folklore

In Medias Res

Harry Potter as Hero-in-Progress

Mary Pharr

Despite the extraordinary reception of J. K. Rowling's books among millions of readers around the world, not everyone has praised the Harry Potter phenomenon. In an essay with the unsubtle title "Can 35 Million Book Buyers Be Wrong? Yes," Harold Bloom has disparaged Rowling's prose, her readers, and any academics who may like her work. "Is there any redeeming educational use to Rowling?" Bloom asks, and then answers his question with another: "Is there any to Stephen King?"[1] Within this context, Stephen King's own assessment of Rowling seems ironic. In a review of *Goblet of Fire*, King praises the Potter series but asks his own question: "Is there more going on here than fun?" His answer is a succinct "not much."[2] Both Bloom and King have legitimate queries in their first questions. What they miss, however, is that one answer to those queries lies within the questions themselves: at least part of the "educational use," the "more going on" within the Potter series, can be found in its own narrative focus on Harry's "going on," the "education" that is a crucial part of his process of maturation, his development as a hero. That development will begin with Harry's point of origin, but it can mature only through his formal training and increasing experience.

Why do we care about the development of another hero? The question may well be, rather, how could we not care? Humanity has always had a boundless interest in heroes, in those few among us who rise to perform great but arduous deeds. That interest is both innate and universal, representing as it does something individualized within a society and yet wide-ranging among all societies. Joseph Campbell spent a lifetime investigating and describing the expression of this interest, the heroic monomyth "through which the inexhaustible energies of the cosmos pour into human cultural manifestation."[3] The manifestation of such energies

1. Harold Bloom, "Can 35 Million Book Buyers Be Wrong? Yes."
2. Stephen King, "Wild about Harry," 13.
3. Joseph Campbell, *The Hero with a Thousand Faces*, 3.

may emerge in the form of a hero, a figure who represents the intense human struggle for both power *and* wisdom, recognition *and* introspection, grandeur *and* honor. Few of us achieve the rigorous balance of such dualisms, but they endure as more than naive aspirations; they endure as goals to guide us toward our possible best selves. The hero's story has the "thousand faces" made famous by Campbell's work, but it is still *a story,* that is, a narrative process by which things happen to create, to shape, and to demonstrate the hero in action. In this sense, the story always educates the hero, but when the story is also *about* the specific education of the hero, it touches what Gregory Maguire has called "one of the archetypal patterns of fantastic children's literature."[4] And when a work of what is initially regarded as children's literature touches readers of all ages, everyone participates in the pattern.

Harry Potter is a hero whose story is in progress, and it can be no surprise that the center of his story is his development through metaphorical and literal education, as well as through the application of that education to his own expanding experience. For not only is this character a potential representative of the monomyth; he is as well a magical figure growing up within the perimeters of a specific fictional universe that clearly needs new heroes—a need that also speaks to the fears and longings of his millennial-era readers. These readers—we readers—live with a daily, media-driven awareness of the interconnectedness of our world, of its vulnerability as a whole to individual acts of violence and mayhem. The England inhabited by Rowling's characters is fantasy, but fantasy, as D. W. Harding noted, "only highlights what is true of all fiction, that it is a convention of communication."[5] In this respect, Harry is the representative of many a "real-time" child's wishful dream and many an adult's private yearning for *someone* to come along and be able to do *something* to help an imperiled world. For the sake of his readers' emotional and psychological well-being, Harry must continue on into his heroism—but that heroism also has to have had a beginning.

Oftentimes, for a hero, that beginning lies within one's heritage. Heroes may seem to come from nowhere, but they are seldom just the luck of the draw; they are more traditionally the deus ex machina of the universe, the intervention of the past into the present in order to preserve the future. Biologically, genetically, an embryonic hero is likely to come from appropriately strong roots, good DNA; mythologically, he is the scion of earlier heroes whose qualities are enhanced by a new environment's fresh rigors and opportunities. Thus, although only a boy, Harry walks in a line that extends for thousands of years and through numerous narrative structures, a line

4. Gregory Maguire, "Lord of the Golden Snitch," 12.
5. D. W. Harding, "Psychological Processes in the Reading of Fiction," 64.

including figures as seemingly disparate as Gilgamesh (the son of Uruk's King Lugalbanda), Arthur (the son of Britain's King Uther Pendragon), Kal-El (the son of Krypton's great scientist Jor-El), and Luke Skywalker (the son of Jedi Knight Anakin Skywalker).

Despite their heritage, however, legends are not always honored in their first youth. Early in his story, Gilgamesh is a royal wastrel; in some of the best-known versions of his legend, Arthur is initially a little-noticed teenage squire. Kal-El is, of course, sent to Earth as an infant alien whose identity is hidden under the guise of farm boy Clark Kent, while Luke Skywalker is a real—if frustrated—farm boy at the beginning of *A New Hope*. All of these young men, however, long for something—for a destiny created by the extraordinary heritage they cannot yet comprehend. Like them, Harry is the direct heir of an exceptional father, of the wizard James Potter, who with his wife, Lily, died saving their only child. Thus, when his friend Hagrid wants to compliment Harry on his heroism, he tells the boy that Harry has done just what his father would have done.

Often less considered but potentially just as significant is the hero's maternal lineage. In Harry's case, it was his mother's love that specifically saved him from death as an infant. Evil sorcerer Lord Voldemort speaks of Lily Potter's deed as a "foolish sacrifice," but even this Dark Lord has to admit that a mother's sacrifice can unleash "old magic" (*Goblet of Fire*, 653). Lily's ancient female magic preserved her son for future greatness even as it also badly damaged Voldemort by destroying his body—thus giving the world time to rest and recuperate in the endless war of good against evil. Harry's heritage runs deep and wide—and the only cost to his parents was their mortal lives.

Not that the Potter boy knows anything about this heritage at first. He begins his life in ignorance, but to become a hero he must move toward an awareness of his own potential. Gilgamesh at least knows that he is powerful, though he does not truly know what it means to be human. Arthur and Luke, conversely, have some sense of their own humanity but know little of their potential. Kal-El treasures his adopted humanity even as he knows he is more than human; his task is to find some way to integrate his two halves. As for Harry, he seems to be like Arthur and Luke: instinctively decent but initially unaware of both the mysteries within his past and the powers in his person. Nonetheless, something is different here—a fairy-tale quality that Rowling adds to the mix. For although he shares the frustration felt by earlier embryonic heroes (especially the orphans—whether real ones like Frodo Baggins and Kal-El or circumstantial ones like Luke), Harry is still exceptionally young when he initially encounters great evil. Like the African hero Mwindo, he is only an infant when he first becomes involved in the struggle against Voldemort, but unlike Mwindo (who is born mature in mind and magic), baby Harry has no consciousness of his potential. Only at age eleven does Harry consciously accept a role in his destiny. At that age, he cannot be expected to know much about humanity—his own or anyone else's. He just knows that he *has* to go to Hogwarts School of Witchcraft and Wizardry. All heroes learn, but much of Harry's education will be scholastic as well as experiential. His incipient greatness will be marked by the rigors of that process.

Moreover, despite his youth, the Potter heritage calls Harry to become a seeker whose episodic quests for knowledge are unified by the grand themes of self-discovery and selfless valor. That combination is important, for if a hero is to be complete, he must come to know more than himself and his own potential; he must also come to know the value of other creatures, great and small. So it is that King Arthur comes to understand the value of a round rather than a rectangular table, the emblem of chivalrous community above that of monarchial hierarchy. And so it is that rather than simply discovering the truth of the Sorcerer's Stone or the Chamber of Secrets, Harry must use his burgeoning knowledge for the good of others, whether in defense of a solitary groundskeeper unjustly accused of infamy, or in defense of the remains of a murdered boy whose ghostly wish is to be returned to his grieving family—or in defense of the whole world of wizards and Muggles against the Dark Lord's absolute evil. In other words, Harry must not only be powerful but also empathetic, able to feel as well as to do.

Harry comes by both his frustration and his empathy honestly, each a response to—or a means of escaping from—the nonmagical family that raises him after his parents have died. Actually, "raises" is the wrong word here; "torments" is the more appropriate verb for the Dursleys' treatment of Harry. They are Harry's only blood relatives, yet in their own way, Vernon, Petunia, and Dudley Dursley are each as monstrous as any of Voldemort's minions—and their monstrosity is crucial in Harry's early development. Cousin Dudley is grotesque, greedy, sneaky, and stupid—the kind of kid whose birthday demand is for more than the thirty-eight presents he got last year, but who also has trouble figuring out that two more gifts added to this year's thirty-seven will equal thirty-nine. So fat that his posterior droops over kitchen chairs, Dudley has for years quite literally thrown his weight around, regularly beating up his smaller cousin merely out of mean-ness. No wonder that an exasperated Hagrid casts a spell that leaves Dudley with a pig's tail, the implication of poetic justice clear even to the rustic gamekeeper.

As for Dudley's parents, they are equally horrendous. Petunia Dursley al-ways hated her wizard sister with a vehemence that was only a thin disguise for envy. Vernon Dursley is the consummate prig and hypocrite, disgusted at the thought of something unconventional in his family. The Dursleys have lied to Harry for years, telling him his parents died in a car crash and never mentioning his magic heritage. For a time, they force Harry to sleep in a cupboard, literally putting the familial secret in the closet. Even when Harry gets a small bedroom, Uncle Vernon puts bars on its windows and locks on its door—making Harry the prisoner of Privet Drive. Only the Dursleys' fear of Harry's increasingly visible ties to his parents' world keeps them from imposing worse restrictions. That fear does not, however, prevent them from further humiliating Harry. While showering the porcine Dudley with lavish presents, the Dursleys give their nephew (when they remember him at all) special-occasion gifts such as a pair of old socks or a single tissue.

Obviously, the Dursleys stand as caricatures of cruelty, Dickensian figures given one more turn of the screw—a pretty thorough turn that can be seen in the lie they use to hide Harry's attendance at Hogwarts: they tell people he attends "St. Brutus's Secure Center for Incurably Criminal Boys" (*Prisoner of Azkaban*, 19). The hyperbole here is characteristic of the way Rowling uses the Dursleys. Never really frightening but always nasty and absurd—they are a way for the author to preserve both real sympathy for Harry and the easily accessible humor of her narrative. Those who are supposed to be normal are so preposterous that we are immediately prompted to like not only their victim but also the metanormal world he is entering.

In terms of Harry's development as a hero, the Dursleys have a further, more complicated significance. By abusing Harry, they predispose him to identify with the abused. Rowling makes clear that such identification could become dangerous: Harry learns enough magic to wreak havoc on the family were he so inclined, but his Potter heritage calls him, instead, to go beyond the obtuse and angry Dursleys, to seek a more important fate. Like his power, his compassion has its roots in the heroism and sacrifice of his parents; the Potters died, however, before he could ever know them as living ethical guides. If their name serves as his entrée into the world of wizardry, his childhood deprivations must serve as a gateway into empathy. Even before he starts his formal education as a wizard, he enters that gate, as when he sympathizes with a caged boa constrictor, whose plight he perceives as "worse than having a cupboard as a bedroom" (*Sorcerer's Stone*, 27). A Parselmouth, Harry can talk to snakes, but what matters is that he can also feel for these creatures so often also branded as "incurably criminal." Almost two years later, he tricks the vicious wizard Lucius Malfoy into freeing a house-elf named Dobby. House-elves are effectively slaves, and Harry has known his own kind of captivity with the Dursleys. True, he will later be reluctant to become involved with his friend Hermione's attempts to free all house-elves, but many house-elves themselves also appear uncertain about these attempts and so are reluctant to accept Hermione's efforts—at least initially. What is certain is that Harry finds a way to free an elf who most assuredly wants liberty. And on being freed, the grateful and overly effusive Dobby sobs, "Harry Potter is greater by far than Dobby knew!" (*Chamber of Secrets,* 339). He is also greater than he could have been with a more comfortable—hence more parochial—childhood. He has learned empathy from the old school of hard knocks, and he is not a boy to forget his early lessons.

This empathy accounts for Harry's fundamental, "underprivileged kid makes good" appeal, but it's only the start of his education. Rowling has been very clear on the bildungsroman aspect of her series, having said of Harry, "I do want him to grow up."[6] He cannot grow from abused orphan to adult hero in the foolish world of the Dursleys; he must move on. Most heroes journey as part of their development. Sometimes, the voyage is undertaken with reluctance, as when Achilles and Odysseus sail away from Greece to their destiny in Troy, or when Frodo leaves the Shire to find his own fate in Mordor; sometimes, it is simply a natural part of things, as when Kal-El/Clark Kent moves from Smallville to Metropolis, from Superboy to Superman. As for Harry, he needs to find an extraordinary setting that will provide him an education in pragmatic magic and hard truth. Thus, he journeys each year to Hogwarts, a castlelike school perched on a mountain between a black lake and a forbidden forest. More than a fairy-tale backdrop for the wizards and witches of the Potter universe, Hogwarts is the nexus between the agony of their past and the uncertainty of their future—and not even its headmaster knows all its secrets. As a school, moreover, Hogwarts is a fundamentally serious place (though as everywhere in this series, the seriousness is balanced by humor). For Harry Potter, Hogwarts is a place of tests: some academic, some practical, and some moral. Many of these tests include adventure, danger, and choice—heady stuff that forces Harry to grow up or fail. And failure in a universe of magic is all too often fatal.

It is true that all of us are continually tested in diurnal reality—but not against fiends like Voldemort and Malfoy or with the help of friends like Hagrid and Dobby. Harry's world is chock full of fantastic others, creatures fundamentally different from those found in the mundane world of fact, creatures that almost always participate one way or another in the testing process. The Potter series has dragons, of course, mighty creatures quite capable of testing any hero. Of more consequence, however, is that Hogwarts itself is a locus for magical figures of every degree of sentience and significance: sorcerers, ghosts, banshees, animagi, centaurs, werewolves, hippogriffs, grindylows, boggarts, merpeople, sphinxes, and dementors among them. The challenges posed by this fantastic catalogue are explicit and often

6. J. K. Rowling, interview by Malcolm Jones, 59.

perilous. But the empirical knowledge imparted to the hero by his encounters with the catalogue is vital if he is to grow in wisdom as well as strength.

To obtain that experiential knowledge, he must survive even the encounters for which he is initially ill prepared—the ones that require machinery and technique as much as heritage and empathy. Like any wizard, Harry must learn to handle extraordinary machinery—transformative potions and powerful wands—but the use of such machinery is seldom self-evident. Like everyone else, the Potter boy must learn use and technique from masters, and education is never really free—not even for a natural like Harry. He must practice the skills that will let him face increasingly arduous trials. At Hogwarts, Harry has multiple masters, some of whom he appreciates (for example, the werewolf wizard Remus Lupin), and some whom he despises (potions professor Severus Snape being the most obvious example), but all of whom he needs. Lupin, for example, patiently tutors him on the Patronus Charm, "highly advanced magic" that can repel even the fearsome, mind-destroying dementors (*Prisoner of Azkaban*, 237). Later, in a terrifying test that Harry only half understands, the charm saves his life and that of his friends when he uses it to fend off a mob of hungry dementors.

Not all Harry's teachers are so accommodating as Lupin. Professor Snape (whose background was evil but who has long been converted to—a somewhat strained—good) has no interest in tutoring a boy whose dislike he amply returns; nonetheless, Snape, too, instructs the boy—and not always in the classroom. Part of his role in the series seems to be to demonstrate to Harry that hasty conclusions are inherently weak. Throughout the story, both Snape and Harry are continually caught in the unfortunate repercussions of mutual misunderstanding, always suspecting each other of skulduggery. Thus, near the end of year one at Hogwarts, the boy is amazed to discover that Snape deliberately chose to help protect him when Quirrell (another of the Dark Lord's minions) tried to curse Harry off his flying broom during a Quidditch game. Yet even this discovery fails to soften the reciprocal antipathy. As late as year four, Snape is still undermining Harry's reputation as something built on a "determination to break rules" (*Goblet of Fire*, 276).

More explicitly and inexcusably, Snape constantly badgers the whole Potter circle, leaving Harry to engage in vivid dreams of revenge. If Snape's petty meanness suggests the limits of conversion, Harry's childish fantasies suggest his own youthful immaturity. Their relationship as a whole implies that unrequited tolerance is a much more difficult skill to acquire than is proficiency with a wand. Still a juvenile, Harry cannot assimilate everything with equal facility, but Snape's unintended "lessons" will surely eventually take hold. If they did not, Harry would never be completely worthy of his heroic heritage.

So Harry has a multiplicity of masters instructing him in different areas with varying degrees of success. Only a few of these masters, however, can serve as his closest advisers, his specific role models in judgment. In certain narratives—not all—such guides in wisdom may seem more than human, ready to help whenever and wherever needed. They respond to the hero's belief in their response: "One has only to know and trust," says Campbell, "and the ageless guardians will appear."[7] Thus, Gilgamesh has Utnapishtim, who teaches him the secret of eternal life and the far more precious truth of mortality. Arthur has Merlin, who shows him the world as it could be. Luke has Obi-Wan and Yoda, the former to introduce the boy Luke to the Force and the latter to train the Jedi Luke in its ways. Through the first four episodes of his story, Harry also has two special mentors: Albus Dumbledore and Sirius Black.

The silver-haired headmaster of Hogwarts and the greatest magus of his time, Dumbledore is precisely the right man to play Aristotle to Harry's Alexander. He is also something of a grandfather figure to the orphaned boy, indulgently allowing him more independence than a father might. In year one, knowing as he must that Harry will use magic devices to break those rules that obsess Snape, Dumbledore still slips Harry the invisibility cloak that once belonged to James Potter; he then allows the boy to find the dangerous, dream-filled Mirror of Erised—powerful tools for a first-year magician to handle. Dumbledore operates by trust as much as by skill, however, and as Harry later realizes, the old headmaster "sort of wanted to give me a chance" (*Sorcerer's Stone*, 302), not just another chance to face his parents' killer directly but to learn his own ability and possibility. In their second meeting, Voldemort is again defeated, but the effort of the combat almost kills Harry. Just as maternal love saved Harry's infant life, however, his connection to Dumbledore saves him now, the wizard rushing to the rescue just as Harry loses consciousness.

This connection between headmaster and Harry intensifies with each passing year, even as each fresh crisis allows Harry more autonomy as a hero, more independence in his quest to reach his own destiny and to secure the safe destiny of untold others. In year two, the headmaster's pet phoenix, Fawkes, comes to Harry's aid in another crisis because it senses his loyalty to Dumbledore. At a moment of near calamity during year three, Dumbledore advises not Harry but his friend Hermione on the time travel the students must use to save innocent lives. Here the old grand wizard shows how well Harry has chosen his companions, for the profoundly intellectual Hermione is better suited than Harry to understand the intricacies of temporal displacement.

7. Campbell, *Thousand Faces*, 72.

As the series progresses, Dumbledore proves to be more than just a wise elder, in much the same way that Tolkien's Gandalf is more than an old counselor. In year four, Harry is apparently on his own during another fearsome encounter with Voldemort; however, once the boy escapes the Dark Lord, Dumbledore saves his student from still another of Voldemort's mad toadies. It's then that Harry sees the normally gentle headmaster at full force, combat-ready, as "a sense of power radiated from Dumbledore as though he were giving off burning heat" (*Goblet of Fire*, 679). Now the wizard has truly become Campbell's "ageless guardian," the powerful patron who intervenes as destiny requires, effectively becoming the hero's unseen shield and companion in arms. Although he never claims mystical status, Dumbledore is more than a mentor in magic; like Gandalf rushing to Frodo's aid, he is also an element of the monomyth; he is the hero's secret strength. But Dumbledore cannot protect Harry the boy forever; when his training is finished, Harry the man must rely on his own strength. Only then will the eternal circle come round, with Harry able to pass on his own heroism, perhaps to create or to instruct some new hero himself.

Sirius Black is not so imposing a figure, but he is critical to Harry's development in a different way: Sirius contributes repeatedly to the growth of Harry's emotional well-being. An animagus able to transform into a dog, Sirius was James Potter's best friend and infant Harry's godfather. As a child, Harry never knew Sirius. It was not the Dursleys who kept the two apart; it was the prison Azkaban. Framed by the traitorous Peter Pettigrew (secretly Voldemort's spy Wormtail) for a mass murder, Sirius has survived long years amid the hideous dementors, his innocent conscience and transformative power preserving him while the guilty around him go mad or die. When he finally finds the stamina to escape, he does so to protect Harry from Pettigrew, whose own animagical power has turned him—literally and figuratively—into a rat. After a dozen years in Azkaban, Sirius is a survivalist whose skills and knowledge Harry needs; more important, however, he's also a direct link to the past Harry cannot himself remember—to the parents whose gifts, sacrifice, and love form the foundation of Harry's heroism. As the living embodiment of what the Potters stood for, Sirius has an attachment to Harry quite different from that of the mighty Dumbledore; thus, the fugitive from Azkaban is the one the boy consults when he worries that his problems are too foolish for Dumbledore's notice. Quite simply, Sirius and Harry are family, both having survived the unsurvivable. Small wonder that Harry longs for the day when Sirius will finally clear his name, for then the godson can move into his godfather's home—if that day ever comes.

All too often for heroes—even for those, like Odysseus and the Cid, who long for their living families—home fires burn brightest when they are most distant. Domesticity is abandoned for adventure, requiring of the hero a certain toughness that is as much a part of him as is his empathy. Joan Acocella believes that one of the major appeals of the Potter series is its "lack of sentimentality."[8] Despite his sympathy for the abused, Harry is no wimp; he has his enemies on Privet Drive and more enemies at Hogwarts, where he doesn't waste time trying to reconcile with the likes of Draco Malfoy, malevolent son of Lucius. The animosity here is palpable—not just a schoolboy clash but a miniature of the enmity between the forces of light and dark. This struggle dominates Harry's life, to the point that Snape is curiously accurate in judging the boy to be an inveterate rule-breaker. Harry has to break rules if he is more committed to right than to regulation. Ironically, that commitment is itself dangerous—or it would be if *right* were determined only by Harry's personal perspective and power, by his still juvenile interpretation of others, backed up by his steadily increasing might. Were that the case, he might have already inadvertently injured Snape—thus impairing his own potential as hero. But Harry's commitment is reinforced by Dumbledore and Sirius, by Hagrid and Hermione, by his best friend, Ron, and all of Ron's bumbling, decent family. They, too, contribute to his development, giving him their collective integrity.

Of all within this circle, Hermione and Ron have the closest contact with Harry on a daily basis. As his peers, they offer him comfort and companionship—a real boon for a developing hero. Gilgamesh has Enkidu, "Sweet France's" Roland relies on Oliver, and Luke has Leia and Han as more than friends, as companions of the heart who let the hero laugh and feel a normalcy otherwise denied him. Such companions are not automatically given to heroes: Beowulf has none, nor do Arthur and Mwindo—and Superman's buddies often seem more trouble than comfort. But if the gift of such friendship is allowed the hero, it humanizes him—adding an element of grace to his tale. Harry is never more likable than when he is joking with Ron or trying to figure out Hermione's independent ways. The three often inadvertently reveal just how young they are by their schemes not only to defeat evil but also to get through the school year as successfully (Hermione) or as simply (Ron) as possible. Harry needs both perspectives, and he's never as anguished fighting Voldemort as he is when he quarrels with these beloved friends. Friendship itself helps Harry grow toward maturity.

Nonetheless, although Harry's masters, guardian, godfather, and friends do all they can to help Harry, they cannot *be* Harry. What clinches the heroic nature of the Potter series is its adherence to the complexity of Harry's moral development. His childhood was miserable; his adolescence at Hogwarts is different but never easy. For beyond the normal tensions of the

8. Joan Acocella, "Under the Spell: Harry Potter Explained," 76.

teen years, Harry rapidly discovers the truth about evil: that it is seductive, potent, and enduring. Speaking for his lord, Voldemort's puppet Quirrell posits evil's creed, beginning with its denial of ethical distinctions: "There is no good and evil, there is only power . . ." (*Sorcerer's Stone,* 291). Harry has power—more each year—and he does enjoy it. Indeed, Acocella goes so far as to state that the "subject of the Harry Potter series is power," how to get it, how to use it, and how to answer the Miltonic questions it brings forth.[9]

Surely the greatest of those questions—raised in *Paradise Lost* when Satan offers the formidable apple of knowledge to humanity—is that of choice. Alan Jacobs astutely perceives that Harry's heroism depends on his awareness of the seriousness and the difficulty of choice, encapsulated in Harry's "recognition that he is not *inevitably* good."[10] As proof, Jacobs points to a year one scene in *The Sorcerer's Stone,* wherein the magical Sorting Hat places new students in the communal house where they belong. The Hat almost puts Harry in Slytherin, where *"cunning folk use any means / To achieve their ends,"* where a boy with Harry's potential "could be great" (*Sorcerer's Stone,* 118, 121). Harry has already had his first run-in with soon-to-be Slytherin Draco Malfoy, and he grips the edges of his stool while mentally refusing the hat's offer. Even so, the temptation posed by the Hat scares Harry, and many months pass before Dumbledore is able to convince the boy that it was choice rather than potential that mattered on the sorting day, that—in Jacobs's words—Harry's "character is not a fixed preexistent thing, but something that he has the responsibility for making" (par. 19). Gradually, Harry comes to know what he has earlier only sensed and what Quirrell will never understand: that good and evil do exist, with choice the thin but crucial wall between them, and power the charm that can make that fragile barrier disappear. This is his school's greatest lesson.

Choosing to fight evil requires as much faith as strength—and with no guarantee of victory. All heroes must face both the temptation of evil and the prospect of defeat, possibly death. Young as he is, Harry, too, must face these challenges. While searching for the Chamber of Secrets, for example, Harry descends into the underworld of Hogwarts, where he discovers that beneath its marvels lie possibilities of power etched into memories of pain and madness. Within the Chamber, Harry comes face to face with the living memory of former Hogwarts student Tom Marvolo Riddle. It seems that the Sorting Hat really does know the houses: fifty years ago, Riddle became the Heir of Slytherin, he who would dominate the dark arts—and try to

---

9. Acocella, "Under the Spell," 77.
10. Alan Jacobs, "Harry Potter's Magic," par. 18 (online).

dominate the world—under the more fearsome name of Lord Voldemort. Riddle wonders at the similarities between himself and Harry: both "half-bloods, orphans, raised by Muggles," both Parselmouths, and, strangely, each boy physically resembling the other (*Chamber of Secrets*, 317). It will take a while before the incipient Dark Lord acknowledges their other similarities: a phenomenal gift for magic and the rare fortitude required to exercise that gift. Yet no matter how often Harry escapes, even defeats his seeming doppelgänger, Voldemort will likely never acknowledge their primary difference: the strength Harry receives from his conscious decision *not* to become another Heir of Slytherin. Like Tolkien's Sauron and Lucas's Emperor, Voldemort cannot conceive of strength derived from the refusal to dominate by power. But such strength is real—as real as Dumbledore's might—and it helps Harry decimate the memory of Riddle.

A year later, Harry confirms who he is becoming when he stops Sirius and Lupin from executing the vile traitor Peter Pettigrew. Thinking of Sirius and Lupin as his father's closest friends, Harry then tells Pettigrew, "I'm not doing this for you! I'm doing it because—I don't reckon my dad would've wanted them to become killers—just for you" (*Prisoner of Azkaban*, 376). By enriching his familial identity with his own resolution, Harry corroborates Thomas Greene's theory that a hero's life "is devoted to informing his name with meaning."[11] Such enrichment, alas, always comes with a price. Soon enough, Pettigrew repays Harry's grand gesture by escaping, returning to Voldemort's service, and (as Wormtail) playing a major role in the Dark Lord's physical resurrection. Even for a hero, it would seem, choice has consequences beyond his reach.

The discovery of his limited reach may be the most painful lesson of all for Harry, but it is vital to his development as a hero. Even the swift-footed Achilles has to learn his limits when he finds that neither his godlike reputation nor his glittering armor is enough to save his best friend's life in battle. Only after accepting the inherent confines of mortality does Achilles become both awesome *and* humane. And in the *Chanson*, only by blowing the *olifant* that will summon Charlemagne does Roland effectively admit that even the most arrogant of heroes cannot defeat all enemies alone. Rowling's young hero is rarely arrogant, but his decision to restrain his friends in the Pettigrew matter indirectly allows Voldemort to unleash his full wrath on innocents, on Hogwarts student Cedric Diggory in particular. The Dark Lord casually kills the sixteen-year-old Cedric simply because the boy is in the wrong place at the wrong time. And Harry can do nothing to prevent the death. He has met his limits, and it is appropriate that this bitter knowledge comes in *Goblet of Fire,* the midpoint book in his story. For Harry is

11. Thomas Greene, *The Descent from Heaven: A Study in Epic Continuity,* 16.

now committed to the trajectory of his progression into mature heroism, and he knows full well what sacrifices it may entail.

Sacrifice, too, is an inevitable part of a hero's story. Sometimes, all that is required is a period of suffering, as when Odysseus and the Cid must turn away from their longed-for domestic tranquility to the demands of their heroic exploits. At other times, though, more than suffering is demanded: Achilles and Roland lose first their best friends to death, then their own lives; Beowulf, too, dies in service, leaving like the others a miserably uncertain future for his people. For someone like Arthur, the sacrifices expand until they swallow all the hero has labored for—the very kingdom and culture that he has defended. Yet the sacrifices cannot be avoided. Beginning with Harry's parents and moving on to and no doubt beyond Cedric, the Potter series is littered with such sacrifices, each imposed on those who value goodness more than life. At this point in the Potter series, no reader knows how many and how much will be lost in the war against evil, but all readers must admit—as Dumbledore does—that the denizens of Harry's world are "facing dark and difficult times" (*Goblet of Fire*, 724).

Thus, we leave Harry at a somber moment in his development. Nonetheless, to focus exclusively on this moment would be to misstate the uniqueness of the Potter series. Just as it is both a children's and an adult's series, it is also both solemn and quite funny. The humor, too, is a part of the educational process within the book, but here, perhaps, the education is aimed toward Rowling's audience, serving both an empathetic and a cathartic function. The humor's empathy is another link between characters and readers, a link suggesting that we readers could, perhaps, be at least a little like these heroes in their greatness if they are sometimes like us in our folly. As for catharsis, George Lucas well understood this need when he added the droids as a prime source of humor in the Star Wars series. They repeatedly break tension—just as Nearly Headless Nick and Moaning Myrtle do within the Potter series. One of Rowling's most remarkable attributes as a creator is her ability to move from the absurd to the momentous with ease.

And so the series continues, its hero's development currently in medias res. More and more, Rowling's narratives are recognizable for their adherence to heroic patterns and for the remarkable protagonist her title character is becoming. Harry is not a hero simply because his parents were heroes; heritage is a crucial starting point but never an end unto itself. Rather, Harry is a hero because he is willing to engage in the defense of all that is constructively human. To turn that willingness into action, he has had to find the right education, and in the extended environment of Hogwarts and its environs, Harry has the time and space, the mentors and equipment to make the transition. There, too, he has met those who, like Voldemort and the Malfoys, have chosen to assault humanity rather than protect it; these meetings have also been part of his education, teaching him what he could become if he falls prey to his own ego and power.

Already, Harry's development has moved him beyond the boundaries of diurnal reality, beyond the circumscribed setting that is the world of the Muggles—and also the world of Rowling's readers. Yet Harry the extraordinary young wizard also remains touchingly human, limited as all humans are but developing the will and the judgment to direct his quest toward a defense of others who are less than he—toward a state that is the stuff of his readers' best dreams. Harry's age and his tale's readability may have led a somewhat desperate *New York Times* to create a restricted "children's literature" list of bestsellers, but the Potter series truly has a global appeal.

He is also a welcome figure in an age crammed with pseudo-heroes. With his slight physique, his glasses that *don't* disguise a secret Adonis, and his personal anguish over ethics, Harry is the antithesis of today's wrestling-style "heroes" who cross the line between good and evil with dull, misleading regularity. Yet he is as much a representative of the new millennium as are the wrestlers, the rappers, the TV hosts, the pro athletes, the fuzzy New Age characters who dominate the electronic universe. Like them, Harry requires no erudition to appreciate. Like them, he has crowd-pleasing skills that set him apart and allow him to triumph in public competition. Like them, he rebels repeatedly against the petty tyranny of irritating regulations. And like them, he is a phenomenon who has roused both ire and confusion within critical and popular comment.

Unlike them, Harry's character (in both senses of the word) is progressing, each new book suffusing him with the wisdom of a myriad of earlier heroes, each new adventure refining that wisdom with modern knowledge. Ruth Nanda Anshen has described modern knowledge "as a means of liberating mankind from the destructive power of fear, pointing the way toward the goal of the rehabilitation of the human will and the rebirth of faith and confidence in the human person."[12] Harry Potter functions as a deceptively simple emblem of this ideal, which connects wonderfully with the old ideals of the monomyth. Through the education of her hero, J. K. Rowling encourages people to enhance their sense of awe, to think about the nature of the universe, to ponder the possibility of moral action—and to read of their own free will. As she teaches Harry, so he teaches us all.

12. Ruth Nanda Anshen, "World Perspectives," xi.

Of Magicals and Muggles

Reversals and Revulsions at Hogwarts

Jann Lacoss

Mr. and Mrs. Dursley, of number four, Privet Drive, were proud to say that they were perfectly normal, thank you very much. They were the last people you'd expect to be involved in anything strange or mysterious, because they just didn't hold with such nonsense.

—*Harry Potter and the Sorcerer's Stone*

The world of Harry Potter is rife with mystery. J. K. Rowling, in creating intriguing scenes of heroism and hysteria, not only captures imaginations for an enticing read but also incorporates life lessons through her characters and events. Several folkloric elements and devices help make the series extraordinarily popular: folk groups, rites of passage, reversals, boundary crossing, and taboo themes play significant roles in helping children deal with changes in life and prepare them for appropriate social roles. Consciously or unconsciously, Rowling includes these in relating Harry's adventures to her readers.

From the beginning of the series, Rowling introduces her readers to a culture that differs markedly from their own. Wizarding society is described in a fashion that entices the audience to want to be a part of it. This society can be seen as a distinct folk group, with a cultural identity paralleling that of a national group. The characters in the series also undergo rites of passage similar to those children and adolescents go through in real life.

Certain elements of the series are presented in extraordinary contexts, turning them upside down or inside out with regard to how they are normally viewed, as they might be construed in a child's imagination. Such reversals depict life as it should not be, in order to reinforce socially acceptable behaviors. The preadolescent and adolescent children who constitute the main audience of the series are at a stage where they may question social norms and parental and social behaviors. The Dursleys present a particularly clear example of this, reinforcing the notion of parental love and support by demonstrating the opposite behaviors and their effects. In using several instances of reversals, Rowling shows her audience some ambiguities of life and, more subtly, the way things should be.

Liminal, or boundary-crossing, people and objects commonly appear in folklore and ritual, and they are included in the Potter books. People with out-of-the-ordinary powers, who can apparate and disapparate at will, and items with unexpected functions such as fireplaces that act as transportation conduits exemplify such transitional qualities. Because children, who are in a transitional stage of life, relate to boundary-crossers, the prominence of such people and things appeals further to them.

Children, especially preadolescents and adolescents, embrace taboo topics and themes as they learn socially acceptable behaviors and social norms. Violence and murder, magic and mysticism, and the very nature of evil are enticing yet frightening topics to consider, even for adults. Most parents naturally prefer that their children not see or even discuss murder, mayhem, or evil of any sort. Yet children are exposed to this regularly through the mass media and entertainment venues. The world of Harry Potter approaches these taboos in terms and under circumstances that children can more easily understand than the six o'clock news. Rowling draws distinctions between good and evil and presents very negative events in relatively nonthreatening ways. Rather than learning about death by racking up carnage points in "Doom," Potter fans see the consequences of senseless murders by vicariously experiencing the emotions felt by Harry and others who have been influenced by Voldemort's actions. Rowling allows an open discussion of evil by having characters confront it on a regular basis and even by naming it.

The Potter series also resembles folktales in certain ways. Tales present difficult concepts (for example, violence, conflicting feelings, taboos) in terms that children understand. They also tend to follow a relatively standard sequence of actions, as does the Harry Potter series.

Folk Groups in Harry Potter

As readers are introduced to the wizarding world, they meet a culture that differs considerably from their own. They encounter another folk group—that is, people who belong to a society with traditions and folkways that seem unusual and sometimes bizarre. Folk groups share common elements that form the foundation for cultural communications.[1] They comprise groups of people who have mutually accepted traditions. That is, their members have certain specific traits in common that identify them with the group as a whole. Outward indicators may include costume, verbal interaction among members, and foodways. They also tend to share certain rituals. Each folk group has its own body of folklore.[2] Using the guidelines

1. Barre Toelken, *The Dynamics of Folklore*, 51.
2. Jan Harold Brunvand, *The Study of American Folklore*, 39–41. As an example, American folk groups can be classified into six major types, based on occupation, age,

that indicate delineations of folk groups, children can be seen as a distinct group, based on age, social position, and biological and mental developmental stages. Likewise, the wizards in the Harry Potter series are a folk group, and child wizards constitute a subgroup. J. K. Rowling has, either consciously or unconsciously, drawn from a knowledge of how folk groups are constituted in building her wizard society.

The wizarding world is a secret society that is entered only through necessary rites of passage. It is not exclusive; anyone with the gift can join, whether Muggle- or wizard-born. Wizards have a specific form of dress and a special vocabulary, and they tend toward certain occupations. Though they eat regular food, it is not always prepared in the usual (that is, Muggle) way. The secrets of the group are kept so well that Muggles are, for the most part, unaware of the very existence of the wizarding world. In fact, wizards keep Muggles unaware through quite elaborate means: anti-Muggle precautions are taken to extremes to hide the existence of wizarding schools and the Quidditch World Cup, for example.

Costume often indicates membership in a certain group. Many professions have distinct uniforms or dress codes to set their members apart from the rest of society and lend them credibility. People tend to accept that a person wearing a white band inserted in the collar is a member of the clergy. In the reader's world, police officers, firefighters, and doctors can easily be recognized by their dress. Similarly, social groups have dress codes: people who play almost any team sport wear either official or unofficial uniforms, as do bowlers, tennis players, and golfers. Members of ethnic groups may wear identifiable clothing to indicate membership in the group: Orthodox Jewish men may sport yarmulkes; Indian women may wear saris; Irish dancers may don traditional garb when performing folk dances. In the wizarding world, members of society wear robes, which set them apart from nonwizards. Some Muggles find this dress intriguing, and others consider it odd and disquieting, as evidenced by Mr. Dursley's reaction to the people that he deems to be strangely attired at the beginning of *Sorcerer's Stone:* "As he sat in the usual morning traffic jam, he couldn't help noticing that there seemed to be a lot of strangely dressed people about. People in cloaks. Mr. Dursley couldn't bear people who dressed in funny clothes. . . . He'd forgotten all about the people in cloaks until he passed a group of them next to the baker's. He eyed them angrily as he passed. He didn't know why, but they made him uneasy" (*Sorcerer's Stone,* 3–4). Mr. Dursley's unease with the cloaked individuals may occur mostly as a result of his general uptightness, but it may also stem in part from his nonmembership in the

---

family, gender, region, and ethnicity. Each group may have its own jargon, rituals, and mode of dress.

group. Humans tend to fear things (and people) that differ from them and that are unknown; hence the ostracism of various cultural groups in society as a whole. Clothing alone is enough to set these people apart as nonmembers of "normal" society. This seemingly odd introduction to wizards has its benefits for the audience. By setting them apart at first as an unknown, dangerous, and potentially feared group and then turning them into the desirable culture, Rowling makes wizards intriguing to her young readers.[3] In any event, wizards are immediately distinguished as belonging to a culture distinct from that of Muggles.

Specialized lexicon constitutes another main indicator of a folk group. When folklorists work to define a people as belonging to a specific group, they collect any distinctive terminology used primarily by group members in order to distinguish a specialized informal vocabulary.[4] The wizard's general vocabulary includes words foreign to Muggles: apparating and disapparating, Floo powder, Gryffindor/Slytherin, dementors. Even individual character names are foreign to Muggle readers, or they have different connotations. Rowling draws on other languages for some; others have roots in or similarities to known words: Albus Dumbledore, Rubeus Hagrid, Severus Snape, Sirius Black, Voldemort. It is notable that wizarding vocabulary is not widely known in the Muggle world, and vice versa. In *Sorcerer's Stone,* Harry begins to learn the terminology of his new folk group, as he has to decipher new words when he hears them or experiences their effects (for example, Muggle, Floo powder, Quidditch). These terms have crept into the reader's lexicon as well. The *Wall Street Journal* and *Newsweek* have reported instances of Potterisms being used in the workplace.[5] This indicates the desire of the reading audience to join the wizarding folk group. While readers cannot (as far as we know) apparate and disapparate, they are able to pick up the folk lexicon with relative ease.

Within a group's lexicon, secret languages may emerge. To an outsider, the group's entire specialized vocabulary may seem like a secret language unto itself. Children create secret languages in order to create a common bond and define themselves as a folk group and within their subunits. By these languages, special terminology, and certain pronunciations, group members recognize others like them and connect socially.[6] Throughout the series, we see Harry learning the verbal expressions of wizardry and incorporating himself into his new group. This vocabulary parallels a secret

3. I refer to young readers as opposed to older readers–adults who have become pleasantly addicted to the series.
4. Brunvand, *Study of American Folklore,* 79.
5. Matthew Rose and Emily Nelson, "Potter Cognoscenti: All Know a Muggle When They See One"; Malcolm Jones, "Why Harry's Hot."
6. Brunvand, *Study of American Folklore,* 37.

language. Knowledge thereof helps incorporate the readers of the series into yet another "in crowd": those privy to the wizarding world. Readers relate to the terminology of wizardry on two levels: they see the young wizards being integrated into their particular society/adult world, and they themselves are being incorporated vicariously into the world of wizards (wizard "wannabes"). Young readers easily relate and adapt to the new terms, as they are often in the midst of creating their own codes. Older readers reminisce, on some level, about their own anti-languages created in childhood as they assimilate the unfamiliar vocabulary.

Some of the language that Harry learns as he is incorporated into his new group deals with abstract concepts rather than concrete objects. While learning new terms for new items is relatively easy and draws on roots of words that he (and the reader) may already know, the group has also created an even more specialized vocabulary to describe and enact various spells: Riddikulus, Expecto Patronum, Accio, Imperio, Expelliarmus, Engorgio, to name a few. The creation of terms (as opposed to the adoption of already known terms for different purposes) is yet another indicator of a folk group that sets itself apart from the rest of society.[7] By drawing on words and roots from other languages, Rowling gives the reader terms that are meaningful on a higher level. Older readers especially try to discern the meanings of the names and spells.

The young wizards are further delineated at Hogwarts when students are sorted into subgroups, to which they will relate and belong for the duration of their studies and possibly beyond. The houses into which they are sorted resemble fraternities and sororities, in that there are rituals associated with each. The reader is privy only to the goings-on in Gryffindor, so examples from that house shall be used. I mention these rituals as further indicators that the wizarding world comprises a distinct folk group and as a precursor to discussing the liminality of both the young wizards and the target audience. Adding to the secrecy and jargon of the subgroups, students in each house need passwords to enter their dormitories. The passwords consist of words known in the Muggle world, but they are often obscure or used in odd combinations: Caput Draconis, Fortuna Major, pure-blood, Lemon Drop, and Cockroach Cluster, for example (*Sorcerer's Stone*, 130; *Prisoner of Azkaban*, 152; *Chamber of Secrets*, 221; *Goblet of Fire*, 579). Only those who belong to the specific houses or the places to which they apply know these.

Ghosts constitute another concrete example of a folk group in the Harry Potter series. There exists the general group of ghosts: spirits of the dead, and within that main group, subfactions. In *Chamber of Secrets*, Nearly

---

7. M. A. K. Halliday, *Language as a Social Semiotic: The Social Interpretation of Language and Meaning*, 164.

Headless Nick is upset at his deathday party because he has been excluded from the Headless Hunt (122–39). Only ghosts who have been completely beheaded may join this exclusive faction. Nick notes his lack of total beheadedness for his segregation: " 'Half an inch of skin and sinew holding my neck on, Harry! Most people would think that's good and beheaded, but oh, no, it's not good enough for Sir Properly Decapitated-Podmore' " (*Chamber of Secrets*, 124). Nick is barred from the group because he cannot meet this rigid physical standard. Ghosts also have distinct foodways, and the cuisine at Nick's deathday party depicts a reversal. Ghosts are the opposite of humans: noncorporeal and nonliving. Their food appropriately reflects this opposition: rotten fish, burnt cakes, moldy cheese, maggoty haggis (*Chamber of Secrets*, 133).[8] This particular reversal simply emphasizes the nonhumanness of the group members; it is not a necessary characteristic of a folk group in general. That there is particular food associated with the group, as well as the notion of some kind of requisite physical characteristic (such as that one must be dead to be a ghost) indicates that this is an exclusive group.

Children understand that group membership is often desirable, at least to have a sense of belonging, and that certain things must be done in order to join a group. Belief and custom enter into initiations. For secret clubs, kids may make up a certain handshake, require a particular marking such as a handkerchief or fake tattoo, and perhaps create a language known only to club members. They thus recognize the intricacies involved in the magical aspects of Harry's unofficial education.

The wizarding world can be likened to a club or folk group. Readers want to join. By learning "folk" ways (that is, the ways to be a wizard), readers perceive themselves as in the club. Recognizing other members as having the same secret knowledge is a treat. Readers want to be wizards, and in particular Gryffindors. In light of the unusual dress sported by wizards, it is noteworthy that the Harry Potter Halloween costume was quite popular in 2000, and merchandise related to the series is currently ubiquitous. Current web sites allow visitors to put on the Sorting Hat or visit Flourish and Blotts. The uninitiated will no doubt find the sites' vocabulary confusing, but devotees immediately feel part of the in crowd.

Rites of Passage

Apart from the folk group of wizards, Hogwarts students can be seen as belonging to a transitional, or liminal, group. "Born" wizard children are

---

8. This is reminiscent of the house spirit (*domovoi*) found in Russian culture. They eat nondesirable food, like to work, and dress in rags. For more on the *domovoi*, refer to Linda Ivanits, *Russian Folk Belief*, 51–58.

in transition between the world of childhood and the adult world, as is the target audience. For Harry and Hermione, the transition is twofold: they also must learn about and adapt to the wizarding world. All of the students must leave their families, spend time with special guides who will train them in the ways of the main folk group (i.e., wizards), and learn enough to be reincorporated into the general group as full-fledged members. This rite of passage is divided up in the same way that school is for children. Experiences throughout the academic year help the children become incorporated into adult society. This occurs incrementally, with the lessons of each year coinciding with developmental stages. Aside from the obvious childhood parallels, Hogwarts students also learn about their particular culture and society.

As in any rite of passage, three stages are involved: separation, transition, and incorporation.[9] The main rite of passage throughout the series involves transforming the children into upstanding members of wizarding society. In the big picture, they leave home to pursue their studies (separation). During their years in official education at Hogwarts, they are treated both as children and adults simultaneously, as they learn to handle more responsibility (transition). They will, by the end of the series, graduate Hogwarts and rejoin adult wizarding society (incorporation).

Within the principal rite, subrites may occur. Each subrite includes the same three stages. As with Muggle children, the ritual process is divided up into age groups or school years. The latter serves the best equivalent for the purpose of Hogwarts comparison and exemplifies the tenets of a rite of passage. Each year at Hogwarts can be viewed as a rite of passage. Harry's first year serves as a prime example of this rite. During year one at Hogwarts, Harry and his cohorts separate from normal society. For Harry, this means leaving a somewhat traditional though dysfunctional home. Often rites of passage into the next stage of society involve some kind of territorial journey. That is, those being incorporated are taken by their guides to a place set apart from the rest of society.[10] This spatial transference often occurs by special means. For example, in American weddings, the bride, who is in transition from bachelorhood to married life, may be transported to her wedding in a limousine. Schoolchildren are often transported to school in a special bus. Similarly, Hogwarts students travel to school aboard the Hogwarts Express, which leaves from an extraordinary place: Platform 9¾, which, by Muggle reasoning, should not even exist. They embark on a relatively long journey to a place far removed and well hidden. Once there, all students travel up to the campus by special means. First-year students embark on a frightening trip across a presumably sea serpent–infested lake, and

9. Victor Turner, *The Ritual Process*, 94–95.
10. Arnold van Gennep, *The Rites of Passage*, 15.

older students journey via horseless coaches. The extraordinary means of transportation employed to take children to Hogwarts typifies the unusual ways that wizards transport themselves. For Muggle-born wizards, the journey to school prepares them to accept unorthodox forms of transportation: brooms, Floo powder, apparating and disapparating. Thus Harry's journey to Hogwarts constitutes the initial part of the separation stage of the ritual process.

The separation stage continues with the first-year ritual of the Sorting Hat. Each student is immediately put into an official subgroup, in the form of a house assignment. Members of each group will share the transitional experience. Some houses are more desirable than others to certain types of people, depending on reputation and family tradition, but all are presumably equal. Slytherin, for example, is made up mostly of children from old wizarding families. They consider themselves superior to the other houses because they are "born" wizards. Once the students are sorted into their houses, separation for this rite is complete.

The transition stage, when the students learn to contribute to adult wizarding society, occurs at Hogwarts. Once there, Harry begins both formal and informal lessons—traditional, official means of education and unofficial, extracurricular lessons—about the wizarding world. The difference between this and Muggle schools lies in the subject matter of the classes, which represent reversals of the conventional social order (at least to the readers). Through classes such as Potions, Care of Magical Creatures, and Defense against the Dark Arts, the students learn how to use their innate powers appropriately. Moral lessons accompany practical ones: students are subtly encouraged to use their powers to fight against dark wizards and are not outwardly taught the Dark Arts.

As with Muggle children, unofficial lessons come in the form of breaking rules, going on adventures, and making friendships and alliances. Young wizards have magical means to do all of this and often learn valuable extracurricular lessons in the process. Informal lessons thus help them learn about getting along with others, living in a more adult environment away from parents, and, probably most important, learning to deal with good and evil (that is, moral lessons).

Transition is the pivotal stage in a rite of passage, and Victor Turner refers to people undergoing these rites as "liminal."[11] They fall between categories, in that they neither belong to their previous group nor have been incorporated into their new group; they are in the process of crossing a boundary. Liminal people are powerful because they often endure hardship and because they have the ability to cross the boundaries set by society. They

11. Turner, *Ritual Process*, 95–97.

also tend to be marked by special dress in society.[12] A bride wears special clothing to denote her status. When students graduate from high school, they wear special clothing to participate in their commencement procession. Likewise, young wizards wear the robes that are characteristic of adult wizard society. They are further separated from society by moving into living quarters that are separate even from those of their teachers. The children live alone in their liminal groups, in places that appear to be on the periphery of the castle: Gryffindor is located in a tower (outer periphery), and Slytherin is in a basement dungeon (lower periphery). During the transitional period, students are not allowed to live within the confines of society; they are on the fringe, not having crossed the boundary back into society.

Young readers can also be seen as liminal in that they are currently being incorporated into adult society. In the Harry Potter series, they can vicariously test boundaries and encounter the unreal in the story lines. Childhood is a time for testing the real and unreal and finding one's place. The real world does not allow for magic to occur (as far as our Muggle mindset will allow), yet children want to believe and often have no problem accepting that fantastic occurrences are indeed real. Folklore provides one outlet for them to explore the real and unreal. Ghost stories and legends provide excitement in testing these boundaries, and children sometimes have a hard time ascertaining which pieces of information therein are credible. In the Harry Potter books, young readers find an author who validates their needs. Rowling provides a means to explore problem areas in a safe environment. Whereas ghost stories and urban legends are exciting in their potential to be true, Harry's world, while quite frightening at times, remains safe in that it exists within the confines of each book. Once the book is closed, the dark magic remains safely within.

Incorporation for each subrite occurs at the end of each term, when the children are transported (again by special/magical means—the Hogwarts Express) back to Platform 9¾ to spend the summer with their families. That each school year represents a subrite and is not the total incorporation into society is evident in the Decree for the Reasonable Restriction of Underage Sorcery: "underage wizards are not permitted to perform spells outside school" (*Chamber of Secrets*, 21). Young wizards are not yet recognized as fully functioning members of society.

As noted, children regularly go through rites of passage as they mature. They change groups according to age, and religious and social practices train them for adulthood. In the Muggle world, successful transitions are marked by various school graduations, receipt of a driver's license, and buying new clothing for school, to name a few. Children can relate to the rites

12. Ibid., 170–71.

of passage depicted in the series, as they parallel those that they experience as they mature. This gives young readers a point of reference—common ground with the characters.

Food in Harry Potter

Foodways also indicate specific folk groups. We associate certain foods with age, ethnicity, and region: babies eat special food (often packaged specially); fortune cookies exemplify Chinese food, and stereotypically, southerners have a taste for fried chicken and collard greens. For schoolchildren, cafeteria food even holds special meaning. Similarly, particular foods are found the wizarding world: Fizzing Whizbees, Jelly Slugs, and Acid Pops exemplify special food for young wizards (*Prisoner of Azkaban*, 200). They are intended to be consumed quickly and totally, which is indicative of traditional folk foods.[13] In addition to the sweets preferred by the children in the series, food served in the Hogwarts dining hall meets these criteria. It is prepared by special means (house-elves), appears by special presentation (empty platters suddenly fill), and is meant to be consumed quickly and totally (by hungry schoolchildren).

Although the food depicted in the wizarding world outside of Hogwarts is not prepared by the children, it is prepared by those within the folk group: other wizards. This is done by traditional (i.e., Muggle) and nontraditional means. Ron's mother cooks certain foods, such as sausages, traditionally. "Mrs. Weasley was clattering around, cooking breakfast a little haphazardly, throwing dirty looks at her sons as she threw sausages into the frying pan" (*Chamber of Secrets*, 34). She uses magic to prepare others and do other tasks. "Mrs. Weasley slammed a large copper saucepan down on the kitchen table and began to wave her wand around inside it. A creamy sauce poured from the wand tip as she stirred" (*Goblet of Fire*, 58–59). "She flicked her wand casually at the dishes in the sink, which began to clean themselves, clinking gently in the background" (*Chamber of Secrets*, 34). In these cases, the preparation methods have ritual significance, rather than the food itself. Wizard food, with the exception of children's treats, does not differ considerably from its Muggle counterpart. Its potential magical origins, however, set it apart. It is notable that in cases where mainstream members of the folk group do not prepare the food, members of an affiliated group, house-elves, create it. Food can thus be considered yet another indicator of folk group in the wizarding world.

Reversals to Reinforce Social Norms

What if a broom could fly? Do owls actually deliver messages? What if people really could transform into animals? Rowling piques the imaginations

13. Brunvand, *Study of American Folklore*, 591.

of her readers by forcing them to think outside the bounds of the Muggle world and question the apparent uses of everyday objects. Similarly, she allows the reader to glimpse Muggle technology from a non-Muggle standpoint. Regular post baffles wizards: Mrs. Weasley covers an envelope with stamps to ensure its arrival (*Goblet of Fire,* 30–31). Policemen become "pleasemen" to Amos Diggory (*Goblet of Fire,* 159). Muggle technology is so foreign to the wizard world that it is placed off-limits and referred to as "artifacts." Although Muggle artifacts are one of Arthur Weasley's hobbies, the automobile that he covertly owns has been enchanted to fly (*Chamber of Secrets,* 25). Although he has learned to use the car in a culturally appropriate manner, his sons, who are not as familiar with Muggle culture, transform it to conform to their own understanding of how things should work. Even the phrase "the M word" holds different meaning for both groups. For the Dursleys, "the M word" is Magic and therefore forbidden; for wizards, it is Muggles, and their technology is strictly controlled. Rowling bridges the gap between folk groups (i.e., Wizard and Muggle) by showing reversals from both groups.

Transition is often marked by reversals; that is, things that are turned around so that they seem to do the opposite of what they are supposed to do. Reversals exist to reinforce the societal norm. The 1990s television show *Married with Children,* for example, employed reversals regularly, with scenes of neglected family life, intending to show how life should not be. The wizarding world is replete with reversals.

Ordinary objects for Muggles have extraordinary uses in the wizarding world. One form of reversal evident in the series is seen in normal items that are instilled with magical powers. Fireplaces provide warmth, but they also serve as transportation portals (with the help of Floo powder). Owls provide an essential service for wizards, and animals in general may not be what (or whom) they appear to be (for example, animagi). Wands, which are basically sticks that have been doctored to include magical elements, hold deep power when brandished correctly. Broomsticks not only sweep but fly. They are for sport, rather than transportation, as they are too visible to Muggles for the Ministry of Magic's comfort. The fastest broomsticks even carry names reminiscent of racecars: Nimbus 2000, Cleansweep 7, Firebolt. Books may be animated to reflect their content: *The Monster Book of Monsters* bites its readers until its spine is stroked (*Prisoner of Azkaban,* 52–53). Trees such as the Whomping Willow can attack people (*Chamber of Secrets,* 75–76). By depicting things in extraordinary ways, the "normalness" of the everyday is subconsciously reinforced, and readers exercise their imaginations.

The Muggle world starts out as normal (if dysfunctional) for Harry, but as soon as his transition starts, it turns into a quaint and backward place. Hogwarts becomes his true home. Whereas for many Muggle children school represents work, and they may even resort to feigned illness to avoid attending at times, for Harry the opposite is true. He prefers school to home. This is understandable, as the Dursleys present an undesirable home situation. When we first meet Harry, he lives in a closet under the stairs. Although he is eventually allowed to live in a real bedroom, he is often banished to it, with little contact outside his nuclear foster family. He wears Dudley's oversized hand-me-downs from infancy to his teenage years, and Christmas presents arrive in the form of a fifty-pence piece or a tissue (*Sorcerer's Stone*, 200, *Goblet of Fire*, 410). In civilized society, many of the Dursleys' actions represent child abuse. Parents are expected to care for their children (or charges, in Harry's case), and they may even give more than they should, especially in this age of designer clothes and high-priced sneakers. Young readers likely relate to Harry's feeling of not fitting in, although they also probably realize that his home life is rather extreme. By depicting how things should not be, Rowling reinforces the notion of how they should be. Ron Weasley's family, by contrast, reflects a "normal" family: the parents love and support their children even when they've misbehaved, there is always plenty of food, and each child has his/her own space, albeit small. Although there are no designer clothes, the children (even Ron's friends) know they are loved.

Sirius Black represents a reversal employed to demonstrate further to the readers that things are not always as they appear. Rowling similarly transposes characteristics usually associated with evil characters onto good ones. Whereas evil characters are often depicted as rather scruffy-looking, Sirius is painted as a criminal and looks fairly haggard but is actually an avatar. Snape is a rather oily, rather untrustworthy individual, yet he saves Harry's life. Lupin is a "good" werewolf. The ferocious, three-headed dog who guards the Sorcerer's Stone is called, ironically, Fluffy. Instead of reserving the enticing, nasty characteristics for the bad guys, Rowling distributes the more canonical ones among the heroes. Children are not always scared away by nasty features; they use them themselves in scaring each other with ghost stories. To emphasize that the bad guys in the series are truly malevolent, though, Rowling reserves the truly evil features for them. Voldemort no longer looks human until the end of *Goblet of Fire*. In *Sorcerer's Stone* he is forced to share a body, appearing as a face on the back of Professor Quirrell's head (*Sorcerer's Stone*, 293). His familiar is a giant snake, drawing on biblical imagery associating snakes with evil. The Death Eaters cloak their faces, making them more menacing by hiding their normal features.

Another reversal lies in magical creatures and items. Ordinarily uncommunicative creatures and objects take on human characteristics, and certain animals can understand humans. Hedwig appears to understand enough to communicate with Harry, albeit through nips and reassuring hoots (*Goblet of Fire*, 229). Portraits talk, and their subjects can move, as seen when the Fat Lady abandons her frame after her portrait is slashed (*Prisoner of Azkaban*, 160–61). Similarly, chessmen may be animated to move on their own (*Sorcerer's Stone*, 281). The point of reversing accepted standards in these cases is to reinforce them: in real life, inanimate objects are supposed to stay put. By making such reversals a normal part of wizarding life, Rowling turns around the expectation of horrible consequences seen in ghost stories when things move about under their own power.

For young readers, it is perfectly fine to fantasize about things having extraordinary qualities, but "big kids" know how things should be, and they know that the depictions are products of the imagination. In being privy to this knowledge, they feel that they belong to an older group. Children consider being in on the secret to be an adult trait. To use a children's folklore parallel, when a child passes through a stage (whether age-related or developmental), she or he shuns the folklore of the previous stage. For example, when a child realizes that the Tooth Fairy is really a parent's fabrication, she or he usually does not let younger siblings in on the secret. The child guards this "secret" knowledge in order to feel more a part of the adult world and to join the next group, so to speak. Young readers of the Harry Potter series know that the implausible depictions are just that, but on some level they may feel empowered by the knowledge that it is just make-believe. The delineation between the real and unreal reinforces the lessons learned in their journey toward adulthood.

In a more subtle reversal, adult Muggles are, to a certain extent, equated with children: wizards deem that they don't need to know certain things. They tend to protect Muggles and look at them as lesser, not-so-smart beings that prefer not to see beyond their narrow scope. Thus wizards hide the existence of Quidditch matches and wizarding schools and create rules for using wizard technology (for example, flying brooms or carpets) in Muggle areas.

Boundary Crossing and Taboos

As children grow up, they progressively cross boundaries from one stage of development to another, until they reach adulthood. They see, as they are in each stage, that there are places where some crossover is allowed. That is, boundaries are not always concrete. Adults set boundaries through rules, societal mores, and prohibitions. As children mature, they learn which of these should or should not be broken and when transgressing the rules is acceptable.

The Harry Potter series incorporates several topics that are more or less taboo to children: violence, gross and disgusting items and topics, magic and witchcraft, and the concept of evil (as well as evil incarnate). Young readers find all of these rather enticing, as anything that adults consider off-limits must be worthwhile. Unlike the violence, evil, and unpleasantness encountered in real life, those depicted within the pages of the series are presented safely and in terms that children comprehend.

Children embark upon the same themes in oral lore, especially in telling ghost stories, urban legends, and jokes. By recanting stories and jokes that employ taboo words and themes, they test boundaries and determine what is acceptable to utter or discuss in detail among their friends, in adult family company, and with adults outside of the family. That is, children socialize themselves and are socialized by others with regard to acceptable (and un-acceptable) subject matter by trying it out.

As with ghost stories, the taboo themes in Harry Potter are presented on a level that is not overly scary for children. Rowling omits the gory details found in adult novels and primetime crime dramas. Rather, she leaves the particulars to the imagination of the reader. In so doing, she invokes a safety valve of sorts: the reader's imagination. As with ghost story telling, this means that the listeners only visualize those images that they can handle. When an act is imagined, the audience more easily controls it. The paucity of description lets the audience actively participate in the performance. Each reader experiences the narrative a little differently, yet all share a basic understanding of the actions involved. Each visualizes the act at a level that is acceptable to his/her psyche.[14] Thus the material is "safe."

Violence is not infrequent in Harry Potter. At the very beginning of the series, the reader encounters a situation where a couple has been murdered and their surviving child assaulted. To add insult to injury, which Rowling does adeptly, the scarred child is psychologically and, to a certain extent, physically abused at the hands of his foster family. Voldemort murders numerous people in cold blood, including Harry's parents (*Sorcerer's Stone*) and Cedric Diggory (*Goblet of Fire*). As retold in *Prisoner of Azkaban*, Peter Pettigrew murders twelve innocent bystander Muggles and frames Sirius Black for the crime. Dementors suck souls, leaving shells of their owners. In *Goblet of Fire*, the reader is introduced to the unforgivable curses, spells that are intended to harm people: the Imperius Curse, the Cruciatus Curse, and the Killing Curse. In *Chamber of Secrets*, random students are turned to stone. While the latter transformation is not outwardly violent (in that no murder is involved), it does involve an assault. Draco Malfoy constantly challenges Harry and pulls cruel pranks on others. Although the books are not replete with violent acts, the acts are described, and some are fairly hor-

---

14. Jann Lacoss, "Contemporary Russian Childlore." See especially 228–55, "Things That Go Bump in the Night."

rible. Yet the readers are not inspired to re-create them, as are some children who view violent television shows or movies or listen to violent lyrics.

Why does this series not incite youngsters to violence or desensitize them? First, the plots take place at Hogwarts, a school for wizards that presumably does not really exist. By describing the setting in a fairy tale environment, the reader receives implicit clues that this is not real. It is obviously fantasy. In folktales, a similar "whisking away" is accomplished by the marker, "Once upon a time . . ." Here the marker could be the Hogwart's Express or any other wizardly transportation mode, or, more likely, simply the names of the books: *Harry Potter and the . . .* The title in itself serves the same purpose as the aforementioned folk phrase. It sets the scene as fantasy.

Additionally, there are visible emotional and physical consequences to violent acts. In *Sorcerer's Stone,* when Harry's parents are murdered, their assailant loses most of his powers and almost his life. Good triumphs over evil, albeit temporarily. The audience also sees how horrible Harry's home life becomes with his foster family. His scar puts him in excruciating pain every so often, and he lives in fear of the assailant at times. By revisiting the victim, young readers see that once a crime is committed, its aftermath does not go away. After Neville Longbottom's parents are tortured, we see more consequences: they must live in an asylum, away from their son, and he is sent to live with his grandmother, growing up frightened and withdrawn, as seen in *Goblet of Fire.* After the World Cup riot depicted in the same book, much sorting out is necessary to repair the Muggles whose lives were upset and who were injured. Presenting the aftermath of these events, as opposed to simply depicting violent acts, shows young readers that actions have consequences, and that the crime does not fade from memory.

Magic and witchcraft are outwardly taboo topics for some families. Parents, however, tend to expose their children to magical elements similar to those in Harry Potter long before the kids can even read. Many of the tales that children grow up hearing, which are usually told by parents or grandparents, involve some kind of magical elements. Folk tales speak to children on their level, in terms that they understand. They can easily relate to the views described therein. Students at Hogwarts learn magic as though it were science. Bruno Bettelheim remarks that small children do not have the abstract understanding skills necessary to comprehend adult science, and scientific answers may seem confusing until the child matures enough to think objectively. The magic in folktales plays on existing knowledge and subjective imagination. Tales that include animated objects and magical beings do not seem odd to children, as they draw upon "science," as understood by young minds. Bettelheim further notes that for children, inanimate objects may well seem to have life. Animals may indeed have the ability to interact with humans. Thus talking trees and animals in tales are not odd to young readers. Some of the magic in Harry Potter runs along the same lines. The Whomping Willow in *Chamber of Secrets* can have feelings. Portraits can speak and interact with each other. In a child's perception, why not? Certainly young readers do realize that this is fantasy. After all, the trees and portraits that they see every day do not interact with them. But the possibility is in their worldview. Their imaginations still allow them to see these occurrences as feasible, even if they know that they are not real. Bettelheim remarks that for young children, even stones may be alive.[15] Rowling draws, consciously or unconsciously, on this idea in *Chamber of Secrets* by having the villain turn students to stone. Both the protagonists and the readers easily accept that these stone statues are indeed people and remain sentient.

Rowling's presentation of magic speaks to readers on several levels, making it seem as though it could indeed be real. For younger readers, the magic itself provides explanation enough for supernatural occurrences. It may appear more logical than actual scientific explanations, and it draws on their existing knowledge, that is, on the way that they understand the world around them.[16] For adolescent readers, a more scientific approach seems more credible. Classes such as Potions and Herbology are undertaken with the strict logic inherent to such subjects as chemistry and botany, with emphasis on magical results. This scientific approach may well be the most offending factor for opponents who are concerned about the witchcraft components in the series. Because magic is presented as a logical and exact study, it appears more real to educated minds, whereas when it is presented as pure fantasy, it seems less threatening to adults.

The ongoing battle between good and evil is another potentially taboo topic that the series undertakes. Good is not taboo to children. Adults regularly tell their children to "be good," but for children this is in opposition to "bad." In the series, however, good opposes "evil," which is much more threatening than bad. Evil has a name ("Voldemort"), but no one dares speak it. Even the name itself has been imbued with considerable power. In fact, people cringe at it, and they beseech Harry not to use it, as it is too taboo. Dumbledore alone realizes the power of overcoming a taboo and encourages Harry to call evil by its name. Similarly, adults do not tend to talk about evil with children, though they will define "bad" behaviors.

The violence that children encounter personally tends to consist of schoolyard fights and sibling rivalry. Parental discussions of these events

15. Bruno Bettelheim, *The Uses of Enchantment: The Meaning and Importance of Fairy Tales*, 45–49.
16. Ibid., 48.

may center on telling them to "fight with their words, not their fists." Children thus learn that physical fighting is bad. But they still need an outlet to deal with the emotions that lead to their disputes. Folklore provides such an outlet, giving a vicarious means to approach conflicting feelings.[17] The Potter books serve a similar function. Children are drawn to stories that deal with evil, to varying degrees, in order to allow them to deal with contradictory feelings brought on by disagreements.

Although parents do discuss morals and ethics with their children, they do not always speak in terms to which children can relate. Folktales speak on this level, as do the Harry Potter books. Alan Dundes has observed that "folklore presents a socially sanctioned outlet for the discussion of the forbidden and tabood [sic]."[18] Rowling's books also allow such an outlet. She presents readers with concrete examples of evil, allowing them to confront it safely, in a controlled environment.

Revulsions at Hogwarts

The magical creatures depicted in the books allow children to explore fears and play with preconceived notions of what constitutes "gross and disgusting." Children are enticed by things that most adults deem repulsive. Browsing toy store aisles reveals that contemporary children's toys include Slime and Gak, both of which are neither liquid nor solid (and cross that boundary nicely), Icky Yicky Water Ball, the Hairy Hairball plush toy (which spits up various objects), and Gus Guts (who vomits individual internal organs).[19] Objects that cross boundaries tend to be culturally problematic, especially for adults. Things that cross body boundaries are especially difficult to discuss or even consider. Birth provides a real-life example. It often takes place in a particular locale, with specialists (doctors, nurses, midwives) attending to the "crossing." Non-healthcare professionals prefer not to deal with blood, as it is considered to be a contaminant (it is noteworthy that this belief in American culture predates contamination beliefs associated with HIV/AIDS).

Children view nasal mucus, urine, and feces (for which they have vernacular terms) as problematic. Infants and toddlers do not consider these excretions unclean or taboo; in fact, they explore them openly, much to parents' chagrin. Adults, and later other children, socialize small children not to pick their noses or eat their snot, and preadolescents and adolescents learn not to pop their zits. As children mature, they test some of these boundaries by talking about bodily excretions and questionable subject matter. In

17. Ibid., 52.
18. Alan Dundes, "The Dead Baby Joke Cycle," 146.
19. All of these were found on www.toysrus.com. It is notable that the last two are marked for very young children: ages three and up.

so doing, they are learning acceptable (and unacceptable) social behaviors and demonstrating that they understand taboos. Children are not generally allowed to discuss these topics with others, especially adults. The subject matter thus emerges in an unofficial capacity, specifically in children's folklore. The jokelore of young children focuses on body fluids and jokes dealing with bodily excretions (hence the proliferation of "fartlore").[20] This provides a socially sanctioned outlet to contemplate these substances.

Realizing that such taboo body material is fun for children, Rowling incorporates it into the text. In *Goblet of Fire,* readers encounter Bubotubers. These plants, resembling large slugs, must be squeezed periodically to harvest their pus, which is yellowish-green and is used, ironically, as an acne remedy. The students find them repulsive, but they have mixed feelings about them: "Squeezing the bubotubers was disgusting, but oddly satisfying" (*Goblet of Fire,* 194–95). The characters in this book are at an age (fourteen) where their bodies are changing with puberty. They are being introduced to unfamiliar bodily secretions and seeing physical changes in themselves and their friends. Through such creatures and experiences, readers vicariously deal with material that is analogous to boundary-crossing body fluids. These gross and disgusting organisms and materials are repulsive even to Harry and his friends, but they accept them as necessary parts of life and learn to deal with them. They also provide readers of the same age validation, on some level, that they share their conflicting feelings.

Bertie Bott's Every Flavor Beans present another anomalous substance. They clearly parallel Muggle jellybeans, but flavors can include everything from chocolate and peppermint to spinach, earwax, and vomit (*Sorcerer's Stone,* 103–4). Moaning Myrtle serves as a "helper" to Harry and his friends, although she is a rather repulsive character. She lives in a toilet, picks at her blemishes, and regularly gets flushed. Even Harry does not like to visualize Myrtle "zooming down a pipe to the lake with the contents of the toilet" (*Goblet of Fire,* 463–65).

The Polyjuice Potion that Harry, Ron, and Hermione make in *Chamber of Secrets* resembles concoctions that children may create and dare each other to consume, though it is taken to an extreme. The potion requires nauseating ingredients, including lacewing flies and leeches; Ron finds the active ingredients repulsive. " 'Excuse me?' said Ron sharply. 'What d'you mean a bit of whoever we're changing into? I'm drinking nothing with Crabbe's toenails in it—' " (*Chamber of Secrets,* 165). Toenails are not necessary, in the end—hair will do nicely. Even with all of its repugnant ingredients, the potion tastes like overcooked cabbage (*Chamber of Secrets,* 216).

20. Simon Bronner gives several examples in *American Children's Folklore* (74–77). One such is, "Georgie is a nut/He has a rubber butt/And every time he wiggles it/It goes putt putt." Cf. Mary and Herbert Knapp, *One Potato, Two Potato.*

The young readers of the series are continually in the process of crossing boundaries. They relate, on some level, to the anomalous beings and substances depicted in the books. In considering the people, creatures, otherworldly beings, and out-of-the-ordinary materials, young readers begin to define themselves with regard to what they are and are not. By defining the otherness of the events and creatures depicted, they gain a better understanding of themselves and their own world.

Harry Potter as Folktale

Another reason that children easily relate to the Harry Potter series is that the books mirror a plot and structure form that they recognize from very early childhood: the folktale. The first real stories that many children experience are folktales, told by parents and grandparents as bedtime stories. As children listen to these, they pick up on the subtleties of structure therein. Most caregivers have encountered instances when a child has corrected their version of a tale because "that's not the way it goes." Children know the "correct" way to tell certain tales because they understand, on a subconscious level, how tales are put together.

Vladimir Propp, working specifically with Russian magical tales, deciphered their structure, breaking the tale genre into thirty-one "functions," or actions. Each function represents an action taken by one of the characters. Propp called the principal characters dramatis personae: villain, donor, helper, girl (and father), dispatcher, hero, and false hero. He determined that all magic tales have at least the principal seven of the thirty-one functions (and most have many more), and they always appear in the same order. Folklorists following Propp have discovered that his schemata apply not only to magic tales but also to other types of tales and other genres in several cultures.[21]

The Harry Potter series seems to employ these same functions, although not always quite in the proper order (in the Harry Potter series, they *are* actually quite often in the same order as in magic tales). In fact, each book follows the sequence, and the overall plot of the series also appears to do so. This is not to say that the books were intentionally written like folktales. On the contrary, this implies that the formulas for tales may be learned and sublimated from early childhood. Thus when the books were written, Rowling had an instinctive "road map," so to speak, for creating an engaging tale to which children (and adults) could easily relate. Table 1 parallels Propp's functions with *Sorcerer's Stone* and *Goblet of Fire*.

The dramatis personae also resemble those in folk tales. Propp notes that the players in tales represent slots to be filled: villain, hero, etc.[22] The villain

21. Vladimir Propp, *Morphology of the Folktale*, 19–64.
22. Ibid., 79–80.

Table 1.

Propp Applied to *Sorcerer's Stone* and *Goblet of Fire*. It is noteworthy that
the functions do not always occur in the proper order in each book.

Function #	Function	Harry Potter and the Sorcerer's Stone	Harry Potter and the Goblet of Fire
1.	Member absents self	Harry's parents die	Sirius Black is on the run
2.	Interdiction	Dursleys tell Harry, "No magic!"	Sirius wants to know of any odd goings-on
3.	Interdiction violated	Hogwarts invitation	Harry's scar hurts. He doesn't want to tell Sirius and tones down his letter.
4.	Villain/reconnaissance		World Cup: Death Eaters
5.	Villain receives information		Voldemort gets information on HP and makes plans
6.	Villain attempts to deceive victim		
7.	Victim submits to deception		
8.	Villainy	Sorcerer's Stone is stolen	
8a.	Lack	Sorcerer's Stone is missing	Harry is entered into the Triwizard Tournament ("anti-lack")
9.	Lack made known	Theft is reported in the *Daily Prophet*	Harry protests his entry but must still defend as a champion
10.	Seeker agrees to counteraction		Harry contends (several moves here with contests)
11.	Hero tested	Harry's unconscious spells	First, second, third tests
12.	Hero leaves home	Harry leaves with Hagrid	Harry and champions are removed from the other students for the contests
13.	Hero's reaction to future donor	Harry makes friends with Hagrid	Harry wins/ties 1st task
14.	Receipt of magical agent	Harry buys/is matched with his wand	1. Knowledge: Summoning Charm 2. Bath 3. Portkey
15.	Spatial transference	Hogwart's Express	1. Tent, dragon enclosure 2. Underwater 3. Maze
16.	Struggle	Harry meets Draco Malfoy on train	1. Dragon 2. Merpeople 3. Various 3a. Voldemort
17.	Branding	People notice scar (although Harry was branded earlier)	1. Harry's shoulder cut 2. Harry nearly drowns 3. Harry hurts leg 3a. Wormtail cuts Harry's arm. Scar/headache.
18.	Victory		Cedric and Harry find the Portkey
19.	Initial lack liquidated		Harry finishes tournament alive
20.	Hero returns		Harry is transported
21.	Hero pursued		Voldemort attacks Harry
22.	Rescue		Harry escapes from Voldemort. Not a total victory.
23.	Unrecognized arrival		Harry returns with Cedric's body
24.	False hero	Professor Quirrell	The false Mad-Eye
25.	Difficult task	Retrieval of stone	
26.	Solution	Same as 25	
27.	Hero recognized	Harry notified of magical status	
28.	False hero exposed	Exposure of Professor Quirrell	False Mad-Eye is revealed as Barty Crouch
29.	Transfiguration	End of term/new grade	
30.	Punishment	Of Professor Quirrell	
31.	Wedding		Banquet, but solemn

is Voldemort. The donor varies from book to book, and sometimes there are multiple donors. Hagrid, Ron, and Hermione tend to play the helpers in each book. Harry rescues a damsel in distress (the "girl" in Propp's scheme) in nearly every book: he rescues Hermione from a mountain troll in October of his first year; he comes to the aid of Ginny Weasley in *Chamber of Secrets;* and, in *Goblet of Fire,* he rescues the younger sister of his competitor Fleur Delacour. Harry serves as the hero, and a false hero has emerged at least once: the false Mad-Eye in *Goblet of Fire* appears as a sort of avatar at first.

Because the plots of the books so closely resemble folktale structure, young readers are accustomed to the progression of events. Although this does not happen on a conscious level, children recognize the chain of events. This also makes the plot of each book easier for them to remember.

Conclusions

The folktale structure allows Rowling to communicate her plots in a way that is familiar to both young and older readers. This enhances the comfort level of the audience, in that they have an idea of what should come next. This is not to say that the plots are predictable; because it is not a folktale, the predictability inherent in magical tales is not always present. As a literary creation, it gives the author freedom to reorder the functions so that there are surprises for the audience. Because the basic functions are familiar, though, the books resemble a known and beloved genre of folklore.

Children do not always feel comfortable talking to their parents (or adults in general) about certain topics and unresolved issues, especially those that society deems taboo. They may not even realize that these topics are difficult for them. Rowling approaches these issues, describes them, and portrays adults who want to talk about them. Professors Dumbledore and McGonagall seem especially adept at helping the protagonists deal with the issues involved with growing up, and neither fits the mold of "average" adult. This helps children realize that difficult situations are a part of life and that it is okay to openly discuss whatever troubles them.

The issues depicted in the series include those associated with gaining responsibility as one matures, leaving home to garner experience living on one's own (inasmuch as a boarding school allows), and learning to solve seemingly insurmountable problems. These parallel the rituals and trials that the target readers undergo as they gradually develop into adults and learn good citizenship. Like the characters in the books, preadolescent and adolescent readers are constantly in a state of flux. They are seen as both children and adults simultaneously, their bodies are changing physically, and their relationships grow in complexity as they get older. As liminal beings, these readers readily relate to Rowling's protagonists.

Many children are drawn to things that make most adults cringe. They revel in being able to "gross out" the grown-ups. This stems more from a desire for control rather than a need to nauseate. Children do not hold a great deal of control in their lives. Adults dictate when and where they eat, play, work, and sleep; they feed children food of adult choosing, instead of following the child's tastes (with the possible exception of Happy Meals noted). In school, children must study what they are told, how they are told, and they are given further work to complete at home. Children often don't feel they have much control in life. They understand their position as not belonging to the adult world, and they perceive that they do not quite fit in. Anomalous substances entice them, as they also do not quite fit in. When children embrace such substances as Gak, Slime, Creepy Crawlers, blue applesauce, and purple ketchup, they hold some semblance of control over what goes into or onto their bodies. By including such boundary-crossers as bubotubers, Polyjuice Potion, giant spiders, and Blast-Ended Skrewts, Rowling relates the same type of vicarious control to her young readers.

Apart from the folk group of schoolchildren, to which young readers also easily relate, Rowling has created an enticing culture that many readers want to join: wizards. Through her invention of specific jargon, dress, and foodways, she has sculpted a credible folk group based on existing social models. The wizarding world intrigues the audience to the point where toys, journals, statuettes, and even costumes are available to the Muggle public, for those who wish to be part of the "in" crowd. Because the group is so appealing, the characters are easy for children (and former children) to relate to, and the issues broached speak to the needs of the audience, the Harry Potter series grows consistently, and individual titles remain on best-seller lists. Mr. and Mrs. Dursley may not wish to be involved in anything strange or mysterious, but the audience sure does.

Harry Potter

Fairy Tale Prince, Real Boy, and Archetypal Hero

M. Katherine Grimes

When he was five and a half, my nephew Andrew accompanied a friend and me on a trip. We were reading J. K. Rowling's second book, *Harry Potter and the Chamber of Secrets,* aloud in the car, and every time we got into the vehicle, Andrew said, "Can we read again now?" After bragging that he had read the fourth Harry Potter book—734 pages—"in six days flat," my twelve-year-old nephew Jake announced that he planned to begin the books by J. K. Rowling again. Like many children, he has now read each of the four books in the series at least twice and has seen the Warner Brothers movie of the first book. He eagerly awaits the fifth novel of the projected septology. The grandchild of a friend wanted her parents to have someone read her *Harry Potter and the Goblet of Fire* from England when it came out, presuming the English would get the book several hours before folks in the United States due to the time difference. The editor of this book gave her nephews Harry Potter books for Christmas a few years ago, began the first one while visiting them, and had to stop at a bookstore on the way home to buy her own copy and finish it. She has now read the entire series twice.

Andrew's parents have always read to him, and he is a reader himself. Jake, too, has always been a reader, enjoying Beverly Cleary books as much as playing video games with friends. My friend's grandchild reads, as well. Lana Whited has four degrees in English and nine bookcases full of books. But even children who were not readers before are now devouring Rowling's four novels—1,819 pages total in the U.S. editions—about a little British boy who finds out that he is a wizard, and those children's parents, grandparents, teachers, and aunts are reading the four volumes to find out what all the fuss is about. Those of us who grew up loving books wonder why it took the Harry Potter series to cause children to become enamored of reading, and parents and teachers who had bemoaned young people's lack of interest in literature now ponder the fascination they have with these tomes. When these adults read the books to find the answers themselves, they come away with almost as much enthusiasm as they had witnessed in their children. The true joy of the Harry Potter series is that the books' protagonist is both a bigger-than-life hero and a true-to-life boy, just as the books are both magical and realistic.

Harry Potter books work with almost every group of people old enough to read. Young children read or listen to the books as though they were fairy tales. Young adolescents see in the series some means of coming to terms with the real world. Adults use them as windows on the world of younger people, but also as modern myths to help us understand eternal mysteries. Thus, Harry Potter serves as a fairy tale prince for young children; then, like Pinocchio, he becomes a real boy for adolescents; and, finally, he serves as an archetypal hero for adults.

Harry Potter as Fairy Tale Prince

As psychologist and educator Bruno Bettelheim points out in *The Uses of Enchantment,* second only to a child's parents and other caregivers in influencing that child's understanding of his or her world "is our cultural heritage," and "[w]hen children are young, it is literature that carries such information best."[1] Bettelheim examines fairy tales and their positive effects on young children. He explains that the distance of these tales in time and often in place gives children the comfort to understand the truths imparted by the tales without their having to fear that the stories are literally true. In addition, the larger-than-life elements of classic fairy tales help youngsters face the bafflements of the complicated and subtle real world.

Children of elementary school age and even younger enjoy such stories as "Little Red Riding Hood," "Jack and the Beanstalk," and "Cinderella." Bettelheim's approach to what he calls "folk fairy tales" is quite Freudian. In *The Uses of Enchantment,* he asserts that "a child needs to understand what is going on within his conscious self so that he can also cope with that which goes on in his unconscious. . . . It is here that fairy tales have unequaled value, because they offer new dimensions to the child's imagination which would be impossible for him to discover as truly on his own." Bettelheim believes that fairy tales such as those collected by Jakob and Wilhelm Grimm help children cope with the impulses of their ids and integrate these urges with their egos to help them develop their superegos. He writes, "Myths project an ideal personality acting on the basis of superego demands, while fairy tales depict an ego integration which allows for appropriate satisfaction of id desires. This difference accounts for the contrast between the pervasive pessimism of myths and the essential optimism of fairy tales."[2]

Contemporary literature can have benefits similar to fairy tales, especially if the works are ubiquitous, contain characters and themes that tap into

1. Bettelheim, *Uses of Enchantment,* 4.
2. Ibid., 7, 41.

universal archetypes as well as the specific values of the child's time and culture, and include fantasy. The Harry Potter series meets these criteria; thus, the novels can help children face and understand the truths of their world.

For young children, the Harry Potter books work like fairy tales. They are set in a magical world, with evil characters such as Voldemort and good ones such as Albus Dumbledore. There are even mermaids, dragons, unicorns, trolls, orphans, and witches. Thus, youngsters recognize the books as part of the fairy tale world and Harry as a fairy or folk tale hero, like young Jack, who might break a few rules but is basically good and resourceful, allowing him to triumph in the end of every book.

Bettelheim discusses characteristics and themes of fairy tales as well as their effects on children. Among these characteristics are magic, optimism, and distance in time, place, or both. Themes include the duality of human nature, comprising both the animal-spiritual and the good-evil dichotomies, movement toward autonomy, and even birth and death. Children who read fairy tales, asserts Bettelheim, are rewarded by assistance in understanding their parents and themselves, a better comprehension of good and evil, and the satisfaction of the pleasure principle.

The relationship of good to evil is perhaps the most fundamental question. Little children do not see shades of gray or ambivalence in behavior; instead, they separate the world into good and evil: Albus Dumbledore versus Voldemort, Harry Potter versus Draco Malfoy, the sacrificial James and Lily Potter versus the selfish Vernon and Petunia Dursley. The concept of a loving God and a vile devil makes perfect sense to young ones.

Duality appears as a frequent motif in the tales, as we see in "Little Red Riding Hood," a story of a grandmother who turns into a wolf. Bettelheim explains that children have great difficulty understanding that a person can be both good and bad, especially when that person is a loved one or the child himself or herself. Consequently, they view the different aspects of a person as two different persons altogether—or perhaps as a person and an animal.[3] In the Rowling novels, we meet little Harry Potter as he is arriving at the house of one set of parents, his aunt and uncle Petunia and Vernon Dursley, after his first set, Lily and James Potter, have been killed. This duality, present from the very beginning, is classic in fairy tales: the despised parents who discipline or ignore the child must be separated from the idealized parents who love and care for their offspring. That both qualities can exist in the same parents is too complex for a child's understanding. Fairy tales and Harry Potter books allow them the comfort of detesting one set of parents, the disciplinarians, while remaining loyal to the beloved ones.

3. Ibid., 66–67.

Bettelheim explains that dual parents represent a child's dual feelings about his or her mother and father. The evil stepmother, for example, represents the part of the parent the child wants to hate, the one who imposes discipline and restricts his or her freedom. The fairy godmother symbolizes the idealized aspect of the parent, the one who provides protection and sustenance. Because young children are completely dependent for their very existence upon their caretakers, usually their parents, their first great fear is of abandonment, or being separated from their parents in some way. Bettelheim writes, "There is no greater threat in life than that we will be deserted, left all alone."[4]

The theme of abandonment and the motif of dual or multiple parents pervade the Harry Potter books. Besides the Dursleys and the Potters, Harry has two grandfather figures: the near-perfect Albus Dumbledore and the vile Voldemort. The Dursleys are lowly in a moral way, whereas the Weasleys and Hagrid, though perhaps of a lower socioeconomic class than Harry, are morally superior to many of the novels' other characters. Fairy tales use similar means to help children cope with their attitudes toward their parents and their need for independence from them. As Bettelheim explains, the grandmother and the wolf in "Little Red Riding Hood" represent the two sides of the parental figure. "Cinderella" has three mothers: the dead one, who represents fear of abandonment; the wicked stepmother, representing the mother who shows favoritism to the other children and forces the child to do chores; and the fairy godmother, who makes all the child's wishes come true and represents the idealized parent. We can add the two fathers in some of the Jack tales, as well. When Jack's father is a character in the stories, he often sends the boy out on his own to seek his fortune. In turn, Jack finds a king, a father substitute, who needs Jack's help and rewards him with gold, a portion of his kingdom, or his daughter.

Bettelheim notes in his discussion of the Brothers Grimm's "The Three Languages" that children must often go out on their own to establish their independence. "Being 'cast out,'" Bettelheim writes, "can unconsciously be experienced either as the child wishing to be rid of the parent, or as his belief that the parent wants to be rid of him. The child's being sent out into the world, or deserted in a forest, symbolizes both the parent's wish that the child become independent and the child's desire for, or anxiety about, independence." Stories such as "Hansel and Gretel" help young children cope with the fear of abandonment, while stories such as the Jack Tales, famous to children in the Blue Ridge Mountains through their dramatization by Ferrum College's Jack Tale Players, demonstrate the adolescent who

4. Ibid., 66–69, 145.

makes his own way in the world, an inspiration to children aspiring to independence. The resolution of "Hansel and Gretel" is that the children are reunited with the parents, or the father and stepmother, in some versions of the story. In the Jack Tales and stories such as "The Three Languages," the young person achieves a goal that often results in marriage and ascendancy to the throne. Bettelheim explains, "To have become a king or queen at the conclusion of the story symbolizes a state of true *independence,* in which the hero feels as secure, satisfied, and happy as the infant felt in his most *dependent* state, when he was truly well taken care of in the kingdom of his cradle."[5] Thus, fairy tales do work for both young children and adolescents, even though older children are less likely to continue to experience them.

Bettelheim also points out that sons in fairy tales never take their fathers' kingdoms from them, although fathers do allow their sons to earn their thrones when the fathers are in their dotage, usually, in part, by finding and winning brides.[6] In this way, fairy tales are different from myths, which frequently involve young men's usurping the thrones of their fathers or father substitutes. Albus Dumbledore, then, knows that Harry will not try to take over Hogwarts.

For the young child, the dead father is common in fairy tales. Young Jack rarely has a father in the Jack Tales; Cinderella has none; we hear of no father in "Little Red Riding Hood." In other tales, he is ineffective. In both "Snow White" and "Hansel and Gretel," he abandons his child or children at the urging of his wife. Other fairy tale fathers, such as the one in some Jack Tales and in "The Three Languages," send their children away, enabling them to establish independence. The dead father in the Harry Potter books is like the dead father in "Cinderella"; his absence leaves his child vulnerable to mistreatment by others. For young children, this might represent the father's frequent absence from home due to employment or their fear that he will not be there to protect them when they are threatened. For older children, he represents the possibility of freedom, of making one's own way in the world. Harry Potter's dead parents both abandon him to the mercy of a frightening world and free him to make his own adventures.

Vernon Dursley is the fairy tale father from whom the child wants to escape, the one who treats the child unfairly and ignores him. He helps children understand their occasional animosity to their own fathers, without their having to feel guilty for these emotions, as Vernon Dursley is not Harry's real father. He cares more about his guests and keeping up appearances than he does about his surrogate son and more about his biological son than the surrogate. He provides the contrary to the idealized James

5. Ibid., 98, 127.
6. Ibid., 129.

Potter, whose image is easy to uphold because he is dead. It is possible that Bettelheim would see Vernon Dursley as the ogre in "Jack and the Beanstalk," whom the psychologist calls "the oedipal father." Jack must defeat the oedipal father, Bettelheim argues, in order to "become an independent human being."[7] Harry must defeat, or at least escape, Vernon Dursley in order to become a wizard. In both cases, the boy must move past or defeat his father in order to mature, and because Harry's real father is both dead and admirable, he needs a stand-in whose defeat will not discomfit readers.

Rubeus Hagrid represents the fairy tale hunter, the savior in such tales as "Little Red Riding Hood" and "Snow White." Bettelheim points out that the hunter in a fairy tale is "not a figure who kills friendly creatures, but one who dominates, controls, and subdues wild, ferocious beasts."[8] I would add that the hunter of the past was also a provider; thus to associate the hunter with the father, the protector and the source of food, is logical. Therefore, Hagrid's large size, his association with both caring for animals and killing them, and his befriending Harry and his mates are all plausible associations with the nonthreatening father for whom most children wish.

Sirius Black is like the beast in "Beauty and the Beast"; for a time, the children believe him to be evil, as their community has told them to believe this. But they learn that he is not a threat but a protector, and in the end of *Harry Potter and the Prisoner of Azkaban,* they also save him, as Beauty saves the beast. His being an animagus is also characteristic of fairy tales, in which people turn into swans, ravens, fawns, wolves, hedgehogs, and frogs. A common motif in fairy tales is animals' befriending humans, and vice versa. Often the hero who is kind to animals wins the day. We see examples of this in some versions of "Cinderella" and in "The Queen Bee," in which Simpleton is helped by ants, ducks, and bees, all of whom he has befriended. Sirius Black and fairy tale animals teach children not to fear the animal side of themselves or others and to respect nature. His being Harry's godfather is again a common fairy tale element, in which godparents represent the omnipresence of the dead parents as protectors of their children, as Cinderella's fairy godmother is the manifestation of the heroine's dead mother. Thus, Sirius Black is a comforting presence both to Harry and to young readers.

Voldemort is, of course, the evil fairy tale character, the wicked stepmother, the dragon, the ogre, Bluebeard, the wolf. That he is associated with a snake, one of the most feared and loathed creatures, certainly ensures that readers recognize how evil he is. He represents the feared aspects of the

7. Ibid., 190.
8. Ibid., 205.

father, especially as his connections with Harry are made clear through their connected wands. As Bettelheim explains, putting all the hated characteristics of the father into the evil being allows the child to avoid the guilt of having to hate the real father. Voldemort is the extreme of Vernon Dursley.

Albus Dumbledore is the extreme of Sirius Black. Dumbledore is almost godlike in that he controls the entire school, which is in many ways the center of the wizarding world because the government is ineffective and almost ridiculous. Dumbledore's wisdom and goodness, his forgiving and understanding nature, his courage and selflessness all make him the ideal father figure. His giving Harry James Potter's invisibility cloak connects Dumbledore to Harry's father but also to the kings in tales such as those featuring young Jack, kings who give the hero treasure or a princess in return for his good deeds. As Bettelheim points out, children know that they were created by their parents, and they see the world's creator as like these parents, a god.[9] Dumbledore is more a sustainer than a creator, but he is definitely godlike. Like Sirius Black, he is paralleled in fairy tales by the fairy godmother character, the genie. But so far, he is more nearly invincible than Black and has much more power than most fairy tale characters.

At least as important in fairy tales as the father or father figure are the maternal manifestations, the mother who sends Jack on an errand that begins his transition into a hero, the mother who dies yet leaves Cinderella with means to protect herself, the wicked stepmother who tries to destroy Snow White or keeps Cinderella as a servant, the ogre's wife who saves Jack from the giant, the old woman who helps Ashputtle overcome her mean sisters, and the fairy godmother who sends Cinderella to the ball as a princess. Bettelheim points out that the perfect mother of one's infancy must be left behind in order for the child to achieve independence and selfhood, for she is the most important person in the child's life. Thus, symbolically, the dead or absent mother allows the child to grow.[10] Harry Potter suffers and benefits from a number of such women.

Petunia Dursley is reminiscent of the evil stepmother in folk and fairy tales. As in "Snow White" and "Hansel and Gretel," she is willing to abandon the child entrusted to her care. Perhaps she most resembles the stepmother in "Cinderella," as she overwhelmingly favors her biological child over her surrogate. Taken to the extreme, she is the witch in "Hansel and Gretel." Like the witch, she initially takes in her nephew, but her apparent generosity is a sham. Whereas the witch wants to eat the children, Mrs. Dursley starves little Harry to stuff her gluttonous son, Dudley. Such evil stepmothers and surrogates allow little children to feel justified in their

9. Ibid., 49.
10. Ibid., 219–20.

sibling rivalry and to separate their love for their mothers from their anger at them.

Molly Weasley is like Mother Holle in German folk tales, the ogre's wife in "Jack and the Beanstalk," and the old woman in "Ashpet," an Appalachian version of "Cinderella." Mother Holle rewards with gold the young girl who does chores for her and punishes the sisters, who are lazy and greedy. The ogre's wife hides Jack in an oven and a pot, symbols of the womb. The old woman in "Ashpet" gives the title character fire, a symbol of the mother, as it is associated with the hearth and, thus, the home. In Richard Chase's version of "Ashpet," the woman has things belonging to the girl's mother. Molly Weasley is very much the prototypical mother, having given birth to the magical number of seven children and helping the good Harry by giving him what he needs on his mission: a surrogate family and something that represents familial love and warmth. She is a witch, but she comes to the aid of Harry Potter. For example, she knits him a sweater (or "jumper") for Christmas, just as she does for her sons, and she invites him to her home during a break from school, protecting him from the Dursleys as the ogre's wife hides Jack from her cannibalistic husband.

Professor Minerva McGonagall, as her given name suggests, is the wise woman, the teacher who is also connected with the animal world, teaching transfiguration and appearing first as a cat. It is she who tells Harry that, even as a first-year student, he can play Quidditch. Symbolically, this is Harry's permission to fly, to seek, to aim for his reward, represented by the Golden Snitch. As head of Harry's house, Gryffindor, Professor McGonagall is the closest to a mother the boy and his friends have at Hogwarts. She represents the omnipresence of the mother, there to comfort but also to discipline.

Because his mother, Lily Potter, returns to Harry when he needs her most—her voice is there when he needs to fight the dementors, and her spirit when he needs to fight Voldemort—she is like both the dead mother and the fairy godmother in "Cinderella" and other stories, a supernatural woman who appears when she is most needed. Such tales allow children to idealize their mothers and trust that, even when they are not physically present, they will still care for their children.

Maternity raises the theme of birth. Children want to know where they came from, accounting for their early interest in sex. The circumstances surrounding birth are not commonly presented in fairy tales, although Bettelheim points out a connection in the Brothers Grimm's "Snow White" between the Queen's pricking her finger—blood—and the birth of Snow White; the psychologist sees this as a conception story, explaining that there must be the blood of menstruation and the pricking of intercourse to produce the desired child. He argues that this story helps children to begin to understand sex and birth as related and sex as necessary for birth.[11]

Certainly Cinderella's transformation from girl in the ashes to beautiful princess is a sort of rebirth, as are Sleeping Beauty's awakening from her long sleep and Rapunzel's escape from the womblike tower. Bettelheim writes of Red Riding Hood's being cut from the wolf's stomach as like a caesarean birth, explaining, in part, why the hunter does not kill the wolf during the operation: it might make children fear that birth will kill the mother.[12] Birth and death are often related in fairy tales. For example, Sleeping Beauty is initially condemned to die, but a wise woman changes the curse instead to a hundred-year sleep. In both "Sleeping Beauty" and "Snow White," deathlike sleep is followed by rebirth, a sort of reentry to the world as an adult.

We do not know the story of Harry's birth, but we do know that at age one he almost died but miraculously lived and then magically arrived at the home of his surrogate parents. His story is reminiscent of the blessing of Sleeping Beauty's parents with her birth. However, he is welcomed by the Dursleys with as little joy as Hansel and Gretel's parents appreciate having two more mouths to feed or Cinderella's stepmother likes having a rival for her own daughters.

Death and the threat of death are omnipresent in many fairy tale versions. Cinderella's mother is dead. As punishment for her jealousy and her attempts to harm Snow White, the Queen in the Snow White tale is made to dance to her death. The wolves in "The Three Little Pigs" and "Little Red Riding Hood" are killed in revenge. The Beast in "Beauty and the Beast" threatens to kill Beauty's father. The wicked fairy or wise woman in "Sleeping Beauty" tries to kill the child. The ogre or giant tries to eat Jack, and the witch tries to eat Hansel and Gretel.

Of course, Rowling's novels are also death-filled. Voldemort, the last four letters of whose name come from the Latin word for death, has killed Harry's parents and has tried to kill the boy himself. The first book is all about the desire for immortality and ends in the death of two good, but very old, members of the magic world, Nicolas and Perenelle Flamel. Voldemort kills a unicorn, representing both incredible evil and the destruction of innocence. And in book four, the evil wizard kills one of Harry's schoolmates.

Bruno Bettelheim asserts, "Those predecessors of the hero who die in fairy stories are nothing but the hero's earlier immature incarnations."[13] Thus, Harry outlives those who created him, but, more important, he

11. Ibid., 202.
12. Ibid., 178–79.
13. Ibid., 181.

outlives Cedric Diggory, a boy wizard very much like himself who is strong and brave, but not quite strong and brave enough. Cedric is a foil to Harry, and the dead boy's failure makes Harry's success even more remarkable. It is also a step in Harry's success, as Bettelheim explains the motif.

Our fairy and folk tale heroes suffer, struggle, and triumph: Cinderella is abused by her stepmother and stepsisters, works hard to make it to the ball, and gets the prince in the end. Little Red Riding Hood is eaten by the wolf/grandmother, but is rescued by the hunter/woodcutter. Jack fights off the ogre and gets the treasure. Gretel shoves the witch into the oven, and the girl and her brother return home. In every case, the trial must precede the triumph. In every Harry Potter book so far, such has been the case. Harry must defeat Voldemort just to live at the beginning of *Harry Potter and the Sorcerer's Stone,* and later in that book he must, like Hansel and Gretel, escape the Forbidden Forest, then defeat Quirrell to avoid having Voldemort gain immortality. In *Harry Potter and the Chamber of Secrets,* he must rescue the princess, young Ginny Weasley, and overcome the basilisk, evil in the body of a serpent. The third book, *Harry Potter and the Prisoner of Azkaban,* shows Harry confronting his own fears, battling the dementors to keep his soul, saving his friend and an innocent animal, and overcoming his own desire for revenge by sparing the wizard who betrayed Harry's parents to their deaths. In *Harry Potter and the Goblet of Fire,* our hero rescues his friends from the merpeople and again must fight Voldemort for his very life. Rowling's books show young Harry and his friends in mortal danger time after time, and every time Harry at least temporarily triumphs over those who would destroy him and those he loves, although he cannot always save the people around him. Of course his trials represent to young children the perils of life and the likelihood that they, like Harry, can overcome those dangers and threats. They can do this by choosing good over evil (though not necessarily always obedience over disobedience), by choosing their friends well, and by the good fortune of being the heroes of their own tales, as Harry is the hero of his. There is a sort of egocentrism that blesses these young readers with the optimism Bettelheim finds omnipresent in true fairy tales.

Child readers are satisfied to affirm their perception that adults do not always treat them fairly and sometimes show favoritism to someone else, someone much less deserving. These children look forward to the day when everyone notices that they are special, like Cinderella and Harry Potter. They want to see evil adults punished, like the witch in "Hansel and Gretel," the wicked queen in "Snow White," and Voldemort. They want a fairy godmother or godfather, like the good witch Glinda in L. Frank Baum's Oz series and like Sirius Black. They want a beneficent king, like the one who rewards Jack and like Dumbledore. They want to satisfy their animal cravings for food, especially candy, like Hansel and Gretel's gingerbread house, the feasts that appear on the table at Hogwarts, and the candy they can buy and consume gluttonously on the train to school and at Honeydukes. They want the promise that their uniqueness and perfection will be discovered, like Jack's and Harry's; they also hope their mistakes will not result in drastic punishment in the meantime, as Jack is not severely punished for trading a cow for beans and as Harry is not punished for flying when it is forbidden or for breaking other rules when the result is fortuitous. Fairy tales and the Harry Potter series vicariously provide children with these pleasures and reassurances.

Harry Potter as Real Boy

Freud believed that persons in adolescence enter the genital stage and never leave it. On the other hand, developmental psychologist Erik Erikson postulated that, at about the age they enter puberty, adolescents also enter the psychosocial stage he called identity versus role confusion, leaving it at about age eighteen to enter the intimacy versus isolation stage. Adolescents' search for identity includes their lessening dependence on their parents and increasing identification with their peers. While they maintain the egocentrism of their childhood, perhaps in even greater proportion, they also begin to think more rationally about their futures and to consider issues in a more realistic way.

Consequently, young adolescents often choose to read books that are much more realistic than fairy tales, such as S. E. Hinton's *The Outsiders*, Lois Lowry's *A Summer to Die*, Anne Frank's diary, and Mildred D. Taylor's *Roll of Thunder, Hear My Cry*. They like books about children close to them in age who cope with issues such as going to school, making friends, asserting independence from adults, and seeking their identities. They are certainly not averse to fantasy, but they are integrating it more consciously with their own real lives, resulting in their interest in such books as Katherine Paterson's *Bridge to Terabithia*, in which two realistic children construct a fantasy world, and *Making Up Megaboy*, Virginia Walter's novel in which the protagonist, Robbie, draws a superhero cartoon. Bettelheim explains that some fairy tales, such as "Sleeping Beauty," address themselves primarily toward adolescents, helping them cope with their latent sexuality, for example; however, by puberty most children have moved beyond reading fairy tales, even if these stories are still firmly entrenched in their memories.

J. K. Rowling's books allow for a combination of the fantasy world of childhood with a more realistic world that children in early adolescence are beginning to manage with fewer layers of distance than younger children need. Harry Potter attends school, experiences sibling rivalry, suffers from bullies' attacks, struggles with some of his schoolwork, makes friends, becomes the target of jealousy, and breaks rules, just as most real adolescents do. Because he experiences similar joys and woes, yet triumphs at the end of each book, young adolescents identify with him and feel optimistic about their own lives.

Like fairy tales, more realistic literature with young protagonists offers numerous fathers and father figures as well. *Oliver Twist* alone provides numerous parallels: Vernon Dursley with the beadle; Voldemort with Fagin and Bill Sykes; and Albus Dumbledore and Sirius Black with Oliver's great-uncle. Judge Thatcher in *The Adventures of Tom Sawyer* is a Dumbledore/Sirius Black figure also. Huckleberry Finn's "Pap" is a Vernon Dursley figure who borders on the horror of Voldemort. Atticus Finch in *To Kill a Mockingbird* combines the reality of James Potter with the wisdom of Dumbledore. Ben Weatherstaff in *The Secret Garden* has the kindly natural qualities of Hagrid. Jim in *Adventures of Huckleberry Finn* has some of Hagrid's qualities, too, but he is much more a Sirius Black figure in his special protection of Huck.

That these characters exist in more realistic books indicates that young adolescents are beginning to integrate the qualities in their parents that they had once needed to separate. Thus, Atticus Finch can be wise and good without having to be dead; he can teach his children as well as discipline them. In *The Member of the Wedding,* Frankie Addams can love her father and still hate him for not allowing her to go with her brother after the wedding. Huck Finn can realize that his father is horrible without having to think of his Pap as unrelated to him.

Harry begins thinking about his father and father figures more realistically in later novels, as well. In the first book of the series, Harry, like such fairy tale characters as Lewis Carroll's Alice and Snow White's wicked stepmother, looks into a mirror, the Mirror of Erised, and sees his greatest desire: his parents and other ancestors. But Dumbledore tells the boy to move away from the fantasy world and rely on himself in real life. This advice stands the boy in good stead in interactions with his father and two of Harry's surrogate fathers, his godfather Sirius Black and Headmaster Dumbledore himself. In the third book, Harry receives assistance from his godfather, but he also saves him by turning back time to help him escape those who would lock him up and destroy his soul. In books three and four, the boy looks to his own late father for salvation but finally realizes that, although his father can give him strength, ultimately Harry must save himself. In *Harry Potter and the Prisoner of Azkaban,* Harry summons his father as his patronus to defeat the Dementors, who would suck his soul from his body. His father does appear, in the form of the stag who is his animal manifestation, but Harry also thinks he sees the person of his father. It is not until he understands that he has turned back time that he realizes it is he himself whom he has seen, not his father; Harry has saved himself. In *Harry Potter and the Goblet of Fire*, his father again appears, this time as a ghost spilling forth from Voldemort's wand. Again, his father encourages him and gives him strength, but once more Harry must save himself from the evil Voldemort. Harry's father cannot protect the boy because James Potter is dead. Even Albus Dumbledore, a living wizard and the headmaster of Harry's school, cannot save his pupils. In every book, Harry must fight the demons himself, battling Quirrell, Peter Pettigrew, the basilisk, the dementors, and finally Voldemort directly. Dumbledore's Hogwarts can give Harry the tools and wisdom for the war, but the young man must fight it himself.

Of course, this parallels the life of the adolescent. A child's parents often fight his battles for him, meeting with teachers who seem unfair, calling the parents of bullying classmates, helping with homework, yelling at coaches and referees perceived to be partial to someone other than these parents' child. But the middle school child must learn to advocate for himself, to fight off the bullies and tolerate the injustices of life. If he continues to call for his father, he is perceived by his schoolmates as an effeminate, childish coward. Young adolescents who read the Harry Potter books are aware of this fact but often lack the tools or courage to fight their own fights, which are sometimes overwhelming. Because young Harry can face even greater trials and win, adolescent readers gain confidence that they can, too.

The adolescent's fear of and desire for independence is represented in the maturation novel by the dead or absent mother motif, as well. Harper Lee's *To Kill a Mockingbird*, Carson McCullers' *The Member of the Wedding*, Katherine Anne Porter's Miranda stories, Eudora Welty's *Delta Wedding*, Alice Walker's *The Color Purple*, Charles Dickens' *Oliver Twist* and *David Copperfield*, Mark Twain's *The Adventures of Tom Sawyer* and *Adventures of Huckleberry Finn*, Charlotte Brontë's *Jane Eyre*, her sister Emily's *Wuthering Heights*, and Jane Austen's *Emma* are populated with motherless children. So are Frances Hodgson Burnett's *The Secret Garden* and Johanna Spyri's *Heidi*. The combination the dead mother provides of sympathy for the young protagonist and envy of his or her independence makes this a most successful motif. Reading such novels allows adolescents to retain their love for their mothers and yet move toward adulthood.

Harry Potter certainly joins a large and famous company when he loses his mother. As Dumbledore points out to him, however, it is the strength she imparted to him that literally saved his life when he was a baby (*Sorcerer's Stone*, 299). His mother is not alive to continue to intervene for him, though, and he must make his way without her. Thus, he must tolerate the injustices meted out to him by the relatives who rear him as well as the much more difficult passages of life after he enters adolescence. Like Harry's father, however, Lily Potter appears again when Harry needs her most, emerging as a spirit from Voldemort's wand to encourage the boy when his nemesis attempts to destroy him in the fourth book. Like her husband, too, she alone cannot save her son; he must save himself. Thus, adolescent readers learn both that their parents love them and want the best for them and that young people must fight for themselves, as their parents cannot defeat all their sons' and daughters' enemies.

As they do in fairy tales, wicked surrogates appear in the bildungsroman. Jane Eyre's cruel aunt, who believes her naughty children can do no wrong and locks poor orphaned Jane in the red room, then sends her away as soon as she can, could be the model for Petunia Dursley, if Brontë's character were also ridiculous. Even when the surrogates are not wicked, they are thorns in the sides of their pubescent charges. Tom Sawyer's aunt makes him take cod liver oil; the Widow Douglas tries to make Huck Finn a "civilized" Christian; Scout and Jem Finch have an aunt who tries to mold them into little Southern gentlefolk. Petunia Dursley's conspiracy with her husband to force Harry to behave in ways acceptable to their guests and kinfolk, to deny his very identity, mirrors such attempts to force young people to behave in a culturally approved manner. Adolescents reading such works identify with the pubescent characters in their desires to rebel against adults and the molds into which they are attempting to force the current generation, for adolescents fancy themselves iconoclasts and rebels, with their own identities separate from their elders'. That they mold themselves exactly like the young people around them, with beehive hairdos in one generation, afros in the next, and tattoos and piercings a generation later, does not occur to them as incongruent with their image of themselves as unique, each and every one.

Parallels exist in maturation novels for Molly Weasley, as well, not just for Harry's enemies. For example, the mother of Dickon and Martha Sowerby in *The Secret Garden* is the same kindly woman who loves her family and still has room left over for the orphaned Mary Lennox and the motherless Colin Craven. Often the woman is even more obviously a surrogate mother: Ole Golly in *Harriet the Spy,* Mary Poppins, Calpurnia in *To Kill a Mockingbird,* Dilsey in *The Sound and the Fury,* and Berenice Sadie Brown in *The Member of the Wedding.* As Bettelheim points out, children learn from these surrogates, as well as from such helpers in fairy tales as trees, birds, and other rescuers, that they will be helped in life, even when they feel alone and vulnerable.[14] Molly Weasley, then, with her animal name, joins Hagrid and Harry's other friends in helping the boy through his trials.

Whereas in fairy tales sex is treated only symbolically, if at all, writers in the second half of the twentieth century began to contend realistically with

14. Ibid., 11.

the connection between sex and birth in novels for and about adolescents. Paul Zindel's *My Darling, My Hamburger* shows teenagers the challenges of dating seriously and dealing with issues of intimacy. The allegedly genuine diary *Go Ask Alice* addresses for teenagers, in addition to the dangers of drugs, the difficult possibility of unwanted pregnancy brought on by drug-induced promiscuity. Julius Lester's recent novel *When Dad Killed Mom* hints at incestuous feelings between a father and daughter. However, even in earlier works such as *Oliver Twist* the illegitimacy of the title character is an issue. Of more concern in that work and others is the very real idea that giving birth can kill a woman.

Having taught a freshman seminar in which students talked about how "gross" it is that their parents (or a parent and stepparent) have sex, I believe that adolescents are quite titillated by the idea of sex and that older adolescents believe it is natural for them to have it, but they do not want to associate it with their own births, nor their siblings'. By the fourth book, when Harry is fourteen, he and his classmates begin to show interest in members of the opposite sex. Just as Hagrid and Madame Maxime share an attraction, Harry's friend Hermione Granger finds Viktor Krum to her liking, and Harry himself begins to fancy Cho Chang. Sex is still not mentioned, however, in relation to either the children or their elders.

As it does in fairy tales, the idea of rebirth appears symbolically in literature about and for young teenagers, including the Harry Potter novels. Huckleberry Finn's trip down the Mississippi on a raft is symbolic of rebirth. With his father's death and Huck's release from his father's womblike shack, he is free to be reborn, this time with Jim as his surrogate father. In Bill and Vera Cleaver's *Where the Lilies Bloom,* young Mary Call Luther finds a cave into which she plans to move her family after her father's death. Her finding the cave is a sort of reentering of the womb, and she emerges reborn, ready to move beyond her father's restrictions and make better plans for her family than her father had foreseen. In Jane Yolen's *Briar Rose,* inspired by a fairy tale of the same name, the young woman is rescued after almost being killed in the Holocaust. She is so near death that her memory of her past life is gone, and she emerges from a mass grave an adult with no childhood.

Harry Potter achieves at least three rebirths in the first four of Rowling's novels. The first is his delivery to the Dursleys after he is almost killed by Voldemort. The ending of life with his real parents and the beginning of a second phase with his surrogates is like a second life. He gets a third chance when Hagrid removes Harry from the care of his aunt and uncle, delivering him from the womblike cupboard under the stairs to Hogwarts. Much more symbolic is his dive in *Harry Potter and the Goblet of Fire* to the bottom of the lake to save his friends during the Triwizard Tournament. After eating gillyweed, he can breathe underwater. As the effect of the substance wears off, he emerges from the water like a baby coming forth from the womb, his lungs bursting as he finally reaches the surface and gasps for air. Symbolically, the boy moves from being a baby to being a child, then into adolescence, and finally into young adulthood around the time of initiation in many cultures. Adolescents can understand these symbolic rebirths as periods in their own lives, with their infancy and childhood behind them and their anticipation of adulthood.

These rebirths are often accompanied by symbolic deaths. The loss of young characters' parents, including Harry's, represents the loss of their childhoods, the death of these children's pasts. Other characters also die in novels about and for older children, such as Katherine Paterson's *Bridge to Terabithia* and Carson McCullers' *The Member of the Wedding*. In both of those books, another child dies, a cousin of the main character in McCullers' book and a friend of the protagonist in Paterson's. In both cases, besides literally helping children understand the inexplicability and apparent capriciousness of death, the losses represent the endings of phases in the children's lives. John Henry West's death is the end of Frankie Addams' childhood in *The Member of the Wedding,* the beginning of her movement to adolescence and a more realistic dream. The death of Jess's friend Leslie in *Bridge to Terabithia* also marks the boy's movement away from fantasy and into adolescence.

Young Harry, too, definitely loses any illusion that he will emerge unscathed by his horrible grand adventures when his friend Cedric Diggory dies before his eyes. Besides his parents, who died before Harry could remember, Voldemort's victims are killed far away from the boy, but Cedric dies on Harry's watch, and our young hero is powerless to save him. If Harry had not really understood the power of evil before, he does after this point, and his innocence is lost.

In short, writers of books about and for adolescents do not usually sugarcoat death. It exists, and those left behind grieve. However, life continues despite our grief. Death is perhaps the most impartial of those things that affect us, as it takes away rich and poor, powerful and powerless, and young and old. In almost all novels for and about adolescents, though, it is not our hero or heroine who dies. As we identify with the hero, we feel a bit invincible, learning to cope with the deaths of others but feeling protected from our own mortality. Perhaps that is why nonfictional works such as Anne Frank's diary affect young people so strongly; the heroine does not survive. However, young people do not realize how recent the 1940s were; to them, the Holocaust might as well have been "once upon a time."

On their way to maturity, our more realistic heroes meet and overcome terrors that are perhaps as terrible as being doomed to sleep for a hundred years or taking on the ogre, equally horrible because they are more real. In

To Kill a Mockingbird, Scout and Jem encounter the deadly costs of racism. Oliver Twist faces the abandonment of being orphaned, the betrayal of his protector, and the murder of his real friend. In his autobiographical *Black Boy,* Richard Wright tells about his father's desertion, his mother's illness, and his abuse at the hands of racists.

Even in books with less tragedy, the pangs of adolescence can loom almost as large to young people. Spy Harriet learns what it is like to have almost all her friends turn against her. Frankie Addams' father refuses to let his daughter go with her brother and his bride after the wedding. Young Billy in Wilson Rawls' *Where the Red Fern Grows* loses his dogs.

Whereas Harry's big adventures are fascinating to young adolescents, these readers are equally drawn to the more realistic events in the books. Harry's wearing ill-fitting hand-me-downs and receiving birthday presents that are infinitely inferior to his surrogate brother's ring true to every child who has ever felt jealous of a sibling. His mistreatment at the hands of the bully Draco Malfoy and his henchmen Crabbe and Goyle elicits the sympathy of readers who have been bullied themselves. Ron's jealousy of him and accusation that Harry has cheated when he is entered in the Triwizard Tournament are easily understood by children who have felt special, only at the cost of having their triumph spoiled by the envy of friends. Snape's unfair conduct toward Harry causes children who have felt singled out by those in authority for mistreatment to nod their heads in recognition. The long summer when Harry receives no owls from his friends soothes children who have felt neglected by their own companions. Harry's bafflement when he almost falls off his broom during Quidditch matches the anxiety of children who are not stellar athletes and cannot hit the basket or the ball or the goal. His struggle with some school subjects while Hermione aces every assignment assuages the pains of children whose best work earns only an average grade. When Harry must stay behind at school during Christmas vacation, those children who feel that their parents sometimes do not want them feel a bit of comfort.

The comfort to adolescent readers is that Harry is not perfect. Everything does not always go well for him. Yet in the end, he always triumphs, no matter how misunderstood or mistreated, no matter how gloomy the outlook at any time. And if Harry, the orphan with bad hair and glasses, can make friends, win at Quidditch, be a favorite of the headmaster, overcome the school bully, and be the hero not just of his own life but of wildly successful books, there is hope for every young reader.

At the end of almost every book for adolescent readers, including the first four in the Harry Potter saga, the trial has made the hero or heroine a stronger person, one who is wiser to the world's ways and more in control of self. Thus, we learn through our reading that life is difficult and full of struggles, but that we can weather these ordeals and emerge, not unscathed, but more mature and more capable of enduring the next trials. This lesson seems obvious to us as adults; it is less apparent to children, for whom every new challenge brings a question of whether or not they can withstand, whether or not they are worthy. Consequently, when they see those who appear to be lowly emerging triumphant, their own hope and self-confidence are renewed. So it is with Harry Potter's adolescent fans.

The Harry Potter novels thus far, then, help young people navigate the identity versus self-doubt stage in which Erik Erikson explains they find themselves. Because Harry experiences self-doubt yet finds a heroic identity and functions in a new and strange world, readers of the books about him believe that they, too, can be what my father calls not well-adapted but well-adapting, able to meet new challenges and overcome the hurdles they present. Yes, Harry is larger than life. But he also has a life as a schoolboy, a life that can be overwhelming to him. If he can face it, so can his readers, and they attain vicariously the strength to face their own world.

Harry Potter as Archetypal Hero

Harry Potter novels are so successful that the *New York Times* created a separate bestseller list for children's books to give books written by someone other than J. K. Rowling a chance at the top four spots on the regular list. The Potter series did not catapult to the top just because children read the books. In fact, many of the biggest Pottermaniacs I know are adults. While it is true that many grown-ups are reading the books with their children, others are reading them for their own pleasure. For that reason, in England Bloomsbury issued a separate edition of the first novel with an "adult" cover. How can a book about a pubescent boy have such appeal for adults?

Since humans have existed, adults have attempted to make sense of our world through myth. Pioneering psychological theorist Carl Jung is noted for his study of the world's myths and legends, especially for his discussion of archetypes. Less familiar today is Otto Rank, who applied his teacher Sigmund Freud's theories of dreams and mythology to many of the world's mythical and legendary heroes, both well and little known. According to Robert A. Segal in his introduction to *In Quest of the Hero,* both Freud and Rank believed that myths are like dreams: both are "the disguised, symbolic fulfillment of repressed, overwhelmingly Oedipal wishes lingering in the adult mythmaker or reader." In *The Myth of the Birth of the Hero,* originally published in 1909, Rank wrote what Segal calls "the classic Freudian analysis of hero myths."[15]

15. Robert A. Segal, *In Quest of the Hero,* viii, ix.

According to Rank, hero myths, such as the stories of Oedipus, Moses, and Jesus, contain ten basic elements, eight of which have been fulfilled by Harry Potter, almost the way characteristics surrounding Jesus's birth fit the prophesies in the book of Isaiah:

1. The boy is the son of royal or even immortal parents—Harry Potter's parents are a wizard and a witch;

2. Difficulties precede the conception, and in some cases the mother is a virgin—as of book four, we do not yet know the details of Harry's conception;

3. The child's life is threatened when dream or oracle warns the father or another royal personage that the boy will be a danger—Voldemort, a sort of prince of evil, has reason to fear Harry and tries to kill him;

4. The boy is separated from his parents—Harry's parents are dead;

5. The boy is exposed, often in a basket or other receptacle—Harry is laid on the doorstep of his aunt and uncle bundled like Jesus in swaddling clothes;

6. The boy is put into water, either to kill him or to save him—Harry and the other first-years are ferried to Hogwarts across a lake, and before Harry can be free from the Dursleys, Hagrid must fetch him from across a large body of water;

7. The child is rescued by animals or underlings, often shepherds—Harry is rescued by Hagrid, a gamekeeper, and is later aided by his godfather in the form of a dog and his father in the form of a stag;

8. The baby is suckled or reared by animals or lowly persons—Harry's aunt and uncle, the Dursleys, are lowly persons, as is Hagrid, but in a very different way;

9. The hero is eventually recognized as such, often because of a mark or a wound—Harry's attack by Voldemort has left him with a scar on his forehead, a sign that other wizards recognize;

10. The hero is reconciled with his father (or his representative), OR he exacts revenge upon his father—like the condition about conception, this characteristic has not yet been met in Rowling's novels.[16]

The universality of these characteristics in the world's myths and legends has caused much speculation as to both why they are ubiquitous and why they are popular. Theories about their ubiquity include the concept that they began in one place and spread as people migrated, either because all humans came from a central location with one set of myths, and we carried them with us as we moved throughout the world, or because as we migrated we picked up myths from various peoples, made them our own, and carried them to our new homes.

16. Otto Rank, *The Myth of the Birth of the Hero,* 57.

But why these specific myths? Some postulate that the hero myth symbolizes the fear that the sun/father will die, leaving us helpless like a fatherless boy. Others, such as Freud, believe that all the myths are oedipal, representing our longing to destroy our same-sex parent so that we can be with the parent of the gender opposite ours.[17] The opinions of other theorists are more similar to Bettelheim's theories about fairy tales: just as children both fear losing their parents and desire freedom from them, adults fear losing security and dream of independence and escape.

The myths of our ancestors make clear that another function of the hero archetype is to help establish our connection with God. Like Adam and Eve, we desire godlike wisdom and power, and we want the approval of our father/God. However, we do not wish to obey this father/God; instead, we want freedom. On the other hand, freedom means disconnecting from the patriarch, the deity. Alone, we fear that we will fail. Worse, we fear that we are not worthy of a connection with God, that we are lowly. Hero myths assure us that, while our mothers may be lowly, even animal-like, our fathers offer much more promise: they are noble or even immortal. Thus, we understand that, while we are born animals, we can hold out hope that our souls are immortal.

The Christian concept of the trinity—the father, son, and holy ghost—is clearly relevant to this need, although patriarchal cultures in which Christianity has flourished have perverted the triumvirate. While Bettelheim postulates that the number three, common in myth and tale alike, is related to sex, it seems more obvious that it is really related to the family: the two parents and a child.[18] Thus, we have a father, a mother earth (changed by Christians into a ghost), and a child. It is the child with whom we identify, even as adults. For it is the child, and the child in us, who still has hope that the animal, the weak, mortal part of the person, will pass, leaving the immortal soul, the connection with God.

Adults read Harry Potter books, then, not just to have something to discuss with our children and child friends. We, too, vicariously experience Harry's learning that he is destined for greatness, for a meaningful mission. The boy is not deterred for long by the mundane Dursleys; instead, he is transported to another world, a world in which he is famous and heroic, one that allows him to hear the voices of his parents and have them come to his aid even though they are dead. Just as God tells Moses to lift up his rod and perform miracles, young Harry raises his wand and performs magic. He cannot completely control his world, but he can manipulate it, evade its dangers, and triumph in it. Like children, adults desire these powers,

17. Ibid., 3–5.
18. Bettelheim, *Uses of Enchantment,* 106, 219.

realize they do not have them, but still believe they are attainable. More important, many believe that their earthly selves are temporary, that they are the children of a god, and that they will overcome their earthly fathers, and thus their earthly selves, to be reunited at last with their real fathers, the ones who bestow on them immortality.

Therefore, it is not so much that Hogwarts is like heaven, for it really is not. It has earthly dangers, people such as Quirrell and Draco Malfoy who are certainly not angels, and magic but not miracles. Instead, the point is that Harry is like a heavenly prince. He is nearly invincible, as we know because Voldemort's blows, fatal to Harry's parents, did not kill the child. He is known to all, recognized by his special scar. And he is heroic: brave, good-hearted, loyal, and still humble. We know that we were born human, members of the animal kingdom. But Harry gives us hope that we do not have to stay that way, that we can shuffle off our Muggle coil and move into the magical world.

Almost all archetypal heroes are threatened by their fathers or by some other man, often a royal figure, who has power over them. Oedipus's father, Laius, ordered the boy exposed, as did Paris's father, Priam. Telephus, son of Hercules; Perseus, son of Zeus; and Gilgamesh are all victims of their maternal grandfathers, and Moses is threatened by the Pharoah, the father of his adoptive mother. Jesus is threatened by Herod, the Roman ruler of Judea; Romulus and Remus were also condemned to death by a king.

Harry Potter is threatened not by his father but by the evil Voldemort, the dark lord, who has numerous ties with the boy. First, he and Voldemort have wands with feathers from the same bird, the phoenix named Fawkes that belongs to headmaster Albus Dumbledore. Second, Voldemort has tried to kill Harry, and when he fails, he disappears for a decade. In fact, that defeat almost kills Voldemort. Third, by the end of *Harry Potter and the Goblet of Fire,* Voldemort has been revived by the boy's blood (642–43).

Because it is the father or father figure who has attempted to destroy the child, there must come a time of reckoning between the hero and his attacker. Otto Rank points out that the hero has two choices: to try to reconcile with the father, or to avenge himself against his enemy.[19] Sometimes the tale ends with a combination of these climaxes; the son's assumption of his father's throne is a kind of reconciliation, in the sense that the boy has become the man his father was, but the usurpation is also a sort of revenge or overthrow.

Moses overcomes the man who tried to destroy him, the Pharoah of Egypt, who ordered all male Hebrew children put to death during Moses'

19. Rank, *Myth of the Birth of the Hero,* 57.

infancy and later sentenced the grown Moses to death for killing an Egyptian. Because the Pharoah is Moses' adoptive grandfather, as the child had been found and adopted by the ruler's daughter, when Moses' God sends him to save the Hebrews from their captors, Moses settles a personal score as well as a national one.

Oedipus avenges his father's attempt to have him killed, as well, but he does so unawares; he does not know that the traveler he kills in anger is his father, King Laius of Thebes. Paris of Troy is reconciled with his father, Priam, even though the king had sent a slave to leave the infant Paris to be exposed. The story of Romulus and Remus combines the themes of vengeance and reconciliation. Romulus kills his great-uncle, the king who had tried to kill him and his brother, and is reconciled with his grandfather, from whom he had been long separated.[20]

J. K. Rowling's first four books about Harry Potter give the boy six fathers or father surrogates, each of whom is suggested by a father or father figure in myth and legend, but none of whom is completely satisfactory. Among them, they represent adults' needs to see fathers as both earthly and immortal.

First, of course, is Harry's real father, James Potter, whom Voldemort kills when Harry is only a year old. The boy has great longing to know his father, as we see very clearly in four episodes. The first occurs in *Harry Potter and the Sorcerer's Stone,* in chapter 12, "The Mirror of Erised." The mirror shows those who look into it their greatest desire; for Harry, this desire is to see his parents. In fact, as he looks into the mirror, Harry sees himself, his parents, and his other ancestors. He sees himself in his father, for they both are tall and thin with messy dark hair and glasses. Seeing his family for the first time in his memory, Harry is mesmerized. Rowling writes, "The Potters smiled and waved at Harry and he stared hungrily back at them" (*Sorcerer's Stone,* 208–9). It is also in the first book that Harry is given something of his father's: an invisibility cloak, which allows him to move through Hogwarts without being seen.

Again in *Harry Potter and the Prisoner of Azkaban,* Harry encounters his father. In his Defense against the Dark Arts class, he is learning to fight his fears by summoning a Patronus, the word, of course, derived from the Latin word for "father." The boggart whom he must learn to defeat takes the shape of an evil dementor, a deathlike creature who can suck the soul from a person; when it appears, it causes Harry to hear his parents' voices as he relives the attack on his family by Voldemort. Consequently, the boy is torn between wanting to defeat the boggart/dementor and wanting to hear his parents again.

20. Ibid., 19–20, 34–36.

He learns in chapter 18, "Moony, Wormtail, Padfoot, and Prongs," about his father's experiences as a schoolboy. Young James Potter and three of his friends broke the rules of the magical world by becoming animagi, wizards who turned themselves into animals, without permission. James Potter's alternate self was a stag. Later, in *Harry Potter and the Prisoner of Azkaban,* Harry's father's manifestation as a stag becomes directly relevant. Real dementors are chasing the boy and his godfather, Sirius Black, and Harry summons a patronus. It appears in the form of a stag, and across the lake Harry thinks he sees his own father. As he views the scene from the present looking back on the past, he waits for his father to appear. But he later learns that he and his friend Hermione Granger have turned back time using a Time-Turner, and "[h]e hadn't seen his father—he had seen himself." Subsequently he shouts the spell "EXPECTO PATRONUM" and sees his Patronus, the stag, Prongs, the animal incarnation of his father (*Prisoner of Azkaban,* 411–12).

Although James Potter's death separates him from his son, Harry's feelings about his father are not ambivalent. He identifies with his father and sees him as his protector. Later he tells his headmaster, Albus Dumbledore, of what he thought he saw and says that he realizes his thinking he saw his father was foolish because James Potter is dead. Dumbledore reassures him, telling him how much he looks like his father. He tells the boy, "Your father is alive in you, Harry. . . . [I]n a way, you did see your father last night. . . . You found him inside yourself" (*Prisoner of Azkaban,* 427–28).

The fourth time Harry sees his father occurs during a duel between Harry and Voldemort at the end of *Harry Potter and the Goblet of Fire,* the fourth book in the series. As the two foes hold each other by the power of their connected wands, those Voldemort had killed appear from the end of the evil wizard's wand. Although Harry is astonished at first, by the time Harry's parents appear and speak to him, telling him to run while they protect him from Voldemort, Harry is calm; when his father's head appears, "Harry knew . . . who it would be . . . because the man appearing was the one he'd thought of more than any other tonight . . . The smoky shadow of a tall man with untidy hair fell to the ground . . . and Harry . . . looked . . . into the ghostly face of his father (*Goblet of Fire,* 667). Even in death, Harry's father and mother protect him from his enemy.

Thus, Harry's father has three manifestations: the animal Prongs, the spirit, and Harry's identification with him. Archetypally, he represents the animal part of our nature, the spirit or soul, and immortality through future generations. He is both the father who deserts the child and the one who protects him, the god who puts us in this dangerous world filled with death, including the knowledge of our own at an unknown time, and the god who sustains us and gives us renewed life. Finally, he is the creator who lives on in us.

Vernon Dursley is the first father figure Harry remembers. The epitome of the bad father, Dursley shows strong favoritism to his own son, Dudley, and treats Harry as a pariah, failing to acknowledge his nephew's birthdays, making him sleep in a cupboard under the stairs, forcing him to stay out of sight when guests visit, and forbidding him to speak of his magical gifts. He tries to keep Harry from learning his parents' true identities and hides him when he begins receiving letters telling him to report to Hogwarts. He shouts at Harry during one of the boy's miserable summers on Privet Drive, "I WILL NOT TOLERATE MENTION OF YOUR ABNORMALITY UNDER THIS ROOF!" (*Chamber of Secrets*, 2). In short, Uncle Vernon tries to stifle Harry and keep him from being his true self. Harry's only consolation is that his uncle fears his magical powers. Rowling writes that Dursley treats Harry "like a bomb that might go off at any moment, because Harry Potter *wasn't* a normal boy" (*Chamber of Secrets*, 3). Vernon Dursley represents one aspect of the lowly figure in the archetypal heroic myth. His ordinariness stands in stark contrast to the wizards in Harry's new world at Hogwarts.

Rubeus Hagrid represents the other aspect of this figure. Associated with animals, both as a hunter and a keeper of magical creatures, Hagrid reminds one of the shepherds and cattleherds who take in abandoned children throughout mythology—the shepherds who save Oedipus, find Paris, and visit Jesus at the time of his birth; the cattle herder who saves Cyrus the Great; the swineherd who rears Romulus and Remus; the ox-herders who rear Hercules; and the overseer who rears Gilgamesh. Hagrid is also Keeper of the Keys, a status symbolizing Dumbledore's trust. A wild-looking half-giant, Hagrid is not a brilliant man but a kind one who delivers the infant Harry to his aunt and uncle and the boy Harry to Hogwarts. He continues to befriend Harry and his friends as well.

Sirius Black is Harry's godfather, his father's best friend. Sirius is in hiding because he has been framed for murder, so he befriends Harry primarily through correspondence. However, when Harry is in real trouble, Sirius appears, often in the shape of a dog. Thus, Sirius represents the animals throughout mythology who appear to protect abandoned children: the bear who nurses Paris, the wolf who nurses Romulus and Remus and the woodpecker who guards them, the eagle who saves Gilgamesh, the doe who nurses Siegfried, and the swan who feeds Lohengrin. While it is true that most of the animals who save children are female, the animal who comes to Harry's rescue is male, a father figure. Many children in archetypal hero myths have earthly fathers who serve as surrogates for immortal patriarchs. Joseph, the father of Jesus, epitomizes this father archetype. It is Joseph who saves Jesus by taking him to Egypt when Herod orders male children of the Hebrews killed. Sirius serves in a similar fashion as the earthly protector of Harry Potter, whose father's death deprives the boy of his rightful protector.

Voldemort represents the evil king in the archetypal heroic tale. Like the Pharoah, Herod, Romulus and Remus's uncle King Amulius, and King Hugdietrich of Constantinople who orders Wolfdietrich killed, Voldemort is apparently neither the boy's father nor his grandfather, but an evil person with power who fears losing that power to another and thus attempts to kill the usurper in childhood. However, as noted earlier, Voldemort and Harry share a number of bonds: their similar wands and their shared blood are the strongest. Voldemort's failed attempt to kill the boy also binds them. The symbolic connection of their wands in *Harry Potter and the Goblet of Fire* is particularly fascinating, if the two are not related. Voldemort plans to kill Harry, but wants to play with him first, so he commands him to duel. Reminding Harry of the death of his father, he says, "And now you face me, like a man . . . the way your father died" (*Goblet of Fire*, 660). Then Voldemort attacks Harry with a spell that certainly is meant to call to mind the sacrifice of Jesus, the Cruciatus Curse. When Voldemort halts the curse long enough to taunt Harry, the boy crouches behind Voldemort's father's gravestone, then matches Voldemort curse for curse. As the two foes point their wands at each other, jets of light emerge from each wand and connect, forming one light. This beam lifts both Voldemort and Harry into the air. Harry and Voldemort struggle, and Harry hears the song of a phoenix, noteworthy because his and Voldemort's wands both contain feathers from Albus Dumbledore's phoenix, Fawkes. After a time, ghostly figures are emitted from Voldemort's wand: Harry's friend Cedric Diggory, whom Voldemort has just killed; a man; a woman; and, as noted above, Harry's father and mother. The three Potters, with the help of Voldemort's other victims, are able to overcome Voldemort, and Harry escapes back to Hogwarts (*Goblet of Fire*, 663–68).

At least two points are relevant here. First, those who have been attacked by Voldemort join with his latest victim to foil his attempt. Second, the phallic imagery of the two wands is inescapable.[21] Harry is emasculated when his wand is taken from him, and Voldemort can draw blood. But once Harry's wand is returned, he can block the power of Voldemort. The two beams from the wands of Voldemort and Harry Potter combine both to repel each other and to bind the enemies in a golden web that can transport them and

---

21. Jack Zipes also calls Harry's wand "phallic." Zipes, "The Phenomenon of Harry Potter, or Why All the Talk?" in *Sticks and Stones: The Troublesome Success of Children's Literature from Slovenly Peter to Harry Potter*, 180.

even raise the dead, if only temporarily. Good and evil both attract and repel one another, and good wins, again if only temporarily. Voldemort's wand is rendered useless; he is symbolically castrated, rendered impotent, during this encounter.

Albus Dumbledore is the antithesis of Voldemort. He uses power purely for good, and he, too, assumes a paternal role in the orphaned Harry's life. It is significant that the most admirable and respected character in the Harry Potter series is not a government official but the head of a school, as Rowling clearly suggests that the one who can help shape the minds and character of the next generation of leaders is the most important person in a society. Dumbledore serves that role, mentoring Harry and his friends, serving as a role model, and, most important, taking on the task of rallying all good to fight all evil. We see this at the end of *Harry Potter and the Goblet of Fire,* when Dumbledore sends emissaries to the giants and to the other schools to form alliances to fight Voldemort. Dumbledore is the idealized father, the dream of every child—the father who is godlike: omnipotent, omniscient, and benevolent, always on the side of good. Dumbledore is to Harry what God is to Jesus, what Zeus is to Hercules, what Mars is to Romulus and Remus, perhaps not literally, but figuratively.

Harry, the fatherless boy, has a plethora of father-figures, both positive and negative, one for almost every archetype. He looks to some for comfort and rescue, fears the attack of others, and tries to please most of them.

It is also significant that the mother is the savior of the child in many archetypal myths. Occasionally she attempts to destroy the child herself, as Alcmene exposes Hercules for fear of Hera, Zeus's wife. However, in most instances, if she has any power at all, the mother tries to save the child from his father, his grandfather, or another powerful man. This pattern is almost as common as the male's attempted destruction of the child he fears will usurp him.

Sometimes it is the biological mother who saves her child, as Sargon's mother bore him in hiding and floated him down the river in a vessel that protected him; Moses' mother hid him for three months, then floated him on the river in a basket; and Siegfried's mother put him in a glass vessel to protect him. Often a surrogate mother saves the child, as the Pharoah's daughter saved Moses, Polybus's wife Periböa saved Oedipus, and the wife of the swineherd saved Romulus and Remus.

Harry Potter has three mothers or mother figures. The first is his biological mother, Lily Potter, who like many archetypal mothers of heroes is born of relatively ordinary parents: Lily, though herself a witch, is the daughter of Muggles, the sister of the very ordinary Petunia Dursley. Her child, however, is not ordinary at all, for he is a wizard like his father. This pattern is found in the births of Jesus, Hercules, Paris, and other heroes who have mortal mothers but immortal fathers. The mothers, too, are extraordinary, resulting in their being chosen to have these special children.

Lily is her son's savior. When Voldemort attacks the Potter family, Lily says to him, as Harry hears years later when dementors attack him, *"Not Harry, please no, . . . kill me instead"* (*Prisoner of Azkaban,* 179). Her love for Harry, combined with his own innate greatness, is enough to save the boy from death, just as a few drops of Hera's milk are enough to render Hercules immortal.[22] As Albus Dumbledore tells Harry in the first book, "Your mother died to save you. If there is one thing Voldemort cannot understand, it is love. . . . [T]o have been loved so deeply, even though the person who loved us is gone, will give us some protection forever" (*Sorcerer's Stone,* 299).

Lily Potter returns to Harry when he is threatened by dementors; he hears her voice from the past. He also sees her when he looks into the Mirror of Erised. And when Voldemort tries to kill him again at the end of *Harry Potter and the Goblet of Fire,* the spirit of his mother comes from her killer's wand. It is she who gives him the instructions that save his life. Harry follows her directions, and Voldemort's victims, including Lily Potter, shield the boy as he runs from the evil wizard (*Goblet of Fire,* 667–68). The hero's mother has helped save him again. It is significant that J. K. Rowling's own answer to the question "What would you see in the Mirror of Erised?" was, "I would probably see my mother, who died in 1990. So, the same as Harry."[23] Lily Potter has a parallel in Demeter, for whom the world stopped when she lost her daughter, Persephone, to the god of the underworld and began again only when her daughter was returned to her, though for only part of each year. Like Achilles' mother, who tried to protect her son by dipping him in the Styx, these are women whose lives center around motherhood and who love and try to protect their offspring.

Petunia Dursley, Lily Potter's sister, is Harry's first surrogate mother. Like her husband, she favors her own child over Harry and appears to have very little interest in her nephew. Mrs. Dursley is more reminiscent of the evil stepmother in folk and fairy tales—Cinderella's stepmother is probably the greatest example—than she is of mythical surrogates; however, her type is common in such literature as Charlotte Brontë's *Jane Eyre,* the title character of which has a monstrous aunt who far prefers her own children and locks Jane in a room. In mythology, there are women who conspire with their husbands against children, often in variations on the Oedipus myth,

22. Rank, *Myth of the Birth of the Hero,* 38.
23. J. K. Rowling, "Barnes and Noble Chat with J. K. Rowling," also quoted in Nel, *J. K. Rowling's Harry Potter Novels: A Reader's Guide,* 18.

or even themselves send the children to be exposed. Rank notes that such stories are found even in Christian mythology.[24]

Molly Weasley finds love and room for Harry even with all seven of her own brood to care for. In fact, at the end of *Harry Potter and the Goblet of Fire,* when Harry has won the Triwizard Tournament and survived the attack by Voldemort, Mrs. Weasley is at Hogwarts in lieu of his own family. She is the poor woman whose husband serves the leader, in this case the Minister of Magic, who takes in the foundling, the generous woman who is a foil to the insufferable Petunia Dursley and shows Harry what a mother's love should be. She is like the cattle-herder's wife who saves Cyrus the Great, the swineherd's wife who rears Romulus and Remus, and the gamekeeper's wife who rears Wolfdietrich.

While parents and their surrogates figure greatly in myths, it is the hero or heroine who matters most to us, the person with whom we identify, whose happiness and well-being are our concern. Everyone else in the story matters to us primarily as he or she matters to our hero. We want our hero to live happily ever after, even to be resurrected after death. We care about this person to the extent that the destruction of others, even children, has little effect on us. Consider the ease with which Greek playwrights get us past the killing of Hercules' family, focusing instead on his suffering. Biblical writers move right past all the dead Hebrew children, all the dead Egyptian children, and all the dead people of the world in the story of Noah and his ark. Our hero represents us, and as long as we survive, we can get past the deaths of hundreds of innocents.

However, this does not mean that we want our hero to have an easy time of it. First, ease is not exciting. Second, ease does not aid maturity. One must be tested and withstand the test. We do not want even our gods to be perfect, but we do want them to be triumphant. Our myths and legends make that clear. Hera tries to kill Hercules. Laius tries to have Oedipus left to die. The Pharoah and Herod try to exterminate all little Hebrew boys in their attempts to prevent Moses and Jesus from taking their thrones. But our little heroes are survivors, and we rejoice in their triumph. Later, our heroes try to escape their fates: Hercules almost kills himself after killing his family in a fit of madness brought on by Hera; however, he lives to perform his twelve labors. Oedipus leaves his adoptive parents to avoid killing his father and marrying his mother, only to fulfill his destiny on his biological parents. Complaining that he stutters, Moses begs God not to send him back to Egypt to take on the Pharoah. Even Jesus is tempted to use his power selfishly and asks God to take the cup of suffering from him.

---

24. Rank, *Myth of the Birth of the Hero,* 18.

In the end, however, each hero fulfills his destiny: Hercules performs his labors; Oedipus rules Thebes, even exiling himself to save it; Moses defies the Pharoah and delivers his people to the Promised Land; and Jesus dies and rises from the dead.

Harry Potter, too, experiences the trials of the world's mythological heroes. Attacked as a child by the evil Voldemort, he loses his parents and barely escapes with his life. He endures years of persecution and loneliness in the household of his aunt, uncle, and cousin. Like Hercules, he has his own labors: he must fight a troll, a basilisk, and Voldemort again and again, sometimes in one form and sometimes in another. Like other archetypal heroes, he sometimes asks to be relieved of his tasks, often denying the warning of his aching scar, hoping, like Oedipus, that if he ignores the warning, he can avoid the risk.

But the risk always comes, and Harry faces it directly. He defeats Voldemort time after time and wins battles against the basilisk, the dragon who guards her egg, and Peter Pettigrew. He wins Quidditch matches and the Triwizard Tournament. Like children reading fairy tales and adolescents reading more realistic books, adults, too, identify with mythological heroes and believe that we can stand up against life's slings and arrows.

Rank points out what should be obvious but what might get lost in this discussion: "The myths are certainly not constructed by the hero, least of all by the child hero"; instead, they are "created by adults, by means of retrograde childhood fantasies." Rank explains, "The ego of the child behaves," then, "like the hero of the myth, and . . . the hero should always be interpreted merely as a collective ego."[25]

In short, Rank's theories explain myths the way Bettelheim explains fairy tales: they provide us with allegories to understand our own worst and best impulses, to help us understand birth, death, sex, identity, and good and evil. Mythology also helps adults understand the concepts of God and the soul, the way fairy tales help children understand their relationships to their parents and more realistic fiction for young adolescents helps those children come to terms with their own identities.

Mythology almost always explains birth as a mystical, magical event, one ordained by the gods. Thus, despite Laius's fear inculcated in him by the oracle at Delphi that his son would kill him, he gets drunk and impregnates Jocasta, resulting in the birth of Oedipus. According to rabbinical theology, Moses' parents, too, avoided having a child until their daughter dreamed that their son would save his people. Jesus' conception was not only ordained by God but actually caused by Him, just as Zeus fathered Hercules

25. Ibid., 70–71, 62.

and Apollo. This common archetype, the birth despite many odds, allows the reader or hearer to identify with the hero's special destiny, the idea that the gods wanted the hero's birth—and by extension, our own—so much that they overcame any obstacle to get him and us to earth.

The idea of rebirth, too, appears in myth. When Moses delivers the Israelites from Egypt, he parts the Red Sea and walks his newly freed people through it in a remarkable birth image—the rebirth of a people into their Promised Land. And Jesus and his cousin John the Baptist are baptized in water, conveying upon them or symbolizing a special relationship with God. Of course, Jonah's emergence from the belly of the whale and Noah's family's emergence from the ark after the flood are also biblical rebirths.

Otto Rank cites as one of the characteristics of the hero that he is often put into water, either to send him to his death or to save him.[26] The story of Moses' mother's placing him in a basket and placing him in the Nile, from which he is drawn by the Pharoah's daughter, has numerous parallels, including Romulus and Remus's being placed in a tub on the Tiber, then washing ashore, and the Hindu hero Karna's being placed in a basket and floated down a river into the Ganges, from which a charioteer and his wife save him.[27]

The themes of birth and rebirth are part of understanding ourselves and our identities, as well as the concept of sex. They also make us believe, both as adults and as children, that we have second chances, that we do not have to remain the way we were born. Oddly, these themes combine the ideas of destiny and freedom. If we are destined to greatness, a lowly birth will not prevent us from achieving distinction. On the other hand, even if we are born as though destined for nothing, we can be reborn as persons of eminence and great deeds. In short, we are not doomed by our birth, as Dumbledore tells Cornelius Fudge, the Minister of Magic: "[I]t matters not what someone is born, but what they grow to be!" (*Goblet of Fire*, 708).

The idea of rebirth is also a means of escaping our animal natures. We might be born the same way a calf or even a rat is born, but we can be reborn in a more remarkable form, one closer to the gods. This motif is especially important in mythology, when the birth or suckling mother might be a lowly person or even an animal; the biological parents, though, are noble or divine. Again, the circumstances of our birth are not necessarily our reality, and who we are as children does not limit who we might become as adults. So where does that leave adults? In much religious mythology, our rebirth is expected after our deaths; in short, we might be such animals that we will die an earthly death, but even that will not prevent our achieving our destinies in another world or another life in this one.

26. Ibid., 57.
27. Ibid., 16.

An additional interpretation of the connection of archetypal heroes with animals is that the human acknowledgment of our animal nature is balanced against the desire to believe that we are made in the image of God, the insistence that we have a soul that separates us from the animals. We certainly see this dichotomy in the Harry Potter series. The association with animals is literal in the animagi, the humans such as Professor McGonagall and Sirius Black who turn themselves into a cat and a dog, and in the pig's tail that Hagrid puts on the bottom of gluttonous Dudley Dursley. Hagrid's gamekeeping, Voldemort's sucking the blood from a unicorn, and the children's devouring of food, especially meat—"roast beef, roast chicken, pork chops and lamb chops, sausages, bacon and steak" (*Sorcerer's Stone,* 123)—remind us that we are animals, even predatory carnivores. That Harry's father turns into a stag, a manly beast but prey rather than predator, also reminds us that the animal part of us is the mortal part, the vulnerable aspect of the human being. The connection with animals in childhood, such as the suckling of Romulus and Remus by the wolf, the salvation of Oedipus by a shepherd, even Jesus' association with shepherds, and the delivery of young Harry Potter both to the Dursleys and to Hogwarts by the gamekeeper, is followed by the discovery of the spiritual connection, the father who is a god or the parents who are witches and wizards. Thus we have the two versions of creation in Genesis: the one in which man is made first, in the image of God, then followed by the animals, and the other in which man follows from the animals, in a parallel to evolution. We are both animal and more, as the myths and Harry Potter remind us.

After four books, the circumstances surrounding Harry Potter's conception and birth are still unknown to us. However, birth imagery is quite common in the works. While baby Harry is not placed in a basket in the water, his delivery to Hogwarts contains strong elements of rebirth symbolism, and he later has life-changing experiences with water. When he receives letters announcing that he is to begin school at Hogwarts, his aunt and uncle take him to an island to hide him from whoever is sending the mail. He is carried from the island across the water by Hagrid, just as numerous other heroes are delivered from the water by shepherds, gamekeepers, and other folk who work with animals (*Sorcerer's Stone,* 44–65). In fact, all first-year students—and, significantly, only the first-years—are ferried across water to Hogwarts, a sort of rebirth completed when the Sorting Hat puts them into their new houses. Again in *Goblet of Fire,* Harry has a significant experience with water, this time the lake around Hogwarts School. As part of the Triwizard Tournament, he has the task of rescuing his friend Ron Weasley from the merpeople at the bottom of the lake. He learns of his task by opening a dragon egg under water in a bath (*Goblet of Fire,* 458–66). Then by eating a substance called gillyweed, he becomes capable of breathing through gills, like a fish. He finds his friend, as well as three other captives, and then, after other contestants rescue two of the captives, carries Ron and a child back to the surface, just as he loses the ability to breathe under water (*Goblet of Fire*, 493–504). Again, the birth imagery is unmistakable: like a fetus, he does not need oxygen, but as he is reborn as a hero, a savior of his friends, he must again breathe air.

Birth and rebirth imagery function in three ways for readers. First, they help us establish identity, for it is upon our births that most cultures mark us as individuals distinct from our parents, as unique persons. Second, they reflect our attitude of wonderment toward the idea of sex, especially sex between our parents, a taboo subject for most children and many adults. Third, they allow the opportunity of a new chance, an opportunity most clearly specified in the Christian faith, the idea of being born again, of becoming a new person cleansed of past imperfections or merely of insignificance. As Jesus and his followers are baptized into the kingdom of God, Harry and other first-years are baptized and christened into the kingdom of Hogwarts, ferried across the lake and placed into a house by the Sorting Hat.

Death, the obverse of birth, is even more of a mystery. We have both a fear of death and an obsession with it, partly because no one can really explain it. The threat of death appears at the very beginning of almost every hero myth: Oedipus's father tries to have him killed; the Pharoah tries to have Moses killed—in fact, the Hebrew God slaughters the first-born sons of the Egyptians, making Exodus full of infanticide; and Herod tries to have Jesus killed. Harry Potter, too, is almost the victim of Voldemort's plots to kill him.

To our delight, our hero archetypes always escape the attempted murder. Of course this is comforting: we believe that we, too, can escape early death. However, in *The Hero: A Study in Tradition, Myth, and Drama,* myth ritualist Lord Raglan lists twenty-two similarities among heroic tales, five of which relate to the hero's death.[28] Otto Rank brings us to the hero's triumph, not to his demise. However, most myths and legends do take us to the end of the lives of the heroes. We know that, after killing his father, marrying his mother, and blinding himself upon discovery of his deeds, Oedipus finally dies happy, beloved by his daughters and welcomed into a land of refuge. We know that Moses dies before reaching the Promised Land. We know of Jesus' crucifixion.

Future Books in the Harry Potter Series

The question, then, is whether Rowling will follow the pattern Rank described and end the seventh book at the height of Harry's triumph, or

---

28. Lord Ragland, "The Hero: A Study in Tradition, Myth, and Drama, Part II," 138.

whether she will follow that recounted by Lord Raglan and end with our hero's death. Bettelheim would insist that the last book end with Harry's triumph, not his death. While literature and myths for adults can include the hero's death to help us deal with our own, the idea that all are mortal, so we do not feel so betrayed by our own mortality, Bettelheim echoes J. R. R. Tolkien in insisting that stories for children must end happily, or the child's psyche is too greatly disturbed.[29] If there is something that the great wizard Harry Potter could not overcome, then there is certainly no hope for the ordinary child. The British boy may experience setbacks, but he must not be defeated, and certainly not destroyed.

Thus, if J. K. Rowling follows the path set forth by tellers of fairy tales, Harry will become "king," or at least be on his way to becoming headmaster. He might have prospects of marriage to a woman who is equally wonderful, the fairy tale princess to match his role as fairy tale hero. If the series ends like a fairy tale, Voldemort will be defeated, probably killed by Harry's hand. Harry will save the kingdom represented by Hogwarts from the evil represented by Voldemort, as Jack defeats the ogre or giant, and Harry will be rewarded by Dumbledore, who represents the king.

Perhaps the series will end like maturation novels. In such case, Harry will graduate in book seven, have a girlfriend, and have excellent prospects for the future. Like Huckleberry Finn, he will go forth to find his fortune, or like Oliver Twist he will find a benefactor who will care for him.

Perhaps the series will end like a myth, in which case Harry will have revenge on the evil father figure, Voldemort, or be reunited with a positive father figure, either a resurrected James Potter (not likely) or Albus Dumbledore. Having both endings occur in the final book is not at all unlikely. It is also probable that we will learn that at least one of these men is his grandfather.

The Harry Potter novels are popular because they satisfy our psychological needs. Male or female, child or adolescent or adult, we identify with this boy. He is good but not perfect. He is trying to find out who he is. He commands our sympathy because he is an orphan and lives with cruel relatives. We admire his loyalty to friends, his courage in the face of danger, his kindness to those weaker than himself, such as Neville Longbottom and the elf Dobby. We covet the excitement of his life but feel relief that we are not similarly tested.

Mythology is our earliest form of literature. Fairy tales are probably our second. More realistic narratives came much later, just as more representational painting followed long after the symbolic paintings found in caves. We have much reason to believe that fairy tales grew from mythology and

---

29. Bettelheim, *Uses of Enchantment*, 143–44.

that more realistic literature grew from these tales. Perhaps the early development of mythology stems from adults' desire to explain the world to ourselves. Only later did we feel it necessary to explain it to children. Finally, when we had made our way through the greatest mysteries, such as where the sun goes at night, we turned toward those more mundane ones of everyday reality, such as prejudice.

Now we find all three of these forms of literature in the same series, and we are fascinated. The same works that perform the fairy tale task of helping our children cope with their adoration of and antipathy for us, that help them begin to comprehend good and evil, that help our adolescents see past the present with its bullies and unfairness to a time when they can both fit in with their friends and stand above them—those same works help us, whether we are aware of it or not, to face our animal nature and still have faith that we are children of God with souls that transcend this world.

Harry Potter is Everyboy and Everyman, the Everyman or Everywoman we all know is inside us, whether we are six, sixteen, or sixty, the Everyman who knows he is special, that great things lie in store for him which others do not yet recognize. We are that boy in the cupboard under the stairs just waiting for our letter from Hogwarts, just waiting for Hagrid to come and take us from the humdrum and unjust Dursleys to an exciting, magical world in which our unique heroism allows us to catch the Golden Snitch, look evil full in the face, and win.

III
Harry's Other Literary Relatives

Harry Potter and the Extraordinariness of the Ordinary

Roni Natov

I like the Harry Potter books because they are like real life but more interesting.
— *Melissa Stevens, fourteen*

Harry begins his journey at eleven, an age associated with coming into consciousness, particularly for boys, and particularly in England, when children begin their "serious" study to prepare them for adult life. What Harry discovers on his eleventh birthday is that he is a wizard, that he has powers he intuits but, as is true of most childhood knowledge, does not consciously recognize. He has noticed that strange things happen to him: his hair grew back overnight after his aunt sheared it off; the sweater she tried to force him to wear kept getting smaller when she tried to pull it over his head. A most hilarious scene occurs at the zoo, where the caged boa winks at him, after sleeping through his cousin Dudley's commanding it to move. After Harry somehow makes the glass partition disappear, the snake escapes amidst shrieks from other visitors. Harry does not connect these events with his own power. Like most orphans, he has little sense of having any power at all.

Like most orphan heroes, Harry will need to be unusually sensitive, almost vigilant, particularly since he has been raised by hostile relatives against whom his sensibility absolutely grates. He has to make his own choices, as Rowling points out, without the benefit of "access to adults," the "safety net of many children who have loving parents or guardians."[1]

However extreme this situation, it only epitomizes what I believe at one time every child feels—that she is on her own, unacknowledged, unappreciated, unseen and unheard, up against an unfair parent, and by extension, an unfair world. Justice and the lack of it reign supreme in the literature of childhood, where our first sense of the world is often so astutely recorded.

1. J. K. Rowling, radio interview.

125

"But it's not fair" is a phrase that stands out from my childhood and continues to resonate for me even now. I am reminded of E. B. White's opening to the beloved classic *Charlotte's Web:* " 'Where's Poppa going with that axe?' " White's hero, Fern, protests against the adults' Darwinian treatment of animals, those creatures closest to her child-sensibility: " 'But it's unfair! . . . The pig couldn't help being born small. . . . If *I* had been very small at birth,' " she accuses, " 'would you have killed *me?*' "[2]

And what could be more unfair than losing your parents as a baby? The orphan archetype embodies the childhood task of learning to deal with an unfair world. I am also reminded of Jane Eyre at age ten, thrashing around in her awareness of her unjust treatment at the hands of her aunt and cousins. Harry, like his great Victorian predecessors, is a kind of Everychild, vulnerable in his powerlessness, but as he discovers his strengths, he releases a new source of vitality into the world. He becomes the child-hero of his own story, like Dickens's "favorite child," the orphan hero of *David Copperfield,* whose story begins, "Whether I shall turn out to be the hero of my own life, or whether that station will be held by anybody else, these pages must show."[3] The Harry Potter stories chronicle the process of the child's movement from the initial consciousness of himself as the central character in his story, a singular preoccupation with self, to a sense of his own power and responsibility to a larger community.

Harry Potter has been raised by the Dursleys, who pride themselves on being "perfectly normal" (*Sorcerer's Stone,* 1). That Harry's saga begins with this assertion is a sign that this story will assert the unconventional, even the eccentric. Harry will provide a resistance to normality which, Rowling suggests, is necessary for inclusiveness, for the individual and the community to prosper. Mr. Dursley, director of Grunnings, which makes drills, is a brutal, thick-necked man. His equally nasty opposite, Mrs. Dursley, uses her spindly neck for spying. These are the caretakers of "the boy who lived" through the murder of both his parents and the attempt on his own life. Many are the injustices heaped upon him: he is kept under the stairs, half-starved and half-clothed, and brutalized by Dudley. The Dursleys are also psychologically abusive and provide, conversely, a model of how not to treat children. They treat Harry as though he were invisible, as though he were something that "couldn't understand them, like a slug" (*Sorcerer's Stone,* 22). They withhold the truth of Harry's birth, in violation of a basic tenet of children's rights—one of the many indications that Rowling sees children as people with rights. What they hate in Harry's behavior, in addition to his questions, is anything out of the ordinary. Here Rowling

2. E. B. White, *Charlotte's Web,* 3.
3. Charles Dickens, *David Copperfield,* 1.

emphasizes the preeminence of the imagination of childhood and the need for children to question and dream. So when Harry dreams of a flying motorcycle, it foreshadows his success at Quidditch, a kind of soccer in the sky, and his imminent rise above the chains of conventionality. Normal, Muggle (nonmagical) school is a system that teaches children to hit each other, as if it were "good training for later life" (*Sorcerer's Stone*, 32). There Harry is persecuted by Dudley's "normal" friends, like Piers, who holds Harry's hands behind his back while Dudley punches him (*Sorcerer's Stone*, 32)—because he is different, because he is an orphan, because he is dressed in Dudley's old, shrunken uniforms, which looked like "bits of old elephant skin" (*Sorcerer's Stone*, 35). Aside from his dark cupboard under the stairs, nowhere is Harry safe. And nowhere is he loved, which only provides the urgency for a compensatory endowment of magical powers.

Belying Harry's puny appearance and weak position in the Muggle world is his bolt-of-lightning scar, which marks him, like Cain, for difference and protection against antagonism to that uniqueness. When Harry is most vulnerable, his scar burns painfully, which serves to warn him against proximity of danger. A particularly touching image of Harry's vulnerability occurs at the end of the first chapter, where he is curled fetuslike in sleep, "not knowing he was special, not knowing he was famous . . . that at this very moment, people meeting in secret all over the country were holding up their glasses and saying in hushed voices: 'To Harry Potter—the boy who lived!' " (*Sorcerer's Stone*, 17).

Harry embodies this state of injustice frequently experienced by children, often as inchoate fear and anger—and its other side, desire to possess extraordinary powers that will overcome such early and deep exile from the child's birthright of love and protection. That every child experiences himself as special is obvious, if for no other reason than that everything that happens to him is inherently significant. The world revolves around him; each moment resonates with the potential vitality of the first time, of unexplored territory. As the child grows into consciousness, an inner world serves to witness the extraordinary quality of experience recorded, sorted through, and reflected upon. Along with this consciousness comes the recognition that others may share that experience, in part at least, and that ultimately each child is just another human being on this large, multitudinous planet. I remember looking up at the stars one night in the country and coming to a sudden understanding that contained both terror and relief. My epiphany turned on how small and insignificant I was, coupled with the insight that I was not responsible for the world. I had only a small part to play; the world was long in the making before I entered it and would go on long after I was gone. I remember that my ordinariness, then, offered a perspective and put into sharp relief my need to be special.

The Harry Potter series opens with the infiltration of the ordinary world by the luminous and magical as "a large, tawny owl flutters past the window" unobserved by the blunted Dursleys. Mr. Dursley notices the incongruity of a cat trying to read a map, the first sign that something strange is going on, but with little sense of wonder, he quickly dismisses it. He is aware of a lot of people dressed in odd clothing, which always makes him furious, particularly if they are adults. And although he is oblivious to the appearance of owls in daylight, other people in the street are stunned by this sight. With this startling image of the nocturnal in bright light, Rowling establishes three groups defined by their response to the magic of the world. The Dursleys represent those who are hostile to anything imaginative, new, unpredictable. The Muggles, who notice the owls but are remote from their magical aura, represent a kind of conventional center. Professor Dumbledore, head of Hogwarts School of Witchcraft and Wizardry, an old man with long silver hair and a beard, who appears in purple robes and high, buckled boots, and Professor McGonagall, who has shape-shifted from cat to woman, indicated by her glasses, which bear the identical markings of the cat's eyes, embody the childhood world of magic and awe.

In most popular children's fantasies, the magical world is entirely separate from daily life. In C. S. Lewis's *The Lion, the Witch, and the Wardrobe,* for example, entry into the supernatural takes place through a wardrobe at the back of a strange house during the bombings of World War II and represents the child-heroes' escape into a reimagined and revitalized Christian realm. In Madeline L'Engle's *A Wrinkle in Time* and its successors, *A Wind in the Door* and *A Swiftly Tilting Planet,* the magical world is celestial, in keeping with science fiction and L'Engle's strong religious allegorical allusions. Tolkien's *The Hobbit* and *Lord of the Rings* trilogy take place entirely in a magical world and represent a refuge, an alternative to the real world.[4]

Rowling noted the genius of Lewis and Tolkien, those predecessors with whom she has been frequently compared, but claimed she was "doing something slightly different."[5] Though her stories contain the usual global battle between the forces of good and evil, Rowling, I believe, is essentially a novelist, strongest when writing about the real world. Harry has a psychology; his problems need resolution in the real world. Insofar as he is a real child, with little relief at home, at Hogwarts School of Witchcraft and Wizardry, where the supernatural reigns, he is freer to discover his own powers. In

4. Suzanne Rahn speaks about E. Nesbit as the first children's book author to bring magic into our contemporary world, in which "the protagonists [are] ordinary children." *Rediscoveries in Children's Literature,* 145.

5. Rowling herself mentions E. Nesbit's *The Story of the Treasure Seekers* as particularly influential in her conception of the Harry Potter series in the radio interview mentioned previously.

Rowling's stories, the interpenetration of the two worlds suggests the way in which we live—not only in childhood, though especially so then—on more than one plane, with the life of the imagination and daily life moving in and out of our consciousness. The two realms, characterized in literature as the genres of romance and realism, are located in the imagination, which is, always, created by and rooted in the details of everyday life. In fantasy, always we are grounded; the unconscious invents nothing, or as Freud put it, "In the psychic life, there is nothing arbitrary, nothing undetermined."[6] The realm of fantastic, based on the unconscious, is firmly and inevitably a reconfiguration of everyday reality, transformed and disguised though it may be.

The need for both realms and their interdependence was recognized by Wordsworth and Coleridge in their plan for the *Lyrical Ballads.* In chapter 14 of *Biographia Literaria,* Coleridge noted:

> my endeavors should be directed to persons and characters supernatural, or
> at least romantic—yet so as to transfer, from our inward nature, a human
> interest and a semblance of truth sufficient to procure for these shadows
> of imagination that willing suspension of disbelief for the moment, which
> constitutes poetic faith. . . . [Wordsworth was] to give the charm of novelty to
> things of every day, and to excite a feeling analogous to the supernatural, by
> awakening the mind's attention to the lethargy of custom, and directing it to
> the loveliness and wonders of the world before us—an inexhaustible treasure
> but for which . . . we have eyes yet see not, ears that hear not, and hearts that
> neither feel nor understand.[7]

In the Harry Potter books, magic calls attention to the awe and wonder of ordinary life. Rowling ingeniously enhances and amplifies the vitality of ordinary objects. For example, at Hogwarts, portraits of former headmasters and headmistresses hang on the walls, all "snoozing gently in their frames" (*Chamber of Secrets,* 203). Books bite and argue, "locked together in furious wrestling matches and snapping aggressively" (*Prisoner of Azkaban,* 26)—a literary joke about the Battle of the Books or other debate literature, reminiscent of Carroll's *Wonderland* and *Looking Glass* landscapes. Along with magical wands, cloaks of invisibility, maps that reproduce and mirror actual journeys as they are taking place (like the virtual reality of technology), the things of children's culture—treats like candy, and kids' own particular kind of humor, such as jokes about bodily fluids—are featured. Some of young readers' favorite aspects of life at Hogwarts include Bertie Bott's Every Flavor Beans, consisting of such flavors as spinach, liver, tripe, grass, sardine, vomit, ear wax, and booger. Words themselves suggest the

6. Quoted in Tzvetan Todorov, *The Fantastic: A Structural Approach to a Literary Genre,* 161.
7. Samuel Taylor Coleridge, *Biographia Literaria,* 531.

magical power of language to mean, as well as to evoke and connote. Such passwords as "pig snout," "scurvy cur," "oddsbodkin," suggest treasure and mystery. The characters' names are appropriately allusive and inviting. As Sharon Moore points out, "There are sneaky-sounding s's: Slytherins, Snape, Severus, Sirius and Scabbers. The h's are kind of heroic: Hogwarts, Hedwig, Hermione and Hagrid. The f's are often unpleasant types: Filch and Flitwick. . . . The names that sound French are usually difficult people: Madam Pince, Madam Pomfrey, and Malfoy."[8] Alison Lurie notes, "As in many folk tales, you can often tell a character's character from his or her name, and 'Voldemort' neatly combines the ideas of theft, mold, and death. Harry Potter, on the other hand, has a name that suggests not only craftsmanship but also both English literature and English history: Shakespeare's Prince Hal and Harry Hotspur, the brave, charming, impulsive heroes of *Henry IV,* and Beatrix Potter, who created that other charming and impulsive classic hero, Peter Rabbit."[9] As Harry embodies both the ordinary and the extraordinary, his narratives contain realistic and romantic elements.

Like other questing heroes, Harry must prove himself through a series of tests, each increasingly more difficult. Joseph Campbell noted how the hero's cycle corresponded to the dynamic movement through life stages, particularly the development of consciousness and the discovery of identity. Even the simplest of hero stories, the fairy tales, dramatize the complexity of the life struggles of Everyman/woman/child. For example, both Perrault's and the Grimms's most virtuous, Christianized, and domesticated girl-hero, Cinderella, must revolt against the wishes of the good fairy godmother (without the consciousness that she is doing so, of course). She must forget to leave the ball by midnight, in order that the prince find her and that her rightful place be restored. This tale acknowledges the hero's paradoxical struggle to maintain tradition *and* to subvert it for evolution to occur. Some taboo must be broken, some boundary crossed—this is at the heart of the hero's quest. Harry, who is, as Lurie points out, a kind of Cinderlad himself, must break the very rules at Hogwarts needed to maintain order and its basic values.[10]

The fairy tales of childhood illustrate a most significant aspect of that earliest stage, the centrality of play and the imagination, which, though it receives prominence in childhood, often gets lost along the way to adulthood. Consider "Jack and the Beanstalk," in which the lazy child, Jack, refuses to do his mother's bidding and "forgets" to sell the cow for money,

8. Sharon Moore, ed., *We Love Harry Potter!* 2.
9. Alison Lurie, "Not for Muggles," 4.
10. Ibid., 3.

but rather is enchanted by the magic beans. The tale asserts his right to journey into the sky (the world above the world) and solve the earthbound adult problem of money by stealing the golden harp, hen, eggs—the means of achieving ever-regenerating money and power—precisely what he never could have gotten by selling the cow. Once having used up the modest sum he would have gotten from the cow, he inevitably would have had to go back again to the market with whatever was left to sell, only to return home with fewer resources, thus moving into the cycle of poverty—from which the poor rarely have the power to emerge, any more than children have the power to overcome the authority of adults. The magic beans in this story represent relief from the real problems that are quite beyond the child to solve, but can be, as the story suggests, imagined. Magic embodies the imagination, stands in for what is beyond the power of children, perhaps anyone, to actualize. Often we can envision long before we can create the means to flee or resolve what feels overwhelming. This is particularly true for children.

Harry's supernatural powers invite children to imagine beyond the boundaries of their limitations: what if I could see and hear without being seen or heard? what if I could fly? what if I could read another's mind? With his magic cloak, Harry is invisible; with his Nimbus 2000 racing broomstick, he can fly; he can even, in the fourth book, project himself into Dumbledore's siphoned-off thoughts. Also, like every child, Harry is one among many, represented here by the fact that his classmates are also wizards. While he is good at playing Quidditch, he is just an ordinary player at his school work, nor is he particularly insightful in the way he relates to or understands others. His classmate Hermione Granger, the girl Rowling most closely identifies with, is smarter and more sensitive.[11] Hermione has the most highly developed sense of justice; even though Harry has freed Dobby, the house elf, Hermione alone understands the oppression of the house-elves, as they serve their masters, bowing and scraping, without pay. Part of Rowling's

11. The debate over Rowling's choice and use of a boy hero has been extensive. Christine Schoefer, for example, writes about "Harry Potter's Girl Trouble," claiming that in the Harry Potter novels, "No girl is brilliantly heroic the way Harry is, no woman is experienced and wise like Professor Dumbledore . . . [that] the range of female personalities is so limited that neither women nor girls play on the side of evil," and that Rowling depicts Hermione as working "hard to be accepted by Harry and his sidekick Ron, who treat her like a tag-along until Volume 3." Along with her many supporters, Rowling complains, "What irritates me is that I am constantly, increasingly, being asked 'Can we have a strong female character, please?' Like they are ordering a side order of chips. I am thinking 'Isn't Hermione strong enough for you?' She is the most brilliant of the three and they need her. . . . But my hero is a boy and at the age he has been girls simply do not figure that much. Increasingly, they do. But at 11, I think it would be extremely contrived to throw in a couple of feisty, gorgeous, brilliant-at-math and great-at-fixing-cars girls" (Rowling, "Harry and Me").

genius is the creation of stories about the development of the ordinary boy, as he grows from the start of the series at ten to the age of seventeen. There will be one book for each year, Rowling has announced, with the "hormones kicking in."[12] Gender informs Rowling's vision in that she blends the traditional male quester with the more feminized hero of tales of school and home; these stories are relational, psychologically nuanced, and in that sense realistic.

During a radio interview, a child called in to ask if Rowling could please bring back Harry's parents. Respectfully and sorrowfully, she said she regretted that she couldn't do that. "You can't bring dead people back," she said.[13] She had to set limits on what magic could and couldn't do, since it was important to her to keep these characters real. Even the magical ones are defined by their human as well as magical traits. The real world, then, becomes illuminated by these characters who can span both worlds. For example, teachers at Hogwarts can be imaginative and compassionate; they are also flighty, vindictive, dim-witted, indulgent, lazy, frightened, and frightening. Students are clever, kind, weak, cruel, snobbish. Lessons are inspiring and tedious—as in the best and worst of real schools.

Harry's guide into the magical school of Hogwarts, Hagrid, is a larger-than-life figure, the giant from the fairy tales of childhood, deliverer of the annunciation: " 'Yeh don' know what yeh *are* . . . Harry—yer a wizard' " (*Sorcerer's Stone*, 50). Hagrid is twice the height and five times the width of a normal man, with long, tangled black hair, his face hidden by his beard, with "hands the size of trash can lids," and feet "like baby dolphins" (*Sorcerer's Stone*, 14). He is also careless, drinks too much, and is too sentimental and indulgent in his love for bizarre and grotesque creatures, such as dragons and Blast-Ended Skrewts, who threaten the safety of Hogwarts. Even these creatures suggest the two sides of imaginative writing: dragons are recognizable as mythical fire-breathing creatures, although here Rowling makes them distinct, almost realistic: the baby dragon looks like "a crumpled, black umbrella" with "spiny" wings, and "wide nostrils," "stubby horns, and bulging, orange eyes" (*Sorcerer's Stone*, 235). The Skrewts, sluglike and slimy, are also described in concrete detail, while their size mythicizes them. The movement here between these two poles suggests the force of the imagination of childhood to illuminate reality.

Most of the adventures take place at school, the transitional world situated between childhood and adulthood. It is a liminal space that tests the mettle of the child-hero and, like all liminal landscapes, it represents the "not-as-yet-conscious," what is yet to be, possibility itself, and chance.[14]

12. Rowling, radio interview.
13. Ibid.
14. This phrase was used by Ernst Bloch, *The Utopian Function of Art and Literature*, 103–11.

A burning question for Harry, who has never fit in, not at home, not at "Muggle" school, who has never had the chance to experience friendship—loyalty, competition, finding a place among peers—is how will he succeed in this home away from home, particularly when he has never been at home at home?

Situating the train that takes people to Hogwarts at platform 9¾, between tracks 9 and 10, reinforces the central location of these stories between the earthbound and magical worlds. As Harry transports himself beyond the boundaries of the real world, between tracks 9 and 10, one can viscerally feel his body brace against the shock, his mind unbelieving, as he breaks through what appears to be a solid barrier, as the imaginary may seem in real life. The school and its various accoutrements epitomize, at the same time, the imagination of childhood and the real concerns of children. At Hogwarts, everything is adorned with magic so that, for example, the point of entry into the bank, a warning against the worldly concerns of greed and snobbishness, is heightened by the poetic language on the sign: *"Enter, stranger, but take heed/Of what awaits the sin of greed"* (*Sorcerer's Stone,* 72). There are many such indications of Rowling's abhorrence of the class system, its divisiveness, and the negative potential of specialness. Malfoy, the pale boy with the pointed face, whose sense of self is based on embracing his father's money and social position, is early established as Harry's enemy, just as Ron Weasley, who has to share the little his family has with his six siblings, and Hermione, the mixed-blood daughter of a Muggle and a wizard, are his best friends.

While Hogwarts contains all the offensive and irritating aspects of real life—it in fact mirrors its elitism and petty power struggles—it is also a wondrous and humorous world. Required reading, for example, abounds with hilarious matches, such as *One Thousand Magical Herbs and Fungi* by Phyllida Spore and *Fantastic Beasts and Where to Find Them* by Newt Scamander. The magical Sorting Hat matches each child with her proper house (Harry and his friends are assigned to Gryffindor for their courage), and wands intricately fit their owners. The phoenix that provided the feathers for Harry's wand did the same for Voldemort, Harry is told, linking him to his dark enemy, as Lucifer was God's fallen angel. And there is much darkness in these books. However, it is always rooted in the psychological darkness associated with childhood and human development: with anger, loss, death, grief, fear, and desire. Although initially Harry is elated when he hears the news of his powers, he is also alarmed and bewildered. Hagrid notes that it's hard to be singled out and Harry protests, " 'Everyone thinks I'm special . . . but I don't know anything about magic at all. . . . I can't even remember what I'm famous for" (*Sorcerer's Stone,* 86). Fearful of his power, unsure of how to control desire, or how to recognize and use his gifts wisely—Harry, as Everychild, needs guidance.

Rowling is adept at providing paradigms for thoughtful, courageous, and moral behavior for children, with clear explanations of the accompanying states of feeling. These deeper moments of reflection serve as pauses in the rapid pace of these page-turners. It seems to me that the best mysteries, adventure stories, and romances represent a negotiation between the reckless pace of the narrative breathlessly moving forward and the meditative pockets that provide the space and time to turn inward—to affirm our sense that something memorable is happening to us, something we can retrieve for later, after the book is ended. As is true of our best writers, Rowling draws these opposing realms so seamlessly that they appear to have always been there, side by side, the event and its meaning exquisitely illuminated.

In the first book, *Sorcerer's Stone,* the scene in which Harry comes upon the Mirror of Erised (thinly disguised so children will discover that it represents desire) and sees, for the first time in his life, his family, he aches half with joy, half with a "terrible sadness" (*Sorcerer's Stone,* 209). How fascinating that his friend Ron sees only himself decked out as Head Boy, his own "deepest, most desperate desire" (*Sorcerer's Stone,* 213). Ron, whose strongest wish is to stand out from his five brothers and from Harry as well, assumes he is seeing the future, just as Harry believes he is looking into his past. However, Dumbledore warns that this mirror will not provide any real truth. He warns that it can drive us mad, this "dwell[ing] in dreams"; we could "forget to live." However, he offers that it can help us to be prepared, to recognize this dream state if we come upon it. Rowling has essentially taken the great test of Odysseus, who must hear the song of the sirens but not act on that calling, and reimagined it for children. At its core, Rowling suggests, desire can be both alluring and dangerous. Children need to understand, on whatever level, its complexity. Rowling does not minimize childhood longing. She offers this small allegory with the understanding that the search for identity is reflected in that mirror—as Harry sees his family behind him, and desires only to return again and again to that vision of himself, supported by those who resemble him, smiling at and waving to him. This scene prepares for the ones that follow, in which Harry comes into deeper and darker knowledge, though always returning to this central issue of identity and the protection it promises.

If the mirror reflects what we most long for, it also evokes the fear that accompanies such desire and the loss that engendered it. In *Prisoner of Azkaban,* Rowling focuses on this fear, beginning with the boggarts who take the shape of the thing we most fear. For Harry, as his Dark Arts teacher tells him, it is fear itself, embodied in the dementors, the prison guards of Azkaban. What tortures Harry is his overwhelming guilt and sorrow at his mother's death. At the sight of these gray-hooded figures, Harry hears his mother's desperate cries: "No, take me, kill me instead." Haunted by her pain and feeling guilty that she died to save him, Harry is drawn into intense ambivalence. Rowling explains that even though it was so painful for Harry to hear the "last moments" of his parents "inside his head," these were the only times that he'd heard their voices since he was very young. The desire to be reunited with his parents, though natural and inevitable, serves as a warning, as with the mirror, against remaining in the past, lost in memory or desire. Of course, in addition to exploring Harry's inner demons, here Rowling connects despair with madness and suggests that it is the loss of hope that makes us demented, that promotes criminality and destroys the heart. The dementors, those who are supposed to guard prisoners, keep them in such a state of despair that they don't even try to escape. They suck all joy and hope from you so that you are left with only "the worst experiences of your life" (*Prisoner of Azkaban*, 188).

The antidote for such haunting is happy memories, remembering that which makes children feel safe, loved, confident, good about themselves. More than anything else, a sense of self is exactly what Hagrid was denied in prison, as he tells Harry: "Yeh can't really remember who yeh are after a while" (*Prisoner of Azkaban*, 221). Knowing who you are is at the heart here, the development of the child's consciousness, the narrative of Everychild—the right to knowledge and expression of self. Rowling has spoken about depression as the loss of hope, how it has been her enemy, and how it has informed her depiction of the dementors here.[15] I remember fits of depression as a child, though without any name for that state of mind; it went unrecognized and was buried, along with the shame that accompanied all my unacknowledged feelings. As Sendak claimed, when he was called upon to defend his depictions of frightening monsterlike figures in *Where the Wild Things Are,* most frightening to children is to dream their own figures of fear and find no analog in anything they hear about or read. Children need to see their feelings, particularly the darkest ones, reflected in their stories. Mitigating the darkness of the fairy tales takes away their power to reassure children that they are not alone in their fearful imaginings, that these fears are shared and can be addressed.[16]

As Harry gets older in the books, the emotional challenges become more complex, and Rowling attempts to help children understand them. She

15. In an interview on June 30, 2000, in the London *Times,* Rowling was quoted as describing the Dementors as "a description of depression . . . entirely from my own experience. Depression is the most unpleasant thing I have ever experienced. . . . It is that absence of being able to envisage that you will ever be cheerful again. The absence of hope. That very deadened feeling, which is so very different from feeling sad. Sad hurts but it's a healthy feeling. It is a necessary thing to feel. Depression is very different" (Rowling, "Harry and Me").

16. From an unpublished interview with Maurice Sendak by Geraldine DeLuca and me in 1977.

has captured the familiar sense of childhood shame with the Howlers—loud, public scoldings sent by parents to humiliate and ultimately to control children. For example, Neville receives a letter in the audible form of the voice of his grandmother magnified one hundred times, publicly accusing him of bringing shame on the family. Such exposure is handled with a kind of empathic humor, reminiscent of Woody Allen's adult projection of his mother's face in the sky, publicly denouncing him, a metaphor of adult shame and its childhood roots. This externalized projection mirrors Harry's private, internal moments following his collapse at the sight of the dementors, when he suffers an onslaught of shame. He wonders, "Why had he gone to pieces like that, when no one else had?" (*Prisoner of Azkaban*, 36). Shame separates us, makes us feel less than, different from, others. This aspect of difference, Rowling demonstrates, is deadly. At times she handles it with the acceptance that comes from humor; at times, with a kind of respect that accompanies our most difficult emotional trials.

Children are also led beyond the simple concept of evil as purely "bad guys." In *Prisoner of Azkaban*, Lupin, who is a werewolf, turns out to be a paradoxical figure: a force of good that can be dangerous as well. Rowling's use of the werewolf as metaphor for the split self here is astute and in keeping with the earliest known Red Riding Hood variant, in which it is not a wolf but a werewolf—a fusion of animal and human—that tries to seduce the young girl.[17] What is most interesting here is that the potentially destructive part of the werewolf is humanized and offered with understanding. Rowling establishes his innocence and evokes compassion for him, as he tells his story. Lupin talks about the pain of turning into a werewolf, how isolated he became from others, how in utter despair he turned and bit himself. He says that though his parents tried everything, there was no cure. As Lupin becomes a werewolf when he doesn't take his potion, madness and self-destructive impulses are depicted with a kind of psychological truth. Rowling attempts to humanize the demonic, rather than demonize the human.

The servants of evil are recognizable as frail humans who have grown large because they are adults who are out of control—what is often most terrifying to children. Peter Pettigrew, in *Prisoner of Azkaban*, is grotesque, "like an oversized, balding baby, cowering on the floor" (374), and Voldemort, who represents the generating power of evil, the force of discord and enmity, bears "the shape of a crouched human child, except Harry had never seen anything less like a child . . . no child alive ever had a face like that." Helpless, it is lifted by Wormtail, like a baby, into his arms. The infantile adult, a kind of perverted innocence, childish without anything childlike, is

17. See Jack Zipes, *The Trials and Tribulations of Little Red Riding Hood: Versions of the Tale in Sociocultural Context*, 1983.

most horrifying, particularly for children when it is the controlling force of their lives.

How children take control of their lives—most crucial and central here—is metaphorically represented in several ways. Harry and Hermione watch themselves in a Time-Turner, able to redo an event, to be in more than one place at a time, to go back in time while remaining in the present, to redo their mistakes and save the lovely hippogriff, Buckbeak. Harry tells Hermione, "I knew I could do it this time . . . because I'd already done it. . . . Does that make sense?" (*Prisoner of Azkaban*, 412)—expressing the paradoxical sense of knowing what we didn't know we knew. Even more psychologically profound is the way in which Rowling demonstrates what can be retrieved, even in the final loss—the death of a parent. To protect himself from fear, Harry conjures up a Patronus, an image of his father. As an orphan, Harry will have to provide for himself the father he has never known. Here is a kind of child vision of father atonement. Dumbledore, in such a vision as a father figure, tells Harry: "You think the dead we loved ever truly leave us? You think that we don't recall them more clearly than ever in times of great trouble? Your father is alive in you, Harry . . . you did see [him] last night. . . . You found him inside yourself" (*Prisoner of Azkaban*, 427–28).

This scene represents the only real consolation as well as a possible direction for healing such an early fracture. There are many father/son atonement scenes. Most awful is Barty Crouch's son, rejected by his father, even as he stands before him, pleading in his innocence, "Father! . . . I'm your son!" (*Goblet of Fire*, 596). It is not surprising that, in his confusion and despair, he has become a servant of evil. Rowling also helps children to understand how Neville's parents go insane from being tortured and incessantly interrogated, so that though they are alive when Neville visits them with his grandmother, they do not recognize him. Harry is more fortunate than the others in that he has been able to retrieve something, a touchstone for protection he can carry with him, although he has never had access to his parents. But it is not enough in his state of privilege to be isolated from the misfortune of others. Harry feels for Crouch's son, as images of the pale-faced boy swim up to him from Professor Dumbledore's Pensieve. His compassion extends to Neville too, as he imagines how it must feel for your parents to be alive but unable to recognize or remember you.

The Harry Potter stories center on what children need to find internally—the strength to do the right thing, to establish a moral code. As hero, Harry must go beyond the apparent truth of things and, ultimately, learn to trust what he sees and act on what is right. The tournament of the fourth book, *Goblet of Fire*, departs from the rather simple victories of Quidditch tournaments, where one house at Hogwarts beats the others, Harry serving as Seeker, the primary position, for Gryffindor. In this book, as Hermione points out, the games are supposed to be about making friends with rivals from other teams. Although Ron with partial truth responds, "No it isn't. It's about winning" (*Goblet of Fire,* 423), more is at stake here. The community is larger, more global. What it means to "win" is interrogated. In an expansive leap of feeling, Harry saves his rivals, along with his friends. Voices tell him to save only his own friend, to abandon the others, like Cedric and Krum did. He knows that if he had just rescued Ron, he would have been the first to return. But he resists such individualism. "Differences of habit and language are nothing at all" Dumbledore tells him (*Goblet of Fire,* 723). Harry and his closest rival, Cedric (who took Cho Chang, the object of Harry's desire, to the ball) help and support each other, and finally decide to reach the Cup at the same time, thus producing two winners. While Cedric dies, and thus Harry alone bears the reward, the boys' rejection of the school's either/or policy establishes a new paradigm of sharing, building community, and inclusiveness.

Sharing thoughts and passing on experience is brilliantly depicted in the Pensieve, a basin that holds thoughts. Dumbledore tells Harry that when his mind cannot contain all his thoughts and memories he stores them in the Pensieve. He retrieves them at a later, more convenient moment. He says that he can "spot patterns and links . . . when they are in this form" (*Goblet of Fire,* 597). Harry is literally drawn through a substance that is either "liquid or gas . . . a bright, whitish silver . . . moving ceaselessly; the surface of it became ruffled like water beneath wind, and then, like clouds, separated and swirled smoothly. It looked like light made liquid—or like wind made solid . . ." (*Goblet of Fire,* 583). To understand another's history, one must enter into a liminal state; one must move beyond the established boundaries of self and other, represented by the indistinguishable states of matter. In *Chamber of Secrets,* Harry had fallen "through a page in an enchanted diary, right into someone else's memory" (586). But here the idea is more developed. Thought is depicted as tangible, progressive, dynamic—a series of landscapes to be visited, returned to, and discovered as patterns of meaning. Harry falls through Dumbledore's thoughts about his past, the subjectivity of memory extended to history. When he lands in the courtroom of Dumbledore's memory, "not one of [the adults] noticed that a fourteen-year-old boy had just dropped from the ceiling" (*Goblet of Fire,* 585), reminiscent of W. H. Auden's Icarus, who falls unnoticed out of the sky. But unlike Icarus, who, in his youthful optimism, flew so high that his wings melted from the heat of the sun, Harry's fall is a descent into consciousness, and rather than cautionary, it is visionary. It suggests connection, that we can participate in another's experience, explore another's past, albeit only through the subjectivity of our own vision.

Even the child, without the experience of the adult, without perspective afforded by hindsight, can glean something valuable from the lessons of the past—not those set in stone to be received unquestioningly, but to make meaning of, the way Harry must make sense of the events he witnesses. In this scene of Dumbledore's younger days, Harry first notices how Dumbledore has aged, a perspective that reveals Harry's developing consciousness of time. Each person carries a unique history, some of which can be shared, as when Dumbledore joins Harry in reviewing his thoughts.

Even the idea of reviewing thoughts supports the value of interrogation and reflection. Surely this runs counter to what we are currently being told by television, video games, fast-paced cutting images of MTV and the superficial content of pulp fiction. The Harry Potter books satirize for children the superficiality of this world, its pretenses and human failures, the narcissism of popular culture, the stupidity and cruelty of the press, the rigidity and fraudulence embedded in our institutions, particularly the schools, framed by the unrelenting snobbery and elitism of our social world. The unprecedented popularity of the Harry Potter stories, not only with sophisticated readers of a wide range of ages, but with new readers, those who previously resisted reading, suggests that rather than flat, knee-jerk responses, children are drawn to complexity and reflection—accompanied by the spectacular—integrated, always, in the real and recognizable world it is the child's mission to negotiate and struggle through.

Harry Potter, Tom Brown, and the British School Story

Lost in Transit?

David K. Steege

Pico Iyer, in his essay "The Playing Fields of Hogwarts," describes the similarities between Harry Potter's boarding school and the Dragon School in Oxford that he attended as a boy. He notes that American readers may not appreciate "how much there is of realism, as well as magic, in the exotic tales of young sorcerers being trained at the Hogwarts School of Witchcraft and Wizardry," and details how his own boarding school days are echoed again and again in Rowling's work.[1] By stressing the "realism" of the series, Iyer is suggesting that the Harry Potter novels are based on real boarding school experiences.

Interestingly, the author of the Harry Potter novels did not attend a boarding school herself. Pico Iyer's schooling had much more in common with Harry's than did Rowling's; after graduating from Tutshill primary, she attended Wyedean Comprehensive School, which is what Americans would call a public school. One feature of Wyedean seemingly in common with boarding schools was the institution of "Head Girl," a status Rowling achieved in her senior year. However, the similarity barely extends beyond the title itself. In *Harry Potter and the Prisoner of Azkaban*, Percy Weasley is Head Boy, an exalted position that makes him more pompous than ever, causes his mother to puff with pride that she has had two Head Boys in the family, and leads his authority-flouting brothers George and Fred to steal his silver badge of office and modify the title to "Bighead Boy" (*Prisoner of Azkaban*, 62). For Percy, it is the pinnacle of a lustrous career of school leadership. In Rowling's case, there wasn't much to do in the position except to show a visiting noblewoman around the school fair and to give a speech before the assembled students, a task she dreaded so much she played a record "to cut down on the time that I had to speak to them."[2] In many

---

1. Pico Iyer, "The Playing Fields of Hogwarts," 39.
2. Marc Shapiro, *J. K. Rowling: The Wizard behind Harry Potter*, 39.

ways Rowling's education would be one familiar to the graduates of public schools in the United States.

Yet Rowling need not have experienced boarding schools nor even researched them to portray one in the Harry Potter series. In fact, rather than pointing to real boarding schools as the foundation for Hogwarts, it is more accurate to say that Hogwarts and Harry's experiences there are based on British popular culture conceptions of boarding school experiences, particularly as manifested in the long tradition of what is known as "public school stories." The Harry Potter novels can indeed be added to a very lengthy list of school stories, at the same time transforming the genre so significantly that the books have been able to cross borders with unprecedented success.

There's no doubt that the school setting was uppermost in Rowling's mind when she created Harry Potter. Rowling has spoken of the sudden, clear conception she had of Harry Potter's story, describing how on a train trip, "It just came: bang!" She determined right away to write seven books, because, she says, "I decided that it would take seven years, from the ages of 11 to 17, inclusive, to train as a wizard, and each of the books would deal with a year of Harry's life at Hogwarts."[3] She once commented that "the thing that really got me going on the train was what wizard school would be like. I sat there for hours and just thought and thought and thought. When I got home I started writing and literally haven't stopped since."[4]

Clearly, the boarding school setting is central to the novels, and that is a context the British understand much better than most Americans. Public school stories, defined as literature about experiences at British private educational institutions, especially boarding schools, have a long and rich history. Over the course of the past 140 years, the public school novel has been a genre in its own right, with roots going back even further; the first known boarding school story, Sarah Fielding's *The Governess: or Little Female Academy,* was published in 1749.[5] Naturally, because schools were segregated by gender, public school stories were either boys' school stories or girls' school stories, whose readers were as rigidly divided by gender as the public schools themselves. The most famous early example of a public school novel—perhaps the most famous of all time—is Thomas Hughes's *Tom Brown's School Days.* While perhaps ninety other school stories had appeared between that first in 1749 and Hughes's novel in 1857, the popularity and influence of *Tom Brown's School Days* opened the floodgates to countless public school stories. Jonathan Gathorne-Hardy has noted that

3. Elizabeth Devereaux et al., "Flying Starts."
4. Penelope Dening, "Wiz Kid."
5. Ju Gosling, "The History of Girls' School Stories."

"No other country in the world has this. It is impossible to estimate the size of this literature, but," he believes, "it ran into many thousands of novels."[6] Just recently, in fact, school stories received their own reference manuals, *The Encyclopedia of Girls' School Stories* and *The Encyclopedia of Boys' School Stories,* an event that underscores both the popularity and the extent of the genre.

Many of the public school stories came in the form of a series of novels. While Hughes only managed one sequel, and that one not precisely a school story, *Tom Brown at Oxford,* many later authors wrote six or seven volumes, and some even ran their series into double digits. The champion has to be Elinor M. Brent-Dyer's *Chalet School* series of girls' school novels, which was begun in 1925 and did not end until 1970, when the fifty-ninth volume was published posthumously.[7] In addition to novels, periodicals such as *The Boys' Own Paper,* begun in 1879, fed the appetite for such fare, and a bit later, comics appeared as well and became wildly popular. As Gathorne-Hardy points out, these comics were being devoured by English boys from all classes even between the wars, when the social system that public schools were founded on and celebrated "should have been, and from 1900 on rapidly became, completely out of date."[8] Girls' school stories were also at the peak of their popularity in this era, and although the genre became less popular after World War II, some girls' school novels were in print even in the 1990s.[9]

Although adults, particularly those who went to boarding schools, have enjoyed these stories, the genre became one primarily aimed at juveniles, and was generally highly positive about the public school experience. While Americans might be familiar with a number of adult novels and memoirs highlighting the brutality or stifling conformity in the British public schools, the far more popular juvenile public school novels, though not ignoring the darker sides of school life, concentrated on the salutary shaping of the individual by the institution or on the lighter, more fun aspects of boarding school, such as games and schoolboy misadventures. As critic John Reed points out, in boys' school novels the school itself is as much the protagonist as the individual student, and the structure of many of these novels follows the progress of a boy from his anxious but excited arrival at the school to eventual triumphant but regretful leave-taking years later, after he has risen through the ranks to become a leader, a hero, and a protector of first-years.[10]

6. Jonathan Gathorne-Hardy, *The Old School Tie: The Phenomenon of the English Public School,* 211.

7. Gosling, "History."

8. Gathorne-Hardy, *The Old School Tie,* 219.

9. Gosling, "History."

10. John R. Reed, *Old School Ties: The Public School in British Literature,* 17.

These public school novels, stories, and comics (not to mention, more recently, television programs and films) were very popular even among those who had no public school experiences of their own; middle-class and lower-class British children have been great readers of school stories. As a result, many British readers even today have a picture of public school life that most Americans do not, one derived as much from popular culture as from personal experience.

As Pico Iyer noted, J. K. Rowling's novels deal with the public school experience very directly. More to the point, they use many of the traditions, conventions, and concerns of public school novels and series. That Rowling, like so many readers of school stories, had no direct experience with a public boarding school hardly makes her unusual; several of the most popular authors of girls' school stories, including Enid Blyton, did not attend the kind of institutions they frequently wrote about. Ju Gosling notes that because of this characteristic, "the world of girls' school stories owed more to myth than to reality, and authors read and used characteristics from each other's work . . . and the genre's characteristics developed as characteristics from one author's work became used by other writers."[11] Rowling's own school story series shows this borrowing, development, and, ultimately, transformation.

First there is simply the overall structure of the first novel, *Harry Potter and the Sorcerer's Stone*. In *Tom Brown's School Days*, the protagonist, a bright boy but one prone to getting into scrapes, enters Rugby at about age ten, eager to fit in and in awe of the school. He goes through the first year making a best friend, being bullied by his nemesis Flashman, breaking a few rules here and there while finding ways to thwart Flashman's power, and gaining acceptance in his house through his plucky first game of football; then, as his school career moves on, he becomes the upholder of school values, the protector of the younger boys, and a leader, largely through the guidance of the Doctor (meant to be the great Doctor Arnold), the wise and kind headmaster.

Similarly, in *Harry Potter and the Sorcerer's Stone*, Harry enters Hogwarts at age eleven, eager to be at this wonderful, venerable institution. He spends the first year making a couple of best friends, sparring with the bully Draco Malfoy and his lieutenants, getting in and out of rule-breaking scrapes, and becoming popular through his playing of sports. By the end he has protected the school from an evil wizard and become the hero of his house; moreover, his headmaster, the wise and kind Dumbledore, has been watching him and providing timely aid. And while we cannot yet know

11. Gosling, "History."

what Harry becomes by the end of his school career, we do know that he has begun to follow in Tom Brown's path: in *Harry Potter and the Chamber of Secrets,* he becomes the savior and protector of a younger student, Ginny Weasley, and by the end of the fourth volume, *Harry Potter and the Goblet of Fire,* he is upholding the best values of Hogwarts and wizarding against the darkness of Voldemort and his allies.

Other, more specific elements link the Harry Potter novels to the public school genre, perhaps particularly to *Tom Brown's School Days.* Like *Tom Brown's School Days,* the novel begins with a section on the earlier childhood of its protagonist to establish something of his situation and character. Then both novels show us the preparations for going away to school, involving trips to London, and move to leave-taking scenes. The process of getting the right equipment for school is an element in each book, which takes place early on in *Harry Potter and the Sorcerer's Stone* and a little later in *Tom Brown's School Days,* when Tom Brown and his new friend East first meet and Brown gets a lesson in the proper Rugby headgear: " 'Hullo tho,' says East, pulling up, and taking another look at Tom; 'this'll never do. Haven't you got a hat?—we never wear caps here. Only the louts wear caps. Bless me, if you were to go into the quadrangle with that thing on, I—don't know what'd happen.' "[12] In Harry's case, his introduction to special Hogwarts paraphernalia comes in his foray into Diagon Alley, where he picks up books, a cauldron, an owl, and a wand that has to be keyed to its individual user.

In both texts, the child is eager to go to boarding school but somewhat anxious. Tom feels "the pride and excitement of making a new step in life," but then feels "rather choky" at one point during his leave-taking (90), while Harry, who is understandably happy about leaving his appalling aunt and uncle, is unsure of his fitness for the school and says fretfully, "I bet I'm the worst in the class" (*Sorcerer's Stone,* 100). Tom Brown gets a list of do's and don'ts from his kindly and upright father before he leaves by coach for Rugby; in *Sorcerer's Stone,* it is the Weasley boys who are lectured at and fussed over by their good-hearted mother before boarding the Hogwarts Express train.

Both texts show the boys having a marvelous time on the way to the school. Tom enjoys the novelties of the long journey, from the bumpy but exciting ride itself to the stimulating stories of Rugby boys' pranks, to the unfamiliar and wonderful food along the way—including beef cut "from a mammoth ox" and the special treat of coffee rather than tea (97). He spends time "speculating as to what sort of a place Rugby is" and is "chock full of hope and life," feeling at the end that "he had never spent a pleasanter

12. Thomas Hughes, *Tom Brown's School Days,* 110. Subsequent references will appear in the text.

day" (95, 107). Harry's journey is equally full of incident, whether it is making friends and hearing about the Weasley twins' mischief at Hogwarts or discovering such wonders as trading cards of famous magicians who smile and wave when you look at them or such treats as Bertie Bott's Every Flavor Beans and Chocolate Frogs. He, Ron, and Hermione discuss how they might fit in at Hogwarts, and Harry feels wonderful about sharing candy with Ron. As the journey comes to an end, "Harry's stomach lurched with nerves" (*Sorcerer's Stone,* 111); as Tom is about to see Rugby for the first time, his "heart beat quick" (108). As is typical of public school novels, the school is presented as a daunting but alluring place for first-years.

When each boy arrives at his school, there is great interest in the physical architecture of the place, with long descriptions of the various sitting rooms, halls, and sleeping rooms. The emphasis is on the specialness of these places to the entering student, a sense of wonderful novelty and possibility. Hughes opens the description of the study rooms with a kind of reverence: "Tom was for the first time in a Rugby boy's citadel" (113). Tom "was not a little astonished and delighted with the palace in question" and thinks it "uncommonly comfortable to look at"; the room "had more interest for Tom than Windsor Castle or any other residence in the British Isles" (113–14). In *Sorcerer's Stone,* the room that elicits this awestruck response is the Great Hall: "Harry had never even imagined such a strange and splendid place," lit by thousands of candles floating in the air and "a velvety black ceiling dotted with stars" (116). Whether literally or figuratively, these spaces are presented as magical, where the buildings and rooms themselves show the new students that they have entered into an exclusive, exciting environment brimming with the potential both to absorb them utterly and to help them come into their own.

In each book, as in so many public school novels, we are presented with a school that is largely a world all to itself, isolated from outside influences. In *Tom Brown's School Days,* the coachman talks of Rugby as a "Werry out-o'-the-way place . . . off the main road" (99); Rowling puts Hogwarts, a huge and ancient castle, somewhere unspecified in the north, surrounded by forests and a lake. The public school experience is often described in this way, as one where the outside world is far less important than the microcosm of the institution. While at school, the outside world largely drops away and the hero can concentrate on his own exploits and development. In Harry's case, the isolation of Hogwarts is especially important, for every moment he spends there is one less under the thumb of the Dursleys.

In the microcosm of Hogwarts, central features of public schools can be seen, especially those important in public school literature. Perhaps most obvious is the house system, where loyalty to one's house is paramount. *Tom Brown's School Days* highlights the centrality of house affiliation on

Brown's first night, when "Old Brooke," a football hero who is leaving at the end of the term, gives a lengthy speech in which he pinpoints the reason for his house's athletic success: "It's because we've more reliance on one another, more of a house feeling, more fellowship than the school can have. . . . I believe it's the best house in the school, out-and-out (cheers)" (144). At the end of his oration, Brooke brings tears to his fellows' eyes when he offers his toast to "the dear old school-house—the best house of the best school in England" (147). Hughes, knowing his audience, pleads with "my dear boys, old and young, you who have belonged, or do belong, to other schools and other houses, don't begin throwing my poor little book about the room . . . when you get to this point," because, after all, "would you, any of you, give a fig for a fellow who didn't believe in, and stand up for, his own house and his own school?" (147–48). Similarly, one of the major concerns of the Harry Potter books is house affiliation, beginning on Harry's first night at Hogwarts, during which the Sorting Hat places each first-year in the most appropriate house. By using the device of the Sorting Hat, Rowling makes house affiliation even more integral to her novel than it is to the average public school story, for the hat never places students arbitrarily into one house or another, but picks carefully, based on its reading of the student's inmost character. Thus Hogwarts houses have characters of their own, long-standing and self-perpetuating, a feature present in public school novels but heightened here through magical means.

During the dinner after the Sorting Ceremony, the major plot device involving the house system is highlighted by the Gryffindor house ghost: "So—new Gryffindors! I hope you're going to help us win the house championship this year? Gryffindors have never gone so long without winning. Slytherins have got the cup six years in a row!" (*Sorcerer's Stone,* 124). This rivalry between houses, particularly the competition between Harry's house, Gryffindor, and Slytherin, house of his enemy Malfoy, provides Rowling an opportunity for conflict throughout the series; the struggle to win the house cup dominates much of the first novel and is an element in each of the others. It is in fact only in *Goblet of Fire* that overall school loyalty comes to the fore because it is the first time Hogwarts students come in contact with other wizarding schools. Much more often, house loyalty is the issue. This loyalty becomes a particular anxiety for Harry in *Chamber of Secrets,* when his great worry is that his destiny should have led him to Slytherin rather than to Gryffindor. In fact, when he is briefly left alone with the Sorting Hat, he decides to put it on, "just to make sure it *had* put him in the right House," and when he gets an equivocal answer, "Harry's stomach plummeted. . . . 'You're wrong' he said aloud to the still and silent hat" (209). For Harry, as for Tom Brown and so many schoolboys or schoolgirls, being in another house is unthinkable—it is not just a temporary association but a very real part of one's identity. Again, Rowling emphasizes the connection of identity and house affiliation even more than in the average school novel, for Harry's becoming a Slytherin rather than a Gryffindor would perhaps have meant the difference between his becoming an evil wizard rather than a good one. This is a typical school novel message writ large: the house molds individual character even as individuals help mold the character of the house.

Here too, as in the typical public school novel, we find a system of house-masters (that is, teachers who are responsible for a house) and prefects (older students who help keep order in the house), with housemasters dol-ing out discipline for Harry and company's many—if justified—infractions. In *Tom Brown's School Days,* the most immediate and visible peer authority figure is the praeposter, who, East tells Brown, has certain privileges by dint of his position. East explains why it gets so cold in the rooms at night, de-spite the presence of a fire at the end of the passage: "Jones, the praeposter has the study at the fire end, and he has rigged up an iron rod and green baize curtain across the passage, which he draws at night, and sits there with his door open; so he gets all the fire, and hears if we come out of our studies after eight, or make a noise." The response by the younger boys to Jones's fire hoarding is to steal some time by the fire when he's not there, and simply "to keep a sharp look-out that he don't catch you behind his curtain" (115). The Harry Potter series echoes this sense prefects have of their own privilege and the cautious but less than fully respectful attitude toward them by younger students; Percy Weasley is portrayed as rather self-important and authoritarian and therefore a target for humor, particularly by his twin brothers, as we have seen. Rowling thus perpetuates the com-mon notion of prefects as both important to the house system and yet in a subtle struggle to maintain their position and dignity with the younger students. One wonders, in fact, if later Harry Potter volumes will find Harry, Ron, or Hermione on the other side of that struggle.

Another crucial feature in public school literature is an emphasis upon games, whether football or cricket or rugby. Housemasters and students alike take keen interest in the outcome of matches. As Brooke puts it dur-ing his speech on Tom's first night at Rugby, "I know I'd sooner win two schoolhouse matches running than get the Baillol scholarship any day (fran-tic cheers)" (144). In fact, the chapter in which Tom arrives at Rugby is ti-tled "Rugby and Foot-Ball," and thirteen pages—fully half of the chapter—are devoted to a highly detailed description of a football match. At the end of the chapter, Tom proves himself "a plucky youngster" to football hero Brooke when he dives for a ball and gets the wind knocked out of him at the bottom of a heap of opposing players: "They are hauled and roll off him, and Tom is discovered a motionless body." His reckless sacrifice is noted with approval, and Brooke declares that Tom "will make him a player" (134). His ability at sports is therefore key to his acceptance by others.

The Harry Potter novels follow very closely the school story tradition of making games and sports central to the boarding school experience; some of the most vivid and popular scenes in the series take place on the playing field. Moreover, as with Tom, Harry's ability at athletics proves crucial to his success at school. Although the game of Quidditch may be new, it functions in the novel very much as football does in *Tom Brown's School Days*. When Harry first learns to ride his broomstick, he ends up catching a Remembrall in a daring, last-minute midair maneuver that ought to have landed him in trouble with the redoubtable Professor McGonagall. Instead, she takes him to the captain of the Gryffindor Quidditch team and declares, "The boy's a natural. I've never seen anything like it" (*Sorcerer's Stone*, 151), calling to mind Brooke's approval of new boy Brown at the bottom of that heap. Even the scene where he learns the rules of Quidditch recalls the passage in *Tom Brown's School Days* in which East tutors Brown upon the peculiar rules to Rugby football: "Tom's respect increased as he struggled to make out his friend's technicalities, and the other set to work to explain the mysteries of 'off your side,' 'drop-kicks,' 'punts,' 'places,' and the other intricacies of the great science of foot-ball" (119). Once Harry and the readers learn the rules of Quidditch, we are witness to descriptions of matches nearly as detailed as the one in *Tom Brown's School Days*, the first lasting seven pages (*Sorcerer's Stone*, 185–91). Quidditch plays some part in each of the Harry Potter novels; time and again, Harry's risking life and limb in Quidditch matches earns him respect, even adulation, such as the incident in *Chamber of Secrets* when a rogue Bludger breaks his arm but does not prevent him from catching the Snitch and winning the game for Gryffindor. *Prisoner of Azkaban* features the introduction of Harry's Firebolt, the make of broomstick coveted by every red-blooded Quidditch player, male or female; and in *Goblet of Fire*, the opening chapters of the book revolve around Harry's attendance at an international Quidditch tournament.

Interestingly, Harry and Tom both prove themselves more adept at a sport than at academic subjects. Like Tom Brown, Harry is admired by his peers for his prowess at sports and his out-of-class exploits rather than his classroom brilliance. Both boys seem to be bright but not superlative academically, and their stories, while including classroom experiences, do not center around their winning academic honors; concern about being the best scholar is left to others, such as Hermione Granger in the Harry Potter series. At the end of *Chamber of Secrets*, Harry can't decide which magical subjects interest him, and ends up choosing whatever his best friend Ron does, feeling that, as he says, "if he was rubbish at them, at least he'd have someone friendly to help him" (187).

Instead, the emphasis is on each boy's sometimes reckless courage and wild adventuring. As with many school stories, the focus is often on extracurricular activities, including fighting with rivals and rule breaking. Tom Brown gets into a fight with a bigger but slower-footed boy who has harassed Tom's meek friend Arthur, a fight described with gusto and in great detail by Hughes, who defends fighting with fists as the "English way for English boys to settle their quarrels" (336). In *Chamber of Secrets,* Harry and Malfoy have a duel with their wands in which Harry protects a fellow student from a snake created by Malfoy. Both boys are prone to rule bending and rule breaking, Tom for the fun of it more often than Harry. Both boys tend to be up and about in the night doing things they ought not to be doing when they should be in bed; in Tom's case, his reasons are partly to conduct important business and partly "the excitement of doing something which was against the rules" (213). When Harry and Hermione are caught skulking about the castle, it isn't for the thrill of it but because they are handing over Hagrid's troublesome and illegal pet dragon to more capable hands. Perhaps a closer parallel is Harry's use of the Marauder's Map in *Prisoner of Azkaban* to make it possible for him to visit the nearby town of Hogsmeade, which is off-limits to him but full of temptations.

In any case, the centrality and essential worth of the boarding school experience is stressed in both books when Tom and Harry reveal one of their greatest fears: suffering the ultimate consequence of breaking the rules or not living up to school standards by being expelled. Tom and East are brought to the headmaster, the Doctor, who explains that rules "are for the good of the school, and must and shall be obeyed. Those who thoughtlessly or willfully break them will not be allowed to stay at the school." Tom and East "hurry off horribly scared: the idea of having to leave has never crossed their minds, and is quite unbearable" (237). The love of school and the feeling of belonging it gives students runs deep, and expulsion is an effective threat. Harry frets about being asked to leave numerous times in the series with a sense of fear and hopelessness we understand only too well, considering the bleak alternative of life with the Dursleys. Harry sounds very much like Tom when he is described as "scared out of his wits that he was about to be thrown out of school" (*Chamber of Secrets,* 205).

What, in fact, is so valuable about the boarding school experience that readers should agree that expulsion would be a terrible fate? What lessons are such places teaching, according to their chroniclers? Certainly building friendships, proving a good friend, separating from those who hold the wrong values and thus showing one's true character are all central to public school novels, including the Harry Potter series. In part one of *Tom Brown's School Days,* Tom and East build a friendship and prove strong enough to rebel against the unfair rule of Flashman, even at the risk of becoming victims and outcasts, but also spend a lot of time causing minor trouble, which eventually leads to the Doctor's threat. It is in part two that Tom's essential goodness shines through, when he is given responsibility for a younger boy, George Arthur, and becomes his friend and protector. He even gets East, who was initially skeptical of Arthur, to like this more refined, delicate lad. And he develops in other ways through this friendship—he is willing to follow George Arthur's lead and pray publicly at bedtime and in the morning; as Hughes says, "It was no light act of courage in those days, my dear boys, for a little fellow to say his prayers publicly even at Rugby" (255). He endures sneers and laughter, only to win respect in the end. The Harry Potter books also focus on the forging and testing of friendships, from Harry and Ron's alliance against Malfoy to their eventual acceptance of Hermione as an equal, despite Ron's initial distrust of this somewhat rule-bound, fussy scholar. Many times one or more of these three face contempt, ridicule, resentment, or unjustified accusations of wrongdoing from others—such as when they suspect Harry of being allied with evil after he proves able to speak to snakes in *Chamber of Secrets*. Rowling repeatedly shows them enduring adversity and ultimately winning respect and friendship.

On a larger scale, Harry defends those who are Muggle-born—that is, born into families without other magicians—from the class snobbery and malice of Malfoy and Slytherin House. Time and again Malfoy stresses the superiority of the old, wealthy wizarding families, those in whom the magic runs strong, while Harry befriends Hermione, a Muggle-born girl, and Ron, who is not Muggle-born but is quite poor and of low social standing. One might imagine that this bias against the wealthiest and most privileged students would be absent in a book like *Tom Brown's School Days,* but interestingly enough, Flashman is precisely the Malfoy type: a high-handed bully who sneers at those he considers inferiors and holds power partly "by dint of his command of money" (202). Hughes goes to great lengths in opening chapters to extol the virtues of country landowners of modest means and even the more common folk and to criticize those with "too much over-civilization and the deceitfulness of riches" (62). He praises Tom when, as a boy, he and his brothers played with village boys "without the idea of equality or inequality," adding that it would never enter their heads "till it's put there by Jack Nastys or fine ladies'-maids" (79). Thus his attitude is not so very far from Rowling's, with her sense of sympathy for the Weasleys and Grangers in the boarding school setting.

Both Hughes and Rowling also stress the important ties between the hero and the headmaster, an adult mentor who helps the hero develop into a functioning, useful young man of good character. Tom, Harry, and their friends find themselves often working around their teachers, occasionally covering up their exploits or simply trying to pull the wool over their eyes, as in *Goblet of Fire,* when Harry and Ron begin making up dire predictions out of thin air to pass Divination and placate Professor Trelawney: " 'Next Monday,' [Ron] said as he scribbled, 'I am likely to develop a cough, owing to the unlucky conjunction of Mars and Jupiter.' He looked up at Harry. 'You know her—just put in loads of misery, she'll lap it up' " (221). Tom Brown goes further, at least in the beginning, where he considers the masters "as a matter of course, his natural enemies," for he often fails to do his work steadily and well (189). But both the Doctor and Albus Dumbledore are adults our heroes come to trust and value, and who in turn support, protect, and guide the boys. They are portrayed as moral, fair, kind, and unusual men who at times face criticism from within and without but always have the best interests of their school at heart. Old Brooke, very early on in *Tom Brown's School Days,* defends the Doctor to his somewhat skeptical housemates, who are afraid he will dismantle their old customs: "and he's a strong true man, and a wise one too, and a public-school man too" (147). He is indeed a strong man, and one who is flexible enough to let boys be boys—during morning chapel after a rather wild night, the Doctor "knows better than anyone when to look, and when to see nothing . . . there's been lots of noise and no harm done; nothing but beer drunk, and nobody the worse for it" (152–53). At the same time, he knows when serious talk or timely action is necessary to aid a boy's development, as when he speaks of rules and expulsion with Tom and East or gives Tom care of George Arthur. Similarly, Rowling presents Dumbledore as beloved by some but not all—certainly not by Slytherin House or some of the board of governors, who suspend him temporarily in *Chamber of Secrets.* Harry and his friends, naturally, remain loyal to him throughout. His ability to discern when to nurture, when to pardon, and when to exert his power rivals or surpasses that of the Doctor. He takes special care of Harry, passing on Harry's father's Invisibility Cloak, calling him into his office when he feels Harry needs special attention, and not punishing Harry when the rule breaking isn't significant or was done out of self-defense or for the good of others. These two boarding school novels do not simply dismiss all adults or see them as impediments, but emphasize the necessity of strong, wise adult mentoring to the development of the students.

Ultimately, then, the Harry Potter novels have one more trait in common with many other public school novels, seen especially strongly in *Tom Brown's School Days:* a tradition of providing a moral tale as well as a ripping good yarn. Hughes staunchly defends his practice of "preaching" in *Tom Brown's School Days* in his preface, noting that many have said his book is on the preachy side: "Why, my whole object in writing at all was to get the chance of preaching! When a man comes to my time of life and has his bread to make, and very little time to spare, is it likely that he will spend almost the whole of his yearly vacation in writing a story just to amuse people? I think not" (9). Rowling in interviews speaks of the morality in her books, even if it is of a gentler, subtler kind than Hughes employs, and even if amusement is surely a large part of her design. She mentions "the moral heart" of the first book, and says that "the moral point becomes clear towards the end of each book," adding that "the morals tend to come quite naturally, often as I approach the end I realize what I've been writing about."[13] Naturally, when an explicit moral is presented, as in *Chamber of Secrets,* it is voiced by Head-master Dumbledore, who tells Harry gently that "it is our choices . . . that show what we truly are, far more than our abilities"—probably a sentiment that Doctor Arnold would have approved (*Chamber of Secrets,* 245). In the larger sense, the Harry Potter books are about the great struggle between good and evil, kindness and cruelty, friendship and enmity, all as filtered through the experience of a boy who is constantly learning and coming into his own. And certainly on its most basic level, *Tom Brown's School Days* is about the same struggle, even if the terms there are Christian, with Tom becoming a true Christian first, then bringing his friend East into the fold. While many school stories do not operate on this grand level, the message that the school is a wonderful place to grow and develop is a common one, and the Harry Potter books add to this tradition of portraying the pub-lic school experience in this positive light; they are part of what Jonathan Gathorne-Hardy calls that "great body of glorifying literature."[14]

Obviously, Rowling's books are more popular than the typical public school novel—stunningly so. One could argue that the school story ele-ments actually contribute to their popularity in Great Britain and other countries where public boarding schools are a long-standing part of pop-ular culture. What happens, though, when the average American reader encounters the boarding school elements in the series? The background of public school literature is not in the consciousness of most Americans, nor are Americans particularly inclined to glorify private boarding schools. At the very least, American readers are not likely to pick up on the school story traditions in the way British readers—particularly adults—might very well do, leading one to think that something would be lost in translation for Americans.

One related debate involves the changes made for the American editions of the series. Most of these are minor, such as altering the word "football" to

13. Dening, "Wiz Kid"; "Enchanting Chapters in the Life of a 'Modern-Day C. S. Lewis.'"
14. Gathorne-Hardy, *The Old School Tie,* 212.

the word "soccer," but one change involves the title of the first book, which was *Harry Potter and the Philosopher's Stone* in Great Britain, a decision that some critics decried as part of the dumbing down of cross-cultural artifacts for American society. After all, the philosopher's stone is a very specific magical object with a rich historical and literary background, while a sorcerer's stone doesn't have any but the vaguest connotations and denotes nothing in particular outside of the novel. It's generic. So, when Americans read Harry Potter novels, are they only getting the sorcerer's stone level of understanding? What, if anything, is lost in transit? These novels are unimaginable as American books, not because of the fantastic elements but precisely because of the boarding school elements. And yet I would argue that not as much is lost as might be imagined, because Rowling transforms and tweaks the public school story's conventions in ways that invite American readers into that world.

Simply in terms of today's audience, Rowling's books modify and modernize the tradition so that it is more pleasing to contemporary readers in general. Her school reflects today's Britain, for one: it is a coeducational institution with an ethnically diverse student body, one where individuality is important. Looking at much of the online material for the great public boarding schools, one can see that these are all current trends. Moreover, because the houses themselves are coed, a female professor can be housemaster of male students, such as Professor McGonagall of Gryffindor, and a male professor can be housemaster of female students, such as Snape of Slytherin. This brings the configuration closer to one familiar to contemporary readers, and certainly to students at American public schools.

Rowling also softens the darker side of public school life: there's no victimization of younger students by older ones—nothing at all like the practice of fagging (older boys forcing younger boys to be their servants) as seen in *Tom Brown's School Days*. Rather than an older boy as nemesis, like Flashman, Harry has to contend against one his own age, and he holds his own against Malfoy quite nicely from the start. Instead of physical punishment for rule breaking, there are simply points taken off of one's house total and minor tasks to do. The first year, usually portrayed as rather difficult even if ultimately rewarding, as it certainly was for Tom Brown, is simply lots of fun for everyone. And for Harry, escaping his nasty relatives means that Hogwarts is far better than home. No one expresses any homesickness, in fact, a contrast to Tom, who occasionally is saddened by thoughts of his saintly mother. The food is wonderful, appearing magically from thin air, and the castle, though a bit cold, is a terrific place to explore, with its hidden doors, secret shortcuts, and disappearing staircases. And when it comes to academics, instead of hearing about struggles to learn dull Latin and Greek, as we do in *Tom Brown's School Days*, we are treated to such topics as Defense against the Dark Arts, Charms, Potions, and Transfiguration. Even the most boring class, History of Magic, is taught by a ghost, and the class perhaps most like a literature seminar, Divination, pokes delicious fun at the professor, a gloomy over-interpreter of tea leaves and crystal balls. To sum it up, after reading the Harry Potter novels, what child—or adult—wouldn't want to go to boarding school at Hogwarts?

Moreover, by making this a school for witchcraft and wizards, she transforms much of what might be familiar to British readers and off-putting to American readers into elements that are new and delightful for all. The prime example of this transformation is the sport that is so important in the book: it is not football or cricket or rugby but Quidditch, an entirely new game played high in the air with flying balls and broomsticks. The final episode in *Tom Brown's School Days* is a cricket match, including detailed descriptions of the action. Naturally this kind of scene would not go over well with American readers—in fact, it is unlikely that even a soccer match as climax, despite its increasing popularity in the United States, would be received with enthusiasm. On the other hand, the descriptions of Quidditch matches, whose rules are carefully explained, are some American readers' favorite scenes. She has taken the notion of games, so central to public school novels, and used them in a way that includes non-British readers.

Perhaps more significantly, British public school novels have often glorified English culture and to some extent the English elite classes. One cannot imagine a book about those who go to Eton or Winchester being very popular with American audiences today. In its original form, particularly, the boarding school novel put strong emphasis on the role of the public school in developing virtues thought especially English. *Tom Brown's School Days* is full of pride in many things English, from the landscape to the character of its mothers to its "good English cheeses" and its "beer and skittles" (59–60). Hughes writes of the virtue of "silent endurance, so dear to every Englishman—of standing out against something, and not giving in," and later announces that "almost all English boys love danger" (94, 105). Tom's father wants schools to turn out a "brave, helpful, truth-telling Englishman, and a gentleman, and a Christian" (91). Rowling makes no attempt to single out any trait as particularly English. While she would agree that, like Hughes and so many other authors of school stories, her prime interest is in the development of character over the learning of academic lessons, she has steered far away from naming this education as an English one, even though the world outside Hogwarts is the England of today, its students are clearly from Great Britain, and its traditions are largely those of British boarding schools.

Yet instead of glorifying things British, at least in any overt way, Hogwarts glorifies instead the culture of magic and those elite who have magical powers. Hogwarts is not so much England as it is a non-Muggle, nonordinary world, where the children and their teachers are both extraordinary and yet as familiar as those we might meet on any playground in the Western world. Because of the fantastic elements at the core of the series, Americans do not mind that Hogwarts is an elitist school that favors abilities largely dependent upon the vagaries of one's genetic makeup. Issues of class snobbery and privilege, certainly present in British school stories, can be explored with equal interest by Americans when the classes are wizards and Muggles. Interestingly, Rowling's good characters all respect their wizard friends who are Muggle-born, yet they tend to find Muggles themselves a bit plodding and dull at best and, at worst, loutish and crass like the Dursleys. The world of Hogwarts, like the world of Rugby, is a brighter, livelier world than that of ordinary folk, and its denizens are both as recognizable as our friends and yet special in attractive, exciting ways. Note too that Rowling lets Harry have it both ways—he is unschooled in the ways of magic, Muggle-raised and tousle-haired, and yet a marked child, a golden boy with fabulous ability already at Quidditch and extraordinary powers, even for a wizard. American readers might not be able to identify with the very British Tom Brown, son of a country squire, attending an exclusive boys' school, but Harry is another matter entirely. This is distinctly a post-Empire public boarding school, where British power and pride are not on display in a school with a distinctly British public school flavor.

The school might also get some of its universal appeal from its humorously conservative elements. Oddly enough, for all its differences with the Rugby of Tom Brown's day, Hogwarts reminds one of a nineteenth-century institution in its lack of up-to-date technology. At Hogwarts technology is simply missing, replaced by magic. We don't find computers, phones, television, VCRs, DVDs, or video games. Entertainment consists of Quidditch, magical versions of chess, and getting into misadventures with dragons, trolls, and unicorns. The curriculum partakes heavily of such medieval topics as alchemy, and they are taught in a very old castle. This is about as retro as it gets, and apparently it appeals to a lot of technology-dependent, cyber-smart children and adults. Of course, this old-fashioned world, minus the magic, is the one found in the glory days of the public school novel, where Classics was the main topic and science labs frowned upon.

In fact, what Rowling's novels do to the public school story is to preserve those elements that are fun and reasonably comprehensible to any Western reader while deleting the distasteful and the more culturally specific. In 1941, Edward C. Mack presented the main plot of the traditional boys' public school novel:

> [A] boy enters school in some fear and trepidation, but usually with ambitions and schemes; suffers mildly or severely at first from loneliness, the exactions of fag-masters, the discipline of masters, and the regimentation of games; then makes a few friends and leads for a year or so a joyful, irresponsible and

sometimes rebellious life; eventually learns duty, self-reliance, responsibility, and loyalty as a prefect, qualities usually used to put down bullying or overemphasis on athletic prowess; and finally leaves school, with regret, for the wider world, stamped with the seal of the institution which he has left and devoted to its welfare.[15]

One cannot know Harry's ultimate fate at Hogwarts, but the description of the earlier days shows how Rowling has both used and transformed the elements of this basic plot, emphasizing the more fun and positive aspects of the experience while maintaining a sense of struggle and conflict. As a result, we have the return of the boarding school novel, updated and modified for contemporary readers in ways so appealing that we are left envious, wishing we too had received that invitation to enter Hogwarts and become boarding school boys and girls. In new guise, the genre made popular by Tom Brown has been revivified by Harry Potter, allowing it not only to cross the Atlantic successfully but also to conquer those American readers for whom boarding schools are unfamiliar and the public school story completely unknown.

15. Reed, *Old School Ties,* 18.

Greater than Gold in Gringotts

Questions of Authority and Values

Crowning the King

Harry Potter and the Construction of Authority

Farah Mendlesohn

Attempting to write a critique of a body of work that is clearly unfinished is a challenge to any academic. The Potter series is a work in progress: inevitably, as any competent futurologist knows, attempts at prediction alter the future predicted. The intention in this paper, however, is to focus as much on that process of construction—incomplete as it may be—as it is to center on what has actually been achieved.

Examining the political structures of children's texts is a task always open to attack. Children's texts are not *supposed* to be ideological. Open espousal of ideology is more often linked to the children's books of Red China than those of Western Europe. In reality, most of the major classics of Western children's literature, and specifically of children's fantasy, have been rooted in systems of authority and belief. Charles Kingsley's *The Water-Babies* (1863) and C. S. Lewis's *Chronicles of Narnia* (*The Lion, the Witch and the Wardrobe*, 1950) are unabashedly Christian; *The Wizard of Oz* (1900) outraged much of the American public for its anarchic and populist values, while E. Nesbit's *The Story of the Amulet* (1906) flaunts its author's socialism.

Superficially, Rowling stands apart from these classics. There is no obvious political or evangelical intent other than relaying an oft-told tale about the battle of good against evil. She is not an authoritarian writer with a message to be propounded via the morality tale, nor is she seeking to create a society or world that can, through its mere depiction, inspire us to change. To demand that she do any of these would clearly be an unacceptable imposition from critic upon author. However, while Rowling clearly does not intend to engage with ideology, its role in her work is inescapable. Rowling's Harry Potter books are rooted in a distinctively English liberalism that is marked as much by its inconsistencies and contradictions as by its insistence that it is not ideological but only "fair." Its ideology is its very claim to a nebulous and nonexistent impartiality. The ideological structures of Rowling's work focus on a manipulation of this uncritical construction of "fairness." The denial of ideology, which forms a significant element of the

159

text, promotes a willing suspension of intellectual rigor. This contributes to promoting a particular understanding of authority while simultaneously undermining the coherence of the texts. Further, it leads to a rejection of the subversive opportunities available to the fantasist, exemplified in the works of Lewis Carroll and others: if a world is fundamentally fair and rational, subversion is politically unnecessary. We can see this in both Tolkien and Lewis, whose fundamental message remains that fairness and happiness can best be achieved when rules are obeyed and heroes decided by destiny. That the definition of fairness operated both by these writers and by Rowling is constructed around the actions of the hero means that it is easy to ignore the further implications inherent in the text.

The structures of a genre themselves reflect ideologies, and even where an author sets out to deliberately subvert those structures, this subversion remains an engagement with those ideologies. Thus L. Frank Baum deliberately subverted the moral intentions of the children's fantasy in *The Wizard of Oz*, creating a populist political fable rather than Christian inspirational uplift, with a protagonist who is an admirable, individualistic, and rather selfish child rather than a cooperative do-gooder. However, he at the same time retained the dominant structure of nineteenth- (and twentieth-) century fantasy and with it the neo-imperialism that assumed the inherent superiority of certain racial types. The extent to which he was embedded in a particular ideological structure was incisively revealed by Gregory Maguire's masterful reworking of Baum's parable in *Wicked* (1997). However, Baum's moral subversion is revealing for my argument in what it tells us about the fluidity of boundaries between genres. While the moral message of *The Wizard of Oz* ran counter to the complex Christianity of other fantasists such as George MacDonald, it was firmly within the tradition of the European fairy tale as exemplified by Hans Christian Andersen.[1] In this tradition, leadership is intrinsic, heroism born in the blood, and self-interest simply the manifestation of those powers that ensure a return to order. It is this structure that is encoded throughout the Potter texts.

Two relevant fairy tale narratives are relevant here. In the first, the youngest prince follows his two brothers on a quest in which they have already failed. His "fitness" is shown by his kindness to the poor, unwashed, and unwanted, and by his bravery, which is usually augmented by gifts from the first group. The second narrative is essentially identical save that the hero is poor. Here, too, he demonstrates his fitness, but often trickery is involved, a comment, perhaps, on the essential trickery that lies behind the

---

1. China Miéville points to MacDonald's awareness of the "radical contingency" of good and evil and his decision, at the end of the Princess and Curdie books, to point out that the goodness of his protagonists does not guarantee the probity of their descendants (Miéville, e-mail).

acceptance of aristocracy in the first place. The author who has been most subversive within these tropes is Diana Wynne Jones. *Howl's Moving Castle* begins with the lines, "In the land of Ingary . . . it is quite a misfortune to be born the eldest of three. Everyone knows you are the one who will fail first, and worst, if the three of you set out to seek your fortune."[2]

But while feminist fantasists such as Jane Yolen, Robin McKinley, and Patricia McKillip have reworked the conventions, much modern genre fantasy refuses to deviate from the established assumptions, although new tropes have emerged. The most common new trope to emerge in the nineteenth century, unquestionably a reaction to that century's revolutionary turmoil, was the displaced prince: hidden from view, the exiled prince grows up unaware of his inheritance until either he is informed of his people's need and earns back the throne, or he is informed only *after* he has earned back his throne. In the nineteenth century the adventures of Bonnie Prince Charlie and of Charles II became the subject of high romance. The "princes in the tower," ignored for much of the sixteenth and seventeenth centuries, became the subject of high tragedy. All of these heroes represented a popularization of absolutist monarchy just when it was about to disappear from the European political stage, overwhelmed by the demands of the new capitalist aristocracy. Ironically, the true message of this romanticism, the assumption that fitness to rule is genetic, was essential to the establishment and co-option of this new order. Capitalism needed romance to establish it as a normative value.

More important, perhaps, has been the ideological impact of the structural shift from fairy tale to fantasy. In the classic fairy tale, while the act of traveling provides the tools and proof of the hero's fitness, it is the final application and the proving that are of interest. Thus in "The Twelve Dancing Princesses" the soldier's journey provides him with the means to follow the princesses, but the adventure succeeds his journey. In the modern fantasy, increasingly, the adventure *is* the journey. Similarly, for the soldier in the fairy tale, the crucial choices take place at the end of the story, but in the modern fantasy, the crucial choices are played out, bit by bit, as the journey unfolds. A recent attempt to revert to the last act finale approach, in David Eddings's series *The Mallorean,* proved a damp squib, as the "choice" was unbelievably obvious, foreshadowed by the four previous books.[3]

In the modern fantasy, if the getting there has become the focus of the adventure, it has also become the focus of what it means to be a hero. While most modern fantasy has been unable to avoid hereditarian assumptions, it has at least moved toward presenting the adventure itself less as a proof

2. Diana Wynne Jones, *Howl's Moving Castle*, 1.
3. *The Seeress of Kell* is the fifth book in David Eddings' series.

of blood right than of a growing into strength and maturity that comple-
ments the assumed birthright. However, circumstance of birth has retained
its narrative power, and Rowling, as we shall see, has created a hero and a
moral structure in which the rights of birth, while simultaneously denied,
underpin the structures of heroism that are the basis of her ideological universe. In a rather heated discussion on the Internet, Andy Robertson declared "Harry Potter is a Returning Prince who gets his worth 100% from
heredity and genetics."[4] Robertson advocated the appreciation of Potter
as a blow for traditionalism. However, he rejected the assertion that the
entire *articulated* dynamic of the Potter books is of worth, self-proof, and
the ridiculousness of hereditarian assumptions. What, then, did he mean?

The main plot of the Harry Potter books is, as Robertson has pointed
out, that of the returning prince, deprived of his heritage by the actions of a
usurper, who has come to reclaim his throne, and with it, herald a new age
of happiness. In constructing such a plot, Rowling has had no hesitation in
manipulating all the established tropes in constructing the romantic hero
of modern fantasy. Michael Moorcock has noted that "Almost all romantic
heroes and heroines are wounded children." But not since the nineteenth
century have orphans been portrayed with such extreme relatives with any
other intention than parody: *James and the Giant Peach* comes to mind. The
classic example of this extreme treatment is in Frances Hodgson Burnett's
A Little Princess: Sara Crewe, coincidentally black-haired and green-eyed,
is banished to an attic because she no longer has money. Here she, too,
learns magic, although of a more metaphorical kind, until her true nobility
of heart and blood is discovered. The relegation of Harry to the cupboard
under the stairs, the apparent starvation, and the Dursleys' insistence that
their nephew wear the shabbiest of clothes, all combine to make him the
most mistreated of mistreated princes. It also seems rather unlikely, given
the Dursleys' desire to maintain face in front of the world.[5]

However, despite this, and specifically because the trope she is employing is that of the returning prince, Rowling does not create the classic
"wounded child" of heroic fantasy. Instead, Harry Potter is relentlessly nice.
Harry, unlike Sara Crewe, has been brought up entirely by people who hate
him, and who have half starved him and in other ways abused him (although
it is not clear whether or not he has been beaten). Yet he is, almost incom-
prehensibly, a nice child.[6] Niceness is bred into the bone and is a function

4. Andy Robertson, "Fictionmags."
5. Michael Moorcock, *Wizardry and Wild Romance: A Study of Epic Fantasy,* 81;
Roald Dahl, *James and the Giant Peach; A Little Princess* was first published as *Sara Crewe, or What Happened at Miss Minchin's* (1887).
6. Frances Hodgson Burnett's *The Secret Garden* (1911) offers a much more realistic picture of the nature of a neglected child.

simply of self. Like another best-selling children's novelist, Roald Dahl (see *Charlie and the Chocolate Factory,* 1964, and *Matilda,* 1988), Rowling is playing a double game: niceness will, eventually, be rewarded, and thus we are persuaded that we, too, should try to be nice, but the hidden message is that niceness is a function of inner royalty and one is either born with it, or one is not. Compare this to the hidden prince, Ben, in Eva Ibbotson's 1994 children's fantasy, *The Secret of Platform 13.* Ben is brought up in an almost identical household, with hostile characters represented by a hugely over-fed pseudo-sibling (Rowling is rather fond of using obesity as a shorthand for moral dissolution: see Malfoy's companions Crabbe and Goyle, whose gluttony allows Harry, Ron, and Hermione to drug them [*Harry Potter and the Chamber of Secrets,* 161].) However, Ben's niceness is created by the care and determination of the old nanny that at least one child in the household should be properly brought up.[7] In contrast, Harry is "naturally" nice, and we are left in no doubt that this is his royal inheritance.

From the beginning, we are told that Harry's parents were some of the most powerful magical people of their day, an attribute which, despite all the evidence—Harry's incompetence in potions class for example, and Hermione's greater success in the exams—we are expected to assume he has inherited. Instead of demonstrating power, he demonstrates "gifts" in the most materialist sense. In the first book his popularity is assured by his inheritance of sporting ability *and* the gift of a new, supercharged broom by a wealthy well-wisher (Quidditch, like polo, is a game for the moneyed, it seems). In the second book, *Chamber of Secrets,* his success depends on a magical cloak inherited from his father; in the third, *Harry Potter and the Prisoner of Azkaban,* on the gift of a magical map. In the fourth book, he has "inherited" the ability to withstand a curse, and the best touch of all, he has "inherited" part of Voldemort, which is crucial in the wand selection that helps him to withstand the villain. This is important: it means that at no time does Harry act with anything that can be called his own or the result of hard work and application, as is the case with, for example, Lloyd Alexander's Taran, all of whose gifts (the ability to use a sword, to apply a magical tool, to organize an army) are the direct result of endless hours of *learning,* the realization that love and loyalty matter and the willingness to help someone defend a sheepfold not his own. Nor, as in Baum's Oz, does magic act to encourage Potter to self-development, but instead operates as metaphor *for* self-development. The result, as Diana Waggoner has observed of Roald Dahl's Charlie, is that the reader "knows that . . . [he] is deserving and noble because Dahl tells him so, not because he can see Charlie behaving in a noble manner . . ."; we know the punishment of

7. Eva Ibbotson, *The Secret of Platform 13.*

his enemies is appropriate because our protagonist is allowed to approve.[8] This perception is reinforced by the presence of that staple of fairy tale and fantasy, the companions.

Where Harry's success does not rest on inheritance (whether material or genetic), it rests instead on the attributes of his companions. Repeatedly in the Potter books, it is not Potter who displays ingenuity, intelligence, or bravery, but his companions: the redoubtable and brilliant Hermione; the kind, reckless, and incredibly strong Hagrid; the faithful and dogged Ron. This is no coincidence, nor is it simply a children's author attempting to demonstrate that friendship makes one strong. Traditionally, fairy tale and fantasy have surrounded the hero with companions (some of whom, like Cedric Diggory in *Harry Potter and the Goblet of Fire,* have proved expendable), but the role of the companions has been twofold. First, they provide their skills to enable the hero to achieve specific things for which the *hero* and not they take the credit and the prize.

The second role of the fantasy companion *but not* of the fairy tale companion has been to teach life's lessons: to bring the hero into maturity by teaching him new skills, drawn from their strengths and new wisdoms from their application. David Eddings' *The Belgariad* offers one of the best modern examples of this, as Garion, the hero, is effectively brought up by a range of characters who teach him skills that he finds useful, but also lend their own powers to his cause.[9] Garion becomes more active in the last two books, increasingly applying the lessons himself rather than relying on a companion. A nicely subversive version of the same pattern can again be found in Lloyd Alexander's Prydain sequence, in which Taran's companions share their weaknesses, not their strengths, and each gains enormously in wisdom from this.[10]

However, Rowling, so far, has employed only the first, fairy tale, aspect of this trope, with little implication that Potter learns from the services his companions offer. Where, for example, he applies Hermione's advice, it is presented at the same level as the application of the cloak of invisibility. Hermione, in fact, is not even accorded the status of "companion" as such until the third book. In *Chamber of Secrets* Hermione finds the vital clue but is paralyzed by the basilisk and thus excluded from the adventure. But Hermione is crucial to Harry's success in the *Chamber of Secrets,* providing

8. Diana Waggoner, *The Hills of Faraway: A Guide to Fantasy,* 53.

9. *Pawn of Prophecy* (London: Corgi, 1983), *Queen of Sorcery* (London: Corgi, 1984), *The Magician's Gambit* (London: Corgi, 1984), *Castle of Wizardry* (London: Corgi, 1984), *Enchanter's End Game* (London: Corgi, 1985).

10. *The Book of Three* (London: Heineman, 1966), *The Black Cauldron* (London: Heineman, 1967), *The Castle of Llyr* (London: Heineman, 1968), *Taran Wanderer* (London: Fontana Lions, 1979), *The High King* (London: Fontana Lions, 1979).

him with the disguises he needs. In the inter-school magic competition in *Goblet of Fire,* Hermione similarly provides Harry with the secret talisman, in this case knowledge. Hagrid and Dobby also fit within this construction: both assist Harry to cheat in competition, Dobby with the information about herbs, Hagrid with a secret look at the dragons. Both lend their intrinsic qualities to Harry's service. In both cases, if Harry learns anything, it is patronizing sympathy for their mistakes and simplicities, even while he accepts what is offered. He has not, so far, developed any of the empathy or admiration for Dobby that Taran developed for his similar companion, Gurgi. In the *Chronicles of Prydain,* Gurgi functioned as an alternative model of bravery. Unlike Dobby, he was not a figure of fun, but operated as perhaps the most important support for the hero, not merely as foil.

The structure of companionship in the Potter books has two effects. First, these companions function as courtiers: their talents are, by extension, their prince's talents, and their deeds reflect his glory (one of the best manipulations of this trope can be found in John Barnes's witty novel, *One for the Morning Glory,* 1996). But second, the role of the companions, combined with the hereditary nature of Potter's own intrinsic qualities, creates a peculiarly passive hero to whom things happen, which he suffers and bears, but who rarely proceeds in a proactive manner. Potter does not search out trouble, nor does he willingly enter upon quests, yet he is presented at various times as a shining prince, first through the recovery of Neville's Remembrall (*Sorcerer's Stone,* 145) and then through Colin Creevy's embarrassing hero worship of him in *Chamber of Secrets* (96, 98) as well as the more purposeful underwater rescues of *Goblet of Fire.* However, his bravery, so far, has been to act upon Hermione's advice or, as twice in *Goblet of Fire,* to act out of ignorance, only to be rewarded for his foolishness. He may have shown moral fiber, but that does not mean that he had more moral fiber than those who listened to the instructions. But then, Harry Potter is the prince, and however contrived, the prince must always be the victor even if this involves ignoring the use of magic in the Muggle domain: another child would have been expelled. Fairness and justice may be bent so that the prince remains what we are repeatedly told he is, the nice boy: the role of his companions is intrinsic to creating moral authority around the person of Harry Potter.

Hagrid's position is particularly interesting in terms of the class structures of the book. Hagrid, more than any other character, fits the requirements of the 1950s lower-class sidekick and shapes the presentation of Harry. The 1950s sidekicks came in a range of presentations. The number one sidekick, Dan Dare's Flamer or Jet Morgan's Mitch (in the BBC radio series *Journey into Space,* 1953–1955), was allowed to be of the same social status but secondary in confidence, machismo, looks, and general charisma, and he generally deferred to the hero. This sidekick's role was to reinforce the hero's decisions without ever threatening his leadership. Ron very comfortably fits this role. However, many of these heroes had a second sidekick, usually of marginal social status, and very much more obviously servile. Of a distinctly lower social class than Harry, and belonging to a minority "ethnic" group (he is a half giant), Hagrid is both the outsider and the deferential friend. If we look for a literary comparison, he is the equivalent to Dan Dare's Digby, or Jet Morgan's Lemmy (the Jewish radio operator). Like Lemmy and Digby, he is dignified with only one name (as is Dobby). Hagrid is an egregious portrait of an underclass ne'er-do-well whose magical incompetence can be traced to his mixed blood. Hagrid lacks agency and he lacks real intelligence. More to the point, his attempts to exert agency result in chaos from which Harry and his friends must rescue him. Hagrid, like Dobby elsewhere, is continuously infantilized to an extent that it brings into question what Hagrid was ever doing at Hogwarts and, more to the point, what he learned there, for whatever else Hogwarts achieved, it clearly did not succeed in smoothing out Hagrid's accent. For no apparent reason, Hagrid speaks with an accent rather more than a few social notches below that of his schoolmates, his former schoolmates, and the teachers with whom he has spent more than twenty-five years. Whatever his social origins, association with the school would have changed that to some degree, at the very least, removing the most obvious class markers, but it is more in keeping with the structures of the novel that Hagrid's social origins (and the focus of much prejudice) are demonstrated with every word he speaks, that his lack of intelligence and self-control actually *fulfill* the stereotypes associated with his ethnicity, thus permitting Harry and his friends to demonstrate their "tolerance" and to show that Harry is a "good chap."

Rowling's books have received praise precisely because they are compounded of anachronisms. The Old Englishness of wizardry is a source of humor, from Mr. Weasley's obsession with newfangled Muggle inventions to the befuddled wizard of book four in his mismatched clothes: it is a form of humor that ranges from the affectionate to the derisory. In terms of the authoritarian structures of the book, however, this Old Englishness places Rowling in the company of Tolkien and of Lewis in constructing their fantasy worlds as a lament for old England, for the values of the shires and for a "greener" and simpler world.[11]

One way in which we can understand Rowling's otherwise rather confusing structures is to place her works within the Tory version of fantasy as

11. Meredith Veldman, *Fantasy, the Bomb, and the Greening of Britain: Romantic Protest, 1945–1980,* 54–91.

outlined by Moorcock, Waggoner, and Grant.[12] In this construction of the fantastic, fantasy is both escapist and consolatory. It is hostile to the "real" world but not subversive of it: consolatory (rather than strictly happy) endings are mandatory, and the fittings and furnishings of the fantasy world are nostalgic.

Some of this is material: the use of the steam train at King's Cross, for example, which surely comes into the category of misuse of magic on Muggle artifacts but which helps to re-create the atmosphere of the prewar boys' school story, complete with sweets shared in old-fashioned closed carriages and feasts at the beginning and end of term.[13] The moral conflict within the Potter books is between different structures of authority and differing ideologies of conservatism. Rowling has no real problem with authoritarian figures or with hierarchies. What is in dispute is how they are constructed, and in many ways, this is a battle between versions of Toryism and is thus built upon 1980s politics. On the one hand we have the aristocracy (Malfoy and ilk) posited as closed and bigoted. On the other hand we have the Dursleys, the epitome of a certain type of aspirationalist Thatcherite shopkeeper/middle-class business family as described by the decades' alternative comedians. Both are rejected by the Dumbledores and Weasleys, who see them as unacceptable extremes and who claim for themselves the moral high ground of moderation.

The Dursleys' suburbia was loathed by the likes of Lewis, who saw it as confining to the imagination and inviting the ruin of real England (see the character of Eustace Grubb in C. S. Lewis's *The Voyage of the Dawn Treader* [1953]). To both Tolkien and Lewis, the suburbs, with their emphasis on newness, were radically *anti*-conservative: rejecting communal greens for grain elevators and feudal dues for the financial lures of capitalism. Even the rather twisted socialism of the Grubb family, with their ideas of scholastic equality and vegetarianism, are framed as radical threats to the genuine England. Rowling's use of this trope is both convenient and unnecessary, in that her "real" villains are the aristocracy: the Malfoys and their cronies.

Superficially, in her introduction of Potter as the outsider and Malfoy, the aristocrat, as the school villain, Rowling distances herself from the conservative tradition. In reality she, like school story writers and fantasists before her, simply reconfirms its validity, both by the superficial appearance of egalitarianism—Potter's success—and by the use of liberal characters to reinforce the status quo. Thus, while open contempt is expressed by Dumbledore and the Weasleys toward the Malfoys and their emphasis on pure

12. Moorcock, *Wizardry*, 125; Waggoner, *Hills of Faraway*, 33; and John Grant, "Gulliver Unravels: Generic Fantasy and the Loss of Subversion," 23.

13. I am a regular commuter on the Reading to Waterloo line, which still uses these carriages. They are not pleasantly nostalgic; they are bitterly cold.

blood, both are quick to point out that the Weasleys and the Potters are from some of the oldest magical families in England. And Hogwarts as public school is crucial to this aristocratic structure that underpins the novels: as far as we can tell—and in the great English tradition, finance is not a topic to be discussed openly—Hogwarts is a British public school (a misleading nomenclature, as British "public" schools are funded by fees paid by parents, although to confuse the issue, they have the status of charities, not businesses). In the first book Harry worries about how he will afford the school and is reassured by Hagrid that he has enough money. The need for money to secure a good education is a given: Dudley's school, Smeltings, is sneered at neither because of its cost, nor because it is a poor educational establishment (Dudley's report makes this clear), but because it is a *fake*. It is a "minor" public school, aspiring to compete with the likes of Eton and Harrow in the construction of "traditions" such as the Smeltings' Stick, but it makes itself ludicrous in its self-conscious competition. In the eyes of Tory England, it commits the unforgivable sin of vulgarity.

However, if Hogwarts *is* a private school, and this is very unclear, Hermione is presumably on a scholarship. Hermione's family is comfortably off (they are dentists) but they are not wealthy, and average public-school fees, which include the cost of boarding, are currently running at the annual cost of a medium-sized car. In the conventional school narrative, this would be Hermione's story of struggle against adversity and for acceptance (and in one sense it is, since "Hermione's story" is essentially one of learning conformity to a new social milieu). However, it is Potter who has the status of the special and treasured pupil in the way he is treated by the teachers, while it is Hermione who receives the treatment often meted out by peers to the scholarship pupil, who nevertheless is denied the compensation of status through intellect. On a number of occasions her position as perhaps the brightest child in the school is used to humiliate her: we are expected to believe, for example, that she is unable to tell a cat's hair from a girl's hair (*Chamber of Secrets*, 225), and that her intelligence precludes emotional sensitivity, although it is Hermione who helps Harry to understand why Ron is resentful in the fourth book. When, in *Prisoner of Azkaban*, she receives special attention for her abilities, given extra classes and the ability to manipulate time, this proves to be an opportunity to humiliate her and to emphasize her inability to be "sensible" rather than excessive. At other times, she is ridiculed in contexts where Harry could defend her, but chooses not to, such as when George Weasley, who has failed most of his exams, insists she is speaking only for herself when she suggests that younger members of the school would simply not have learned enough to compete for the Triwizards' trophy (*Goblet of Fire*, 256).

In contrast, although Malfoy may seek to challenge it, Harry's place in the school appears secured by his heredity. Harry is a legacy. His social place is assured both by his own history and the presence of his father. One aspect to understanding what is happening here is the very school structure that Rowling has adopted. Irrespective of the situation in U.S. schools, it has long been a given in British schools that hard work and application in the classroom are not admired by either students or, frequently, by teachers. Hard-working students are swots or scholarship pupils (note that both are true for Hermione), and although they may be a credit to the school, they do not succeed where it really matters, on the sports field. Put bluntly, Harry is set up as the gentleman scholar: he works hard enough that his natural talent will take him through, but he is never shown at the top of the class, as this, a position occupied by Hermione, is despised as too showy for a gentleman. We know Harry is bright because we are told he is, but it is to be taken for granted: he is a "natural," in both work and play, and therefore, although he needs to practice whether in the school room or on the Quidditch field, he rarely needs to exert himself. The structure of the books around a school year and examinations may disguise this, but all of Harry's important magical adventures focus on his talents and not his learning.

Although the Malfoys are always held up as the epitome of evil, the blame is, as has already been indicated and will be discussed further below, placed on their bad blood and not on the structures of aristocracy. In fact Rowling goes to great lengths to deflect attention from the hierarchical and hereditarian ideas with which she litters her novels. By placing almost as much blame on her Thatcherite bourgeoisie, she obscures the construction of the class structure in the books. We are invited to choose, not between aristocracy and their allies, the new rich, and revolutionary change, but between two competing visions of aristocracy. The "good guys" in this structure are the similarly aristocratic (they come from a long line of magical families) Dumbledores, Weasleys, and Potters. In the persons of Professor Dumbledore and Mr. Weasley, we are presented the "real" England of Bilbo Baggins and the Shire. When Rowling presents her Wizard Civil Service, it is in the model of an imagined nineteenth century in which younger sons served for the privilege of service (only this way can the Weasleys' poverty be explained) and in which fairness and scrupulous honesty combined with a particular type of stupidity were the hallmarks of a particular sort of English civil servant manifested in book three as Barty Crouch: a man so upright that he condemns his own child to the prison in Azkaban. As China Miéville has argued, this is "a quintessentially English aristocratic outrage at the ascendancy of bourgeois culture, deflected onto the petty bourgeois inspectorate able, to the aristocracy's profound distaste, to dictate terms for its masters (the sanitary inspector and fire-prevention officer are representatives of that great British whipping boy, the officious minor functionary)."[14] This type of Englishness is further exemplified in Quidditch, a game that combines the public school enthusiasm for rugby with the class structures of polo and that re-creates, unsurprisingly, the English school tradition which prizes the games captain over the head boy and sports agility over mere intelligence and diligence. But finally, this linkage creates a vision of fantasy in which aristocracy is allied with the country gentry in the care of the inferior; a High Toryism or modern liberalism where everyone is nice, and tolerant; where women are in the home and use their magic to speed the cooking and cleaning (Mrs. Weasley in *Chamber of Secrets*, 34) and where differences are accepted but we all know who is inferior to whom and treat them nicely because they *are* inferior (the William Hague understanding of toleration). Here, finally, is where we reach a number of particular knotty problems in the authority structures of Rowling's novels.

The visibly articulated structure of the Potter novels is that birth into a magical family is no guarantee either of magical ability or of quality of character. Potter, the headmaster Albus Dumbledore, and all the other characters we are invited to admire share this apparent belief. However, two characters puncture the structure: Filch, the unpleasant janitor, is the only complete "squib" we meet (*Chamber of Secrets*, 145). Lockhart, also thoroughly unpleasant, appears to have overrated his magical abilities. Both of these characters are laid open to ridicule: Lockhart, understandably, for trying to be more than he is, but Filch for attempting to better himself (*Chamber of Secrets*, 128). For all the claim that magic is a poor measurement of character, we meet no one within this world who is both nice and nonmagical.

The role of the school story in the construction of British self-perceptions has been discussed elsewhere but here it is enough to understand that at the heart of the school tale and of British self-perception of "character" is the idea of fairness, played out most particularly on the sports field. If a man prove himself honorable on the sports field, he is worthy of trust. Rowling clearly understands this trope. Draco Malfoy, our visible representative of youthful malevolence, is a liar and a cheat, and his team, the Slytherins (programmed, according to the judgment of the hat, to be nasty) are quite willing to turn a Quidditch game into a bloodbath. But twice the Slytherins are the victims of miscarriages of justice clothed in the language of fairness. First, at the end of *Sorcerer's Stone,* the house cup victory that should be

14. China Miéville, "The Conspiracy of Architecture: Notes on a Modern Anxiety," 13.

theirs is snatched from them by the award of excessive numbers of points to Harry, Ron, and Hermione. Each receives fifty points, in a context in which points have usually been deducted (admittedly unfairly) and awarded in fives and tens, apparently as direct compensation for losing fifty points each for releasing a dragon. Dumbledore, for whatever reason, fixes the result (*Sorcerer's Stone*, 305–6). And frankly, one has to have some sympathy for Snape. The flattery of Harry by the wizard world is easily as unpleasant as that of Dudley by his parents. A very particular construction of justice and fairness is being erected here, which requires that those at the receiving end accept a certain set of givens as somehow natural.

The hereditarian assumptions of Rowling's novels are also bolstered by the ever-present destinarianism of Hogwarts and its world. Although Albus Dumbledore and other good people preach moral freedom, the evidence is all around Harry that very little is about personal choice. The visible illustration of this sits in front of him once a year: the Sorting Hat. The role of the Sorting Hat is to tell people what they are and what they may become. That Harry gets a choice is entirely due, as we later learn, to his contamination by Voldemort, so that his "choice" is actually between two heredities or destinies. It is not a free choice.

The extent to which the hat is constructing a social order is most vividly depicted by Hufflepuff: a house dedicated to the sidekick and creating the mentality of the faithful follower. The faithful follower is one of the last bastions of Tory, Tolkienian England. He is Sam Gamgee in *Lord of the Rings*, Bunter in the Lord Peter Wimsey mysteries of Dorothy L. Sayers, or Tumnus the Faun in Lewis's *The Lion, the Witch and the Wardrobe*. As the fantasy author China Miéville has observed, the heyday of the English sidekick is definitely "pre-thatcherite but post-feudal: the officer class's dream of the loyal batman who is allowed in the mess hall, differentiated from serfs by being 'chums,' at least to some degree." To make it worse, "because they are *not* slaves they *choose* their own subordination. The stereotype is defined by its subservience, but *within* a (capitalist) framework of class-mobility or denied in hereditarianism." Hufflepuffs, technically equal, are, according to the hat, "Loyal, hard-working and true . . ." (*Sorcerer's Stone*, 118). But they can never be leaders because somehow they are not fully human, and it is perfectly acceptable to kill off Cedric Diggory, captain of the Hufflepuff Quidditch team, in order to provide our hero with a motive to hold out, and in order to allow Dumbledore to deliver his "consolatory" speech, which closes *Goblet of Fire*.[15] For those readers who know their *Star Trek*, members of the Hufflepuff house wear the red shirt. They are doomed by their very association with those they follow.

15. China Miéville, e-mail; Moorcock, *Wizardry*, 126.

And to add to all this, it is simply not possible to accept that people are in Hufflepuff because this is their true character. If this were the case, Hermione should be in Ravenclaw, where those of a " . . . ready mind . . . of wit and learning, will always find their kind" (*Sorcerer's Stone*, 118). Her very presence in Gryffindor is a fix to ensure Harry his courtiers. Thus the house structure manipulates and molds. And finally, if the Sorting Hat predicts rather than controls, it is inconceivable that the House of Slytherin be even tolerated. The hat could assess and expel on the very first day.

A more subtle, and perhaps insidious, example is in the matter of Quidditch. As I have already indicated, although this is never stated, Quidditch is a rich man's sport: like polo, in which the expense of horses limits participation to those with money or those sponsored by money, Quidditch players with old brooms can never compete with those in possession of the latest technological marvels. Yet the possession of these is the source of contention and condemnation. When the Malfoys present the Slytherin team with new brooms, this is presented as cheating; when Harry receives a new, high-powered broom, it is framed as simply good fortune that rectifies a perceived injustice. No comment is made that he now outpowers the competing seekers. This is a sport in which money matters, but in which the moral universe makes some expenditures more acceptable than others. The issue seems to be not how money is used, but who has it.

This equation is reinforced when we look at two related issues: Harry and the Dursleys, and Harry's relationship with Ron. Rowling's depiction of the Dursleys is frankly ridiculous. We are allowed no moral ambiguity. The Dursleys might not be nice, but their moral turpitude is underlined with a bright, red brush. However, the ridiculousness of Rowling's coruscation of the Dursleys disguises a rather unpleasant truth: when Harry's parents died, they left him substantial amounts of money. In normal circumstances, any court would release some portion of that money for his care. Instead, Harry's proper guardians, the wizards and their government, deliberately choose to leave him to unknown relatives who are expected to care for him without recompense or assistance. The moral issue is cloudy. I am sure we all hope that if our children had to be looked after by others it would be done with absolute altruism. But equally, the impression is that the Potters were *rich* in the wizard world. The money *can* be exchanged (*Chamber of Secrets*, 57), yet no provision was made for the financial support of their child. What is Harry's, is Harry's, but his status as the foundling prince implies that what is Harry's will be preserved. And while the Dursleys are vile, the wizardly decision not to provide financial support for their care of Harry is not based upon this judgment, for the wizards provide no evidence that they have taken this into account.

The second issue is that of Ron Weasley. The Weasleys are poor. Why this should be so, this reader fails to understand: Mr. Weasley is a senior civil servant, the equivalent to a Whitehall "mandarin," a role that pays rather well in Britain. His two eldest boys are in well-paid and prestigious employment. Does he have a secret vice, gambling on Quidditch matches for example? But perhaps his poverty is a deliberate indication of his moral stature? If so, it is simplistic. Lloyd Alexander managed this much more effectively with a complex cast of characters whose relative wealth shaped their choices but did dictate their moral compass. Poverty in the Rowling books is all too often used as a shorthand for moral virtue; hence Harry is not simply neglected but positively starved. It is worth noting that Tom Riddle/Voldemort's poverty is less the issue than abandonment by his mother, which is continually contrasted by the loyalty of Harry's parents to their child.

Clearly the Weasleys act as Potter's moral compass, but there are still uncomfortable issues. For all his supposed generosity, Harry Potter does not often use his money to assist Ron. By this I do not mean extravagant presents, but it would be quite within Potter's power to give Ron birthday and Christmas presents that nicely judged his own spending power and Ron's desires. Instead, while we see Harry being given presents, we don't actually hear what he gives to others. His discomfort with his wealth is portrayed, but it remains a cozy, liberal discomfort, not the basis for action. This liberalism points us to another interpretation of the money issue: discussing money is not *polite* in Britain. Only the nouveaux riches (the Dursleys) and the arrogant (the Malfoys) either discuss money or regard it as an indicator of character. Consequently, as Merja Makinen has argued, what we may be reading is less the equation of poverty with moral value, than an assumption that those of genuine value disregard the presence or absence of money as a force in their worlds.[16]

Throughout the novels, there is a tendency for Harry's friends to defer to him. Both Hermione, who is brighter, and Ron, who is better acculturated, wait upon Harry's opinion to validate their actions. This is disguised, ironically, by the comments of Draco Malfoy on this very point. Malfoy operates as the competing prince, contending for attention, for the ideological agenda and for the right of inheritance (see *Chamber of Secrets*). Effectively, anything Malfoy sneers at must in reality be good, so that we are encouraged to disregard the way the world of friendship very literally spins around Harry. Note that Malfoy's relationship with his friends mirrors that of Harry—we are allowed to see them as courtiers, but because

16. Merja Makinen, e-mail to Farah Mendlesohn.

Hermione and Ron are nicer, and Harry less inclined to bully, it is easy to ignore the fact that the relationships are essentially the same. This is clearest in the first of the books, in which Harry's friendship with Hermione is grudging and his willingness to humiliate her in public is no better than Malfoy's treatment of his acolytes (*Sorcerer's Stone*, 148). But later, it becomes clear that Harry does not seek out friends. Ron, Hermione, Hagrid, Colin, and Dobby all seek out Harry, and two of these, Hagrid and Colin, are engaged in hero worship, reinforcing the sense that these are courtiers as much as friends. Dobby fits another, even more dubious role. If, as I have already argued, Harry's main quality as hero is to be the "decent chap," and Hagrid is his batman, then Dobby acts as the "admiring noble savage" whose role in the nineteenth and early twentieth centuries has been to assist such decent chaps out of scrapes while demonstrating their own emotional dependence.[17] I will return to this last point in the final section of this chapter because, as I will explain, it has disturbing ramifications.

But deference has a dual function. I have already discussed the extent to which it creates Harry as the character of the prince, but in addition it functions to create the mirage of social mobility. The message of the book is that both Hermione, the born outsider, and Ron, the socially marginal in an aristocratic world, can succeed and get ahead, but hidden in this is the extent to which their social success is dependent upon Harry. When Hermione refuses to speak to either of the boys in the first book (*Sorcerer's Stone*, 164, 171), it is she who is isolated by the decision, and it is partly pity (and, if we are less generous, need) that encourages Harry to reextend the hand of friendship. Again, Malfoy sees this clearly, consequently encouraging us to disregard it as a factor in the moral order of the novels, but we are shown very clearly in the tensions between Harry and Ron in the third book that Ron both gains and loses in the construction of his moral fiber by the extent to which his social prominence in the school is dependent upon Harry.

The situation with Hermione is more complex. She herself is much more anxious to make her own way, but we are continually shown her dependence on the social hierarchies. Throughout the book, Hermione is accepted in the social structure of the school only because she is Harry's friend. Some of this (as has been considered by Eliza Dresang elsewhere in this volume) is entirely an issue of gender. Hermione is the bossy know-it-all girl and thus doomed to be disliked by her peers. She can be liked only by association, or when she chooses to conform, and will never be permitted to be anything other than a second in command. But in *Goblet of Fire*, Hermione achieves separation from Harry and attention solely for herself. The attention she receives is predicated first on the magical equivalent of plastic

17. Moorcock, *Wizardry*, 76.

surgery (299, 405, 414), a gender issue of which I feel Rowling should be ashamed, and second, on the attention paid to her by the only figure presented as more exciting than Potter, Viktor Krum the Quidditch player. Leaving aside the issue that Hermione gains unconditional approval primarily via male attention (note my earlier comment that her efforts at intellectual self-improvement are often derided), the point needs to be made that she is also drawn into the cozy social world of wizardry by the approval of a high-status insider. Ron Weasley, despite his insider position, cannot validate her because *his* status is not high enough. The structure of social acceptance remains hierarchical.

School stories, however, are inevitably hierarchies, and it is pointless to criticize Rowling simply for her re-creation of this, although it should be pointed out that her decision to operate within these conventions is not inevitable. That archconservative Enid Blyton succeeded in creating a convincing pupil-run democracy in her *Naughtiest Girl* stories, which remains impressive to this day. However, the structure of authority within Hogwarts is informative in that it confirms the emphasis on essentially conservative social and fantastical structures.

At Hogwarts, Dumbledore, the headmaster, is the man in charge, but the final arbiters are the school governors, to whom Dumbledore owes deference and presumably on behalf of whom he runs the school (although there are some hints that the Ministry is in charge). However, while we are *told* that Dumbledore is responsible to the governors, in practice they appear to be in awe of him. Dumbledore is as much a deferential employee as was Merlin. The employee is more powerful than the employer. Our acceptance of this judgment is made palatable by the clearly greater wisdom that Dumbledore possesses and his insistence at the end of *Goblet of Fire* that he is championing the world against a dark threat. This is reinforced by two tactics: first, the retention of Snape, a man manifestly unsuited to be a housemaster—and his retention in this position is serious grounds to question Dumbledore's wisdom, as is his employment of Lockhart, whom he presumably taught—but whose real role is to highlight Dumbledore's fairness, or at least his willingness to cheat on behalf of Gryffindor House (but not, interestingly, for either Hufflepuff or Ravenclaw). The second tactic is to continually undermine Professor McGonagall, an extremely competent woman, presumably, to have reached such a position, but who is shown as prim where Dumbledore is broadminded, rigid where he is flexible, and unfair and hasty where Dumbledore is shown to be willing to listen and fair at least where Harry is concerned. It is possible to see in Dumbledore a parallel to Harry; both actually demonstrate little of their purported superiority, but both are presented against a background in which they emerge the moral victors. I will return to this point in greater detail, but nowhere is this clearer than in *Goblet of Fire,* where only Dumbledore does not tell Hermione that the elves wish to be slaves. His comment that she simply doesn't understand and is going about things the wrong way, and his employment of Dobby, make him seem radical in comparison, but the truth is this is only because his foils are so extreme. Finally, Dumbledore's power is only ever hinted at. He is as powerful as Voldemort but too noble to use this power: a balance which seems to equate active power (and perhaps knowledge) with evil and apparently validates both Dumbledore's and Harry's passivity. One question worth considering, however briefly, is whether this will allow Hermione to be cast as potentially evil. To what extent will her role be to be held in check by the less clever or powerful, but the more moral, Harry?

Because Dumbledore is all-wise, these books, for all that they are presented as children's books in the school tradition, actually limit childhood autonomy, cutting across the tradition that the school story trope offers space for children to test the boundaries and exert independence. Although Dumbledore is often passive in deeds, he is the individual who outlines the nature of the moral battle that is taking place, usually in his conversations with Harry, and at the end of the fourth book in his discussions with his colleagues. That Dumbledore fulfills the archetype of Gandalf is blindingly obvious but still significant in that it prepares us for Dumbledore's prophetic, galvanizing, and consolatory role at the end of *Goblet of Fire,* which might otherwise detract from the protagonist status of Harry. Instead, Harry and his friends, as the books proceed, increasingly find themselves involved in other people's concerns. In part this is a product of Rowling's desire to place Harry at the center of a global struggle, but whereas in conventional fantasy, such as Susan Cooper's *The Dark Is Rising* sequence, which similarly places children at the heart of a global battle between good and evil, the hero comes to act increasingly without adult support, in books three and four Harry is gathering around himself a coterie of adult protectors and champions including Dumbledore, Snape, Black, and Lupin, who seem to obviate the need for Harry to do anything.[18] This is evident in the denouement of the fourth book: Harry is assisted by adult ghosts until adult rescuers arrive. We don't immediately see this because, as I have already pointed out, natural immunity—rather than the range of skills which the fantasy hero usually develops—is praised as a sign of great bravery. The truth is that Harry could have done little beyond what he did. He was not asked to hold out against temptation because he was asked to give up nothing.

18. Note that the last two names are incredibly ham-fisted examples of foreshadowing: they indicate transformations that in *all* cases, whether as animagus or a werewolf bite, emerged after naming age.

Harry's life was in danger, but there was nothing *but* resistance he could offer. Nothing would have saved his life. We already knew that Harry had a natural talent for resisting the curse. Bravery is about choice, and Harry, in this situation, had no choices. If we were looking for the truly brave in *Goblet of Fire,* it is to Neville we should look.

Rowling's world of fantasy is one of hierarchy and prejudice. In the awe and wonder of the magical world, it is easy to miss the point that attitudes to the nonmagical range from contempt to at best patronizing curiosity. The debate between good and evil in these books has little to do with arguments for egalitarianism. Voldemort and his followers, who despise and wish to control all Muggles, are opposed not by espousers of Muggle liberty, equality, and fraternity, but by an understanding that Muggles are a naturally inferior species to be protected and cared for, if only because they occasionally throw up a magical "sport" like Lily Potter or Hermione. The debate is between slavery or house pet status, as evidenced by the passage of the Muggle Protection Act (*Chamber of Secrets,* 51).

The most tolerant attitude we are shown is that of Mr. Weasley, who finds Muggles, and their ways of managing without magic, intensely interesting, but who refuses to accept that in many ways Muggles are cleverer *because* they do not have magic. The very ignorance that the wizards display over Muggle activities is only explainable in terms of hierarchy. Wizards and Muggles live alongside each other. We are informed in book three that there is only one completely Muggle-free (that is, inhabited by wizards only) village. It is almost inconceivable, therefore, that wizards should be so ignorant of Muggle lifestyles. It only works if we frame it in terms of segregated and imperialist hierarchies, in which it is the norm that those who regard themselves as superior are oblivious to the lives of those they control: the madam in South Africa, the colonial governor in the Indian bungalow. All these people felt little need to understand those they ruled. The disrespect shown to Muggles is clearest in the fourth book: during the Quidditch tournament, no one seems to object to the alacrity with which Muggle minds are wiped. While this is obviously taken from the film *Men in Black,* it does not excuse the sense in which Muggle memories seem expendable and it is perfectly acceptable to control Muggles in ways that are explicitly condemned in book three. If any excuse is offered, it seems to be that Quidditch takes precedence over morality.

The position of Muggles in this construct begins as merely background, but by the end of the third book it is clear that the dispute over the treatment of Muggles is central to the political struggle between Voldemort and Dumbledore. In addition, all the evidence so far indicates that the dispute over Muggles extends into the treatment of other, *magical* creatures, and here I am aware that I am treading on very dangerous ground, for this is as yet an uncompleted work and some of what I suggest is happening may yet be negated in later books.

Although this is a magical world, not all magical creatures are equal. In reality we are in a world of apartheid in which magical creatures other than humans are denied wands (*Goblet of Fire,* 132) and are presumed guilty of a crime simply by being found in possession of one (which helps to explain Madame Maxime's reluctance to acknowledge her background) and in which some magical creatures are denied the rights to homes (see the "de-gnoming," *Chamber of Secrets,* 35–37, and note that these are *sentient* beings with language) and in which others are slaves.

The issue of slavery first appears in *Chamber of Secrets.* Dobby, a house-elf, serves a family he dislikes. It is *terribly* important, in the context of the fourth book, *Goblet of Fire,* that we are clear that a house-elf *cannot* leave of his own volition. If we relied entirely on the fourth book, it would be easy to see the house-elves as bound entirely by their own loyalties. They are not. In *Goblet of Fire,* Sirius will agree with Hermione that the way to measure a man is by his treatment of his inferiors, but he never questions the actual position of the elves or their duty to serve (525). Charm and graciousness to one's inferiors, as Ron demonstrates at Hogwarts (*Goblet of Fire,* 377), is the sign of a gentleman, but the dependence of one's inferiors, and their very inferiority, is taken for granted.

Dobby is freed by magical means: Harry ensures that his master presents him with a sock (*Chamber of Secrets,* 338), thus fulfilling the edict that house-elves are freed only if they are *given* clothes. Simply taking garments will not work, and the garments must come from their masters. Thus house-elves are tied in a kind of bondage that is peculiarly difficult to break even if they wanted (*Chamber of Secrets,* 28, 177). Self-liberation (unless Rowling changes the rules, which may happen) is explicitly denied. These slaves *cannot* produce a Harriet Tubman, but must wait instead on the dubious assistance of a William Lloyd Garrison, convinced of the power of moral suasion, or the reluctant intervention of a Lincoln. It is thus fortunate that, with the exception of Dobby, who according to Winky has "ideas above his station" (*Goblet of Fire,* 98), the house-elves do not wish to be freed.

Of the all the structures of authority within the Potter books, this is the one that I find most difficult to accept. Given the fact that the Potter books are not yet complete, I accept entirely the probability that by the end of the series the elves will be freed. Dumbledore's insistence that a moral victory can only be won morally and hence without the assistance of the Dementors seems to imply this (*Goblet of Fire,* 604). I also suspect that the elfish insistence on slavery will prove to be an elfish tactic entirely designed to help the right side win—which will of course make Dobby look irresponsible. In the meantime, however, we are presented with a world in which all the moral authorities appear to approve of slavery and in which the slaves are presented as happy, simple souls who merely wish to serve their families to the best of their ability. No one who has seen *Birth of A Nation* (1915) or *Gone With the Wind* (1939) could fail to recognize the resemblance between the relationship of Scarlett O'Hara and Mammy, and of "Master Barty" and Winky (*Goblet of Fire,* 683). Much of the plot of *Goblet of Fire* hinges on the loyalty of a house-elf—a mammy whose first loyalty is to her charge. House-elves seem not to be expected to have larger loyalties to abstractions such as good or evil. Their loyalties are only to their masters, and their enslavement absolves them from responsibility. Thus the house-elves, for all their competence, are infantilized. The image is reinforced by the characterization of Dobby as the "happy darky," making jokes, causing mischief, and of Winky, miserable when freed. Without some stories of elf rebellion, which might parallel the very real evidence that has survived from slave narratives and masters' reports, the images of Dobby and Winky neatly confirm Stanley Elkins's long-discredited argument for the Sambo complex, in which oppression creates a range of childlike behavior and remakes freedom into a punishment for the institutionalized.[19]

When Dobby reappears in *Goblet of Fire,* he is having a hard time. A free house-elf, he is discovering what Frederick Douglass discovered 150 years ago: a skilled slave is a desirable thing, but a skilled freedman is an unwanted troublemaker. Dobby cannot get work because he wants to be paid for it. This, if nothing else, demonstrates that Hermione is right. The whole system *rests* on the enslavement of elves. If this were not the case, someone like Mrs. Weasley, who bemoans the fact that she has no house-elf (*Chamber of Secrets,* 29), could at least supplement her household needs with paid elf labor. In the end, Dobby finds refuge at Hogwarts, but he is clearly a charity case. Further, his freed status is undermined both by the attitude of other elves and by the disparagement of what he buys. Somehow, Dobby's socks are more trivial than Harry's candy or broomstick repair kit. The contempt heaped on the way Dobby dresses parallels neatly the way "pickaninnies" and maidservants were mocked when they dressed up in what was available or created their own fashions away from the control of their masters (*Goblet of Fire,* 375–76). However, and to reinforce an earlier point, things could be worse for Dobby—he could be treated like a "common goblin" (*Goblet of Fire,* 98).

If it is in the nature of elves to be servants, why are they so clearly owned? Why can they not *choose* for whom they work as do the house

19. See Stanley M. Elkins, *Slavery: A Problem in American Institutional and Intellectual Life* (Chicago: University of Chicago Press, 1959); Herbert Aptheker, *American Negro Slave Revolts* (New York: International Publishers, 1963); William Loren Katz, *Breaking the Chains: African-American Slave Resistance* (New York: Atheneum, 1990).

spirits of tradition? But we are clearly shown that Hermione is wrong and that elves do not resent their slavery: while Dobby may be happy, Winky hates freedom. She is a "proper" house-elf and indicates her misery in her uncleanliness and drunkenness, proving that house-elves do not want freedom and servants should be kept away from alcohol: everyone knows that house-elves cannot cope on their own (*Goblet of Fire,* 377). When Dobby announces the joys of freedom, the other elves edge away from him. It is the only hint we have that he might be endangering them. The open implication is that they think he is mad. When they force the children out of the kitchen, one senses that nasty things may happen to Dobby (later in the book). It is also clear that the elves think Dobby should have stayed with his master, even though that master is bad (*Goblet of Fire,* 381).

Hermione, discovering that Hogwarts is run by house-elves, is incensed and determines to campaign for their freedom. Hermione's objection to the system of slavery on which the magical world rests seems entirely reasonable, yet, whatever Rowling's eventual intentions, Hermione is undermined at every turn with arguments straight from the American antebellum South. Ron argues that the house-elves are happy (*Goblet of Fire,* 125) and that they like being bossed around. Mr. Weasley claims to agree with Hermione but insists "now is not the time to discuss elf rights" (*Goblet of Fire,* 139) and has brought up at least one son, Percy, who believes that the only issue is that house-elves should be unswervingly loyal (*Goblet of Fire,* 154), while Fred warns Hermione not to talk to the elves as it will put them off their cooking (*Goblet of Fire,* 367). Hagrid, whose own position as a half giant opens him up to discriminatory assumptions, dismisses Dobby with "you get weirdoes in every breed." Hagrid feels it would be unkind to liberate the elves. It is "in their nature" to want to care for humans. And we know that Dumbledore is paying Dobby. Why can't he change the terms and conditions for all house-elves; he is supreme master at Hogwarts—or is Ron right that they don't want to be free? At best Dumbledore is a gradualist, like Jefferson, which is a fine position for the slave owner, but not so good for the slave. Further, Hermione is made to look very silly in her campaign (*Goblet of Fire,* 224–25), while Ron, with his continual emphasis that the elves like being slaves, seems to be the sane, mainstream one. Again, Hermione's assertion that the elves are brainwashed makes her look silly, and undercuts her basic argument (*Goblet of Fire,* 229). Whether intentionally or not, Rowling has replicated the 1860s opposition to immediatist abolitionism, making the liberators look extremist and the unhappy slaves the victims of "agents provocateurs." When Ron teases Hermione, his teasing is a conspicuous attempt to bully her into conforming (*Goblet of Fire,* 377). Whether it works is unclear, but Hermione herself is shown up as a hypocrite when she fails to question the provision of the tournament banquet (*Goblet of Fire,* 416–17).

The only indication that Rowling may be playing games with us is with Ron's casual comment: "We've been working like house-elves here" (*Goblet of Fire*, 223). It is obvious that Rowling wants a liberal approach—she is *not* advocating slavery—but it is the inconsistency of the liberal at work here. She cannot help but use the stereotypes and lacks the inventiveness of, say, the slave relationship in Diana Wynne Jones's *The Homewardbounders* (1981). However much the house-elves may turn out to be happy if they are freed, it will never take away the impression of "happy darky" that is created by the character of Winky. Unlike, for example, Gurgi, a superficially similar character in Alexander's Prydain sequence, there is little example of growth, or of humanity. And to conclude, while Rowling may well be seeking to educate children on the iniquities of slavery, the fact that house-elves absolutely cannot free themselves, but must be freed by others, creates a dynamic in which all justice must be offered from above, rather than taken from below.

Conclusion

The structure of J. K. Rowling's books is predicated upon a status quo and a formal understanding of authority in which hierarchal structures are a given. What is at stake, and potentially vulnerable, is never the hierarchy itself, but only he who occupies its upper reaches. Justice, in Rowling's world, rests first on "niceness": as long as the "proper" people are in charge, justice will be achieved without social upheaval or divisiveness. Radicalism, as embodied in Hermione, is irrational, ignorant, and essentially transient. Stasis and a conformity to a certain status quo bolster success, justice, and peace, whereas positive action to change matters is always ascribed at best to foolishness and at worst to evil intent. Thus the hierarchical structures actually support heroic passivity and deny the characters agency. But the second support for justice in the Potter books is "entitlement": those who are entitled through heredity appear to receive the greatest level of "justice," whether this be assistance in the House Cup, excusal from punishment, or survival through the death of others. This is disguised both by consolatory rhetoric and through the extension of "entitlement" to the friends of those entitled in a line of patronage clothed as friendship. The result is a muddled morality that cheats the reader: while the books argue superficially for fairness, they actually portray privilege and exceptionalism, not in the sense of "elitism" but in a specifically hereditarian context that protects some while exposing others; they argue for social mobility while making such mobility contingent on social connections, and they argue for tolerance and kindness toward the inferior while denying the oppressed the agency to change their own lives. In this they embody inherently conservative and hierarchical notions of authority clothed in evangelistic mythopoeic fantasy.

What Would Harry Do?

J. K. Rowling and Lawrence Kohlberg's Theories of Moral Development

Lana A. Whited, with M. Katherine Grimes

British writer J. K. Rowling's wildly famous character Harry Potter, star of four bestselling books so far, goes to school like any other child. However, the school he attends, Hogwarts School for Witchcraft and Wizardry, is unlike any real or "Muggle" school, for Harry and his classmates study subjects such as Transfiguration, Divination, Defense against the Dark Arts, Potions, History of Magic, and Care of Magical Creatures. Because of Harry's magical pursuits, the books have come under attack from the religious right, who fear that putting such notions as witchcraft into children's heads will lead youngsters away from the beliefs they are taught at home and in religious institutions, perhaps resulting in weakened morals and, consequently, inappropriate behavior. At the heart of conservative Christians' objections is what psychologists call "desensitization," the concern that exposure to something will lead to increased tolerance for it. Karen Jo Gounard of the Family Friendly Libraries group calls the Harry Potter series a "door-opener," implying that the books serve as a gateway into a taboo world that children might otherwise avoid or postpone encountering.[1] Conservative Christians also object to the dichotomy Rowling establishes between the Muggle and magical worlds. Compare Harry to Dudley Dursley, Minerva McGonagall to Petunia Dursley, or Hagrid to Vernon Dursley, and it isn't hard to decide whose side Rowling is on. In general, nonmagical characters are ciphers at best and villains at worst, inhabitants of a black-and-white world that contrasts sharply with the colorful magical world. To what child would the idea of flying around on a broom during gym class or changing oneself into a cat not appeal, if only imaginatively?

It is easy to trivialize such religious-based objections to the Harry Potter books, and, in fact, many writers, amateur and professional, have done so.

---

1. Quoted in Kimbra Wilder Gish, "Hunting Down Harry Potter: An Exploration of Religious Concerns about Children's Literature," 269.

For example, writing for the *Times* of London, India Knight says that the ban of the books by St. Mary's Island Church of England Primary School in Kent "proves, yet again, that some people would not know a marvelous role model if it turned round and bit them on the behind." In an appearance on Cable News Network's *Larry King Live,* Rowling spoke with less sarcasm but echoed the incredulity, as she said, "my feeling is that their objection is utterly unfounded." Some of those most vocal about kicking Harry Potter out of children's libraries and classrooms have not read the books, and those who would censor Rowling's books without reading them have a credibility problem that makes them an easy target, especially for intellectuals.[2]

While reconciliation between the Potter-banners and the censor-censurers is unlikely, it is important to note that the positions of both camps are predicated on the same basic premise: that reading is a powerful influence on the moral development of children and adolescents. Whether a person argues that a child reading the Harry Potter series is likely to plot the triumph of evil, like Voldemort, or to launch a personal campaign to promote the welfare of the disenfranchised, like Hermione, the underlying implication is that our own attitudes and behaviors are influenced by the experiences of characters we encounter in books. Voldemort and Albus Dumbledore are, after all, contraries, not contradictions. One opinion that meets with universal agreement is that it is good to see more children becoming regular customers at bookstores and libraries (also like Hermione), and even those who object to Rowling's books on religious grounds or who feel the books lack real literary merit acknowledge that Harry has drawn children's noses into books.

Perhaps, then, a more valuable exercise than condemning or championing the Harry Potter books would be to examine them in light of the examples of moral and ethical decision-making Rowling provides for young readers. Probably the most influential research on children's moral reasoning is that conducted by psychologist Lawrence Kohlberg at Harvard University in the 1960s and 1970s. Applying Jean Piaget's approach to cognition to the development of moral reasoning, Kohlberg's work resulted in a six-stage model. Kohlberg would probably maintain that, rather than mire in questions of what specific morals or values a child might derive from reading Harry Potter, we should consider what experiences of moral reasoning Rowling's books might offer young readers. Although Harry's dilemmas involve creatures and settings quite different from the "real" world, Rowling puts him in the position of deciding between or among quite realistic alternatives, and Harry's saga ultimately provides an effective illustration of Kohlberg's theories.

2. India Knight, "The Trouble with Harry"; J. K. Rowling, "The Surprising Success of Harry Potter."

Lawrence Kohlberg Meets Harry Potter

Educators and theorists in the field of education have debated since the time of Socrates the appropriateness of moral education in schools and the means of achieving it. Lawrence Kohlberg's doctoral research involved studying children's moral reasoning by confronting them with moral dilemmas, and he subsequently applied the theories he formulated from these and other studies to the school environment. Kohlberg conducted studies on moral reasoning with children and young adults, mostly boys. His general method was to present a child with a scenario involving a person facing a moral dilemma and then ask the child to discuss what the person should do and why. The scenario Kohlberg used most often has come to be known as "the Heinz dilemma":

> In Europe, a woman was near death from a special kind of cancer. There was one drug that the doctors thought might save her. It was a form of radium that a druggist in the same town had recently discovered. The drug was expensive to make, but the druggist was charging 10 times what the drug cost him to make. He paid $400 for the radium and charged $4,000 for a small dose of the drug. The sick woman's husband, Heinz, went to everyone he knew to borrow the money and tried every legal means, but he could only get together about $2,000, which is half of what it cost. He told the druggist that his wife was dying, and asked him to sell it cheaper or let him pay later. But the druggist said, "No, I discovered the drug and I'm going to make money from it." So having tried every legal means, Heinz gets desperate and considers breaking into the man's store to steal the drug for his wife.[3]

It is important to note that Kohlberg's main focus was the reasoning the child exhibited in attempting to resolve the dilemma, not the specific solution the child suggested. As Thomas Berendt, author of *Child Development,* explains, Kohlberg "would have had little interest in whether or not you thought Heinz should steal the drug. He would have been very interested in *why* you thought Heinz should or should not steal it."[4] So whether the child argued that Heinz should not steal the drug because he might get caught or that he should steal the drug because he needed his wife to cook for him, these responses would both typify reasoning at low levels, as they are based on what is best for Heinz and therefore exhibit reasoning primarily motivated by self-interest.

From this research, Kohlberg developed a scheme of moral maturation with three levels: Preconventional, Conventional, and Postconventional. In addition, each level has two stages; thus, there are six stages of development in all. The terms of the levels and stages are Kohlberg's.[5]

3. A. Colby and Lawrence Kohlberg, *Theoretical Foundations and Research Validation. Standard Issue Scoring Manual,* 1.
4. Thomas Berendt, *Child Development,* 614.
5. Kohlberg, *The Philosophy of Moral Development,* xxviii.

Level I: Preconventional
   Stage 1: Punishment and Obedience
   Stage 2: Instrumental Exchange
Level II: Conventional
   Stage 3: Interpersonal Conformity
   Stage 4: Social System and Conscience Maintenance
Level III: Postconventional
   Stage 5: Prior Rights and Social Contract
   Stage 6: Universal Ethical Principles

Moral Development at the Preconventional Level

The first level, the Preconventional, contains two stages. During the first, Punishment and Obedience, young children learn to do what adults and older children want them to do in order to avoid punishment. They adopt an attitude of "might makes right" because it seems the safest. If they can figure out what grown-ups want and do it, they can avoid punishment. Presented with the Heinz dilemma, children reasoning in stage one would say that Heinz should not steal the drug because he could be arrested and sent to jail or that he should steal the drug because he would probably get away with it. Either way, avoiding negative consequences is the key motivation.

The character in Harry Potter's world who best exemplifies stage one morality appears early in *Harry Potter and the Sorcerer's Stone,* sticking his head in the door of Harry's train compartment on the first trip to Hogwarts. He is Draco Malfoy, son of a Hogwarts board member. In the four Harry Potter books published so far, Malfoy never acts out of any motive except "my daddy's an important person so I can get away with this." In book one, Malfoy steals perpetual underdog Neville Longbottom's "Remembrall," a gadget sent to him by his grandmother to keep him from forgetting important things. When a professor appears, Malfoy finally returns the remembrall, muttering that he was "[j]ust looking" (*Sorcerer's Stone,* 145). When Neville subsequently breaks his wrist during his first broomstick practice, Malfoy makes fun of him, seizing the remembrall again and zooming off on his own broomstick. Harry finally intimidates Malfoy into dropping Neville's ball by threatening to knock him off his broomstick. Harry knows that the only tactic that will work with the bully is based on the reasoning that characterizes Kohlberg's stage one—"might makes right."

An adult character who illustrates the "might makes right" approach is Harry's uncle Vernon Dursley, in whose care Harry has been left after his parents' death. Dursley presumes that the strong-armed approach will work with Harry, at whom he roars, "I WARNED YOU! I WILL NOT TOLERATE MENTION OF YOUR ABNORMALITY!" (*Chamber of Secrets*, 2; emphasis Rowling's). The Dursleys lock Harry in a room under the stairs, thinking they will prevent him from practicing magic, and once, when Harry tries to leave, his uncle restrains him by grabbing his ankle. However, Dursley has misjudged Harry, for the young wizard is far beyond the "might makes right" stage, and he bides his time at the Dursleys', waiting out his tedious summer vacations broken only by occasional rescues by his magical friends. As an adult, Dursley is not actually in stage one himself, but he obviously thinks that Harry is and, therefore, that threatening his nephew will work.

Vernon Dursley's son Dudley, Harry's cousin, illustrates the second stage on Kohlberg's scale, Instrumental Exchange. During stage two, children do what they think they should in order to get what they want. A child learns to share his toys so that his playmate will share hers with him. The attitude is "you scratch my back; I'll scratch yours." An interesting example of stage two reasoning in Kohlberg's study was the Inuit child who said Heinz should steal the drug so that his wife could recover to cut his fish (i.e., prepare his food) for him. Alternately, a child in stage two might say Heinz should not steal the drug because he isn't the one who needs it.

At the second stage, children begin to understand the concept of fairness and can divide a treat such as candy equally among friends. Dudley Dursley, however, has no friends. Instead, he trades the behavior his parents want for their approval and favors, especially food. Not surprisingly, one of his first words is "won't!" (*Sorcerer's Stone*, 6). In *Harry Potter and the Chamber of Secrets*, Dudley taunts Harry by asking him why he hasn't gotten birthday cards from his school friends. When Harry responds angrily, frightening Dudley with stereotypical magic words such as "hocus, pocus," Dudley runs to his mother to tattle and is rewarded with an ice cream cone. Dudley appears in only two chapters of *Harry Potter and the Goblet of Fire*, by which time his gluttony has made him obese (27). Because he has outgrown the largest school uniform made, he is on a strict diet, allowed one quarter of a grapefruit for breakfast. Not surprisingly, he is usually out of sorts, and when the Weasleys arrive to collect Harry for the Quidditch World Cup and George and Fred drop toffees on the floor, Dudley sucks them up like a Hoover, unaware that they are charmed and will make his tongue swell. Even at age fourteen, Dudley's main interest is still what's in it for him.

Kohlberg found reasoning at the Preconventional level to be most common among children younger than nine. In *Sorcerer's Stone*, Harry and his classmates are eleven. Thus, even in the first book of the series, Draco Malfoy should be reasoning at the next level, the Conventional. However, even in *Harry Potter and the Prisoner of Azkaban* and *Harry Potter and the Goblet of Fire,* by which time students in Harry's year are thirteen and fourteen, respectively, Malfoy has achieved only stage two. In *Prisoner of Azkaban,* Draco stands by while the Ministry of Magic plans to behead a hippogriff that cut him because the boy disregarded appropriate handling practices. The creature's impending execution does not cause Malfoy any moral discomfort, as the boy knows his own injury will lead his father, a school governor, to call for the dismissal of Hagrid, one of Harry's protectors. Thus, Draco can bask in the limelight of his father's bullying. When, in *Goblet of Fire,* Hagrid introduces the students to another magical creature, the Blast-Ended Skrewt, Malfoy asks, "What's the point of them?" (196). The clear implication is "why should we take care of creatures if they don't do something for *us?*"—a question which illustrates stage two reasoning.

A frightening example of adults still functioning at the stage two level comes in the Quidditch World Cup section of book four. As the Dark Mark, the sign of Voldemort, is conjured in the night sky, a group of "Death Eaters" (Voldemort's supporters) terrorize a group of Muggles by floating them along over the campsite and enjoying their terror and humiliation, even turning one woman upside down, so that her underwear is revealed to gawkers below. The prejudice that fuels the Death Eaters' harassment of anyone who isn't a "pureblood" is also a stage two concept: if they can belittle everyone who isn't 100 percent wizard, those who are "pureblood" (or who think they are) can think they belong to a more exclusive group. That Draco Malfoy has adopted the stage two reasoning of his father and the other Death Eaters is apparent in *Chamber of Secrets* when he predicts that the attacks will get worse: "Bet you five Galleons the next one dies" (267). Malfoy has even thought of a way to benefit from his prediction— a wager.

Another adult who sometimes functions at the Preconventional level is Peter Pettigrew, called "Wormtail" in book four. Pettigrew is a former friend and schoolmate of Harry's father James Potter, and Harry learns in book three that it was Pettigrew who betrayed his parents by revealing their whereabouts to Lord Voldemort on the night they were killed. Confronted by Sirius Black and Remus Lupin (the remaining two members of James Potter's foursome), Pettigrew argues that he betrayed James and Lily Potter because Voldemort would have killed him if he had refused. This is a textbook example of stage one reasoning, practiced by someone who cannot be swayed by higher moral principles (such as loyalty to friends) because he is preoccupied with his own safety. Sirius Black knows Pettigrew well enough to see his real motivation: his loyalty to Voldemort gave him a sense of self-worth he previously lacked. Black had thought Pettigrew was the best confidence man for the Potters precisely because Peter seemed "a weak, talentless thing"; however, "Wormtail" regarded the betrayal of James and

Lily Potter as an opportunity to win Voldemort's favor, and in describing Pettigrew's motivation, Black articulates pure stage two reasoning: "you never did anything for anyone unless you could see what was in it for you" (*Prisoner of Azkaban*, 370).

Another good example of Pettigrew/Wormtail's stage two reasoning comes toward the end of *Goblet of Fire*, when Wormtail must mutilate his own arm to complete the cocktail of bone, flesh, and blood Voldemort needs to regenerate. The human flesh the Dark Lord needs must be volunteered, and in order to extract Wormtail's willingness, Voldemort has promised him a perfect arm later on. Voldemort keeps his promise several pages later, only after the Death Eaters have gathered round, evidence that he, too, is motivated by stage two reasoning; he chooses to heal Wormtail's arm in front of the other Death Eaters to reinforce their appreciation of his power (Voldemort fluctuates between this motive and the reasoning of stage one, "might makes right"). Although a reader might sometimes be inclined to argue that Wormtail serves Voldemort out of a stage three motive—loyalty—Voldemort knows better, telling Wormtail that he returned out of fear of Voldemort's allies, not loyalty (*Goblet of Fire*, 649).

Moral Development at the Conventional Level

The second level in Kohlberg's scheme is the Conventional. At this level, children begin to be much more aware of abstract concepts of morality and social expectations and to conform their actions to the conventions they perceive around them. Again, there are two stages. The first is Interpersonal Conformity. During this, the third stage, children learn to do what earns them praise. Being told "You're such a nice girl!" or "What a good boy you are!" is sufficient at this stage to elicit desired behavior from children. It is at this stage that motivation begins to be important to children and they understand that accidents with bad consequences (knocking over a glass of milk unintentionally, for example) are not wrong in the same way as intentional bad acts, such as knocking over a glass of milk in a fit of pique. At this stage, a child begins to be able to put himself or herself into another person's place in the sense of the Golden Rule. Children in stage three confronted with the Heinz dilemma would say that Heinz should steal the drug because it is for his wife, whom he is supposed to love, or that he should not take the drug because then people will think that he is an honest person. At this stage, adolescents and adults act in accordance with the expectations of others, as they perceive them.

Harry and his friends function comfortably at the stage three level. When he has just met Ron Weasley on the Hogwarts train, Harry buys a lot of candy to share with his new friend, whose family's modest means Harry has already perceived. In *Chamber of Secrets*, Harry, because of his celebrity, is given signed copies of a new professor's books, but he promptly gives them to Ginny Weasley, Ron's sister, perceiving that it will ease the family's burden of buying textbooks for five children. But Ginny and Ron are more privileged in another way: they share their large, loving family with Harry, and the Weasleys often provide Harry a hiatus from the drudgery of life at the Dursleys. In *Goblet of Fire,* when the school champions' families are invited to watch the third task, Harry is surprised when Molly and Bill Weasley (Ron's mother and brother) show up to serve as his surrogate relatives. In the same book, Harry clearly demonstrates a stage three motive, loyalty, when he regrets writing to his godfather, Sirius Black, about his scar hurting because he fears Black's return will put the fugitive in jeopardy. The only living person to whom Harry feels deeper loyalty than to Sirius Black is his headmaster, Albus Dumbledore. In fact, at the end of *Chamber of Secrets,* Harry is able to defeat a basilisk that has been terrorizing the school when Dumbledore's phoenix, Fawkes, arrives to assist him. Dumbledore tells Harry after the ordeal that only a demonstration of "real loyalty" could have summoned the bird. Dumbledore notes the fidelity associated with the phoenix on several occasions (*Chamber of Secrets,* 332, 207).

However, while Harry usually functions at the stage three level (or higher), he at least once reverts to stage two thinking; when he is inside the maze attempting the third task in *Goblet of Fire,* he hears Fleur Delacour scream and briefly thinks, *"One champion down"* (*Goblet of Fire,* 625). Harry's reaction to Fleur's distress as something advantageous to him is a temporary regression, probably induced by stress.

In *Exploring Harry Potter,* Elizabeth D. Schafer argues that Hermione and Ron serve as Harry's Knights of the Round Table or Merry Men, and they "appear unremarkable . . . stereotypical of most children their age."[6] It is clear by Halloween of their first year at Hogwarts that the three will be loyal to each other, when Harry and Ron battle a troll to rescue Hermione, and she lies—says she was stalking it because she'd read about trolls in books—to deflect blame from her friends. "[F]rom that moment on," Rowling writes, "Hermione Granger became their friend" (*Sorcerer's Stone,* 178–79).

Although one would have to take issue with Schafer's characterization of the intelligent, well-read Hermione as "unremarkable," Ron does seem "stereotypical," particularly where his moral reasoning is concerned. In fact, Ron is perhaps the best example of stage three reasoning in the Harry Potter series, as loyalty is his preeminent virtue. In *Sorcerer's Stone,* although he has known Harry only a few weeks, Ron is prepared to serve as Harry's second in a wizard's duel with Draco Malfoy, a role he has to explain: "A

6. Elizabeth D. Schafer, *Exploring Harry Potter,* 51.

second's there to take over if you die." In the climax of the same novel, Ron demonstrates that he is a worthy second when, in the human chess match, he allows himself to be captured by the white queen so that Harry can checkmate the king and get through a passageway and on with their search for the Sorcerer's Stone (154, 283).

At the stage three level, much importance is placed on interpersonal relationships, as Ron demonstrates when Harry discovers his parents in the magical Mirror of Erised and Ron begs to look in the mirror, too. The value Ron places on loyalty to those he loves is often clearest when he perceives that others are disloyal. For example, in *Goblet of Fire*, Ron stops speaking to Harry for a few months after Harry's name is selected by the Goblet of Fire for the Triwizard Tournament. Ron refuses to believe that Harry didn't break the tournament rule about eligibility and enter himself, and, although Hermione explains away Ron's reaction as jealousy, Ron more likely feels that Harry made a decision which excluded him. Only after Ron watches Harry confront the dragon, when he realizes the real danger his best friend faces by virtue of being selected a champion, does he come around. In the same book, when Hermione shows interest in the Durmstrang champion Victor Krum, Ron lectures her that she is *"fraternizing with the enemy"* (*Goblet of Fire*, 421; emphasis Rowling's). When Hermione assures Ron that Harry is secure in her loyalty and that the point of the tournament is the opportunity to mingle with young people from other schools, Ron reverts to stage two: "No it isn't! It's about winning!" (*Goblet of Fire*, 423). This temporary regression aside, throughout the four volumes published so far, Ron seldom acts out of a motive other than loyalty, a classic stage three trait.

Ron Weasley also illustrates conventional moral reasoning when it comes to social norms. He is hesitant to join Hermione's campaign for the house-elves' welfare, arguing a rationalization commonly used to defend slavery: that the elves not only accept but welcome their servitude and, furthermore, would be lost without their masters (*Goblet of Fire*, 224). Later, he explains to Harry the prejudice against half giants, an attitude he has clearly internalized: "they just like killing, everyone knows that" (*Goblet of Fire*, 430). Even at fourteen, in his fourth year at Hogwarts, Ron largely borrows his ethics from the society around him rather than forming them for himself.

As Hermione's attitude about the Triwizard Tournament makes clear, she also demonstrates the interpersonal emphasis of stage three. She values her friendships, and she shares her remarkable knowledge with Ron and Harry, because she is better at school than any of the other children in her year and because, as a lover of books and knowledge, she is eager to share them with others. Hermione's association with Victor Krum in *Goblet of Fire* effectively demonstrates the value she places on interpersonal relationships—to wit, that a friendship with someone she likes is more important to her than the interschool competition Victor and Harry are engaged in.

But a more problematic aspect of Hermione's character has been pointed out by several writers. Often, in moments of real danger, Hermione becomes emotional, sometimes bursting into tears. As Harry and Ron fight off a troll early in their first year, Hermione, nearly faint, shrinks against a wall, then sinks to the floor in fright and remains there while the boys dispense with the troll. In the climax of *Sorcerer's Stone,* Harry urges Hermione to return to Ron as Harry moves on through passageways, anticipating a confrontation with Severus Snape and, possibly, Lord Voldemort, and Rowling describes a stereotypically feminine reaction, as, lip trembling, Hermione embraces Harry and declares, "Harry—you're a great wizard, you know . . . oh Harry—be *careful!*" (286–87). When Harry and Ron begin speaking to each other again after the first task in *Goblet of Fire,* Hermione "burst[s] into tears" (358). Cultural critic Christine Schoefer writes in *Salon,* "Like every Hollywood damsel in distress, Hermione depends on the resourcefulness of boys and repays them with her complicity. . . . Again and again, her emotions interfere with her intelligence, so that she loses her head when it comes to applying her knowledge."[7] It isn't difficult to see that Hermione's emotional, often cheerleaderish manner would grow old with feminist readers. She is always there, after Harry drags himself out of another peril, to say something along the lines of "Harry, you were brilliant!" (*Goblet of Fire,* 358).

Hermione's emotional devotion to Harry touches on what has been the primary objection to Lawrence Kohlberg's work, a complaint described by his protégé and colleague Carol Gilligan, author of *In a Different Voice: Psychological Theory and Women's Development* (1982). Gilligan criticized Kohlberg's methodology because the subjects of his interviews were all male and he generalized, from their responses, theories about the moral development of people in general. Gilligan felt, as Kohlberg himself explains, "that morality really includes two moral orientations: first, the morality of justice as stressed by Freud and Piaget and, second, an ethic of care and response which is more central to understanding female moral judgment and action than it is to the understanding of judgment and action in males." Gilligan and Kohlberg's disagreement is essentially over whether stage three reasoning, based on an "ethic of care," is inferior to stage four reasoning, based on an "ethic of justice." Gilligan's allegation, in other words, is that Kohlberg considered reasoning whose basis is the individual welfare of friends and loved ones as inferior to reasoning based on the concept of justice for all

7. Christine Schoefer, "Harry Potter's Girl Trouble."

society. This disagreement is not likely to be resolved, as it touches on age-old stereotypes of the sexes and as subsequent theorists who got involved in trying to argue one position or the other, such as Lawrence Walker and Diana Baumrind, tended to line up along gender lines.[8]

However, the application of Gilligan's objection is significant to the criticism of Hermione. One might well ask whether those who criticize her emotionalism, particularly her enthusiastic support of Harry, side with Kohlberg in the debate, viewing Harry's attempts to keep the dark forces in check as superior to, for example, Hermione's attention to the feelings of Neville Longbottom. In *Sorcerer's Stone,* when Hermione decides to petrify Neville rather than risk his following her, Harry, and Ron, she first apologizes to Neville (273). Hermione, in fact, often combines stage three motives with higher-order reasoning, as we shall see. She is also smart enough to know that different levels of reasoning work with different people. For example, when she has known Harry and Ron only a few weeks, she instructs them that they should stay in their own house after curfew rather than exploring the castle because otherwise they would surely be detected and Gryffindor would lose points. Thus, she considers the boys' late-night excursions "very selfish" (*Sorcerer's Stone,* 154). Although earning points in the inter-House competition is more mercenary than Hermione's usual motivation, she clearly expects Ron and Harry's loyalty to Gryffindor to keep them in check.

Kohlberg thought that, while most children move to the conventional level around the age of nine, some adults never move beyond it. Like the real world, the realm of Hogwarts and the Muggle world beyond provide plenty of examples of adults still in stage three. With the exceptions of when he is acting forcefully toward Harry (stage one) and when he orchestrates a dinner party for his boss in order to make the biggest deal of his career (stage two), Vernon Dursley generally functions at the level of Interpersonal Conformity. He is obsessed with what other people think of him, which explains why the owls continuously bringing Harry mail in book one concern him. In book four, he is anxious to know whether the Weasleys will be stopping by to pick up Harry in a car, fearing that they will employ some mode of wizard transportation that calls attention to them all. In fact, it is almost as though harboring a wizard in his home violates Mr. Dursley's concept of *himself,* as he forbids any mention of Harry's "abnormality."

In *Goblet of Fire,* the reader encounters a character who, in order to preserve his social standing, paid a very heavy price—his own son. In a flashback scene involving a magical device, Harry learns that Bartemius Crouch,

8. Lawrence Kohlberg, *The Psychology of Moral Development,* 339; Lawrence Walker, "Sex Differences in the Development of Moral Reasoning: A Rejoinder to Baumrind"; Diana Baumrind, "Sex Differences in Moral Reasoning: Response to Walker's Conclusion That There Are None."

a Ministry of Magic official, allowed his son to be sent to Azkaban, the dreadful wizard prison where repulsive creatures called Dementors suck out people's souls, rather than risk humiliation by attempting to defend him. Fortunately for Crouch, he can betray his son while giving the impression that his motivation is at the stage four level of observing rules—in this case, not making an exception for his own son. But his true motivation, as Harry learns, is his own reputation, a stage three concept. Another adult character who conforms her actions to the opinions of others is Madame Maxime, head of Beauxbatons School, who will not admit her ancestry—even to Hagrid, who fancies her—because of the prejudice against half giants. Finally, it is interesting that even the two house-elves who emerge as individual characters act at the stage three level: Winky, who does not want to behave in a manner disappointing to her employer, Barty Crouch, even after he has fired her, and Dobby, who, out of loyalty, supplies Harry with the gillyweed he needs for the second task of the Triwizard Tournament.

At the second stage of the Conventional level, adolescents and young adults believe in what our report cards once called "citizenship": obeying rules and laws in order to maintain harmony in society. This is called the Social System and Conscience Maintenance stage; a person in it has moved beyond doing good only in interpersonal relationships and desires to maintain a more abstract social order. Stage four–based arguments about the Heinz dilemma might be that Heinz should not steal the drug because the right of the pharmacist to his own property must be preserved if society is to be orderly or, alternately, that "Heinz should steal the drug because people must be willing to save others if society is to survive."[9] "Conscience," in stage four reasoning, becomes the internalization of society's dictates and precepts; this is the principle that Freud called the superego. Usually adherence to the social order results in good, but when citizens obey the law no matter what that law is, we have horrors such as the Holocaust.

By far, the character who best illustrates this level is Percy Weasley, a Hogwarts prefect and, later, employee of the Ministry of Magic. "Percy loves rules," says Ron in *Goblet of Fire,* and that is a perfect statement of stage four reasoning (534). (In fact, Ron alleges that if Percy knew the story of Mr. Crouch's son, he would argue that Crouch had to let his son go to Azkaban or risk accusations that he had bent the rules.) Percy is a perfect candidate for prefect, and he is proud of the badge that designates him as a guardian of rules, sometimes appearing from his dormitory to investigate nighttime mischief with the badge fastened to his bathrobe. After serving as Head Boy during his final year at Hogwarts, Percy moves on, in *Goblet of Fire,* to a Ministry of Magic office, where one of his first tasks is studying whether the regulations governing cauldron thickness are sufficient. He is

9. Berendt, *Child Development,* 616.

equally loyal to the rules outside Hogwarts, as he argues with Hermione that Mr. Crouch's house-elf, Winky, should obey her master strictly because of his rank within the Ministry (154).

That spat aside, Percy gets along with Hermione better than almost anyone else, as Rowling herself observes (*Goblet of Fire,* 141). This is true because Hermione is, herself, quite rule-bound, fearing above all else that she, Harry, or Ron will be asked to leave the school. When Harry and Ron sneak out of the Gryffindor common room for a midnight duel with Draco Malfoy in *Sorcerer's Stone,* Hermione, clad in her bathrobe, invokes rules and authority, threatening to tell Percy, who is a prefect (155). When Harry turns Malfoy into a ferret early in *Goblet of Fire,* Hermione cuts short Ron's enjoyment with her observation that Professor McGonagall was right to intervene, as Malfoy could have been injured (207). When Neville reports that Malfoy has been terrorizing him, Hermione urges him to tell Professor McGonagall (*Sorcerer's Stone,* 218). After Harry writes to Sirius to say that he probably only imagined his scar hurting, Hermione upbraids him for lying (*Sorcerer's Stone,* 229). Her tendency to point out violations of the rules extends even to the Hogwarts faculty. For example, when their fourth-year Defense Against the Dark Arts teacher, Professor "Mad-Eye" Moody, announces that he will subject each student to the Imperius Curse, Hermione objects, "but you said it's illegal, Professor" (*Goblet of Fire,* 230). Hermione is destined to be Head Girl.

Because Harry understands the importance of order in his society, he obeys the rules of the magic world even when he is sorely tempted to break them. We see this at the beginning of *Chamber of Secrets* when the Dursleys have imprisoned his snowy owl, Hedwig, cutting off any hope of communication with his friends from Hogwarts. Despite his loneliness and his awareness of the owl's misery, he does not disobey the prohibition against using magic in the Muggle world. Harry's internalization of the rules of the magic world cause him confusion in *Sorcerer's Stone* during the first day of flying practice. Although his teacher, Madam Hooch, has forbidden the children to fly while she is gone, Draco Malfoy ascends on his broomstick while playing keep-away. Because Draco has Neville's Remembrall, Harry flies after him, observed by Professor McGonagall. Although Malfoy is scolded for disobeying, McGonagall is so impressed by Harry's flying ability that, instead of punishing him, she praises him and suggests that he might assume a prominent position on his house's Quidditch team. Despite his pleasure, Harry is confused by her disregard of a rule that her colleague made.

Harry and his friends also have the ability to prioritize rules. For example, in *Chamber of Secrets,* after Ron and Harry miss the Hogwarts Express at the beginning of the term, they decide to fly Mr. Weasley's car. Although Mr. Weasley has broken a Ministry of Magic rule in making the car flyable and could get in trouble with the Misuse of Muggle Artifacts Office if Ron and Harry are seen, Ron reasons that they must use the car in order to observe another rule: they are due at school, and even wizards-in-training can use magic to get out of a jam (69). It is noteworthy that Ron's reasoning is a justification *not* for breaking a rule but for how their use of the car might not be perceived as a violation. As such, it is an example of stage four or rule-observant reasoning.

The importance of rules is underscored in the Harry Potter novels by the presence of a number of authorities, most notably the Hogwarts faculty and officials of the Ministry of Magic. With few exceptions, Harry's professors enforce rules and deduct points from the houses of students who break them. Even Severus Snape, whose behavior toward Harry is somewhat mysterious, is a strict guardian of rules where Harry is concerned, if only because of the delight he takes in penalizing Harry and his friends when they break them (Snape is less vigilant about the behavior of his Slytherin House charges). In fact, the more famous Harry becomes, the more Snape seems to delight in having leverage over him; in *Goblet of Fire,* Snape reminds Harry that no matter how much publicity the young wizard attracts, he is "nothing but a nasty little boy who considers rules to be beneath him" (516). That Ministry of Magic officials are rigid about rules is apparent in *Prisoner of Azkaban,* when they plan the execution of the hippogriff Buckbeak because he assaulted Draco Malfoy, regardless of arguments about how Malfoy provoked him. Harry is allowed to participate in the Triwizard Tournament even though he's underage because, as Barty Crouch confirms, it is a ministry rule that anyone whose name comes out of the Goblet of Fire competes for the championship. Percy Weasley's study of cauldron thickness in *Goblet of Fire* also suggests the specificity of the ministry's regulations. Finally, the presence of Quidditch matches in all the books adds another layer of rules to Harry's environment. Sports is a notoriously rule-bound realm, and Quidditch is more complicated than most. All these aspects of the Harry Potter books suggest that Harry and his friends function in an environment where rules are prominent and important.

Moral Development at the Postconventional Level

Some adolescents and most adults reach a third level in their moral development, at which point they are willing to break rules if they feel a higher principle is at stake. Kohlberg called this level the Postconventional. Reasoning in this stage goes beyond what one is taught into a kind of morality that one discovers, even crafts, for oneself. Again, Kohlberg postulates two stages. Stage five is called Prior Rights and Social Contract. During this penultimate stage, people realize that rules and laws exist for mutual benefit and by mutual agreement—what Abraham Lincoln called "government of the people, by the people, and for the people." Thus, when the laws are unfair or when one side doesn't keep its bargain in an agreement, the contract no longer binds and the laws should be overthrown or even disobeyed. The attitude of a person in stage five is generally utilitarian. Henry David Thoreau explains this concept in "Civil Disobedience." So does Thomas Jefferson in "The Declaration of Independence." The Civil Rights movement was based entirely on this idea.

With regard to the Heinz dilemma, a person reasoning at the stage five level would be most likely to say that Heinz should steal the drug because preserving his wife's life is a higher good than obeying the law or, as Thomas J. Berendt puts it, "the right to life takes precedence over any person's right to property." Berendt maintains that an adult reasoning at the stage five level "should *not* say that Heinz should not steal the drug."[10] The principled rule-breaking characteristic of stage five is very different from the rule-breaking of twins Fred and George Weasley, which is motivated only by what amuses them or gets them something they want (generally stage two motives).

Kohlberg asserts that a few people reach a final stage, Universal Ethical Principles, in which they realize that some moral truths are absolute, that there is a higher law that should be obeyed. Martin Luther King makes this argument in "Letter from Birmingham Jail" in his distinction between just and unjust laws: "A just law is a man-made code that squares with the moral law or the law of God. An unjust law is a code that is out of harmony with the moral law. . . . An unjust law is a human law that is not rooted in eternal law and natural law." The "Universal Declaration of Human Rights" also acknowledges this concept. However, some theorists believe that no one except Jesus and a few other important religious figures have ever reached this stage; other theorists think that Gandhi, Mother Teresa, and Martin Luther King also reached it.[11]

It is important to note, however, that Kohlberg did not provide useful examples of stage six morality as distinct from stage five. Berendt theorizes that this is because none of the young men in Kohlberg's longitudinal study achieved a level beyond stage five; thus, he and his colleagues were not able to incorporate guidelines for identifying stage six reasoning into their scoring manual. Berendt concludes that "researchers are left, in practice, with only one Postconventional stage of moral reasoning"; thus, this discussion of Postconventional reasoning will be somewhat generalized but mostly confined to examples at the stage five level.[12] The salient point is that

10. Ibid., 616.
11. Kohlberg, *Philosophy,* xxviii and 409–12, and Kathleen Stassen Berger, *The Developing Person through the Life Span,* 347–48.
12. Kohlberg, *Philosophy,* 617.

reasoning which advocates rule-breaking in observance of universal and inviolable ethical principles occurs at the very highest level that Kohlberg and his associates could identify.

J. K. Rowling provides Harry with two models of behavior at the Post-conventional level, at least one of whom may be at Kohlberg's nebulous stage six: the falsely accused Sirius Black, who is Harry's godfather, and his remarkable headmaster, Albus Dumbledore.

Of course, Harry's most significant mentor is Dumbledore, a figure almost universally revered in the wizarding world. When Dumbledore is temporarily suspended and called to the Ministry of Magic at the height of the mysterious and terrible attacks in *Chamber of Secrets,* the reaction underscores the esteem in which he is held. While he is away, an atmosphere of near hysteria pervades Hogwarts, and the minister himself, Cornelius Fudge, declares that if Dumbledore can't stop the attacks, the situation may be hopeless (263). Part of Dumbledore's effectiveness with young people is that he, like Lawrence Kohlberg, is much more concerned with *why* students behave as they do than with the behavior itself. At the end of *Sorcerer's Stone,* Harry learns that Dumbledore does not subscribe to one of the most prevalent codes among magical folk, that Voldemort should be called "He-who-must-not-be-named." Instead, Dumbledore instructs Harry, "Call him Voldemort. . . . Always use the proper name for things. Fear of a name increases fear of the thing itself" (298). The prohibition on Voldemort's name might seem a stage four concept—keeping the wizarding world intact by not invoking the name of its primary threat—but it is actually grounded in superstition, a stage one concept, having at its base the need for self-preservation. Nevertheless, it is a significant example for Harry of his headmaster's willingness to go against the grain.

In the four books published so far, Dumbledore gives Harry and his friends plenty of instruction in knowing when and how to break the rules. At the end of *Chamber of Secrets,* after Ginny Weasley has unknowingly allowed Voldemort access to the castle through her involvement with Tom Riddle's diary, her father gives her a typical "I've warned you about this" authoritarian lecture. Dumbledore, however, reasoning that Ginny has suffered enough and that Voldemort has duped more experienced wizards, declines to punish her (330). Then he turns to Harry and Ron, who fully expect to be expelled because they and Hermione have violated a number of school rules, including stealing items from Professor Snape's office to make a Polyjuice Potion. But Dumbledore, grateful that the students have rid the castle of the basilisk and the more dangerous threat of Voldemort's return, declares that his threat to them simply illustrates that authority figures must sometimes suspend the rules. Instead of expulsions, Harry and Ron get awards and points for their house (330–31).

In their third year, Dumbledore presents Harry and Hermione with the opportunity to be agents of justice. Confronted with the impossibility of convincing the Ministry of Magic authorities of Sirius Black's innocence, Dumbledore authorizes Hermione and Harry to use a nearly always forbidden form of magic—turning back time in order to change events—to alter Black's fate. The sanctity of the rule he is allowing them to break is reinforced by his admonition, *"You—must—not—be—seen"* (*Prisoner of Azkaban*, 393). Using an hourglass-like gadget that Hermione has been allowed so that she can enroll in simultaneous classes, the two young people reenact the events of the previous three hours, realizing in the interval that they can also save Buckbeak from execution. The hippogriff, a cross between a horse and an eagle, becomes, by virtue of its ability to fly, the agent of Sirius Black's escape, and Harry and Hermione return to the castle, undetected, just in the nick of time. Albus Dumbledore, the man charged by the Ministry of Magic with the responsibility of enforcing Hogwarts' rules, not only allows Harry and Hermione to break a nearly inviolable precept but also *tells them how to do it.* His actions are guided by a motive not unlike Martin Luther King's, the notion that man-made (or, in this case, wizard-made) laws can be broken if a higher moral law, such as justice, is at stake.

At the conclusion of *Goblet of Fire*, Voldemort's return to a physical form prompts Dumbledore to violate more regulations or conventions. Minister of Magic Cornelius Fudge expresses reluctance to enlist the giants' aid because of the prejudice against them, fearing that he would be ousted from his position. Fudge's motive is a combination of stage three ("What will people think of me?") and stage two ("What will it cost me?"). Dumbledore responds with a stage five argument, that "it matters not what someone is born, but what they grow to be!" and then, probably realizing that stage five reasoning will not work with Fudge, dangles a stage two carrot: that if Fudge follows Dumbledore's advice, the wizarding community will remember him as one of the top ministers of magic ever (*Goblet of Fire*, 708).

Another principle Dumbledore appears to hold as universal is honesty. The value he places on truth is established in *Sorcerer's Stone* when Harry approaches him with questions about Voldemort. Dumbledore tells him that truth "is a beautiful and terrible thing, and should therefore be treated with great caution." There are some questions he will not be able to answer for good reasons, he says, adding, "I shall not, of course, lie" (298). At the conclusion of the Triwizard Tournament, Dumbledore reinforces the high value he places on honesty in announcing to the student body that Cedric Diggory was killed by Voldemort. Aware that the Ministry of Magic and many students' parents will frown on his disclosure, Dumbledore reasons that the truth and Cedric's legacy require his candor—and he explains his reasoning to students. Facing the prospect of Voldemort's return, Dumbledore becomes Winston Churchill, delivering a "we are all facing dark and difficult times" speech to prepare his pupils for the coming battle with the forces of evil (*Goblet of Fire*, 723–24). As Churchill stood in the House of Commons and implored his fellow Brits to behave in the Battle of Britain so that subsequent generations would be able to say "This was their finest hour,"[13] Dumbledore urges the students that "if the time should come when [they] have to make a choice between what is right and what is easy" they should "Remember Cedric Diggory" (724). It is interesting that, in preparing the young wizards for the battle ahead, Dumbledore focuses on how to conduct oneself at the moment of moral decision-making. It is abundantly clear by the end of *Goblet of Fire* how well Albus Dumbledore is preparing his charges—Harry, especially—for their roles in the conflict between good and evil.

Toward the end of *Prisoner of Azkaban*, Harry gains a second mentor when he discovers that Sirius Black is his godfather. When Black confronts Peter Pettigrew about betraying Harry's parents, Pettigrew's reply reveals his "what's-in-it-for-me" reasoning: "[W]hat was there to be gained by refusing [Voldemort]?" Black screams, "Only innocent lives, Peter!" When Pettigrew protests that, had he refused to tell Voldemort where the Potters were, Voldemort would have killed him, Black retorts, "THEN YOU SHOULD HAVE DIED . . . RATHER THAN BETRAY YOUR FRIENDS!" (374–75). It is important to point out that Black urges the protection not merely of one's friends, a motive which might evidence stage three reasoning, but of an abstract concept: innocence. This is certainly stage five reasoning, possibly stage six.

Toward the end of *Prisoner of Azkaban*, Harry himself moves toward the realm of stage five reasoning. He is presented with an opportunity to kill Peter Pettigrew, the person who, rather than the falsely suspected Sirius Black, betrayed Harry's parents and consequently caused their deaths. Despite the fact that Harry feels he should want to kill Pettigrew, he is incapable of this action. And when two of James Potter's old schoolmates volunteer to kill Pettigrew themselves, Harry finally intervenes to spare his parents' Judas and instead turns him over to the prison authorities. Pettigrew grovels at Harry's knees, but Harry quickly upbraids him. He is not exercising mercy, the young wizard notes; rather, his motivation is his awareness that James Potter would not have wanted his son and his friends "to become killers" just to exact revenge on Peter Pettigrew (376). It is interesting that as Harry perceives a stage five concept—killing a person is wrong because it makes the perpetrator a killer—he reverts to a stage three motive: my duty as a son is to do what my father would have me do. He is

13. Winston Spencer Churchill, speech before the British House of Commons.

not yet mature enough to function completely at stage five (as many adults in the books and in real life never are), but he clearly shows potential to do so—at the age of thirteen. (Kohlberg theorized that adults who achieve Postconventional reasoning usually do so *after* age twenty-five.)[14]

By the time he arrives at Hogwarts for his fourth year, Harry demonstrates that his reasoning at the Postconventional level in *Prisoner of Azkaban* was more than a fluke. When he realizes that all the champions except Cedric Diggory know that the first task in the Triwizard Tournament will involve confronting dragons, Harry finds an opportunity to tell him. When Cedric expresses surprise, Harry explains that fairness can only be achieved if all four champions know the task ahead, so that they are "on an even footing." Harry's instinct is validated a page later when Professor Moody praises his decision to tell Cedric about the task. Further evidence that the fairness principle is worth upholding comes when Cedric returns the favor by giving Harry a clue about the second task. During that task, when Harry is about to free his hostage (Ron) from the merpeople and ascend to the surface of the lake, he notices that Beauxbatons champion Fleur Delacour's sister is still a hostage with Fleur nowhere in sight and time running out. So he frees Ron *and* the little girl and drags *both* to the surface. When Ron derides Harry for thinking the girl was actually at risk, Harry protests that he couldn't be expected to leave a child in danger. Although he later learns that Ron is right, Harry's action is heroic, based on his assessment of the situation and the fact that the gillyweed helping him breathe underwater is losing effect. During the third task, when he hears a scream he thinks is Fleur's, he unselfishly stops to look for her, before reverting to the stage two reaction, "One champion down." His self-centeredness doesn't last long, however, for a short while later, when he and Cedric emerge almost simultaneously into the clearing where the Triwizard Cup stands, Harry's reaction is not to grab it but to say to Cedric, "Go on, take it. You're there." Cedric instead urges Harry to take the cup, and, when Cedric initially steps into the clearing, instead of claiming the cup immediately, he turns at the sound of Harry's battling a giant spider to see whether Harry has been hurt. Finally, the two boys, agreeing on what they perceive to be a higher good—a victory for Hogwarts—decide to take the cup together (*Goblet of Fire*, 341, 342, 503, 625, 632). Their ability to put the welfare of others before the glory of the Triwizard Championship and each boy's willingness to admit that the other may be more deserving of the cup is, particularly to those of us in the sports-crazed culture of the United States, quite amazing. If Ron were present, a reader knows what he would say to Harry: "Are you crazy? Get the Cup!"

14. Berendt, *Child Development,* 616.

Like Harry, Hermione is also functioning comfortably at the Postconventional level by their fourth year at Hogwarts. In fact, Hermione functions more consistently at that level, with fewer regressions, than any other character who is not an adult. That Hermione is willing to break rules for what she perceives to be a higher good is clear from her willingness to mix the Polyjuice Potion necessary to solving the mystery of Tom Riddle's identity in *Chamber of Secrets,* as well as from her use of the Time-Turner in *Prisoner of Azkaban* to attend classes that meet simultaneously and then to save Buckbeak and Sirius Black. (It should be noted that Hermione's use of the Time-Turner is technically approved, first by Professor McGonagall and then by Albus Dumbledore, but it is still a device that is ordinarily forbidden; thus, her conspirators insist on secrecy.)

In *Goblet of Fire,* Hermione moves on to challenge a standard rule of the wizarding world—that house-elves work as unpaid servants. When she establishes her Society for the Protection of Elfish Welfare (S.P.E.W.), she declares that wizards have been abusing elves for centuries and that she can't believe that elf servitude wasn't abolished before her time. Hermione's crusade is a clear allusion to slavery and worker's rights campaigns, and she stands her ground despite teasing from her classmates, her close friend Ron included. In addition, Hermione has a clear awareness of bigotry and the harm it does. When Ron and Harry tell her Hagrid is half giant, Hermione says that people simply become hysterical about giants as well as werewolves, adding that such an attitude is "just bigotry." In *Prisoner of Azkaban,* Hermione is one of werewolf Remus Lupin's strongest advocates. Hermione also demonstrates that she is willing to go against the hardest principle for teenagers to violate—the opinions of their peers. When Ron accuses her of disloyalty to Hogwarts because of her friendship with Viktor Krum, Hermione reminds him that universal understanding is a higher good than sectarian rivalry, that the purpose of the entire tournament is to foster understanding among young wizards from different cultures. By the time she is fourteen, Hermione is functioning rather consistently at the stage five level, obeying the rules consistent with her internal moral code and breaking those that are not. It will be interesting to see how she navigates the rules that violate her conscience when she becomes a prefect, a development that seems assured.

Kohlberg originally asserted that people progress through stages and never reason in a stage more advanced than the one they are in at the time; nor do they step back, so that a child who has reached stage three will not regress to stages one or two. However, later studies indicate that certain circumstances, such as going to college, can cause a person to regress as much as two stages.[15] In addition, it is common knowledge that a person—

15. Robert E. Grinder, *Adolescence,* 288.

a child in particular—will occasionally behave like a person lower on the developmental scale in situations of great stress, such as Harry's temporary lapse ("One champion down") in the maze. It is also important to note that just because children and adolescents—and even adults—have reached certain moral stages, they will not necessarily reason in that stage in every instance. For example, children can progress to stage four, in which they generally believe that the rules of society are right and should be obeyed, but will shoplift if their friends encourage them to do so because loyalty to fellows may supercede loyalty to a broader, more abstract concept of society. However, once they achieve the principled level of stage five, regression is less likely.

In addition, Kohlberg also points out that while those who reason at the highest levels are usually intelligent, intelligence does not guarantee high moral reasoning: "you have to be cognitively mature to reason morally, but you can be smart and never reason morally."[16] The "Dark Lord," Voldemort, is a perfect example of that. As the student known in *Chamber of Secrets* as "Tom Riddle," he was a prefect and received an award for special services to Hogwarts, by his own account "brilliant . . . [a] model student" (331). Clearly, he had potential to do great things, had he only picked up some scruples along the way. Although he can concoct plans that gain him (or his associates) access to the highly secure Hogwarts castle, Voldemort is incapable of reasoning morally beyond the stage two level. This is because achieving his ultimate goal, immortality, drives all his actions. In pursuit of this goal, we learn in *Goblet of Fire,* he has killed his own father. When the Death Eaters return to him, the revived Voldemort reminds them, "You know my goal—to conquer death" (653). While it is clear that he will do whatever it takes to achieve that victory, Rowling has made clear, much earlier in Harry's education, that immortality is to be subverted to higher principles. When Harry regrets the destruction of the Sorcerer's Stone, which conveys immortality, and the resulting death of its creator, Nicolas Flamel (who, at 665, with his 658-year-old wife, Perenelle, has benefited from the stone's elixir), Dumbledore assures him that there are more important things than living forever and that "humans do have a knack of choosing precisely those things that are worst for them" (*Sorcerer's Stone,* 297). Flamel's willingness to give up his (albeit long) life in order to prevent the stone's doing further harm stands in marked contrast to Voldemort's selfishness.

Of course, one of the difficulties in the process of developing moral reasoning is that those around us constantly exemplify reasoning at all levels, and even exemplars of virtue may be inconsistent or ambivalent. This is just as true at Hogwarts as it is in the real world, and those in positions

16. Kohlberg, *Philosophy,* 138.

of authority—the faculty—are no more likely to be consistent role models than the students. This is made very clear in the difficulty of maintaining a Defense against the Dark Arts teacher on the Hogwarts faculty. In *Sorcerer's Stone,* the mysterious Quirrell turns out to be allied with Voldemort. The second DADA professor, Gilderoy Lockhart, is too preoccupied with his own celebrity to teach students to ward off dark magic. The third, Remus Lupin, who turns out to be a close friend of James Potter, is the one exemplar among the DADA professors thus far (although, as a werewolf, he would be generally perceived as an inappropriate role model). In *Goblet of Fire,* just when it appears that Alastor "Mad-Eye" Moody also has it in for Harry, it turns out that his body has merely been "borrowed" by a schemer. This twist prevents Moody, who ordinarily has Dumbledore's complete confidence, from serving as a model as well.

Even Albus Dumbledore and Minerva McGonagall are inconsistent as paragons of scrupulousness, as both can be caught functioning at the Conventional level. Although Dumbledore is Rowling's Great Wise Wizard, he oversees a realm where house-elves are in servitude, and after the launch of the S.P.E.W. campaign in *Goblet of Fire,* it may be difficult for some readers to understand how Dumbledore tolerates an abuse that troubles a fourteen-year-old. McGonagall at least once functions as low as the stage two or three level, when she bends the eligibility rules to put Harry on the Gryffindor Quidditch team. Professor McGonagall is clearly motivated by what she and her house are likely to gain from having Harry on a broomstick—the House Cup. Because her reasoning is influenced by loyalty to Gryffindor, Professor McGonagall might be reasoning at stage three rather than stage two, but no higher. Also, whereas Dumbledore permits Hermione the Time-Turner in the climax of *Prisoner of Azkaban* so she can turn back time and prevent a miscarriage of justice, McGonagall has approved her use of the device at the beginning of the third year so that Hermione can attend classes scheduled simultaneously. In this case, McGonagall allows the breaking of a rule not in service of a moral imperative (as does Dumbledore in the case of preventing the hippogriff's execution) but simply as a convenience for Hermione. Certainly passion for education is a good, but when Hermione is constantly exhausted and irritable with her friends, McGonagall's decision seems questionable. In addition, in *Goblet of Fire,* Harry is permitted to enter the Triwizard Tournament although he is underage, for no better reason than because the cup spit out his name. Dumbledore and McGonagall endorse his entry, although it is clear that the tasks will be dangerous.

In fact, the tasks in the Triwizard Tournament are merely the apex of a running theme throughout all four novels, the imperilment of the Hogwarts' students, often with the sanction or ambivalence of the faculty. In *Sorcerer's Stone,* Harry and Ron, on condition of punishment for violating a curfew, are sent into the Forbidden Forest at night with Hagrid to look for whoever or whatever is killing unicorns. It would seem prudent to have Hagrid search for the predator himself or with other well-armed adults, but such is not the case at Hogwarts. Quidditch, the school sport, subjects players to zooming around on broomsticks high above the ground, aiming missiles called "Bludgers" at each other. At least once per novel, Harry or a teammate must visit the school nurse, Madam Pomfrey, to have bones "re-grown." In *Chamber of Secrets,* a basilisk roaming freely about Hogwarts castle begins petrifying students, including (eventually) Hermione. In Care of Magical Creatures class, Hagrid routinely subjects his pupils to creatures that bite, scratch, and sting. The hippogriff in *Prisoner of Azkaban* is origi-nally indicted for having inflicted an injury on Draco Malfoy, but only when Malfoy's father, contacted by his son, registers a complaint. The height—so far—of the danger to students is reached in *Goblet of Fire,* when the house champions—the exemplary students from each school—are subjected to the tasks of stealing an egg from a brooding she-dragon, recovering class-mates from the bottom of the school lake, and negotiating a maze rife with giant spiders and creatures that blast fire. All the while, because of the boarding-school environment, the parents of these students are oblivious to the peril their children experience. In a posting to the ChildLit listserv group, Jane Yolen questions the credibility of this atmosphere in *Chamber of Secrets:* "Here one has a school (forget about the magic for a moment) run by a man that all agree is kind, generous, smart, etc. Kids in the school (and sometimes teachers) are falling like flies. Are the parents called? Is the school shut down? Are kids sent home while the disasters are sorted? If this were any other school but Hogwarts, the answer would be yes. Yet this goes on FOR AN ENTIRE TERM." This apparent mishandling of crisis situations is, Yolen says, "the hardest pill to swallow" in the novels.[17]

For Harry and his friends, moral maturation means negotiating the maze of these conflicting models. The presence in the books of models chil-dren should not emulate, including the behavior of some authority figures, has been viewed by some readers as a troubling aspect of Rowling's work. Certainly conservative Christians feel that some aspects of the characters' behavior—Harry's included—are not imitable. But the inclusion of char-acters functioning on all levels of Kohlberg's scale ensures that the world created by J. K. Rowling is the real world, for all its magical attributes. De-spite the fact that memories (such as Gilderoy Lockhart's) can be erased, that people can apparate or become animagi, and that time can be turned back, magic is not miraculous in Harry Potter's world. Even with a wand that is the twin of Voldemort's, Harry cannot permanently defeat the "Dark

17. Jane Yolen, "Aesthetics of Harry."

Lord." Remus Lupin can be treated but not cured. Sirius Black must remain on the run. Harry's parents cannot be resurrected. Bones may be regrown in the hospital wing, but injuries to the psyche or the soul such as those inflicted on Barty Crouch's son are not easily repaired. In a confusing world such as Rowling's, as in the real world, one can depend on knowledge, represented by Hermione; on loyalty, represented by Ron; or on scruples, which Harry increasingly represents. But, of course, even these can be put to misguided purposes. It remains, for Harry, and for a young person reading about him, to navigate the maze in hopes of moving closer to the center and farther from the obstacles and dangers.

Moving Through the Maze

Lawrence Kohlberg believed that children between the ages of ten and eighteen progress through more moral stages than people at any other age because they are beginning to test their independence and have developed more formal reasoning abilities. For them, a black-and-white world is replaced by one in varying shades of gray.[18] If Kohlberg and other psychologists are right that young people experience the bulk of their moral development between the ages of ten and eighteen, then what they read during those stages is vital, not only for them, but for the rest of us, who will eventually live in the world they run. Children who read J. K. Rowling's books are encouraged to elevate themselves above the bully Draco Malfoy, whose name calls to mind the draconian measures used by those in power to keep others oppressed. The dreaded Dursleys, too, are morally retarded; and, yes, Dudley is a dud. Young readers are encouraged to move with Harry Potter and his friends Ron Weasley and Hermione Granger into the Conventional level of Kohlberg's scheme, in which one treats one's friends kindly and tries to make the society—wizard, in this case—function smoothly and fairly. What a young person encounters in Harry Potter's world is a boy who is loyal to his friends, sensitive to outcasts and underdogs, respectful of his teachers—when they deserve his respect—aware of the moral dimensions of a decision, and capable of realizations that move him along toward adulthood. Finally, adolescents may be inspired to aim for the Postconventional or principled level, emulating such role models as Sirius Black, who teaches that black can, in fact, be white, and Albus Dumbledore, who, like the albumen, or egg white, suggested by his first name, nourishes the yolk of these young wizards and witches, preparing them to hatch into a world they know how to improve.

Readers such as William Safire, who finds the Harry Potter series insubstantial, and conservative Christian parents who object to the books on

18. Berger, *The Developing Person*, 347.

206 Lana A. Whited, with M. Katherine Grimes

moral terms should reconsider Rowling's work in the light of Lawrence Kohlberg's work. Kohlberg maintained that there are three ways of provoking moral development in children and young people. First, they need the friction of cognitive-moral conflict, what Thomas Berendt calls "cognitive disequilibrium."[19] It is important, at any stage, for children to have opportunities to discuss alternative resolutions to moral conflict and their consequences. It is helpful for them to hear the arguments of people reasoning in stages higher than theirs. The second method for helping children develop morally is to present them with opportunities for role-playing, particularly opportunities that challenge them to take different perspectives and explore new viewpoints. Finally, children who live in a community characterized by justice move through stages of moral development more rapidly than those who do not. This concept has been applied successfully to schools, with students being actively involved in formulating standards for community learning (and, in the case of college students, community living).

It is easy to see how the Harry Potter novels provide all three of the opportunities Kohlberg described. Fiction, by its very nature, allows the reader to see life from others' perspectives and to contemplate how he or she might resolve dilemmas not present in his or her own life. One of the primary reasons that religious teachers such as Jesus use parables or anecdotes is to provide disciples the opportunity to evaluate the decisions and actions of the primary character in the narrative. Religious activities such as Sunday school in Christian churches provide an opportunity for children to discuss these parables and other narratives, an undertaking that addresses Kohlberg's first method of nurturing moral development: provoke discussion of moral conflict. Good parents will create the same opportunities for children reading Harry Potter, and many young readers will discuss characters' actions with their friends. Because Rowling's books lend themselves to such discussion, clergy members such as Jonathan Marlowe, a Methodist minister in Monroe, North Carolina, have developed children's ministry programs using the Harry Potter books as texts. Toward the end of "Hunting Down Harry Potter," Kimbra Wilder Gish (herself a member of a conservative Christian church) suggests that rather than banning Rowling's books from their shelves, parents who object to the depiction of magic might use the volumes "as a learning experience," allowing children to read the books and then discussing "what [they] find of concern . . . and why." Gish says this method has the increased benefit of "adding to the joy of reading for pleasure, an understanding of what it is to be a thoughtful reader."[20] This position is

19. Berendt, *Child Development*, 622.
20. Jonathan Marlowe, "Harry Potter's Magic Less Dangerous Than Ours," 9A; Gish, "Hunting Down Harry Potter," 270.

akin to Mary Wollstonecraft's argument in *A Vindication on the Rights of Woman* that rather than interdict the works of the "stupid novelists" who "miseducate" women by providing negative images and role models, we should encourage young women to read these works in order to learn what behaviors and attitudes to avoid. In other words, young readers should be encouraged to develop their own critical faculties and judgments, to work through the "cognitive disequilibrium" with appropriate guidance.

But even children not fortunate enough to have opportunities for discussing Harry Potter in organized groups can profit, developmentally speaking, from the series. When Harry and his friends experience moral conflict, they always talk their way through it. There is probably no better example than Harry and Cedric Diggory's extended discussion over who deserves the Triwizard Cup, a prize they decide to share. When characters such as Draco Malfoy act in accordance with lower levels of moral reasoning, Harry and his friends always condemn those actions. Rowling provides young readers with models of moral decision-making via the characters who inhabit her magical and Muggle worlds. The experience of reading, then, provides the opportunity for the role-playing Kohlberg called for, and readers can see how the members of an essentially just community—Hogwarts— react when their community is threatened. The justice characteristic of this community is guaranteed by the presence of Albus Dumbledore, but even Dumbledore knows that what he represents is more important than who he is. When he is temporarily suspended in *Chamber of Secrets*, he reminds Lucius Malfoy that removing the headmaster does not remove his influence: "you will find that I will only *truly* have left this school when none here are loyal to me" (264). Young readers respond to the goodness of the Hogwarts community, a realm where good and evil are nearly always clear (even if their agents sometimes aren't); this accounts for why children write to Rowling asking how they can enroll at the school.

The positions of adults thrilled to see young people reading Harry Potter and of conservative Christians who would intercept the books are what Aristotle called "corollaries," or opposites in a spectrum, not contradictions. There is common ground: both camps endorse the concept of reading as a fundamentally powerful experience. If we grant that books can change our lives, we must concede the possibility of both constructive and destructive change. There *are* books that may not be appropriate for some children, for a variety of reasons. A good reason for delaying some children's experience with Harry Potter might be the series' darker elements—not magic, but the death of Harry's parents, the treatment of young Barty Crouch at the hands of his own father, the basilisk's near-fatal attack on Ginny Weasley, and the death of Cedric Diggory. Children too young to understand death may be unnecessarily traumatized by these developments, just as some children taken to see Disney's *The Lion King* were too young to comprehend the death of Simba's father. In a *USA Today* article published a few weeks before the release of *Goblet of Fire,* booksellers and librarians expressed concern that too many parents were buying the series for children younger than eight, an action bookstore proprietor Diane Garrett calls "completely inappropriate."[21] Parents and educators must use their judgment about when children in their care are ready for this material. But for young people who are mature enough to understand the darker aspects of the books, and certainly for those in adolescence who, Kohlberg would remind us, experience so much movement through developmental stages, Harry Potter should be near the top of the reading list.

21. Deirdre Donahue, "Some Want Harry to Vanish till Kids Are Older," D1.

Gender Issues and Harry Potter

Hermione Granger and the Heritage of Gender

Eliza T. Dresang

"People are in names, names are in people," asserts Hermione Gant, protagonist of H.D.'s posthumously published novel, HERmione. Hermione Gant could well have been speaking for Hermione Granger, the central female character in the Harry Potter books. Hermione, as both a name and a persona, has raised considerable interest among literary critics and the public in general. Initially the commentary focused on easy-to-resolve issues such as how to pronounce her name (Hur MY uh nee). Although Viktor Krum mispronounces Hermione when he first calls her "Hermy—own" and then he calls her "Hermy-own-ninny" in J. K. Rowling's *Harry Potter and the Goblet of Fire* (418–19), no general "making fun" of Hermione's name occurs in the books. It stands throughout the narrative as unique yet accepted. Moving on beyond her name, more substantive discourse has focused on feminist issues in relation to both Hermione and other less central female characters in the books. Reviewers, literary critics, and other readers have pondered the question of gender representation. "Well I was just wondering about the sexism in the series. Do you think it exists, even when J. K. Rowling is a woman?" queried one thoughtful thirteen year old.[1] An analysis that addresses feminist issues against the background of previous significant mythological and literary characters bearing the name Hermione responds to these uncertainties and suggests the legacy that she and Rowling may leave for future readers.

Mythological and Literary Heritage

Collectively, several mythological and literary Hermiones provide a heritage for Rowling's Hermione, one of Harry Potter's two best friends.

The Significance of Naming

Rowling frequently gives her opinion on the importance of names in the Harry Potter books:

1. Hilda Doolittle (H. D.), *HERmione*, 131; J. K. Rowling, interview by Christopher Ludden; "Do You Ever Get the Feeling the HP Books are Sexist?" ("Yellow Cherry").

I love names, as anyone who has read the books is going to see only too clearly. . . . Snape is a place name in Britain. Dumbledore is an old English dialect word for bumblebee, because he is a musical person. And I imagine him humming to himself all the time. Hagrid is also an old English word. Hedwig was a saint, a Medieval saint. I collect them. You know, if I hear a good name, I have got to write it down. And it will probably crop up somewhere.[2]

The names of most of the 127 characters in the Harry Potter books have a tie to some appropriate external meaning. Reading the glossary of names is amusing in and of itself.[3]

Rowling has contended on several occasions that Hermione "was most consciously based on a real person, and that person was me. She's a caricature of me when I was younger." It is not surprising that Rowling gave careful thought to the name of this quasi-autobiographical character. Rowling's degree from Exeter in French and Classics provided a rich resource for the name she chose for her personal representative in the book. Granting this character a distinguished literary tie through her uncommon name whose source Rowling cites as Shakespeare's *A Winter's Tale* gives her the legitimacy and strength among her peers that the main male characters gain either out of heredity (Ron) or endowment (Harry). Hermione is called by her surname, "Granger," alone far less often than either "Potter" (Harry) or "Weasley" (Ron). Although this may represent a gender-based custom, it highlights the name Hermione and gives less attention to Granger, an English surname meaning "tenant" or "farmer."[4]

Ursula Le Guin's Earthsea quartet reveals the deep significance of "naming" in modern fantasy; the naming around which her writing centers refers always to the given name, not the surname. In the first book of the series, *A Wizard of Earthsea,* Duny's real name, Ged, is revealed to him in order for him to be able to embark on his hero quest. Ged subsequently learns the "real names" of everything, knowing that this knowledge will give him power. In the second book, *The Tombs of Atuan,* five-year-old Tenar is taken from her parents to a desert-like island where she serves the Nameless Ones, and her own name is taken away. The gift that Ged bestows on her is the return of her name. The importance of naming surfaces again in the fourth

2. J. K. Rowling, "The Surprising Success of Harry Potter."
3. Rudolf Hein, "Harry Potter Glossary."
4. Rowling, "Surprising Success"; Lindsey Fraser, *Conversations with J. K. Rowling,* 31. See the complete original version of William Shakespeare's *The Winter's Tale.* Harry Potter has a quite common British surname and a given name with a distinguished and appropriate meaning—"Lord, ruler of the House"—but no apparent literary ties. Harry's heritage as the privileged wizard among his peers affords him no need for the attention drawn to Hermione through her heritage of an out-of-the-ordinary, rich-in-literary-history name. (Hein, "Harry Potter Glossary").

book, *Tehanu*.[5] In this story, Therru is given her real name, Tehanu, by Kalessin the dragon, who is her father. Le Guin bestows names in the Earthsea quartet in various ways but always with the sense that gaining one's proper name is the ultimate act in achieving one's true identity.

Hermione's role in the Potter books has some similarity to that of the characters in these high fantasy books by virtue of the significance of her name and the accompanying gender issues (to be discussed later in this chapter). Like Tehanu, it is clear that with the strength of her purposefully chosen name, Hermione cannot be weak or inconsequential.

Although Rowling cites a Shakespearean character as the inspiration for the name Hermione, a particularly fascinating feature associated with several outstanding literary Hermiones is the intertextuality among various works in which they appear, leading to the supposition that several of the Hermiones, rather than any one alone, may have influenced Rowling's naming or shaping of her literary character. However, an examination of this intertextuality is not based on speculation of Rowling's intentions but on the resemblance that I find among this community of fictional women that stretches across several thousand years and between their composite portrait and Rowling's Hermione. I agree with David Lucking's statement in his analysis of Shakespeare's *Coriolanus*, "the history of a name will also be the history of an identity."[6] A contextual placement of Hermione Granger adds depth to understanding this character and assists in analyzing her role in the magical world of Hogwarts.

The Mythological Hermione

Hermione, the female form of Hermes, messenger of the gods, god of science, trade, and eloquence, is immortalized in Greek mythology as the daughter of Helen of Troy and Menelaus, King of Sparta. She is a daughter and a wife whose destiny is in the hands of her father and her two husbands.[7] The last of classical Athens' great tragic dramatists, Euripides, brings the goddess Hermione into literature and reveals more of her character through his play *Andromache*, written 428–424 B.C.E. Andromache, captive of Troy, has borne a son to Hermione's husband, Neoptolemus, and the angry goddess accuses Andromache of causing her own infertility. Euripides' reputation as a dramatist with profound psychological insight is borne out in the

5. Ursula LeGuin, *A Wizard of Earthsea; The Tombs of Atuan; Tehanu: The Last Book of Earthsea*. *Tehanu* won the Nebula Award for the best science fiction book published in 1990.

6. David Lucking, " 'The Price of One Fair Word': Negotiating Names in *Coriolanus*."

7. Hein, "Harry Potter Glossary"; "Hermione," *Encyclopedia Mythica*. Menlaus's pledge of Hermione to Neoptolmus is mentioned in *The Odyssey of Homer*, translated by Allen Mandlebaum, 65.

denouement of this play, and the Hermione who emerges shows a strength of intellect, determination, and the ability to achieve her purpose, even if it is through a male god. This strength of Hermione created twenty-five hundred years ago sets the stage for the Hermiones to come.

The Saint Hermione

The Bible introduces Hermione as a prophetess in the "Acts of the Apostles." The daughter of Philip the Deacon, she became a martyr at Ephesus and was canonized in 117 A.D. Her feast day is September 4. St. Hermione contributes to the cumulative portrait of women with this name that lead their lives with a certain determination and resilience, an intellect that gives them problem-solving ability as well as dedication to achieving their purpose.

The Shakespearean Hermione

The Hermione referenced by Rowling comes to life in the Shakespearean play *The Winter's Tale.* As in the myth, in this comedy of the early seventeenth century, choices made by the males in the play circumscribe Hermione's actions. She is declared unfaithful by her husband, Leontes, King of Sicilia, and imprisoned, although she is pregnant with a daughter who is born while she is confined. The daughter, Perdita, left to die, is found and raised by a shepherd. Hidden for twenty years by her attendant, Paulina, Perdita brings Hermione "back to life" when she returns, and Leontes, long repentant, receives both with joy. Shakespeare's sources for names in *The Winter's Tale* are largely from Greek and Roman origins, including works by Plutarch and Ovid.[8] Thus this seventeenth-century Hermione has ties with both the mythological Hermiones and current literary examples.

The Hermiones of H. D. and D. H. Lawrence

The Hermiones created by two early-twentieth-century British authors who were at one time involved in a tryst complete the influential literary environment from which an analysis of Rowling's Hermione emerges. The poet and novelist Hilda Doolittle, known more commonly by her initials H. D., wrote an autobiographical novel, *HERmione,* devoted to a struggle with the signifying of nomenclature. The novel, written in 1927, was published posthumously fifty-four years later and uncovered in the Beinecke Library at Yale University by her daughter Perdita (named after the daughter in *The Winter's Tale*). Perdita's introduction to *HERmione* characterizes her mother as a split personality, like the character Hermione in H. D.'s book: "Names, people; split dimensions. The protagonist is a divided personality, Her and Hermione. Hermione of Greek mythology, daughter of

---

8. Amanda Mabillard, "Shakespeare's Sources: *The Winter's Tale.*"

Menelaeus and Helen. Also, most significantly to me, Shakespeare's misunderstood heroine of *The Winter's Tale,* mother of Perdita. . . . I recognize one certainty in my future. I'll never escape the past."[9] What does H. D. herself have to say about her name and her heritage? Within the space of two pages in her novel, she connects her fictional alter ego with a Greek heritage, with the Shakespearean Hermione, and with an Eastern tradition. Throughout the novel/story of herself, H. D. struggles with the meaning of this name that represents what and who she is, how it is in her and she is in it, never quite reconciling the competing forces of emotion, mystery, creativity, and rationality. These aspects of her personality, like the aspects of her name, war with one another throughout her life. With the linking of her name to Greek, Shakespearean, and Eastern sources; the strong tie between her name and her search for identity and agency; and the autobiographical nature of the novel, H. D.'s Hermione is a linchpin among the various literary Hermiones and an important part of the literary backdrop behind Hermione Granger.

From 1914–1918, H. D. had a close but, according to her biographer Barbara Guest, nonsexual relationship with the writer D. H. Lawrence, who in 1919 published his novel *Women in Love.* Interestingly, and perhaps coincidentally, one of the four female protagonists in Lawrence's philosophical novel of relationships bears the name Hermione. In her analysis of the relationships among the four women in *Women in Love,* Danica Vukovi makes an observation relevant to the understanding of Hermione Granger. She describes Lawrence's Hermione as a woman who "wants to 'know' everything intellectually and control everything," words that could easily be written about Rowling's Hermione.[10]

The Literary Heritage of Hermione Granger and Gender

This exploration of the linking among the various well-known mythological and literary Hermiones and the variety of their backgrounds creates a conducive environment in which to examine critically Rowling's Hermione Granger. For the reader versed in literature, the possible literary ties add a depth to Rowling's choice of an "unusual" name that makes it more than simply unusual. A name in its own right unusual, yet one that has been recorded in works by Homer, Euripides, the author of "Acts of the Apostles," Shakespeare, H. D., and D. H. Lawrence, carries a certain dignity and sense of historical and psychological significance that cannot easily be discounted. The existence of a piece of literature in which the heroine focuses

9. H. D., *HERmione,* xi.
10. Barbara Guest, *Herself Defined: The Poet H. D. and Her World,* and H. Hernandez, *A Brief Biography of H. D.;* Danica Vukovic, "Bonding and Separating of Female Characters in *Women in Love.*"

almost obsessively on the origin of her name and its significance in her life reinforces this supposition.

Both the mythological and the Shakespearean Hermiones were at the mercy of the men who controlled their lives, yet they were strong women who used their wits and their position to seek their due in life. Their twentieth-century heirs are much more in control of their own destinies yet still not entirely free of male dependence.

The long, distinguished literary history of the name Hermione leaves an impression of connection and belonging. The intertextuality of its use increases the sense of a "community" of Hermiones all with some aspects of their lives, but far from everything, in common. Rowling's Hermione has a comfortable place in this distinguished literary heritage.

A Feminist Analysis of the Heritage of Gender in Harry Potter

The examination of the "inherited" symbolic importance of Hermione's name has set the stage for an analysis of the heritage that Hermione Granger may leave to the future. Her legacy from the past sheds light on this examination of the meaning, development, and treatment of Hermione's persona in the Harry Potter saga.

The Basis for the Analysis

Feminist theory takes as givens the premises that society is patriarchal and that women do not occupy a position of political, economic, or social equality, creating difficulties and barriers for both genders. Feminism advocates for the rights and interests of women unfettered or undeterred by the patriarchal structure. Feminist theory provides various frameworks from which to examine, explain, and understand how gender affects all aspects of life, primarily focusing on females as the more disadvantaged gender, but also analyzing how the patriarchal structure negatively affects males. The end purpose of understanding and applying the feminists' point of view is to eliminate inequality for women and improve the lot of everyone.

A misconception held by some, however, is that a unified feminist perspective exists. Rosemarie Putnam Tong in *Feminist Thought* provides an articulate chronological characterization of the various types of feminist analysis. Although Tong is optimistic that at some point the labels given to various "schools of thought" will be dropped, for now "they help mark the range of different approaches, perspectives, and frameworks a variety of feminists have used to shape both their explanations for women's oppression and their proposed solutions for its elimination." Starting in the eighteenth century with Mary Wollstonecraft and other liberal feminists, Tong traces the shape of feminist thought through radical-libertarian and radical-cultural feminism, Marxist and socialist feminism, postmodern feminism, existentialist feminism, psychoanalytical and gender feminism, multicultural and global feminism, ending with what she labels the most radical, ecofeminism. Although she presents the schools of thought chronologically, Tong describes these various groups and subgroups as a kaleidoscope—when a new train of thought appears, the old one does not disappear, but continues to coexist, although possibly in modified form. Originally, Tong says, the ephemeral nature of any one pattern, any one movement, seemed negative. Later she came to understand that change and growth are essential and are, in fact, what make feminist thought vital. Ultimately, she concludes that "not the truth but the truths will set women free."[11]

Because feminist literary criticism draws from general feminist theory, it, too, is kaleidoscopic. Within the various movements, specific and somewhat rigid "truths" exist—those that Tong refers to as the good, the true, and the beautiful—but the overall picture varies both by theory and by reader. According to feminist critic Chris Weedon, "How the feminist critic fixes meaning will depend on the framework within which she reads a text. Texts may be read, for example, as expressions of women's experience already constituted in the world beyond fiction, as an essentially feminine subjectivity . . . which seeks to reassert itself through the discursive strategies of fiction, or as specific examples of the construction of gender in language." Roderick McGillis, in *The Nimble Reader: Literary Theory and Children's Literature,* expresses these various feminist perspectives in yet another way: "But, just how does a feminist reading of a children's book proceed? Well, it proceeds along one of several possible paths: an examination of the presentation of the female in literature, a reading of archetypes from a feminine perspective, an examination of feminine values and community, a focus on patriarchal modes of subject construction and ways of resistance." Roberta Seelinger Trites expresses these same thoughts: "Referring to 'feminism' in the singular implies erroneously that what is actually a polymorphous and polyvocal set of theories, movements, and political actions has a unified number of principles."[12] In other words, no one feminist approach to literary texts exists.

Among the theoretical (and pragmatic) approaches to feminist thought cataloged by Tong, the one that most readily accepts a variety of perspectives

11. Rosemarie Putnam Tong, *Feminist Thought: A More Comprehensive Introduction,* 1–2, 279. See also Mary Wollstonecraft, *A Vindication of the Rights of Woman.* This book was originally published in 1792. According to *Webster's Collegiate Dictionary,* tenth edition, 1995, the word "feminism" was coined in 1895, but the precepts of liberal feminism, focusing on the rights of women, were clearly laid out in the work of Wollstonecraft.

12. Chris Weedon, *Feminist Practice and Poststructuralist Theory;* Roderick McGillis, *The Nimble Reader: Literary Theory and Children's Literature,* 156; Roberta Seelinger Trites, *Waking Sleeping Beauty: Feminist Voices in Children's Novels,* 143.

is postmodernist feminism. In this analysis of the Harry Potter serial novel, I take a postmodernist approach. According to Tong, "Postmodern feminists . . . remind us that as bad as it is for a woman to be bullied into submission by a patriarch's unitary truth, it is even worse for her to be judged not a real feminist by a matriarch's unitary truth . . . As I see it, attention to difference is precisely what will help women achieve unity."[13] In adopting the postmodern approach, I accept the "other" stance of the females in the Harry Potter books, but I do not regard it as negative, as the existential feminists might. Rather, I regard it as an opportunity to observe whether or how females may find strength and agency despite their marginalization. I borrow from a number of the feminist frameworks named by Tong and several of the "questioning stances" mentioned by Weeden and by McGillis, none of which I propose is the "one right or best way" for analysis of feminist issues. What I provide rather is a selective yet multifaceted view of gender issues in these books.

What Is a Feminist Children's Novel?

"What is a feminist children's novel? Defined simply, it is a novel in which the main character[s] is empowered regardless of gender." This definition is offered by Roberta Seelinger Trites in *Waking Sleeping Beauty: Feminist Voices in Children's Novels.*[14] However, she makes a caveat in giving this definition: that the emphasis of feminist analysis has been far more on female protagonists than on males. One parameter that I place on my analysis due to time and space is to examine only the lives of girls and women in the Harry Potter books, fully acknowledging that feminism concerns itself with the issues raised in relation to all humanity, not women alone. Using the term "feminist novel" denotes a conclusion rather than merely an analysis from the point of view of feminist theory. Therefore, in *Waking Sleeping Beauty,* Trites identifies what she considers feminist novels and explains why. In this essay, I ask the question "Is this a feminist novel?" from a variety of viewpoints.

To guide my analysis and focus upon issues from various feminist perspectives, I turn to Kay Vandergrift, who has developed a model of Female Voices in Youth Literature (figure 1) through the extrapolation of feminist themes from general feminist theory, feminist literary theory, and feminist

---

13. The postmodernist approach is somewhat akin to the one I advocate in my book *Radical Change: Books for Youth in a Digital Age* in which I note the similarity between the Radical Change theoretical approach to children's literature and that of many contemporary feminists with "the openness, connectivity and interactivity of the digital world . . . in the tradition of the female" (238). Tong, *Feminist Thought,* 279.

14. Trites, *Waking Sleeping Beauty,* 4.

theories of child and adolescent development.[15] The model is a graphic representation of the themes she found in these three basic disciplines.

Vandergrift struggled with the visualization, wanting it to be nonhierarchical with discrete yet overlapping parts. The result is something that resembles flower petals that overlap but move outward from the center in a layered set of concentric, circular pieces. Vandergrift describes the model as "organic in nature, almost as petals of a stylized flower from which individual elements can be removed for independent study without destroying the totality of the organic form." Concerning her model, Vandergrift asserts, "As an organic form, it is expected that this model will be modified

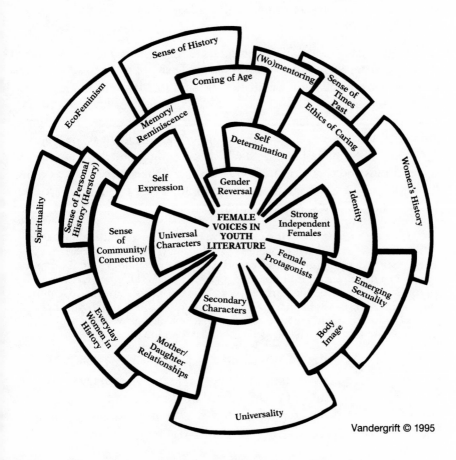

Vandergrift © 1995

Figure 1. Female Voices in Youth Literature

15. Kay E. Vandergrift, "Journey or Destination: Female Voices in Youth Literature," in *Mosaics of Meaning: Enhancing the Intellectual Life of Young Adults through Story.* For further information see http://www.scils.rutgers.edu/~kvander/model.html.

by those who use it, growing and changing as young people and adult intermediaries find their own connections between literature and feminist theory." In this spirit, I have altered some of Vandergrift's categories, combining, expanding, or adding to them with others suggested by the work of Roberta Seelinger Trites.[16] Drawing upon the components of Vandergrift's mosaic model (V) and the dimensions in Trites's (T), I assembled the following gender issues to examine from a feminist perspective in the Harry Potter saga:

> Role construction [subverting stereotypes (T); examining archetypes; language (T); gender reversal (V); strong independent females (V)]
> Self-determination (V); agency (T);[17]
> Sense of community/connection (V); interdependency (T)
> Ethics of caring (V)

In applying her model, Vandergrift takes into account both the writer and the reader from a feminist stance.[18] I have chosen not to do this. Numerous comments from the author convince me that Rowling did not *consciously* write these texts as feminist, that is, to advocate for or promote equality or empowerment for females; she has said repeatedly that Harry sprang "fully developed" into her mind; she never gave thought to making him "Harriet." She emphasizes that she is concentrating on telling the story as she envisions and creates it, not as readers would like to see it. She defends her choice of female characters with no apologies for them. They are there because they tell the story as she wants it told:

> I was writing the books for six months, before I stopped and thought: Well, he's a boy. How did that happen? Why is he a boy? Why isn't it Harriet? And number one, it was too late, Harry was too real by then for me to try to put him in a dress. That wasn't going to work. And then there was Hermione—and Hermione is an indispensable part of the books and how the adventures happen. And she is so much me that I felt no guilt about keeping the hero who had walked into my head. You know, it was uncontrived. It wasn't conscious. That's how he happened. So I kept him that way.[19]

I will *not* critique Rowling's writing as an essentially feminine subjectivity that seeks to reassert itself through the discursive strategies of fiction. Moreover, I carry out this analysis based on what I perceive that Rowling has done, rather than determining what she should or could have done.

---

16. Vandergrift, *Mosaics*, 20; Trites, *Waking Sleeping Beauty*.
17. It is under this topic that I will touch upon the structure of authority that is expanded upon elsewhere in this book in Farah Mendlesohn, "Crowning the King: Harry Potter and the Construction of Authority."
18. Vandergrift, *Mosaics*, 21–22.
19. Rowling, "Surprising Success."

Hermione: Role Construction

In order to analyze Hermione and the roles of other female characters in the Harry Potter books, it is essential to differentiate between a caricature and a stereotype. Rowling has said repeatedly that Hermione is "a caricature of me when I was younger."[20] A caricature is a representation in literature or art that implies somewhat ludicrous exaggeration of the characteristics or features of a subject; that is, it is not "real life" but an exaggeration of real life. It is based on an individual, not a group. On the other hand, a stereotype is something conforming to a fixed or general pattern, a mental picture that is held in common by members of a group and that represents an oversimplified opinion or an uncritical judgment, and sometimes is associated with a negative prejudiced attitude, although some stereotypes have roots in positive images. A stereotype is based on a group, not an individual.

I propose that, from a feminist point of view, it is possible for a character presented through a caricature to be empowered in her role, while it is possible for a stereotypic character to be thus empowered only if she consciously subverts the stereotype. Rowling intended to construct Hermione's role as a caricature or exaggeration of herself, rather than a general stereotype of eleven- to fourteen-year-old girls. She believed herself to be writing about an individual, not depicting a group. She only partially succeeds, as sometimes her caricature bleeds over into a stereotype of girls Hermione's age.

Rowling has constructed a role and developed a caricature of her own life with Hermione in two ways. The only obvious role in the first three books is that of highly intelligent, overachieving, somewhat annoying student. We are introduced to Hermione less than midway through *Harry Potter and the Sorcerer's Stone* when she encounters Harry and Ron on the train to Hogwarts. Immediately after they meet, she informs her traveling companions that she has done a great deal of background reading on the history of magic and the dark arts. Further, she informs them that Harry Potter is mentioned in two of the books she's read, so she knows everything about him. Rowling has mentioned this type of exaggerated behavior when discussing Hermione in interviews. We see almost immediately that Hermione has not yet learned how to share what she knows about either life or learning in a manner that does not aggravate her listeners. Later in the journey, in a somewhat know-it-all manner, Hermione lets Harry and Ron know that they had better put their robes on and prepare for their arrival at Hogwarts. This is a caricature rather than a stereotype because, as the story moves forward, Hermione learns to apply her knowledge in a more reasonable and appropriate way, and her knowledge becomes a valuable asset. The extreme behavior serves as an introduction to a more fleshed-out role

20. Ibid.

for her by the end of book one, developed further throughout books two and three and on into four. In book three, Hermione doubles her course work, becoming irritable and reclusive at times because she has ten subjects to study at once. This is, however, an important plot device, because near the end, Hermione uses her "secret," the Time-Turner that Professor McGonagall gave her so that she can take two courses simultaneously, to run time backwards to save Buckbeak from execution and Sirius Black from the Dementors (*Prisoner of Azkaban*, 395–402). Hermione's compulsion to study is a legitimate beginning place for helping her develop into a strong character; after her year of double studies, she realizes her workload is "too much" and gives the Time-Turner back to Professor McGonagall. This is one milestone of Hermione's learning how to reconcile her love of learning with the limitations of life.

The second aspect of Hermione that is rooted in Rowling emerges in the fourth book—Hermione's social concern on behalf of the house-elves—in a "bigger than life" manner as usual. Rowling worked for Amnesty International in London for two years, researching human rights issues in Africa. According to an article in the *London Guardian*, "[Rowling's] heroine is the writer Jessica Mitford," whom she admired not only as an author but also as a civil rights activist.[21] Mitford spent more than thirty years producing nonfiction that exposed self-serving practices related to birth, prison, death, and social injustice, and she actively opposed the Vietnam War. If Rowling admired Mitford and her writing, it makes sense for her to lead the character who represents herself in the Harry Potter saga into social activism. Rowling's real life role in relation to social activism again is raised to the level of caricature, at least initially, in the role given to Hermione. Ron taunts Hermione about her role in this cause. "What are we now, then, the House-Elf Liberation Front? I'm not barging into that kitchen and trying to make them stop work. I'm not doing it" (*Goblet of Fire*, 374).

Hermione's role is constructed by her actions within the confines of the story and by the language that Rowling uses to describe her behavior. Catherine Belsey represents the poststructuralist approach to literary criticism, which asserts that subjects are constructed by language in their environment—by exterior forces rather than interior unique identity.[22] Readers must overcome the language Rowling imposes on Hermione when she is not describing her in the "intellectual, problem solver" role to see Hermione as empowered in her role as a "strong, independent woman." The stereotypic part of Hermione's role constructed by Rowling relates to the hysterical and fearful, whining behavior that Hermione exhibits, and specifically to the language that Rowling employs to describe this behavior.

21. Simon Hattenstone, "Harry, Jesse, and Me."
22. Catherine Belsey, "Constructing the Subject: Deconstructing the Text."

Despite the fact that, in the world of witches and wizards, magic reigns supreme, Hermione, a Mudblood (of Muggle or nonwizard descent) employs her acquired knowledge of magic (rather than her innate ability at it) to "save the day." Some of Hermione's ability IS innate; she's a witch, not a Muggle. She is a prime example that information brings power, and she sees this at work repeatedly in her life at Hogwarts. Yet throughout her role development thus far, Rowling allows Hermione to lose sight of her own strength and revert to stereotypic behavior, and she facilitates this by employing gender-related stereotypic words to Hermione's behavior again and again. Repeatedly Rowling has Hermione "shriek," "squeak," "wail," "squeal," and "whimper," verbs never applied to the male characters in the book. For Hermione the bossy, assertive champion of rights and problem solver, these words, at least in some contexts, seem unbelievable and completely out of character; for example, " 'Ron! Ron! Are you all right?' squealed Hermione" (*Chamber of Secrets*, 113). Adverbial phrases are often no better—Hermione acts "in alarm," "hysterically." Throughout the books, Hermione often bursts into tears (all right in some circumstances but overdrawn in others). The language that constructs the roles played by Harry and Ron is much calmer, more reasoned, despite the fact that Hermione is the problem solver. In employing this technique, Rowling departs from her own experience—does she think it is necessary to portray girls as fearful, even though she herself was not? Rowling tells the *Guardian* reporter, "I never cried, I felt like it, but I never did." The reporter comments: "Rowling is one of life's copers."[23] So is Hermione. Her hysteria and crying happen far too often to be considered a believable part of the development of Hermione's character and are quite out of line with her core role in the book. They add nothing to an understanding of her persona or its individual caricature, nor, for the most part, anything to the story. Thus, they can only be interpreted as "how [silly, weak] girls act," which is unfortunate from the point of view of feminist analysis.

How damaging are these stereotypical aspects of Hermione's role? According to Rowling, readers see Hermione as strong and able to take care of herself. Between books three and four, Rowling let the word out that a significant character would get killed in *Goblet of Fire*. Rowling describes the speculation about which character this might be that preceded the book's publication: "Mostly they [the kids] worried about Ron. As if I'm going to kill Harry's best friend. What I find interesting is that only once has anybody said to me 'Don't kill Hermione,' and that was after a reading when I said no one's ever worried about her. Another kid said, 'Well, yeh, she's bound to get through OK.' They see her as someone who is not vulnerable."[24]

23. Hattenstone, "Harry, Jesse, and Me," 32.
24. J. K. Rowling, "A Good Scare."

There is some evidence that as Hermione's caricatured self becomes stronger in its own right, Rowling, consciously or unconsciously, is letting go of the stereotypical language and giving her the freedom to subvert the stereotypical behavior assigned to her in the early books. Hermione cries less readily and is described less frequently using the weak verbs and adjectives in book four than in any of the previous three books. She "shrieks" and "squeaks" only once, does not wail or squeal at all, and is not described as "timid" in *Goblet of Fire,* compared to more than fifteen such descriptions in *Prisoner of Azkaban.* Alternative, stronger (if not always pleasant) verbs and adjectives are employed in *Goblet of Fire.* Trites refers to this as subverting stereotypes, something that can occur during the course of a book, even if a character is not empowered at the beginning. "If she does not already know how to speak for herself, she learns in the course of the novel. If she does not already know how strong she is, she learns. If she does not already know how to combine the strengths traditionally associated with femininity with the strengths that have not been, she learns."[25] Not all feminists agree with this androgynous approach to feminism. While radical-libertarian feminists believe both men and women should be androgynous, that is, have access to the full range of so-called male and female characteristics, radical-cultural feminists look more to the enhancement of the so-called female qualities. Although the series is not finished, by book four Hermione seems to be in the process of combining both masculine and feminine traits and thereby subverting the stereotypes imposed on her in earlier books.

It is not precise to discuss Hermione as the hero in an archetypical hero tale because she is not the protagonist of this tale. However, the multi-layered, multifocused nature of what is happening in this novel gives some license to look at Hermione as a second hero, for the hints are clear in book four that she has her own quest to follow. This quest may or may not merge in subsequent books with that of Harry. Here the Le Guin quartet comes back into play, for the first three books are written in a typical masculine archetypical struggle, following the rules of physical prowess, perfection, and a straight line to achieving goals. Speaking of the first three books, Le Guin says, "In all three books, the fundamental power, magic, belongs to men; only to men. . . . The establishment of manhood in heroic terms involves the absolute devaluation of women."[26] However, by the time she writes *Tehanu,* her writing style has undergone a metamorphosis, and she breaks many of the rules of the common archetypical drama. Although it is mere supposition at this point, Hermione's story and her possible move toward a heroic venture are set out in the feminist pattern of *Tehanu,* not

25. Trites, *Sleeping Beauty,* 11.
26. Ursula Le Guin, *Earthsea Revisioned,* 9, 11.

that of its masculine predecessors. In this sense, Hermione's role construction might be described as a female archetype by the denouement of the saga. At this point it is impossible to tell.

One way that authors have attempted to depict strong, independent female characters is through role reversal, that is, by placing women in adventurous roles that have typically been the province of men. The virtue of role reversal may have grown out of existentialist feminism, whose most articulate proponent was Simone de Beauvoir. Her seminal work in feminist study, *The Second Sex,* described women as "the other," the second or lesser sex. De Beauvoir concluded in some cases that adopting roles played by men was the way to equalize power rather than accepting subjugated roles created by men. Robin McKinley's *The Blue Sword,* in which the female protagonist assumes the role of a male, is an example of this technique. This is not the technique employed by Rowling in constructing a role for Hermione. Her strength in the story is not achieved by construction of a typically male role for her. To this point, she does not attempt to be "Ged," nor is she the strong but to-be-rescued Tenar in the second of Le Guin's novels. It remains to be seen whether or not she is as much of a feminist heroine as is Tehanu.

Hermione: Self-Determination and Agency

Put quite simply, this analysis looks at just how much self-determination Rowling affords Hermione. Since Hermione's character seems to be developing in unexpected ways as she gains maturity, it is particularly difficult to say anything definitive with the story only partially told. An answer depends on speculation from threads of evidence offered.

Mendlesohn's essay in this volume is a detailed analysis of the structure of authority in the Harry Potter books. She concludes, "While the books argue superficially for fairness, they actually portray privilege and exceptionalism, not in the sense of elitism, but in a specifically hereditarian context that protects some while exposing others. In this they embody inherently conservative and hierarchical notions of authority clothed in evangelistic mythopoeic fantasy." According to most radical and contemporary feminists, "the feminist notion of a social order [is one] free from hierarchy and exclusion, the hierarchical nature of the fantasy world and its exclusiveness [are] inherently anti-feminist ideals."[27] There must be a caveat to this statement in that not all feminists see hierarchy as specifically male. However, radical-cultural feminists, postmodern feminists, multicultural and global feminists, and ecofeminists would most likely agree with this characterization of male structure. Clearly the administration of Hogwarts is hierarchical and neither Hermione nor any other females have the greatest power

27. Mendlesohn, "Crowing the King," 181; Elizabeth A. Messe, *Crossing the Double-Cross: The Practice of Feminist Criticism.*

or prestige in the story. Because Mendlesohn's analysis is thorough and because the structure of authority at Hogwarts is visibly anti-feminist, I will not consider the structure of authority itself but rather will focus on how much license Hermione and other females have within the confines of this structure. Are they completely subjugated to the patriarchic structure, or do they have some room to develop their own interests and standards, to "be themselves"?

Mendlesohn asserts that Hermione, a witch born of Muggles, is socially acceptable only because someone of higher status, that is, Harry Potter, draws her into the story. Furthermore, she finds that "Hermione is made to look very silly" in her campaign for the house-elves in book four.[28] If I were using the Marxist or socialist feminist framework or approach for this analysis, I might agree with Mendlesohn about the inevitability of suppression of the weaker in an inherently hierarchical structure. However, from a postmodern feminist point of view, looking at ways that females gain agency when they do not have it (as is often the case), I find evidence in the text to be considerably more optimistic about Hermione's self-determination than does Mendlesohn.

In addition, Rowling, through naming and personal identification, suggests that she intends for Hermione to be a strong character who continues to gain strength and self-determination rather than finding it transient. Some textual evidence exists that Hermione will negotiate a place of power in the Hogwarts hierarchy. At this point, I make my case on what we know about Hermione and her interior self-determination that propels her forward despite the barriers she has to overcome, such as her Muggle blood, the male dominance in the hierarchy of the Hogwarts world, and her sometimes overbearing personality. It must be pointed out that many feminists, including existentialist feminists and radical-libertarian feminists, would make no apologies for the overbearing, somewhat obnoxious way Hermione has of dealing with the world, pointing out that men have had the license to act in this manner without castigation.

From the very beginning when she is chosen for Gryffindor House, we know that Hermione has more to her character than merely being smart. The song of the Sorting Hat, the magical chapeau that intuits where each student belongs, tells the eagerly waiting first-year student that she might belong in Gryffindor, "Where dwell the brave at heart/Their daring, nerve, and chivalry/Set Gryffindors apart" (*Sorcerer's Stone*, 118).[29]

---

28. Mendlesohn, "Crowning the King," 180.
29. In *Goblet of Fire* we find from the Sorting Hat that among the four founders of Hogwarts, it was Gryffindor who founded the tradition of the hat to carry on the selection of students for houses after the founders were gone (177).

Harry notes that sometimes the hat shouts out the house to which some-one belongs at once and at other times it takes a little while to decide. It took the hat almost a minute to place Seamus Finnigan. It had a difficult time with Harry Potter, wavering between Gryffindor and Slytherin. But with Hermione, it shouted out Gryffindor without hesitation. From what we know about Hermione's propensity to "wit and learning" (*Sorcerer's Stone,* 118), the characteristics of those in Ravenclaw, we might assume that to be her fate. That there was not a moment's hesitation by the Sorting Hat foreshadows for the reader that Hermione will have "daring, nerve, and chivalry." These are all signs of self-determination, in the case of Hermione, against the external odds of initially acting chiefly as Harry's agent. It is no mistake that Hermione was sorted rapidly by the hat.

Hermione's agency develops slowly. She refuses to be deterred from her purposes, whether it be learning, admonishing about rules, or, as I believe we will see, championing the underdog. Although in the first mutual ad-venture the friends have with the troll, the boys rescue Hermione, in all subsequent adventures she plays a decisive role. She first wins the respect of Harry and Ron through her use of knowledge to solve many of the trio's difficulties. Harry is clearly not as knowledgeable and adept at analytical thinking as Hermione, even though he has endowed magical powers that she does not possess. Her first opportunity to save the day comes with her discovery that Nicolas Flamel, alchemist and friend of Dumbledore's, is the maker of the Sorcerer's Stone—a stone that makes gold and stops its pos-sessor from dying. As the three friends try to find their way to the Sorcerer's Stone, they must pass through obstacles set up by the faculty. Hermione is able to solve Snape's spell because it is based on logic. As Hermione points out, "A lot of the greatest wizards haven't got an ounce of logic, they'd be stuck in here forever" (*Sorcerer's Stone,* 285). Hermione has vocalized just why she will succeed despite being born to Muggles—she is not only learning magic, but she has logic, the logic missing sometimes from her friends, Harry and Ron.

Determined action is another element of Hermione's agency in her own fate. Hermione's feelings can clearly be hurt, as, for example, in *Sorcerer's Stone* when she overhears Harry saying no one can stand her and Ron not-ing that she has no friends, and subsequently she turns away and hurries off in tears. Nonetheless, Hermione sticks to what she believes. The on-going saga of Hermione's cat, Crookshanks, is a signal from Rowling that Hermione will stand up for her rights despite "bucking the crowd," and even if it means losing one of the two friends she has at that point. Could it be that Crookshanks is named after the radical reformist and caricatur-ist George Cruikshank, who illustrated Dickens's novels and who agreed with Dickens on the need for social reform? Will Crookshanks play a role with Hermione in her struggle for social reform? Is this a foreshadowing? Should we think of Crookshanks as a sort of daemon of the type that appear in Philip Pullman's *His Dark Materials* trilogy? Does his determination tells us something about the character of his owner—tough, brave, and unwanted? In *Prisoner of Azkaban*, Sirius Black pinpoints Crookshanks as highly intelligent (rather than mad, as some might think).

There are two instances of Hermione's "Crookshank-like" intelligent and determined personality in *Prisoner of Azkaban*. The first is when she tells Professor McGonagall that she thinks Harry's new Firebolt broom is from Sirius Black, and Professor McGonagall confiscates it to be sure it is safe, making both Harry and Ron furious with Hermione. Just as the boys decide to apologize, Scabbers, Ron's rat, disappears, and Ron again becomes quite angry with Hermione. Although it is clear that Hermione suffers from the alienation that results in each case, she sticks to her principles. Of course, in the end she is vindicated about Crookshanks, who senses all along that Scabbers is evil. Both of these actions are signs of a female with her own agency.

One of the first signs that Hermione is going to stand up for the downtrodden is shortly after Hagrid has received word that Buckbeak the hippogriff is going to be executed. Hagrid has his face buried in a handkerchief when Malfoy says sarcastically, "Have you ever seen anything quite as pathetic?" (*Prisoner of Azkaban*, 293). Although Harry and Ron make threatening moves toward Malfoy, Hermione gets there first. With fury, she slaps him in the cheek and demands that he never say anything of that sort to Hagrid again. After this action, Hermione remembers she is a witch and pulls out her wand, combining now her logical, physical, and magical powers (one page after which she "squeaks"—entirely out of character). Malfoy has met his match.

But it is in book four that we find Hermione's self-determination coming to the forefront. She has taken on the case of the house-elves, who are slaves of the wizards. It is true that both her friends and the faculty ridicule her for her actions, that she is made to seem extreme and unreasonable, and that initially the house-elves seem worse off for her efforts to help. This is, however, precisely what happens when any individual advocates for massive social reform. History documents that those who opposed slavery were not enthusiastically welcomed or even understood by most of their contemporaries. Rowling has set up Hermione's character from the moment that she is chosen for Gryffindor to be brave at heart, to show daring, nerve, and chivalry, an indication that she may continue her advocacy for the house-elves despite her own misgivings or those of others.

Hermione asserts her independence socially from her friends also by going to the Yule Ball with Viktor Krum from Bulgaria—one of the four students chosen to participate in the Triwizard Tournament. It is her trump card when Harry and Ron seek her out at the last minute to attend with them, yet another sign that she is becoming her own agent, free from being merely Harry Potter's friend. And who can worry about a girl who takes on the bully of the tale with sarcasm: "Twitchy little ferret, aren't you, Malfoy?" (*Goblet of Fire*, 404).

Rowling seems to have successfully, thus far, developed an emerging adolescent who appears armed to withstand the most dangerous gender-related pitfall and not retreat into silence, intimidated by the masculine world. The most typical and one of the most dreadful and long-lasting things to happen to young women as they reach adolescence is for them to "lose their voices," symbolic of their losing their self-confidence and their agency. Lynn Mikle Brown and Carol Gilligan's *Meeting at the Crossroads: Women's Psychology and Girls' Development* is a study of preadolescent girls and how they lose their voices "at the crossroads" of becoming young women. Psychologist Mary Pipher's *Reviving Ophelia: Saving the Selves of Adolescent Girls* also documents this adolescent silencing and the disastrous results. Joan Jacobs Brumberg, professor of history, human development, and women's studies at Cornell University, addresses this same issue in "When Girls Talk."[30] She reviews a number of recent books in which young girls do speak out on topics such as incest and other abuse, drug use, self-mutilation, anorexia, sexuality, and issues about school. She suggests that, although numbers of girls are now finding their voices, they do not have the connections with others or the adult world they need. Referring to the issue of articulated voice in children's literature, Trites says, "A chief characteristic of feminist children's novels is that they define relationships that foster community as an arena in which children of both sexes can safely articulate their voices."[31] Hermione sometimes has difficulty with her own articulation—she is "put down" throughout much of the first two books for her studying. However, this teasing tapers off considerably as Harry and Ron perceive how valuable her knowledge is to them. By the end of book three, she is lauded by Professor Lupin as the cleverest witch of her age that he's ever seen. Later in book four, Hermione is derided because of her concern for house-elves. Overall, however, there is ample evidence that Hermione is growing stronger and more articulate rather than retreating into repressed silence. Whether she is developing the autonomous, individualized girlhood observed by Brumberg even when young female adolescents do speak out remains to be seen.

30. Joan Jacobs Brumberg, "When Girls Talk." One such book, a follow-up to that of Mary Pipher, is Sara Shandler's *Ophelia Speaks: Adolescent Girls Write about Their Search for Self.*
31. Trites, *Waking Sleeping Beauty*, 99.

Hermione: Sense of Community/Connection

One of the characteristics of females pointed out by Carol Gilligan of Harvard University and numerous other researchers is their sense of connection and community. Tong labels Gilligan's form of feminism a type of radical feminism known as "gender or cultural feminism," akin to psychoanalytic feminism, but capitalizing on the inherent gender strengths of being female rather than cataloging the weaknesses as in a Freudian approach. Gilligan finds it is "in women's nature" to be communal. She observes that "women perceive and construe social reality differently from men and . . . these differences center around experiences of attachment and separation."[32] According to Gilligan, this is not a weak position, but one of strength because intrinsic to this interdependence is a strong sense of responsibility. Women have wrongly been perceived as weak when in fact their strength is simply not defined in masculine terms.

Where does this enter the analysis of Hermione? Rowling tells us that, from the moment of the troll trauma, Hermione became Ron's and Harry's friend. Sharing this adventure served as a catalyst for their bonding. The three friends clearly respect one another, and each contributes to the relationship, as is shown by how each of them takes a lead role in solving one of the mysteries set up by the faculty to protect the Sorcerer's Stone (although Hermione's knowledge initiates the search). Hermione does miss out on fairly substantial parts of the adventures of Ron and Harry in book two. In *Chamber of Secrets* Hermione mistakes a cat's hair for that of Milicent Bulstrode, transforming herself into part cat rather than into Milicent. Later in the same story she is turned to stone. She is in the infirmary when the most exciting action takes place. However, before she is taken off stage, Hermione contributes to the denouement of both adventures—it is Hermione who reads about the transfiguration spell that later backfires on her with the wrong hair, and she is the one who suggests using this spell to get information from the Slytherins. It is also Hermione who suggests that Tom Riddle's diary might be written in invisible ink. Other than these two instances in book two, however, her time on stage seems fairly equivalent to that of Harry's other friend, Ron.

A more important question, perhaps, is whether Hermione receives anything from this relationship that helps in her own development. According to Trites, "Almost every feminist children's text shows some sort of community being built. . . . What really matters, then, about the focus on relationships in feminist children's novels is the way these novels demonstrate people interacting, gaining strength from each other, and being strong in their relationships." The emphasis here is "interdependency" rather than

---

32. Gilligan, *In a Different Voice: Psychological Theory and Women's Development*, 171.

dependency. What is affirming about the friendship among Harry, Ron, and Hermione is that it is heterosexual but largely not sexual—the three friends care for one another in an interdependent manner.[33] There are numerous examples in the books that show an interdependency among the group—if anything, Harry and Ron are more dependent on Hermione than she is on them. Many of the adventures involve the three together trying to solve a puzzle. Rowling constructs a friendship community in which Hermione demonstrates her own innate abilities and the honing of them through her study.

What is notable, however, from a feminist point of view, is the almost complete isolation of Hermione from anyone else other than Harry, Ron, and Hagrid. She is essentially without the context of "sisterhood"—she has no female friend; she is not particularly at ease with her female teachers; and, although her dentist parents are mentioned several times, we know nothing about her family except that they went to France on vacation one summer. This is in stark contrast to Harry, whose birth parents as well as the family in which he grew up are well known to us as readers, and to Ron, whose siblings and parents have large roles in the stories. When we think of Hermione as a witch-in-training, the lack of a female community seems odd, as forming a supportive community, largely of women, is a hallmark of witches and Wicca.[34] Although this is clearly not what the author intended for the story, nonetheless when looking at it from a number of feminist perspectives, it does nothing to strengthen an often-referred-to feminist characteristic—a closely knit, supportive, same-gender community. The multicultural, global, and ecofeminists put particular emphasis on community. While the radical-cultural feminists or gender feminists put the most emphasis on sisterhood, from the very beginning of liberal feminism with the suffragettes, female bonding has played a role in many (but certainly not all) feminist stances.

Hermione: Ethics of Caring

Closely related to the feminist issue of community (or lack thereof) is the moral development of females, particularly the ethics of caring. This ground

33. Trites, *Waking Sleeping Beauty,* 99. Ron is based on a person who was a close friend of Rowling's. She says, "Ron, who is Harry's other best friend, he's a lot like my oldest friend, who is a man called Sean. I was at school with him and the second book is dedicated to Sean" (Rowling, "Surprising Success").

34. For information on modern witches and Wicca, see *The Witches' Voice Inc.* Rowling has repeatedly said, however, that the witches and wizards at Hogwarts—as real as they seem—are not intended to be authentic in any way other than in her imagination. It is the fear that they are that caused the Harry Potter books to receive the most censorship challenges in statistics collected by the American Library Association during 2000 and prompted the counter-censorship group Muggles for Harry Potter (now known as KidSPEAK).

for discussion, however, becomes more controversial as it enters the realm of societally constructed traits versus biological determinism. While radical feminists adhere to biological determinism, radical-libertarian feminists see overcoming it with androgyny (male and female traits embraced to the advantage of both genders), while radical-cultural or gender feminists argue that women should capitalize on it and protect it. The research of Carol Gilligan suggests that Hermione seems to embrace more of an androgynous model of moral and ethical development that has decidedly "male" components. In her study of women, Gilligan finds that the concept of morality is concerned with the activity of care and that moral development centers around understanding of responsibility and relationships. Men, on the other hand, understand the morality of fairness and tie moral development to the understanding of rights and rules. In essence this boils down to care versus justice and a focus on others versus structures. One of the issues with this characteristic is whether women learn to care for themselves as well as others. Hermione's taking care of herself in getting to the Yule Ball seems one instance in which she is capable of doing this. Gilligan states that her research provides a very different female moral perspective from that of Lawrence Kohlberg, whose study focused primarily on boys.[35] More in line with Kohlberg or what Gilligan suggests as the masculine view of morality, Hermione's stance against the mistreatment of the house-elves seems to be more from a sense of injustice (everyone should be treated the same) than of what might be called care (no one should be hurt).

However, although Hermione's sense of "right and wrong" is clearly often based on rules and regulations, relationships actually hold the upper hand. As much as Hermione hates breaking rules, she lies to protect her friends. The friendship among Harry, Ron, and Hermione was first solidified when Hermione deliberately lied to Professor McGonagall about what happened with the troll in the girls' bathroom to protect her friends from the teacher's discipline. Clearly this action was done out of caring rather than justice. Later, in *Prisoner of Azkaban,* Hermione takes the lead in rescuing Buckbeak from execution, out of a sense of caring for him and her friend Hagrid. The question of whether, in balance, Hermione is acting from what Gilligan and others have described as a female morality of caring (often overlooked, unheard, or disdained by men) rather than a male morality of justice or whether she is achieving an androgynous balance must be left to future analysis. She is only in early adolescence, so it is too soon to tell. Another characteristic noted by feminists who advocate for a biological determinism in women is looking inward for knowledge. Hermione does not fit this

35. Tong states that "when I wrote the first edition of this book [*Feminist Thought*], I was both impressed and overwhelmed by the diverse range of views within the radical feminist community" (2); Gilligan, *In a Different Voice,* 19. Kohlberg's work on moral development is the subject of Lana Whited's essay elsewhere in this book.

"female model." She is not contemplative; she constructs her knowledge almost entirely from external sources, rarely using "female intuition." She even forgets to use magic at times. " 'HAVE YOU GONE MAD?' Ron bellowed. 'ARE YOU A WITCH OR NOT?' " (*Sorcerer's Stone*, 278). Possibly Hermione may end up with what Belenky et al. call a "constructed knowledge," integrating what she knows intuitively with what she has learned from outside sources.[36] But so far, Hermione seems prone to what some feminists characterize as a "man's way of knowing"—perhaps even more so than Harry, who doesn't "know" what to do but depends on his "magic intuition"—and a "man's way of negotiating society." In either case, she is full of self-determination and insistent upon her own agency as much as possible within the structure of authority in her magical world.

Hermione—Two Other Feminist Issues

Body image, a serious adolescent issue for young women, is only cursorily touched upon in the Harry Potter books. The most sexually provocative women are the Veela, who appear at the Quidditch World Cup and momentarily mesmerize Harry (*Goblet of Fire*, 103). Hermione seems to care little about her appearance until book four. The major issue of appearance is Hermione's teeth, which have already been described as larger than average. Then Malfoy points his magic wand and they start to grow. Later in a discussion of who is going with whom to the Yule Ball, Ron notes that Hermione's teeth are no longer fangs but "all . . . straight and—and normal-sized" (*Goblet of Fire*, 403). At the Yule Ball, Rowling gives us Harry's "take" on Hermione—he sees her sleek hair, her filmy dress, her regal way of walking, and her newly reduced teeth all as extremely attractive.

Here Harry's admiration for Hermione is shifting from her brains to her looks—and Hermione has purposefully concentrated on her body image. Radical-libertarian feminists maintain that females have the right to do whatever they want to with their bodies, while radical-cultural feminists would more likely disapprove of using the body in this manner to attract male attention. This is a minor incident, a paragraph among thousands. Is it a turning point? Is this a "red flag?" As with other developmental issues, it's simply too soon to tell.

The other feminist issue that may be surfacing through Hermione's concern for the house-elves is one common to contemporary feminist perspectives—inclusiveness and concern for all types of repression and marginalization rather than that of women alone. Vandergrift's model includes both "body image" and "Eco-Feminism" as pieces in her "Model of Female Voices in Youth Literature." Ecofeminism is the most radically inclusive form of feminism and in this sense joins multicultural and global

36. Mary Field Belenky, et al., *Women's Ways of Knowing: The Development of Self, Voice, and Mind.*

feminism. According to Tong in *Feminist Thought,* realization of this affinity of women's issues with others in marginalized positions represents the major revision of her book, first published at the end of the 1980s. Tong states, "I now understand the extent to which all systems and structures of oppression interlock, reinforcing each other and feeding off of each other's venom" (278).[37]

Up to this point the Harry Potter saga has seemed to be about a magical wizard world in which concerns rested on good versus evil in the sense that Voldemort portrays evil—a nebulous but threatening menace. Hints that good versus evil may go beyond this come when the issue of "Muggle" versus "witch or wizard" blood is raised several times throughout the first four books. The trio of main characters has one pureblooded wizard (Ron), one mixed blood (Harry), and one Muggle-born or, in derogatory terms, "Mudblood" (Hermione). By creating a main character of each type, Rowling provides a clue that purebloodedness is not to be the "ideal" in this world. But the "blood heritage" has not yet become a "cause for crusade."

However, in book four when Hermione comes forth forcefully with her Society for the Protection of Elfish Welfare (S.P.E.W.), the issue of an extended sense of social conscience enters the story. There are implied questions of race here, although Rowling has not put emphasis on racial differences per se (no racial or ethnic discrimination is directed toward Lee Jordan, Cho Chang, and Parvati Patil). The issues raised and comments made about Muggle blood, giant blood, and elf suppression represent racial as well as class discrimination in these books.

It is difficult without the remaining three books to analyze this from a feminist point of view, but if Rowling is going to emphasize these issues more in books to come (which I suspect she is), then a feminist analysis of the books would have to include acknowledgment of this inclusiveness.

Minerva McGonagall: What Kind of Character?

The only other female character with a significant and ongoing role in the Harry Potter books is Minerva McGonagall. McGonagall is neither a caricature nor a stereotype but a strong, independent female. Christine Schoefer writing in *Salon* magazine says, "The only female authority figure is beady-eyed, thin-lipped Minerva McGonagall, professor of transfiguration and deputy headmistress of Hogwarts. Stern instead of charismatic, she is described as eyeing her students like a 'wrathful eagle.'" Mendlesohn describes McGonagall as "unfair and hasty."[38] I propose that McGonagall

---

37. Hermione's actions, which become more and more outward-directed by book four, parallel the development of feminist movements—toward a more inclusive, comprehensive concern for others, Tong, *Feminist Thought,* 278.

38. Christine Shoefer, "Harry Potter's Girl Trouble"; Mendlesohn, "Crowning the King," 175.

is, instead, the epitome of fairness, the second in command who provides stability and discipline so that the first in command is freed to be more creative. Rather than contrasting McGonagall to Dumbledore, I contrast her role to that of Professor Snape.

Ron reports to Harry that Professor Snape, who is head of Slytherin, favors those students in his house. Harry wistfully replies that he wishes Professor McGonagall, head of Gryffindor, would favor them. Like Hermione, Professor McGonagall believes in rules but is not chained to them. She breaks a rule early in book one, and wisely so; she does not do it in the spirit of favoritism as do Snape and even the headmaster, Dumbledore. She shows the maturity not to adhere to a rule simply because it is a rule. The incident occurs after Harry's first try at flying. Professor McGonagall observes him at practice, marches him to her office, and introduces him to the captain of the team as a potential seeker, the central player on the Quidditch team. First-years are not supposed to play seeker, but Professor McGonagall immediately sees that enforcing this rule would not be advantageous. She does admonish Harry to play hard or she may change her mind about not punishing him. At the same time, she smiles kindly at Harry and notes that his father, an excellent Quidditch player himself, would have been proud of him. Later McGonagall proves herself not to be rule-bound by letting Hermione use the Time-Turner to extend her studies.

In addition to representing fairness, justice, and dependability in the Harry Potter books, Professor McGonagall also possesses a wry sense of humor, as is captured in several scenes with Professor Trelawney. Following Christmas dinner, Professor Trelawney shrieks loudly when Harry and Ron get up from the table, demanding to know which boy left his seat first. Professor McGonagall remarks, with a touch of sarcasm, that she doubts if it will matter "unless a mad axe-man is waiting outside the doors" ready to slaughter the first student in sight (*Prisoner of Azkaban,* 230).

Professor McGonagall is a strong, ethical woman. She is head of the most prestigious house, Gryffindor, and she is party to all important decisions. The structure of authority, the patriarchal society, places some constraints on her, but she is an empowered female within this structure. She seems to embody "wisdom," thus living up to her given name.

Other Females in the Harry Potter Novels
Looking beyond Professor McGonagall, however, the female landscape at Hogwarts (or in the magic or Muggle world beyond) is somewhat bleak. It must be analyzed as a landscape, as no one character has a large enough role to make or break the story from a feminist point of view. One reason that Hermione may have no female friends is that there are few other girls at Hogwarts with whom she might be compatible. None possess her strength, assertiveness, and wisdom. Many of the background characters are

stereotypes. Certainly Petunia Dursley, a female in the family with whom Harry grew up, is unpleasant in stereotypical ways. Madame Pince, the librarian at Hogwarts, is competent but a worn-out stereotype. Professor Trelawney is more of a caricature than a stereotype but is definitely "ditzy." Reporter Rita Skeeter is is another highly exaggerated caricature. We don't know enough about Madame Hooch, the Quidditch coach, to determine what type of person she is, although the fact that she is female speaks to some consciousness on the part of Rowling not to overbalance the choice roles for males. Professor Sprout, a female science teacher, also steps beyond the bounds of stereotype. Quidditch players, including keepers, are both male and female. Ginny Weasley and Parvati Patel might show some promise for strength beneath their silliness and giggles—Rowling deemed Parvati worthy of going to the Yule Ball with Harry. Fleur Delacour does not perform spectacularly in the Triwizard Tournament, coming in last place after the males. Lily Potter sacrificed herself for her son, Harry, but we know little else about her. Cho Chang, a seeker on a Quidditch team, so far has a minor role. Winky, the house-elf, could be called Weepy or Whiny, as she complains bitterly about her freedom. It's a mixed and inconclusive picture. Here is the perspective of a thirteen-year-old girl who initiated a discussion among teens on the *Un-official Harry Potter Fan Club* web site with the question "Do you ever get the feeling that the HP books are SEXIST?" Her initial post was

> I was just thinking about this and it occurred to me that the most developed and interesting characters are all males, and the major roles in the book are male roles.
> Harry's the hero, Voldemort's the most powerful villain in the world, Dumbledore's one of the best, Moody's the most interesting Auror, nearly the whole Ministry is male, the Weasley twins are the comic relief, Sirius is the wild, fatherly figure . . . and so on. As for the female characters, we have Parvati and Lavender. They are written as giggling (and ditzy?) girls.
> And Hermione? Well, I'll take a poll. Who has the larger part in the story, Hermione or Ron? I'm not saying that I resent the books for being more masculine than feminine, but I was just wondering if anybody else felt there was some sexism. The story's very enjoyable with all the guy characters, but I personally don't like the way the female characters are written. And plus, wouldn't it still have been acceptable if Voldemort had been a woman? A cold, murderous woman that is able to lead evil men. Where's the harm in having a commanding female presence? Oh yes, and the Triwizard Tournament was also something. 3/4 of them were guys and Fleur was given last place. Any comments on that?[39]

The discussion went on for two weeks with a number of young people participating. The group never agreed on what "sexist" means. Most

39. "Do You Ever Get the Feeling the HP Books Are Sexist?" ("Yellow Cherry").

participants defended Hermione and Professor McGonagall. Hermione was characterized as "smart, brave, wise, kind." Another discussant commented that "Hermione is a more powerful witch than Ron is a wizard. Prof. Mc-Gonagall is deffinatly [*sic*] one of my favorite characters, in the top 3. I think her character is really well developed, how she manages to keep stern, and keep the respect of all her students, but at the same time it really shows through how much she cares about them. She's assertive, deals well with every problem, stands up for what she believes in, and she's a great teacher. I think she's awesome!" Yet another teen reader says, "Hermione, Prof. McGonagall (she deserves bigger parts) and Mrs. Weasley (I love her!) are great examples of good, brilliant, brave witches."[40] Some participants commented on the "second tier" role of the women in general. Others, in response to the original questioner, cited Crabbe, Goyle, and other male counterparts as comparable to the blander females. With many thoughtful points and counterpoints, the general consensus was that the books are "a little bit sexist," but basically just good stories and okay. In balance, taking an overview of the entire Harry Potter world, I agree with one young reader's perception:

> The wizard world as portrayed by JKR is an ironic image or a copy of our own society. I don't mean this is the "message" behind it all, it's just why it's so funny—just think of the style of the newspaper articles, the organization of the ministry and of the school, how Fudge talks exactly like all politicians do . . . so if the wizarding world is full of allusions, irony and satire about our own world, it's very likely to mirror those social mechanisms and institutions and opinions that we consider as sexist. And so it does. The ministry is such a male-dominated thing BECAUSE OUR MINISTRIES ARE. There are very few witches in leading positions anywhere BECAUSE IT'S THE SAME WITH US. It's part of the ironic representation of the Muggle world in its parallel, the Wizarding world.[41]

The one area in which Rowling falls below a mere reflection of the world as it exists is in her use of verbs and adjectives when she describes girls and women. This has already been discussed in relation to Hermione. Her use of gender-biased words is far more overtly and overly "sexist" than the roles she assigns to girls and women. The pervasive description of girls as silly, giggling, and light-headed undermines her more gender-balanced depiction of girls' opportunities in the patriarchal hierarchy. For example, "Cedric Diggory walked past, surrounded by a large group of simpering girls" (*Goblet of Fire*, 297). There are far more descriptors of this type than justified by the

---

40. "Do You Ever Get the Feeling the HP Books Are Sexist?" ("CherryTea," "Akari," and "AndreaVera").

41. "Do You Ever Get the Feeling the HP Books Are Sexist?" ("Lioness").

social structure that Rowling portrays. It is the major gender-based discord in the books.

If a feminist novel is one that sets up a world to which readers can aspire rather than one that more or less reflects the existing social order, Rowling does not write a feminist novel. She reflects a patriarchal, hierarchical world. Some of the females have the opportunity to be assertive, to take leadership positions, and to be heard, but the males are dominant and are in charge— at least for the time being. The social structure of this magical world as it relates to gender is closer to reality than it is to a vision of a better world—at least through the end of book four. Rowling tells a good tale, but so far it is not a story intended for reformation based on gender issues. Thus, when I take an overall look at gender issues in the Harry Potter series, I conclude that in a general sense it will represent for future generations the far less than ideal reality of the late twentieth and early twenty-first centuries.

The Cinematic Hermione

On November 16, 2001, the much-anticipated film of *Harry Potter and the Sorcerer's Stone* was released by Warner Brothers in the United States and a number of other countries, with a full worldwide rollout by April 12, 2002. Eleven-year-old British actress Emma Watson made her film debut as Hermione. According to screenwriter Steven Kloves, he pleased Rowling by saying, unsolicited, that one reason he wanted to write the script was Hermione. "And," he says, "it's true. I read Hermione and she jumped off the page for me. I was so enchanted by her, because she's difficult and smart and funny, and sometimes unaware that she is being funny. She's a great character to write."[42] Kloves had an unusually active working relationship with Rowling, who often provided guidance about what was a throwaway in the books and what was essential for the yet unpublished tomes in the saga. With a perceptive screenwriter and an author heavily involved in the production, the portrayal of the cinematic Hermione would predictably be closely aligned with that of the literary Hermione.

To some extent this is accurate. Kloves does successfully create the "difficult and smart and funny" Hermione he saw in the book. Upon close analysis, however, Hermione on the screen differs somewhat from Hermione on the page. The cinematic Hermione has been "toned down" in several ways, some of which are subtle. For example, she is not quite the acerbic, absorbed young scholar whom Rowling brings to life in the book. Throughout the book, Hermione makes reference to the exact titles of the tomes she has studied when she offers her insights into a situation. In the film, the specific sources of her knowledge are removed, as are many descriptive passages about the hours and hours she studies and what she achieves, for example,

---

42. "International Release Dates"; Joe Nazzaro, "Scripting Spells," 22.

scoring 112 percent on Flitwick's exam in *Sorcerer's Stone*. Possibly the books' titles and remarks about Hermione's academic achievement seemed like "throwaways" to both Kloves and Rowling, and perhaps they are in the long run, but to the thoughtful reader/viewer, Hermione becomes less a scholar and more a person "endowed" with knowledge. Applying the feminist analysis framework, in the film Hermione seems somewhat less involved in determining her own fate or role. Another subtle omission is the Sorting Hat song—no longer are the characteristics of the Gryffindor students spelled out, taking away the explicit foreshadowing of the hat's quick pick for Hermione. However, gone, also, are the stereotypical adjectives associated with young females, as are some of the gestures and reactions into which they might have been translated.

In comparing Hermione as a film and book character from a feminist point of view, the most damaging omission occurs near the end as the three companions approach the Sorcerer's Stone. In the book, each child gets credit for successfully leading the others in accomplishing an especially dangerous task created to block those attempting to reach the stone. The tasks in which Harry and Ron take the lead remain in the film, but Hermione's task is omitted. Her accomplishment, which involved choosing which of seven bottles is poison, is just to her liking—it requires logical thinking. According to Hermione, many great wizards are lacking in logic and therefore could well miss the solutions to puzzles that she solves. Despite Hermione's contribution to the rescue, in the film it is the two male children who are the saviors at the end, and gone for Hermione is an important self-defining statement. From the feminist analytical framework, this is a blatant, not a subtle, denial of agency, and in fact it seizes from Hermione the opportunity to journey toward establishing her equality with the male characters. She is relegated at this point to the role of sidekick rather than that of co-equal contributor and determiner of her own fate through her own unique abilities. There are several reasons that this scene may have been omitted from the film that have nothing to do with the fact that it was Hermione's task, one of which is that it lacks the intensity and action of Harry's and Ron's episodes and may have been deemed to slow down the momentum that had been built. Nonetheless, it was an unfortunate action for the development of Hermione's character.

The jury is still out regarding an analysis of the cinematic Hermione based on the portrayal of gender. There is even more uncertainty in the deliberation than with the books since only one film has been produced.

Hermione and the Heritage of Gender

What tentative conclusions about legacy can be reached from the first four books, looking backward to Hermione's mythological and literary heritage and forward to the heritage that Hermione leaves to future readers of this saga? Hermione Granger, like all of her literary and mythological antecedents, remains secondary in her role to the males in her story. In this, she does not differ substantially from Euripides' or Shakespeare's Hermiones, although her life is less controlled by men. Her relationship to male characters in the Harry Potter novels is more akin to the contemporary Hermione of H. D. than to the ancients.[43] Hermione Granger does show kinship, however, with the courage and determination of her "ancestors." Like them, she makes her way as a strong female in a patriarchal structure. Euripedes' Hermione stands her ground against her husband's lover; what little we know about St. Hermione shows courage and determination; Shakespeare's Hermione makes a dramatic "comeback" in order to reclaim her rightful position as queen; H. D.'s Hermione seeks strength from her own tripartite literary "heritages."

Hermione Granger starts her journey being somewhat dependent on Harry and Ron, but that dependence grows quickly into interdependence, and there is some evidence in book four that this will develop into independence. Like D. H. Lawrence's Hermione, Hermione Granger uses her intellect to gain control over her own life, but unlike her predecessors, Hermione shows signs of overcoming her unpleasant, bossy nature and of directing her intellectual energy into socially useful causes in addition to solving puzzles for Harry and her friends. To date, Rowling has produced a character who has developed steadily throughout the four books—moving toward an integrated personality with increasing agency. D. H. Lawrence's Hermione has been analyzed from the point of view of female bonding and has been found lacking in terms of lasting "sisterhood" relationships. Hermione Granger has bonded with her male friends, but at this point in the story there is no evidence that she will participate in the community of women that is a fundamental feminist characteristic. Only St. Hermione of the preceding Hermiones showed the "ethics of caring" that may be emerging with Hermione Granger in her house-elves' campaign. It is too early to tell what her "story" for future readers might be in this arena.[44] All in all, Rowling's Hermione stands tall among her literary antecedents.

43. Kate Millett, a radical-libertarian feminist who wrote the influential *Sexual Politics,* describes D. H. Lawrence as one of the worst perpetrators of patriarchy's female sexual suppression. Hermione Granger does not relate to the Lawrence character in this dimension, only in her intellectual approach to life.
44. Vukovic, "Bonding and Separating of Female Characters in *Women in Love.*" In response to Christine Schoefer's harsh review of Rowling's females in Salon.com, Lis Langley makes this concluding comment about the gender heritage of Rowling's books: "But in the end, it's a good idea to take a reality check on the sex roles. Harry, male, is made up. Dumbledore, male, is pretend. J. K. Rowling, female, is very real, a gazillionaire, owner of a superior imagination and a way with words. . . . If that is what it's like to be 'only a woman,' who wouldn't enjoy being a girl?" From Lis Langley, "Charmed, I'm Sure."

One predictor of what Hermione Granger may become "when she grows up" comes from another character in the books, Professor Minerva Mc-Gonagall. Not only do Hermione and Minerva share mythological roots through their names, but Rowling also links them in her text. " 'You're not telling me you *did* fly here?' said Hermione, sounding almost as severe as Professor McGonagall" (*Chamber of Secrets*, 84). One of the teens in the online sexism discussion makes this link also: "A word about the 'strong women,' Hermione and Prof. McGonagall. They are actually quite similar, ever thought of Hermione taking over McGonagall's teaching job when she's graduated and McGonagall retires?"[45] Minerva was a greater goddess than Hermione and outwitted the male gods around her. Professor Mc-Gonagall has more power than Hermione Granger and to some extent, she is also wiser. There is some foreshadowing, however, that Hermione's role may surpass the adult role that Professor McGonagall now plays, and that it may be more multidimensional. We have no evidence that Professor Mc-Gonagall has any relationship with males beyond her assistant headmaster duties, while Hermione has now moved into interaction with male characters that may go beyond friendship. Professor McGonagall has not revealed any social conscience of the type that Hermione exhibits in book four.

Judging just past the midpoint in the story, I find a great deal of promise that Hermione Granger's heritage for future readers, viewed from a feminist perspective, will hold up as one that meets Trites's definition of an empowered female and that satisfies feminist ideals from a number of perspectives. Hermione seems to be subverting the more stereotypic aspects of her personality and moving toward becoming a stronger, more independent (as well as healthily interdependent) character. She is not likely ever to be a champion for the rights of women in the nineteenth- or early-twentieth-century sense of liberal feminism. Yet, she may exhibit kinship with the marginalized elf population and in her work with them move into an inclusive position adhered to by multicultural, global, or ecofeminists.

From the postmodern view that I proposed to take in this analysis, the marginalized or "other" position of females is enabling rather than entrapping because it allows for change and difference. There is no unified one best way for a woman to be, no feminist ideal that can be articulated and applied. Instead the ideal for a female is to become what she wants to be with concern and respect for both self and others. Hermione is not a feminist model for engagement in sisterhood and is the antithesis of a strong female in the "shrillness" with which Rowling has at times portrayed her. But Hermione *is* seeking what she wants to become with a healthy concern and respect for both self and others.

45. "Do You Ever Feel HP Books Are Sexist?" ("Lioness").

Rowling's Hermione is a strong, intelligent, thoughtful, compassionate female who is not only assisting the males with whom she has an interdependent relationship but also working to become her own agent as well as a catalyst for social change. This is the heritage that Hermione Granger, at the end of book four in the Harry Potter series, leaves readers of the story.

Locating Harry Potter in the "Boys' Book" Market

Terri Doughty

A few weeks ago, in a fourth-year class discussion of gender in children's literature, one student mused, "Would we read the books differently if they were *Harry the Spy* and *Harriet Potter*?"[1] Certainly the heroines of Tamora Pierce and Robin McKinley have shown that anything boys can do they can do better. Also, the Harry Potter books are celebrated for their broad readership: adults and children, boys and girls. Gender does not appear to be an issue. However, reviewers have remarked in particular on the books' appeal for boys, and editorial cartoons across North America have shown boys forsaking their computers and the television for Rowling's tales.[2] No matter who reads them, the Harry Potter books are quintessentially boys' books. As Gregory Maguire notes, Harry is "a boy's boy."[3] He is obsessed with sport (Quidditch); he flourishes in the somewhat homosocial world of Hogwarts (although he does have a female friend, Hermione is usually fussing over her studies, and in the earlier books she often either does not accompany Harry and Ron on their most daring adventures, or frets in a shrill voice throughout the action); and he longs to be worthy of Gryffindor, brave and chivalrous, rather than patient (Hufflepuff), learned (Ravenclaw), or crafty (Slytherin). The film adaptation of the first book highlights this aspect of the novel. Harry's fellowship with Ron is emphasized, and all female students other than Hermione fade into the background. Even the female Quidditch players have almost no lines. The books make use of such standard boy's school story elements as team sports, interhouse competitions, and escapes from the dormitory for midnight adventures.[4]

1. I would like to thank Julie Conroy for allowing me to open my discussion with her question.
2. See, for instance, the selection of cartoons at "Darryl Cagle's Professional Cartoonist Index."
3. Gregory Maguire, "Lord of the Golden Snitch."
4. For a survey of sources tapped for the Potter books, see Wendy Doniger's "Can You Spot the Source," 26–27.

The elements of the classic boy's school story used by J. K. Rowling have led to some criticism. The books have been described carefully by Nicholas Tucker as "backward looking," and more nastily by Anthony Holden as being nothing more than "Billy Bunter on broomsticks."[5] I think these criticisms are outgrowths of a particular cultural climate. We are bombarded by media images of children abandoned, children abused, children who kill; the idea of childhood as a privileged, innocent state has little currency. For many critics, the signs of the times point to a need for children's literature that does not shy from the gritty, ugly, or even dangerous "realities" of contemporary childhood. Michael Cart ends his survey of contemporary young adult literature with a plea that writers address current hard issues facing what he calls "the most-at-risk-ever young adults."[6] Many of Harry Potter's readers presumably fall into this category, as young adult books address readers between the ages of twelve and eighteen, and although Harry begins his adventures at age eleven, he will be seventeen by the time they are done if Rowling proceeds with her projected seven volumes. For those critics who insist on the need for gritty realism, the early Potter books appear woefully lacking: the world of Hogwarts is, despite He-Who-Must-Not-Be-Named, too cozy, too safe. Even at the most frightening moment in *Harry Potter and the Chamber of Secrets,* when Harry appears to be completely at the mercy of Tom Riddle, the boyhood incarnation of You-Know-Who, after Dumbledore has been sent away from the school, Harry is rescued by Dumbledore's phoenix, Fawkes (presumably named after Guy), and the homely Sorting Hat. For some, Harry's safety net of magical guardians and helpers works against the child reader learning how to deal pragmatically with various "real" dangers. It is no accident that Cart's title, for instance, presents a linear relationship that privileges realism over romance (or fantasy). The accusations that the Potter books do not address "real" issues, or that they offer unrealistic solutions to problems, belong to a long tradition of attacks on imaginative literature.

I will return to the issue of fantasy; however, I want to pursue this notion that there is a group of youth in dire need of stories that address "real" concerns. Frequently, the youth seen as being in need are male. Whether they agree with Christina Hoff Sommers that feminism has emasculated North American boys, or with William Pollock that the myths of masculinity are forcing boys into ever more destructive patterns, the critics seem to agree that being a boy is a problem.[7] As Peter Hollindale puts it, "girls at the

5. Nicholas Tucker, "The Rise and Rise of Harry Potter," 221–34; Anthony Holden, "Why Harry Potter Doesn't Cast a Spell over Me."

6. Michael Cart, *From Romance to Realism: Fifty Years of Growth and Change in Young Adult Literature,* 278.

7. Christina Hoff Sommers, *The War against Boys;* William Pollock, *Real Boys.* The two sides are dissected neatly in Nicholas Lemann's "The Battle over Boys," 79–83.

time of writing seem to be making a better job of growing up than boys are. On the whole it is not girls who carry knives, commit assaults, steal cars and crash them. Boys rather than girls resort to negative demonstrations of self-worth. Boys rather than girls currently feel surplus to society's requirements."[8] These generalizations could certainly be challenged, but what is of interest is the perception that boys have a harder time of it than girls. In an excellent discussion of "boyology," Kenneth Kidd shows that the current trend is a replay of discussions at the previous turn of the century.[9] Then, concern about engendering masculinity followed anxiety about the New Woman; today, the "boys in crisis" message follows a period of perceived sustained attention to girls' educational and developmental needs.

The idea that boyhood is a socially problematic stage is paralleled in the world of education and reading. When the American Association of University Women released a report claiming that girls are still disadvantaged in schools, the response was swift: test scores show girls outperforming boys in most categories.[10] Commentators on children's literature take it as a given that boys are more likely to be reluctant readers than girls. It is also sometimes presented as a given that most fiction produced today is aimed at a "girl market." For instance, on her website *Reading Rants: Out of the Ordinary Teen Booklists,* middle school librarian Jennifer Hubert appeals to boys: "Does it seem like all the books are for girls? Are Sweet Valley High and Teen Angels threatening to overwhelm you with their sickening pastel covers? Well, never fear, Best Boy Reads are here! Believe it or not, there are some great books out there for the teen-aged males of the world who like a little more testosterone in their paperbacks."[11] It appears that boys must be coaxed into reading, and just as masculinity defines itself against femininity, books for boys must be defined as the antithesis of "girls' books." "Testosterone" translates into sports, alienation, and violence, at least in the examples listed on the site. The protagonists in these books are under siege. Their problems are "real life" problems with a vengeance: murder, abuse, and sociopathic siblings, to name a few.

So, if boys need a dose of gritty realism, how and why does a seemingly insignificant Cinderfella like Harry Potter earn kudos for "bring[ing] boys back to reading"?[12] A comparison of the Harry Potter books with other "boys' books" currently winning critical attention suggests that, in part, the popularity of Rowling's world may be a reaction against some of the

8. Peter Hollindale, *Signs of Childness in Children's Literature,* 121.

9. Kenneth Kidd, "Boyology in the Twentieth Century," 44–72. See also the opening of Alan Richardson's "Romanticism and the End of Childhood," 23–43.

10. See Dudley Barlow, "AAUW Gender Equity Research: Scholarship or Partisanship?" 46–50.

11. Jennifer Hubert, "Boy Meets Book: Best Boy Reads."

12. Eden Ross Lipson, "Book's Quirky Hero and Fantasy Win the Young."

realism being called for by critics like Cart and Hollindale. I am not suggesting that the Potter books are purely escapist, the equivalent of John Grisham or Louis L'Amour for the junior set, as some reviewers have done; rather, like all good fantasy, they touch on deeply moral issues. Indeed, Rowling addresses many of the same problems treated in contemporary realistic fiction for boys. The one major distinction is that of genre. Another key distinction is the books' attention to issues of masculinity.

The books I will be discussing, Walter Dean Myers' *Monster* (1999), Virginia Walter's *Making Up Megaboy* (1998), and Edward Bloor's *Tangerine* (1997), address a range of age groups, mostly older than those initially targeted as Rowling's readers. However, it is fair to group the Potter books with these, as Harry matures from book to book and his readership grows with him. One of the key elements shared by all of the more realistic fictions is a concern with the problem of growing up male. For Steve Harmon, Robbie Jones, and Paul Fisher, learning to be a man is fraught with dangers and tensions.

In *Monster,* a top-ten selection for the 2000 American Library Association Best Books for Young Adults, the protagonist is concerned in part with what it means to become a man. Sixteen-year-old Steve Harmon tells his story, partly in a journal and partly in the form of a screenplay of his life, in jail awaiting trial for supposedly standing guard during a robbery-homicide. One of the reasons he is even associated with the actual perpetrators of the crime is his half-conscious desire to seem "tough," like James King and Osvaldo Cruz. In Steve's world, among his peers, masculinity has to be performed. This desire is what presents Steve with his dilemma. He insists he was not involved in the crime, yet he *is* guilty of wanting to hang around with the perpetrators to enhance his own masculine status. The prosecutor says that Steve has made a moral decision—Steve wonders just what that decision was, and when he made it. He portrays his confusion as gender-driven rather than moral. Race intersects with gender as well. Myers suggests that Steve is on trial for being a young black man in the wrong part of the neighborhood at the wrong time. Even after his defense is successful, Steve's own attorney avoids his attempt to hug her. Steve feels that everyone sees a "monster" when they look at him, and the novel closes with Steve obsessively recording his life and trying to see what others see when they look in his face.

There is no doubt about thirteen-year-old Robbie Jones's guilt in *Making Up Megaboy:* before the book opens, he has shot and killed an elderly Korean convenience store owner. Instead of figuring out "who-dunnit," we are invited to ponder *why* he did it. The text consists of commentary by family members, teachers, friends, and community members, interspersed with graphics. Robbie himself is a cipher, as he never speaks; perhaps he is Sommers' pathologized, voiceless boy. One thing we do know about Robbie, though, is that he imagines himself as a kind of superhero, Megaboy, who is drawn with bulging muscles, fighting enemies and rescuing "Taragirl," a character based on a girl from his class. The main thrust of the text is to push readers to judge family and society who pass judgment on Robbie while revealing their own biases. The race issue surfaces here as well, as Robbie's mother wants to blame "that Mexican boy who hung around for a while" for being a bad influence on her son.[13] Nonetheless, Robbie's fantasies of masculine empowerment, present throughout the book on the frontispiece, in the body of the text, and on the back endpaper, clearly suggest that he is motivated in part by masculine anxiety. One reading of the shooting, which happens on the day of his thirteenth birthday, is that he wants to show Tara, and perhaps his other peers, that he is now a man: this is his rite of passage.

Both *Monster* and *Making Up Megaboy* raise questions about defining masculinity, the connections between certain ideas of masculinity and violence, and individual moral choices. Rowling raises similar questions about moral choices. As in much fantasy literature, characters in the Potter books choose to align themselves with either the evil Voldemort or with the forces of good, led seemingly by Dumbledore. However, this is not an absolute world, and some of Harry's most interesting dilemmas address the difficulty of distinguishing at times between good and evil. It can be hard to know who is friend and who is foe. Like Steve Harmon, Harry needs to choose his friends carefully. From the first book, in which Quirrell, the Defense against the Dark Arts teacher, turns out to be sharing his body with Voldemort, there are continual surprising allegiances. The notorious Sirius Black, supposedly the betrayer of Harry's parents, was actually framed, and is a dedicated enemy of Voldemort. Perhaps the most shocking revelation, for Harry, is the moment when Snape is revealed as a spy for Dumbledore. Snape, the head of Slytherin House, hates Harry passionately, just as he hated Harry's father and his friends when all were boys together at Hogwarts. Harry in turn dislikes Snape and finds it hard to believe that such an unpleasant person, a Death Eater, is to be trusted.

However, far more difficult for Harry than learning who is and is not to be trusted is learning to trust himself. Harry is somehow linked to Voldemort; after he survived the attack that killed his parents, he was marked with a lightning-shaped scar that aches whenever Voldemort is plotting some evil or is near. Harry also possesses the rare gift of speaking Parseltongue, the speech of snakes, which only Lord Voldemort shares. And Harry's wand is the twin of Voldemort's: both have at their core a phoenix feather from Fawkes. Harry's fears about his own nature are made clear when he encounters the Sorting Hat. The hat has a difficult time placing Harry, and almost

13. Virginia Walter, *Making Up Megaboy,* 9.

puts him in Slytherin, former home of Voldemort (the Heir of Slytherin) and the house that has produced the most Dark Wizards: "You could be great, you know, it's all here in your head, and Slytherin will help you on the way to greatness, no doubt about that" (*Sorcerer's Stone*, 121). It is only Harry's determined resistance to belonging to Slytherin that makes the hat place him in Gryffindor. Draco Malfoy, a Slytherin and son of a Death Eater, frequently taunts Harry, suggesting he made the wrong choice. When Harry finally shares his fear that he might secretly be a Slytherin, Dumbledore calmly agrees that he possesses many qualities in common with Voldemort, but then insists that what distinguishes Harry from the latter is his choice *not* to be like him: "It is our choices . . . that show us for what we truly are, far more than our abilities" (*Chamber of Secrets*, 333). Clearly, Rowling is establishing Voldemort and Harry as opponents who have similar backgrounds and similar talents to illustrate the importance of free will. Voldemort is part Muggle, and as the boy Tom Riddle, he, like Harry, was treated badly by Muggle relatives; this has led to his hatred of Muggles and his desire to destroy all so-called Mudbloods and Muggle-lovers. In a realistic novel, Voldemort might be a Robbie Jones.

Voldemort's history suggests a kind of pop-psychology reading of the abused child who grows up to become a violent offender. Harry, however, is proof that the cycle need not be continued. As you'll read elsewhere in this volume, the series presents Harry with a number of moral choices to make; these rites of passage mark not only his increasing maturity but also his refusal to become like Voldemort. It is easy to hate his nasty relatives, the Dursleys. They are characters out of a Roald Dahl novel (in fact the Ton-Tongue Toffee joke played on Dudley by the Weasley twins is rather like the grotesque fates of the nasty children in *Charlie and the Chocolate Factory*). Harry retaliates against Aunt Marge's insults, but for the most part he comes to terms with the Dursleys (perhaps this is one of the reasons Harry must continue to live with them, as well as because of the protection they afford). By *The Goblet of Fire*, Harry has achieved a standoff with the Dursleys (thanks to the specter of Sirius), and is able to ensure his own comfort with a secret cache of food while the rest of the household is supporting Dudley's "diet." Of course, Harry has more challenging tests. First, when he has the opportunity to kill Sirius Black, whom he believes to be responsible for his parents' deaths, he hesitates. After being interrupted by Remus Lupin, Harry reflects that "his nerve had failed him" (*Prisoner of Azkaban*, 343). More deliberately, he decides not to kill the real traitor, Peter Pettigrew. Finally, during the Triwizard Tournament, Harry refuses to benefit from Hagrid's tip and warns Cedric of the first task. During the second task, Harry refuses to win at the expense of others' lives. He stays under the lake until Hermione and Cho are rescued, and then rescues Fleur's sister and his own hostage, Ron. During the last task, Harry insists that Cedric, able to run to the cup faster than Harry, is the real winner; when Cedric demurs, Harry proposes that they each take the cup. This is one of the most difficult choices Harry has to come to terms with, for the cup is a Portkey that takes both boys to Voldemort, who kills Cedric. Up until this point, Harry's choices have all led to praise and a feeling that right has been done. This time, however, Harry feels guilt for Cedric's death, even though no one blames him. Choices in Rowling's world do have consequences, and they are neither always predictable nor always pleasant.

Like some of the other current books on the boys' market, the Potter books link moral issues to racial and ethnic issues in a reflection of current debates. In the light of the nationalistic and ethnic battles in the former Yugoslavia, or the tribal wars in Rwanda, it is hard not to read Voldemort and his Death Eaters as ethnic cleansers. Supporters of Voldemort wish to promote purity of blood. Mudbloods, wizards or witches born of Muggle parents, like Hermione Granger, are targeted. A number of characters are of mixed blood: along with Hermione, Harry's mother was a Muggle-born witch, and Voldemort's father was a Muggle. Another race, the giants, is also hated and feared by most wizards and witches. When Hagrid is recovering from his shame at being outed as part giant, he insists that Harry must win the Triwizard Cup: "It'd show 'em all . . . yeh don' have ter be pure-blood ter do it. Yeh don' have ter be ashamed of what yeh are" (*Goblet of Fire*, 456). This message that blood does not necessarily tell is reinforced when Barty Crouch, the last heir of a great pureblood family, is unmasked as a half insane servant of Voldemort.

Barty Crouch's family history has another important lesson for Harry and readers. His father, a stern judge of Dark Wizards, became so obsessed with fighting the Dark that he became rather like them. When Harry watches trials via Dumbledore's thoughts in the Pensieve, Crouch becomes grayer and more hate-filled with each trial, until finally he condemns his own son, claiming he no longer has a son. As Dumbledore notes, the Ministry of Magic's use of the Dementors and its willingness to bargain with Death Eaters bring it closer to the Dark. Young Barty, cast off by his father, identifies entirely with Voldemort, and, like Voldemort, he eventually kills his father. Barty represents another path not taken by Harry. Each time Harry chooses mercy, he allies himself with Dumbledore, who is well known for the "second-chances" he gives, such as to Snape and Hagrid. The possibility of redemption is a key positive value in the novels.

Rowling has said on more than one occasion that her books are deeply moral.[14] Certainly they raise a number of the same kinds of questions that

14. For instance, during an online "Chat with J. K. Rowling" on Yahoo, sponsored by Barnes and Noble, Rowling responded to a question about the controversy over her

Monster and *Making Up Megaboy* raise. How does one know whom to trust? How does one trust oneself? What role does environment play in one's moral development? Does one's sense of identity come from blood, ability, or actions? The one issue these works of realism address that does not seem to be present in the Potter books is the matter of masculinity. Harry's problems stem from being Harry Potter, not from being a boy in a world that views young men with suspicion. Yet, by setting Rowling's books against a book also concerned with (among other things) boys and sports, *Tangerine,* we can see that the Potter texts are not gender neutral.

Paul Fisher, like Harry Potter, wears glasses, is small for his age, and has a big desire to belong somewhere. His family, particularly his father, is obsessed with the Erik Fisher Football Dream, the golden career of his football-star older brother. Edward Bloor raises some important questions about the connection between sports and masculine aggression. Erik and his goony friend are stereotypical jocks, trading on their stardom and bullying everyone around them. Erik gets away with everything because of his status on the football team. He is the golden boy, but with a hollow core. Paul calls him a psychopath. However, Bloor gives us enough family history to indicate that Erik needed help he did not get when he was younger. He has never had to accept any consequences for his actions. When he is finally revealed as a thief and, indirectly, a murderer, it comes as no surprise to find he is also responsible for Paul's vision impairment. Our last vision of Erik is of a wild animal caged in a cell. Bloor seems to be deconstructing jock culture.

On the other hand, Paul is also an athlete, but he plays a less glamorous sport, soccer. Nonetheless, Paul's identity formation is very much connected to his sport. Once Paul changes schools and overcomes his white, middle-class bias (it's a little hard to take Paul's saying he feels like he belongs with the minority students, the majority at the new school, because he is a half-blind "geek"), he finds a place on the school soccer team. At first mocked, he wins respect for his ability to take punishment. Covered in mud and blood, Paul is a War Eagle, a member of the brotherhood. At his sport, Paul is just as fierce as Erik. In his journal he records gleefully, "We have destroyed every enemy. We have laid waste to their fields and their fans. There is fear in their eyes when we come charging off our bus, whooping our war cry."[15] By the end of the book, Paul takes pleasure in his new reputation as a "bad dude." It seems as though Paul wants to be like Erik in terms of having recognition.

---

books by claiming that "these books are fundamentally moral (that is how I see them, in any case)."

15. Edward Bloor, *Tangerine,* 165.

However, the paralleling of the brothers and their sports sends some interesting messages. Erik's story seems to come straight from the headlines that connect athletic stars with violence off the playing field. There is the distinct suggestion that, individual pathology aside, Erik's aggressive behavior is encouraged by a culture that values his skill. There is, nonetheless, no simplistic analogy made between violent sport and violent behavior. Paul is shown as participating in equally violent athletic contests, yet he does not translate that aggression into his daily life. Erik represents a certain masculine ideal that is ultimately devalued by the novel. Paul, who establishes boundaries between sport and life, yet who is also willing to cross class and racial boundaries to understand and be understood by the Other, represents an alternative masculine ideal. Physically insignificant, Paul is nonetheless able to compete well at a sport he loves, and he is able to make lasting connections with the students from Tangerine Middle School, particularly the Cruz family. By the end of the book, Paul has found a code of honor by which he can live. Even though he is suspended from school, he is not going to become a rulebreaker for the sake of breaking rules: he will abide by the consequences of a decision he made out of loyalty and a sense of justice.

Harry Potter is another undersized boy who finds confidence through sport. The youngest Quidditch player in a century, Harry earns respect for his skill as a seeker. His flying skills are first revealed when he fights Malfoy to rescue Neville Longbottom's Remembrall, so early on his ability is partnered by his decency. The degree to which Harry is invested in his identity as a successful player is revealed by his overreaction to losing his first match, when he is beaten by Cedric Diggory. Cedric, in fact, becomes a rival to Harry off the field as well as on; both boys are attracted to Cho Chang, and of course both also compete in the Triwizard Tournament. Some might joke that the battle between good and evil is won on the playing fields of Hogwarts, but in Harry's case, his Quidditch training does indeed stand him in good stead. It helps him defeat the Hungarian Horntail dragon in the first task of the championship, and in a more dangerous situation, it helps him evade the Death Eaters in his escape from the resurrected Voldemort.

As in *Tangerine,* extreme valorization of sport and sports stars is criticized in the Potter books. From the beginning, Harry is contrasted by, on the one hand the Weasley twins, who rarely take anything (including Quidditch) terribly seriously, and on the other hand by the comically intense captain of the Gryffindor team, Oliver Wood, who is over the top in his obsession with winning the school cup. There is an even stronger message in the person of Ludo Bagman, a former international Quidditch star. It is tempting to imagine Erik Fisher as a more sinister Ludo Bagman, thirty years or so down the line. Bagman is stupid and amoral. His only talent has been for Quidditch, and now, too old to play, he cuts a rather pathetic figure in his old uniform. He cheats the Weasley twins, and we find through the Pensieve that he managed to cheat the judge as well. On trial for spying for Voldemort, Bagman is acquitted because of his fame; one of the jury members actually asks to congratulate Bagman on his performance in a recent match (*Goblet of Fire*, 593). These are the same false values that allow Erik to flourish in *Tangerine*.

Paul's soccer team and the Hogwarts Quidditch teams are both coed; however, a key feature of playing sport for both Paul and Harry is the entrée it affords into a brotherhood. Paul's teammates actually come to call him "brother," and they are more brotherly toward him than his biological brother is. Through the team he meets Tino Cruz, and eventually he is accepted as a member of the crew at the Cruz plantation; this is tantamount to becoming a member of their extended family. Similarly, although Harry is forever set apart by his scar, identified as the one who defied Voldemort, his playing for Gryffindor integrates him into the community of the house, and he develops a sense of fellowship with other male Quidditch players, save for those from the Slytherin team. We do not see him joking and interacting with female athletes; instead, aside from his friendship with Hermione, Harry's world is mostly a masculine one. During the second task of the Triwizard Tournament, unlike the older boys, Cedric and Krum, Harry must rescue not a girl but his best friend, Ron Weasley.

There are suggestions that Harry and Ron will soon be noticing the opposite sex. I have already mentioned Harry's interest in Cho (which is tangled up with his rivalry with Cedric), and by the end of volume four, Ron has not only noticed Fleur Delacour but also come to recognize Hermione as a female, as well. However, in the first four volumes Harry is more interested in his relationships with "brothers" and father figures than he is in those with girls or women. Mrs. Weasley plays a maternal role, particularly when Harry has been through horrible experiences, but she is a distant supplier of good food and knitted jumpers rather than a key figure in Harry's life. Instead, Harry is surrounded by substitute fathers. Harry is frequently compared to his own father, and he develops filial relationships with a number of his father's friends and former schoolmates. Harry does, of course, have an actual godfather in Sirius, but even before he meets Sirius, Harry often seeks reassurance from Remus Lupin. When Harry doubts himself, it is Lupin who teaches him to find his Patronus, a stag, a connection he shares with his father. (According to Pliny's *Natural History*, the stag is supposed to be able to use its breath to draw serpents from their holes and trample them to death—a suggestive association, given the connection between Voldemort and snakes.)[16] Hagrid also feels somewhat fatherly toward Harry; he tells

---

16. Ivor H. Evans, *Brewer's Dictionary of Phrase and Fable*, 1065.

Harry that, on their first meeting, Harry reminded him of himself as a boy, orphaned and unsure of his belonging (*Goblet of Fire*, 456). Hagrid watches over Harry, providing tea and a sympathetic ear when Harry is troubled, as well as a timely clue about dragons. Finally, his father's former teacher, Dumbledore, is a paternal figure as well. He is the one who provides explanations after Harry's most frightening adventures, and he is also the one who assures Harry that he is growing into the right sort of boy.

In his relationships with adult male figures, Harry is quite unlike the heroes of the realistic novels we've considered. Paul Fisher admires Luis, the eldest Cruz brother, but there are no other adult men in his life who take an interest in him or who encourage his development. His father is of course obsessed with living vicariously through the Erik Fisher Football Dream, and his soccer coach is a woman. None of the adult male voices in *Making Up Megaboy* seems to know Robbie Jones at all, and, although Steven Harmon has a father in *Monster*, his father exists at the extreme sidelines of Steve's life, bewildered by his son's actions and interests. This absence of male role models emphasizes these boys' isolation as they grow. It also suggests that adult men are themselves self-absorbed, absent, or incompetent. It is only by going outside of his class and culture that Paul finds a positive model of manhood. Small wonder, then, that masculinity in North American culture comes to be seen as a problem, or that in extreme cases such as Robbie's, masculinity appears to be pathologized.

The Harry Potter books do not problematize masculinity; this is, perhaps, one reason for their appeal for boy readers. Rowling follows an older narrative tradition, in which her boy-hero comes to maturity supported by a cast of "fathers" who are there when he needs them, but who also let him find his own way when he needs to do that. In this regard, Harry is rather like Jim Hawkins, who interacts with and learns from the models of Squire Trelawney, Doctor Livesay, Captain Smollett, and even Long John Silver. Like Jim, Harry also has adventures on his own, and indeed, in his most serious tests, he must depend upon himself. In the first volume, Harry must face Quirrell/Voldemort alone; again, in *Chamber of Secrets*, although Fawkes heals Harry with his tears and the Sorting Hat gives Harry Gryffindor's sword, Harry alone is responsible for the destruction of Tom Riddle's diary. In this tradition, the boy-hero has the best of both worlds: he has the security of being supported by positive older male role models, and he enjoys both the pleasures and the responsibilities of independence.

It is important to note that Harry does mature over the course of the books, and not only in terms of his moral choices. He grows in wizardly abilities, signaled by his ability to compete with the older and better-trained champions in the Triwizard Tournament. Rowling claims that she has planned all along to move away from a children's series; because Harry ages a year with each volume, she is able to address issues of increasing complexity and maturity.[17] Harry's challenges become more difficult with each volume. In the first book, Dumbledore arrives just in time to assure that Quirrell does not triumph, although he notes to Harry that he was "doing very well on [his] own" (*Sorcerer's Stone*, 296). Next, Harry faces Voldemort's boy self, Tom Riddle, and once again Harry is sent help when he needs it. It is important to note, though, that Dumbledore still gives Harry credit for his victory: "You must have shown me real loyalty down in the Chamber. Nothing but that could have called Fawkes to you" (*Chamber of Secrets*, 332). In *Prisoner of Azkaban*, Harry has to confront the fact that Dumbledore cannot solve all problems: "Harry stared up into the grave face and felt as though the ground was falling sharply away. He had gotten used to the idea that Dumbledore could solve anything. He had expected Dumbledore to pull some amazing solution out of the air" (393). This is a key moment of maturity; every child must at some time come to terms with the fact that adults cannot fix everything. In this case, Harry must provide the solution, with the help of Hermione's Time-Turner. He and Hermione are given a grave responsibility, as Dumbledore tells them that if they are successful, they will be "able to save more than one innocent life" (*Prisoner of Azkaban*, 393). Harry's success in this mission also marks his discovery of his Patronus: instead of being saved by the ghost of his father, he has saved himself, for he has found his father in himself (*Prisoner of Azkaban*, 428). Not only does this suggest that Harry has found a connection with his father, but metaphorically he is ready to father himself; the boy is indeed the father to the man. The fourth volume, right in the middle of the projected series, marks Harry's most serious encounter with Voldemort. He only narrowly escapes being killed, after unwillingly contributing to the resurrection of the Dark Lord. Dumbledore marks Harry's coming into maturity with this battle. Not only does he praise Harry for exceeding his expectations and imply that Harry is as brave as his parents (when he refers to wizards and witches who fell during battle with Voldemort before he was injured), but he notes that the boy has successfully fought a man's battle (*Goblet of Fire*, 699). This, then, has been Harry's rite of passage into adulthood. In future volumes, he is likely to take his place beside the adults fighting Voldemort. Indeed, with Minister Fudge's unwillingness to accept the return of Voldemort, Harry may well fight for adults who will not fight for themselves.

The pleasure of following the adventures of a boy who comes to fight a man's battles is surely one of the pleasures for boys in reading the Potter series. Just as the playing field provides an acceptable place for exercising

17. "Chat with J. K. Rowling."

aggression, so does the endless battle between good and evil. Another element in the books should not be overlooked, however. Unlike high fantasy generally, these books are funny, and funny in a way boys in particular enjoy. There is a lot of gross-out humor here, from Bertie Bott's Every Flavor Beans, which can come in such flavors as "vomit" and "ear-wax," to the Blast-Ended Skrewts, with their exploding bottoms. One of the benefits of having Hagrid as the teacher of the Care of Magical Beasts class is his penchant for monsters and oddities. Looking after unicorns might appeal to girl readers, particularly those who have grown up playing with toys marketed to girls such as "My Little Pony," but it provides little interest for boy readers. At the first Harry Potter movie, my son certainly delighted in the sight of Harry wiping troll "boogers" off his wand. The giant dollops of slimy drool falling from Fluffy the three-headed dog onto the hapless Ron were also well-received by the young boys in the audience. The humor definitely becomes more sexualized in volume four, as the characters, and perhaps readers, hover at puberty. In Divination class, when Lavender asks to have a planet identified, Professor Trelawney answers, "It is Uranus, my dear," whereupon Ron trots out the rather tired but endlessly funny joke still to thirteen-year-old boys: "Can I have a look at Uranus, too, Lavender?" (*Goblet of Fire*, 201). There is precious little laughter in much current realistic fiction dealing with boys' issues. The Potter books manage to address some of the same moral and psychological issues, but with the balm of humor to balance the horrors. When Harry gives the Weasley twins his Triwizard winnings to finance their projected Joke Shop, he comments that any laughs they can generate will be more needed than ever as a counter to the dark times to come when Voldemort makes his next move (*Goblet of Fire*, 733).

Finally, I want to come back to the matter of genre. Michael Cart and others have suggested that the complexities and dangers of contemporary life demand a harsh realism in literature. The assumption here is that only realistic fiction provides engagement with "real-life" issues. I hope I have shown that the Potter books do engage with issues that face boys today, even though few boys will be called upon to fight a basilisk. In *From Romance to Realism*, Cart disdains what he calls the pendulum swing of the eighties, the rise in popularity of the paperback romance, which he sees as part of a reaction against the realism of 1970s literature for young adults.[18] While he celebrates the return of realism in the 1990s, I would suggest

18. This is not the place to engage in debate about the ideological implications of romance reading, but work by Janice Radway and others certainly suggests that the relationship between text and reader is a complex one, and by no means always a disempowering one. See for instance Radway's *Reading the Romance* or Tania Modleski's *Loving with a Vengeance*.

that the popularity of the Harry Potter books into the twenty-first century is a reaction against that realism. As Hugh Crago notes in "Can Stories Heal?" interest in bibliotherapy has led to a concomitant interest in finding realistic fiction to match young readers' lived experiences. However, if, as he suggests, the therapeutic effects of reading are most likely to occur when the reader merges with the text, then we need to look at what causes that merging. Crago argues convincingly that this merging is most likely to occur when "the correspondence [between lived and literary experience] is partly or wholly metaphorical rather than literal. Human addiction to 'story' is an aspect of our symbol-making nature."[19] This suggests that fantasy, which addresses experience metaphorically, is perhaps the most appropriate, or even most satisfying, genre for addressing the psychological needs of readers. The fantastic elements of the Harry Potter books, then, are not necessarily escapist; boy readers who enjoy the books are not avoiding the problems of growing up male. Instead, they may be identifying with those problems on a deeper, symbolic level. According to Perry Nodelman, in the act of reading fantasy, "experiencing something clearly and completely different from ourselves, we become acutely aware of who and what we are."[20]

The series is not yet complete, and we do not know all that Rowling has planned for the remaining three volumes, other than that Harry will continue to grow and mature. Rowling enjoys teasing readers, hinting at dire outcomes, but I would be surprised if the forces of good do not win out, and that brings me to what is probably one of the most satisfying elements of fantasy: hope. Tamora Pierce, herself a gifted fantasist, argues passionately for the necessity of hope in young readers' lives: "one of the things I have learned about [young adults] is that they respond to the idealism and imagination they find in everything they read . . . YAs are also dreamers . . . Here the seeds are sown for the great visions, those that will change the future for us all."[21] I am not suggesting that only fantasy literature offers this. Although both *Monster* and *Making Up Megaboy* leave the reader with troubling, perhaps unresolvable questions and issues, *Tangerine* certainly presents a hopeful ending. Paul Fisher may have been expelled, but he gets a fresh start at a new school; he has a positive sense of family with the Cruzes, and it even looks as though his father will pay him more attention in the future. Indeed, as he drives with his father to his new school, the sight of Mike Costello's memorial tree and the scent of citrus fruit lead Paul to look forward to new life. The two novels share a similar vein, though. *Tangerine*, although presented as realism, has many fantastic elements: Paul is "blind,"

19. Hugh Crago, "Can Stories Heal?" 169. See also Jane Yolen's "Turtles All the Way Down," 164–74.
20. Perry Nodelman, "Some Presumptuous Generalizations about Fantasy," 178.
21. Tamora Pierce, "Fantasy: Why Kids Read It, Why Kids Need It," 179.

but he can see better than the rest of the characters; gothic elements lurk in Tangerine County amid its sink holes and muck fires; and Paul himself is, like Harry, akin to the "brain-over-brawn" heroes of fairy tales. In short, *Tangerine,* like fantasy narratives, demands to be read metaphorically. Harry, of course, has been identified as a male Cinderella: he lives humbly in a cupboard under the stairs, and later in the attic of his hated relatives' home, but is revealed to be a great hero in the wizard world. He is also something of a Jack figure, however, depending on his wits and abilities to defeat a larger, older, more powerful foe. Harry's continued successes, his ultimate triumph presumably waiting in the wings, offer boys a hero to cheer; his victories are their victories.

I would not claim that the Harry Potter books, or that fantasy in general, should be preferred reading. Readers usually find the books they need, whether they be fantasy or realism. In Kit Pearson's *Awake and Dreaming,* her protagonist, a neglected girl named Theo, finds solace in reading not only the fantasies of Edgar Eager but also the domestic realism of Elizabeth Enright. However, I do argue that the Potter books present a balance in the boy book market. Whereas we have seen a critical embracing of gritty "issues" books, the undeniable popularity of the Potter books, hype aside, has reminded publishers and critics alike of the power of fantasy to engage readers, and in particular of the continued appeal of a certain brand of masculine fantasy of empowerment for boy readers. Critical deconstruction of romance reading for girls has yet to be matched by a thorough deconstruction of contemporary masculine romance. The rise of the Potter books reminds us of the need for that work to be done. We *would* read the Potter books differently if they were about Harriet Potter. By celebrating male heroism at a moment when popular culture fears male violence, indeed when boys are seen as killers, Rowling has tapped into a kind of collective unconscious need to be reminded that boys have a path toward maturity to follow, and that they can indeed make it, both with help and on their own. As a mother of a son, I, too, find Harry's adventures reassuring.

Harry's Language

Taking Issue with Words

You Say "Jelly," I Say "Jell-O"?

Harry Potter and the Transfiguration of Language

Philip Nel

Many have criticized the decision by Arthur A. Levine of Scholastic to translate the Harry Potter books from British English into American English. The same month that *Harry Potter and the Prisoner of Azkaban* made its American debut, eleven-year-old Whitaker E. Cohen's letter to the *New Yorker* asserted that children "have large imaginations, and can usually figure out . . . what words mean from their context." When the fourth novel, *Harry Potter and the Goblet of Fire,* was published, Peter H. Gleick's op-ed piece in the *New York Times* lamented the "devolution from English to 'American' English" and suggested that Scholastic's "Americanized" texts contribute to the "dumb[ing] down" of U.S. society. Later that year, Sukanta Chaudhuri's "Harry Potter and the Transfiguration of Language," published in the Malaysian newspaper *New Straits Times,* blamed "the global arrogance of the American" for this act of "cultural reappropriation" that, were it done to a "non-privileged" culture (such as Hindi), would be roundly criticized. For his part, Levine has said, "I wasn't trying to, quote, 'Americanize' them. What I was trying to do was translate, which is something different. I wanted to make sure that an American kid reading the book would have the same literary experience that a British kid would have."[1]

This essay centers around acts of translation both literal and figurative, and the responses to them—not just the "toe-may-toe, toe-mah-toe" pronunciations suggested by the Ira Gershwin lyric, but the differences in cultural heritage and meaning obscured by editorial revisions. Were it possible to create "the same literary experience" for children from different countries, why would it be desirable? That this question does not occur to Levine reinforces Chaudhuri's point. As Martha Bedford, a self-described

---

1. Whitaker E. Cohen, "Hands Off Harry!" 16; Peter H. Gleick, "Harry Potter, Minus a Certain Flavour," A25; Sukanta Chaudhuri, "Harry Potter and the Transfiguration of Language," 5; Arthur A. Levine, quoted in Daniel Radosh, "Why American Kids Don't Consider Harry Potter an Insufferable Prig," 56.

"13-year-old English girl," wrote in response to Gleick's piece, "In England, we have American TV shows, American pop groups and American movies, yet the language is not changed to suit us. The spell-checks on our computers come in American English."[2] In addition to highlighting America's disproportionate influence on global culture and effacing some of the books' Britishness, Scholastic's "translations" result in changes in meaning. Not only is "English muffin" different from "crumpet," but *Sorcerer's Stone* also lacks the reference to alchemy implied by *Philosopher's Stone* in the title of the British edition published by Bloomsbury in 1997. As well as changing the title of *Harry Potter and the Philosopher's Stone* to *Harry Potter and the Sorcerer's Stone,* Levine, in collaboration with author J. K. Rowling, translated "sherbet lemon" to "lemon drop," "motorbike" to "motorcycle," "chips" to "fries," "jelly" to "Jell-O," "jacket potato" to "baked potato," "jumper" to "sweater," and "mum" to "mom" (though, at Rowling's insistence, "mum" was retained in later books). While the fourth Harry Potter novel has largely escaped the zeal of American translators, this subtle blurring of cultural distinctions continues in the Scholastic editions of books two and three.

As Bedford's letter indicates, these acts of translation have repercussions beyond the books themselves, highlighting Americans' blithe ignorance of important differences within British society, as well as Britons' anxieties about U.S. representations of themselves. Though no one has remarked on it, the *New York Times* Bestseller List (which has since banished the Potter books to a new "Children's Bestsellers" list) did something curious in its summaries of the first Potter book. When *Harry Potter and the Sorcerer's Stone* first appeared on the list in December 1998, its description read, "A Scottish boy, neglected by his relatives, finds his fortune attending a school of witchcraft." A month and a half later, "Scottish" had quietly become "British." Though Scotland is indeed a part of Great Britain, one suspects that a Scotsman would notice the switch from "Scottish" to "British."[3] Indicative of U.K. concerns, one reason that Steven Spielberg is not directing the planned Harry Potter films hinges upon translation: he planned some Americanization of the books. Rowling disapproved of his plans for the film, and he did not get the job. Both her disapproval and the widely misreported notion that "Spellotape" was translated as "Scotch tape" ("Spellotape" *was* retained by Scholastic, though "Sellotape" was not) illustrate the uneasiness over the power American companies have to shape the perception of British culture. That is, while all acts of translation can be read as acts of appropriation, the global marketing of Rowling's Potter series makes appropriation

2. Martha Bedford, Letter to the Editor, A30.
3. Bestsellers: Hardcover Fiction," December 27, 1998, and February 14, 1999.

particularly significant. As the series continues to grow in its market value and in its marketing (the second was released in November 2002), these issues will grow increasingly important. There are big bucks and cultural identities at stake, and the latter are more likely to get lost in the translation.

Translating British books for American audiences does not begin with Rowling's Potter series, and Scholastic's revisions must be evaluated in this context. As Chaudhuri reminds us, the original American editions of Dickens's *Martin Chuzzlewit* removed "unflattering references to Americans" so that the novel's U.S. "sales might not suffer nor the box office" when Dickens undertook a reading tour of the States. However, the often extreme degree of American editors' revisions to children's literature in particular— as well as the assumptions behind these revisions—make analysis of Scholastic's revisions to Rowling especially significant. As Jane Whitehead points out in the first part of her thorough, two-part study of this subject, " 'This is NOT what I wrote!': The Americanization of British Children's Books" (1996), "The range of alterations made under the umbrella of Americanization is vast." These changes include: "Titles, setting, character names, . . . culturally specific allusions, . . . in addition to spelling, punctuation, vocabulary, and idiom."[4] Furthermore, the practice of making such alterations is so widespread that it usually passes without comment. For example, there has been little discussion of the fact that Knopf saw fit to publish *Northern Lights,* the first book of British author Philip Pullman's acclaimed *His Dark Materials* trilogy (1995–2000), under the title *The Golden Compass.* So, to some extent, the attention paid to Scholastic's translations of Rowling's series tells us more about the popularity of the Potter novels than about Levine's particular acts of translation. The books are, in this sense, a highly public example of a common editorial practice.

That said, though Scholastic's versions of the first three Potter novels are guilty of some degree of cultural imperialism, Levine has done a much more sensitive job than many of his peers. Whitehead, for example, cites Catherine and Laurence Anholt's *Tiddlers,* published in the United States by Candlewick Press as *Toddlers.* The line "I am sad, I am happy, I want Mum to change my nappy" becomes "I am sad, I am sweet, I can stand on my two feet," effecting so complete a change in meaning that the original British version virtually disappears under its heavy-handed American editor. While some American "translations" of British books go so far as to change radically the author's style and meaning, others take a "signposts" approach. "Children everywhere are keenly interested in, and ready to learn about, other children; and the odder, the better. The editor needs only to

---

4. Chaudhuri, "Transfiguration," 5; Jane Whitehead, " 'This Is NOT What I Wrote!': The Americanization of British Children's Books," part 1.

help with a few signposts," observes Grace Hogarth in a 1965 issue of the *Horn Book*.[5] In general, Levine's goal seems to have been more of the "signposts" method, striving to locate key words and phrases that might confuse an American child, and then inventing a U.S. "equivalent." To his credit, Levine actually worked with Rowling on the translation—a practice that not all editors follow. While their collaboration did not create a text irrevocably damaged by Americanization, the significance of Scholastic's changes extends beyond signposts.

Before examining more fully the deleterious implications of the Scholastic translations, let us look at some of the benefits. In several senses, the Scholastic editions may represent Rowling's final version of the manuscript and, as such, include changes that ought to be incorporated into future Bloomsbury editions as well. That is, considering that Rowling worked with Levine on the Scholastic editions, the discrepancies between the following scenes amount to something other than "Americanization." In Bloomsbury's *Harry Potter and the Chamber of Secrets,* just after Ron and Harry find themselves blocked from entering platform nine and three quarters, Ron suggests flying the car, an act which, he insists, would not violate any wizarding laws. As he explains, "Even under-age wizards are allowed to use magic if it's a real emergency, section nineteen or something of the Restriction of Thingy . . ." The next sentence registers Harry's interest in the idea: "Harry's feeling of panic turned suddenly to excitement."[6] In contrast, Scholastic's edition inserts a brief debate in between Ron's passionately vague justification and Harry's excitement:

> "But your Mum and Dad . . ." said Harry, pushing against the barrier again in the vain hope that it would give way. "How will they get home?"
> "They don't need the car!" said Ron impatiently. "They know how to Apparate! You know, just vanish and reappear at home! They only bother with Floo powder and the car because we're all underage and we're not allowed to Apparate yet. . . ."
> Harry's feeling of panic turned suddenly to excitement. (*Chamber of Secrets,* S 69)

Harry's objection reinforces the notion that Harry is more mature and less likely to act on impulse than Ron is, but it also introduces the magical skill of Apparating. In chapter 9 of *Prisoner of Azkaban,* Hermione lectures her fellow students on the impossibility of Apparating into Hogwarts, and *Goblet of Fire* offers a much fuller exploration of the ability to "just vanish and

5. Grace Hogarth, "Transatlantic Editing," 520.
6. J. K. Rowling, *Harry Potter and the Chamber of Secrets,* Bloomsbury edition, 56. Subsequent references to the Harry Potter books will appear in the text with the designation "B" indicating the Bloomsbury or British edition and the designation "S" indicating the Scholastic or U.S. edition.

reappear," as Ron puts it. If the Scholastic version does represent Rowling's final version of this scene, then it cleverly anticipates a reader's objection (how will Ron's parents get home?) and subtly introduces another dimension of the wizarding world, preparing the reader for its return in future novels.

In the first Potter novel, revising a conversation between Ron and Dean Thomas also enhances the realism in Rowling's fantasy world, doing so not through foreshadowing but by making more explicit the episteme in which the characters' experiences are grounded. Earlier in the novel, Ron and his Muggle-raised schoolmate Dean argue over which sport is more exciting, Quidditch or football ("soccer" in the Scholastic edition)—Ron could not see the excitement of "a game with only one ball where no one was allowed to fly" (*Philosopher's Stone*, 107; *Sorcerer's Stone*, 144). A version of this debate emerges after the Slytherin team captain, Marcus Flint, fouls Harry during a Quidditch match (or "game" in Scholastic's version):

> Down in the stands, Dean Thomas was yelling, "Send him off, ref! Red card!"
> "This isn't football, Dean," Ron reminded him. "You can't send people off in Quidditch—and what's a red card?" (*Philosopher's Stone*, 138)

If the Bloomsbury edition alludes to the differences between Ron's and Dean's respective worlds, the Scholastic edition emphasizes these differences more clearly:

> Down in the stands, Dean Thomas was yelling, "Send him off, ref! Red card!"
> "What are you talking about, Dean?" said Ron.
> "Red card!" said Dean furiously. "In soccer you get shown the red card and you're out of the game!"
> "But this isn't soccer, Dean," Ron reminded him. (*Sorcerer's Stone*, 188)

A subtle change, perhaps, but it does make very clear the different life experiences that have shaped Ron and Dean. In Bloomsbury's version, Ron's immediate reply—"This isn't football. You can't send people off in Quidditch"—leaves open the possibility that Ron already knows that sending a player off the field is a sanction used in a football match. His question "what's a red card?" could indicate merely a lack of awareness that the red card is the formal means for this sanction. However, in Scholastic's version, *all* of Dean's remark catches Ron by surprise. Instead of replying with a reminder that the two sports are governed by different rules, Ron asks, "What are you talking about, Dean?" Only after Dean explains how a red card works does Ron remind Dean of the discrepancy between Quidditch rules and soccer rules. Ironically, the American edition blurs somewhat the cultural specificity of Rowling's original by changing "football" to "soccer," while at the same time making much clearer the specific cultural contrasts between the "Muggle" world and the wizarding one.

Generally and with the exception of once substituting Lupin's name for Black's in *Prisoner of Azkaban*,[7] the Scholastic editions tend to correct errors published in the Bloomsbury editions, a change for which Levine and his fellow editors at Scholastic deserve credit. In the third chapter of Bloomsbury's *Chamber of Secrets,* "Geoge groaned" (B 32); Scholastic's *Chamber* fixes the typo, rendering the line as "George groaned" (S 35). Likewise, when Harry and Ron board the Hogwarts Express in *Prisoner of Azkaban,* Bloomsbury's version tells us that "Harry and Mr Weasley led the way to the end of the train" (*Prisoner of Azkaban,* B 58), which cannot be correct because in the very next sentence they "went back outside to say goodbye to Mr and Mrs Weasley." Scholastic's editors catch the error, replacing "Mr. Weasley" with "Ron," so that "Harry and Ron" lead the way into the train, and the paragraph makes sense (*Prisoner of Azkaban,* S 72). In the first of the Potter novels, we learn that *A History of Magic* was written by Bathilda Bagshot (*Philosopher's Stone,* 52; *Sorcerer's Stone,* 66); however, the Bloomsbury edition of *Azkaban* attributes authorship to Adalbert Waffling (B 7), while Scholastic remains consistent, identifying Bagshot as the author (S 1). These may seem like relatively minor details, but Scholastic deserves praise for its more careful editing and for the handsome design of the American editions. In any case, even if such details appear to be minor, readers are paying attention. In an online chat with Arthur Levine at *USA Today*'s web site, one reader actually asked, "In volume 3 page 1, why was the name of the author of History of Magic changed from Adalbert Waffling to Bathilda Bagshot?" Levine replied that Scholastic did, indeed, catch "a typographical error that (apparently) the British editors missed."[8]

Readers can ask such detailed questions because the Potter books have drawn such a wide following: people are collecting different editions, reading the books many times over, and even publishing books on Rowling herself. There are more than a dozen books about Harry Potter, even though no one had heard of J. K. Rowling before June 1997.[9] The series' incredible

---

7. The passage " 'Then it's time we offered you some proof,' said Black. 'You, boy—give me Peter. Now.' " (266) becomes " 'Then it's time we offered you some proof,' said Lupin. 'You, boy—give me Peter, please. Now.' " in the Scholastic edition (362). The change from "Black" to "Lupin" appears to be an error because Lupin, who is familiar with Ron, addresses him as "Ron," not "boy." Black, who does not know Harry's friend, is much more likely to address Ron impersonally as "boy." Though Scholastic's revision softens the command by including "please" before "now," the line still sounds as if it should be spoken by Black and not Lupin.

8. " 'Harry Potter': Arthur Levine."

9. These books include: Sharon Moore's *We Love Harry Potter!* (1999) and *Harry Potter, You're the Best: A Tribute from Fans the World Over* (2001), Marc Shapiro's *J. K.*

popularity renders its version of Britain *the* most widely known representation of that country at this point in history. Just as Margaret Mitchell's
Gone with the Wind (1936; film, 1939) has provided people all over the
world with an enduring (if inaccurate) image of the American South during and after the Civil War, the Harry Potter novels broadcast a version of
late-twentieth-century Britain that has been absorbed by millions. To echo
the claims of Karin Westman's essay (elsewhere in this volume), though
these novels are fantasy, the worlds of the Potter books—both magical and
Muggle—directly respond to the England of the late twentieth and early
twenty-first centuries. The cultural weight borne by Rowling's novels amplifies the importance of their details, especially those details that have been
"translated" into American English. Some have suggested that Scholastic's
editions merely provide "a vernacular that represent[s] the British nature
of the novels" to make "Harry and Hogwarts seem . . . more realistic to
readers in the United States who lack . . . awareness of boarding school and
British culture."[10] However, replacing British vernacular with what Americans think of as British vernacular diminishes the novels' realism. At times,
when reading the Scholastic editions, the phrase "British simulacra"—and
not "British vernacular"—more accurately describes the translations. For
example, in *Philosopher's Stone,* during the Christmas holidays, Harry and
Ron sit by their common room fire, toasting "bread, crumpets, marshmallows" (146). In *Sorcerer's Stone,* they sit by the fire, toasting "bread, English
muffins, marshmallows" (199).[11] While "crumpets" and "English muffins"
are related, they are not the same. A similarly inexact substitution occurs
when Ron says that he will not "take any rubbish from Malfoy this year" in
the British edition of *Azkaban* (B 64), but tells us he will not "take any crap
from Malfoy this year" in the American version (S 80). You say "rubbish," I
say "crap"? Hardly. The greater degree of vulgarity in the word "crap" hits
the reader with more force than "rubbish" does. Apart from being unnecessary (surely an American child would deduce that "crumpets" are food?) the

---

Rowling: The Wizard behind Harry Potter (2000), Lindsey Fraser's *Telling Tales: An
Interview with J. K. Rowling* (2000, published in America as *Conversations with J. K.
Rowling,* 2001), Elizabeth D. Schafer's *Exploring Harry Potter* (2000), Ben Buchanan's
My Year with Harry Potter: How I Discovered My Own Magical World (2001), Richard
Abanes's *Harry Potter and the Bible: The Menace behind the Magick* (2001), Bill Adler's
Kids' Letters to Harry Potter: An Unauthorized Collection (2001), David Colbert's *The
Magical Worlds of Harry Potter* (2001), Allan Zola Kronzek and Elizabeth Kronzek's
The Sorcerer's Companion: A Guide to the Magical World of Harry Potter (2001), Sean
Smith's *J. K. Rowling: A Biography* (2001), and my own *J. K. Rowling's Harry Potter
Novels: A Reader's Guide* (2001).
    10. Schafer, *Exploring Harry Potter,* 214.
    11. Ibid. Schafer's claim that "Harry consumes crumpets in both British and Amer-
ican editions" may apply to the second, third, and fourth Potter novels, but it clearly
does not apply to the first one.

substitutions of "English muffin" for "crumpet" and "crap" for "rubbish" offer subtle misrepresentations of British language that, over the course of several novels, enact a kind of stealthy vandalism on the source texts.

The distortions evident in translations of British children's books into American English prove that American definitions of multiculturalism do not include Great Britain. As Whitehead notes in the second part of her article, "Many British authors" whose texts have been heavily revised for an American market "feel that, in spite of lip service to multiculturalism, American children are being overprotected from exposure to different cultures." She reminds us that reviewers and librarians rightly insist that Native Americans, African Americans, and Asian Americans be represented accurately, preserving the ethnic and cultural specificity of each group. However, this same standard does not apply to the peoples of Britain, a nation as ethnically diverse as—but quite different from—the United States. Chaudhuri correctly points out that where translators of Indian works once would have Anglicized the material, now they would carefully preserve "each artifact of Indian culture." Yet, she says, "the rules of the game apparently change when the source culture is British and the recipient culture American." Though Scholastic did try to preserve much of the "British-ness" of the Potter series in the translations of the first three novels, the American publisher nonetheless illustrates the double standard delineated by both Whitehead and Chaudhuri.[12]

The words "pitch" and "field" exemplify the ramifications of this double standard. Significantly and unfortunately, the change from "Quidditch pitch" to "Quidditch field" is one of the few terms altered not only in the first three books but also in *Goblet of Fire*, a novel that otherwise remains largely true to its original version. In addition to providing the consonance of "Quidditch pitch" and the internal rhyme in a phrase such as "the Snitch was glittering way above the pitch," (*Prisoner of Azkaban*, B 193, S 261), the word "pitch" links the wizards' sport to a very British sport—cricket, also played upon a pitch. Quidditch clearly refers to sports other than cricket, of course: the fans' devotion parallels that of English football fans, and Harry himself first compares Quidditch to "basketball on broomsticks" (*Philosopher's Stone*, 124; *Sorcerer's Stone*, 167). However, cricket is clearly one of the sporting referents here. That "cricket pitch" and "Quidditch pitch" share the same number of syllables rhythmically reinforces the connection between the two sports, as do the many jokes about how long Quidditch matches can last. The longest cricket test matches have lasted for more than a week, and Rowling comically exaggerates this length

12. Whitehead, " 'This Is NOT What I Wrote,' " part 2; Chaudhuri, "Transfiguration," 5.

of time even further. In *Philosopher's Stone,* Gryffindor captain Oliver Wood tells Harry that Quidditch "can go on for ages," and that "the record is three months, they had to keep bringing on substitutes so the players could get some sleep" (*Philosopher's Stone,* 125; *Sorcerer's Stone,* 169). The words "Quidditch field" reduce the sense of connection with cricket provided by "Quidditch pitch" and remove the poetry of the latter phrase.

Though "pitch" turns to "field" in all of the Potter books, the first three novels undergo more "translation" than the last, the first undergoing the most of all. As a result, during its transformation to *Harry Potter and the Sorcerer's Stone, Harry Potter and the Philosopher's Stone* loses the most in translation. The almost total disappearance of the word "Mum" is a case in point, illustrating how acts of translation efface cultural specificity. Although Hagrid still says "Mum" in the Scholastic edition, the Weasleys' and others' "Mum" changes to "Mom" and Seamus Finnegan's "Mam" becomes "Mom" as well. This sort of inconsistent substitution distorts the dialect and, in so doing, the cultural differences and similarities that characterize the world of these characters. As a child of Irish descent, Seamus should be allowed to tell American readers, "Me dad's a Muggle. Mam didn't tell him she was a witch 'til after they were married" (*Philosopher's Stone,* 93) instead of "Me dad's a Muggle. Mom didn't tell him she was a witch 'til after they were married" (*Sorcerer's Stone,* 125). Furthermore, the word "Mam" reminds us of the distinction between his style of speech and the styles of Ron, Hagrid, and the rest (all of whom use "Mum"). Compounding the effects of this inconsistency, "Mum" remains "Mum" in the American versions of the second, third, and fourth novels, suggesting to American readers either that Hagrid's dialect has begun to rub off on the Weasleys or, worse, that linguistic signs of difference do not matter.

But they do. Rowling deploys signs of social and cultural difference both to value their positive qualities *and* to argue against hierarchies based on such differences. As her use of dialect and of names such as "Pavarti Patil" and "Cho Chang" suggest, Rowling is aware that Britain contains a mix of many cultures. However, Rowling investigates the prejudices that develop and create hierarchies of difference through a mixture of fantasy and realism. Her critique of racism and bigotry resides in rifts between witches and Muggles, in Salazar Slytherin's belief that only children from "Pureblood" wizarding families should be allowed to attend Hogwarts, and in the reaction to Malfoy calling Hermione a "filthy little Mudblood" (*Chamber of Secrets,* B 86, S 112). Issues of social and economic class emerge more realistically, class prejudice represented by the Malfoys' condescending attitude toward the Weasleys and a hilarious parody of conspicuous consumption exemplified by the nouveau riche Dursleys. If in these examples difference becomes a basis for discrimination, in others difference is celebrated—

as in Mr. Weasley's delight in all things Muggle or in the linguistic rich-ness conveyed by the variety of speech patterns the characters use. To blur these differences through Americanization is to diminish both the aesthetic enjoyment and political critiques of the novels.

Lucius Malfoy's disdain for Muggles and for the poor represents an im-portant dimension of Rowling's political message—a message subtly altered (though by no means lost) in Scholastic's translation. When Lucius Mal-foy engineers Headmaster Albus Dumbledore's suspension from Hogwarts during a time of crisis, Hagrid protests, "Take him away, an' the Muggle-borns won' stand a chance! There'll be killin's next!" (*Chamber of Secrets,* B 195). Mocking Hagrid, Mr. Malfoy says he is sure that Dumbledore's "successor will manage to prevent any—ah—'*killin's*'" (B 195). The scene enhances our dislike of Malfoy's snobbery and of his many prejudices. A crucial element in this portrait of Lucius Malfoy is his snide imitation of Ha-grid. However, Scholastic's version changes Hagrid's word from "killin's" to "killin'" (*Chamber of Secrets,* S 263), which, in turn, smudges Lucius Malfoy's cruel mimicry of Hagrid: Malfoy says "'*killin's*'" in the British edition and "*killins*" in the American one. Though the match between British words is exact, the connection between American words is inexact—if he is teasing Hagrid, then Mr. Malfoy should say "*killin'*" just as Ha-grid did. Translation is, of course, an inexact science, but one wonders why Scholastic felt it necessary to modify the dialect in the first place. It is, after all, *dialect.*

Preservation of the original texts may provide only a subtle emphasis to Rowling's moral themes, but offers a great opportunity for children in the United States to learn about children in Britain. The fourth book in the series is the first to explore this chance for a painless introduction to selected aspects of British life and language. Either because the manu-script arrived too late for Scholastic's editors to edit it thoroughly or be-cause the American publisher has come to realize the vast potential for mis-translating, *Goblet of Fire* arrived in the United States looking more like its British version than any other book so far. Perhaps reflecting a change in approach, Linda Ward Beech's Scholastic Literature Guide for *Goblet of Fire* even makes reference to the differences between British and Ameri-can English—unlike Scholastic's guides for the first three, which do not. It includes a worksheet titled "Learning English," which explains, "Harry and his friends speak English, but they don't always use the same words Americans do." On the left-hand side of the page, the exercise prints twelve different "British" words, the majority of which *were* translated in Scholastic editions of the first three novels but remained in British English for *Goblet of Fire;* on the right, the sheet lists American terms for each. The instruc-tions advise the student to "Match each word Harry uses to the one(s) you would say." These words include "mum," "fortnight," "dustbin," "crisps," and "queue" in one column and "mother," "two weeks," "garbage can," "potato chips," and "line" in the other. While the match for "mum" really should be "mom" (as Scholastic itself translated the word in the first Potter novel), the exercise shows the educational possibilities of leaving British children's books untranslated. Referring to American publishers' tendency to translate English books for an American market, author Mary Hoffman asks, "Why shouldn't children know there are other countries where things are done differently?" Though this and the other three Scholastic Literature Guides each include a "vocabulary" list, only this particular guide reminds us that "Like many good writers, J. K. Rowling does not 'write down' to her readers, but expects them to work at comprehending the words she uses."[13] Were the editors to apply this principle to the act of translation, the first three readers' guides—and the Scholastic editions of the first three Potter books—would be better for it, and American children would have the opportunity to learn more about a culture and language different than their own.

Inasmuch as the very idea of translations may stem from a certain arrogance on the part of American publishers, Americans need exactly this sort of education. As Peter H. Gleick argues, "By protecting our children from an occasional misunderstanding or a trip to the dictionary, we are pretending that other cultures are, or should be, the same as ours. By insisting that everything be Americanized, we dumb down our own society rather than enrich it." The effect of such dumbing down is to give offense (albeit unintentionally). When Stephen Spielberg was entertaining the idea of directing the first Potter film, the British press reported that he planned to change "Hogwarts School" to "Hogwarts High," cast the American actor Haley Joel Osment as the title character, and give Harry a blonde cheerleader girlfriend. One article critical of this idea concluded by satirically imagining an Americanized Harry Potter: " 'Howdy,' drawled Harry Potter, and pulled off his Stetson." While these reports of the director's intentions may or may not be true, Rowling did talk to Spielberg and was not pleased with the degree of control he wanted; in the end, Chris Columbus, who pledged fidelity to Rowling's vision and offered to make her executive producer, got the job. As Steve Norris, head of the British Film Commission, puts it, "Harry Potter is something that is weirdly about us. It's culturally British and the thought of it being made anywhere but here sent shudders down everyone's spines. It's like taking *Catcher in the Rye* and setting it

---

13. Linda Ward Beech, *Scholastic Literature Guide: Harry Potter and the Goblet of Fire by J. K. Rowling,* 22; Hoffman quoted in Whitehead, " 'This Is NOT What I Wrote,' " part 2.

in Liverpool."[14] Comments such as these exemplify why Americans should develop an awareness of cultures other than their own. It is, apparently, very difficult for some Americans to recognize that what appears to be a minor change (Hogwarts High?) can provoke great offense.

Discussing the Americanized books, Chaudhuri suspects that a "more insidious motive behind the spelling change . . . is the global arrogance of the American." Multinational capitalism, in which U.S. corporations play a central role, amplify this perceived arrogance. Britons receive plenty of American culture that has not been Anglicized, but the economic imperative of selling to the vast American market gives U.S. publishers the belief that they have license to Americanize British texts. A telling example of such Americanization occurs in the U.S. edition of British writer Jacqueline Wilson's *Double Act* (1998): eager to get money for a trip to a London audition, Ruby sells her china doll for "$30," only to realize that it was worth much more, when her twin sister's "doll went for $900."[15] The publisher's presentation of these figures in dollars rather than pounds highlights the fact that American dollars motivate these translations. Having invented a monetary system unique to the wizarding world ("Seventeen silver Sickles to a Galleon and twenty-nine Knuts to a Sickle"), the Potter books evade any such currency translations (*Philosopher's Stone*, 58; *Sorcerer's Stone*, 75). However, while Scholastic's layout, design, and artwork do make the U.S. editions look more appealing than Bloomsbury's, they also emphasize these books *as* products, designed for public consumption. While there is no way to extricate a book—much less a cultural phenomenon such as the Harry Potter books—from its status as product, Scholastic tends to emphasize commodity more than Bloomsbury does. In Bloomsbury's first Harry Potter book, the characters eat "jelly" for dessert, but in Scholastic's, they eat "Jell-O" (*Philosopher's Stone*, 93; *Sorcerer's Stone*, 125). The change from "jelly" to "Jell-O" emphasizes the product name over the food itself: "Jell-O" is not just flavored gelatin, but a specific brand of flavored gelatin. Even when the item in question is purely imaginary, Scholastic is more likely to capitalize its name, an alteration which suggests a brand name instead of just a generic, commonplace item. Harry eating a big "stack of cauldron cakes" differs from Harry eating a big "stack of Cauldron Cakes" because the capital letters in the latter emphasize Cauldron Cakes' status as product (*Chamber of Secrets*, B 63, S 79). Similarly, changing a "grow-your-own-warts kit" (*Philosopher's Stone*, 150) to a "Grow-Your-Own-Warts kit"

14. Gleick, "Harry Potter, Minus a Certain Flavour"; "Spielberg Plans to Put Harry on the Big Screen"; Adam Sherwin and Grace Bradberry, "Harry Potter Gets the Hollywood Treatment"; Gregg Kilday, "Potter Training," 47–48; Norris quoted in Gareth McLean, "Hogwarts and All."
15. Chaudhuri, "Transfiguration," 5; Jacqueline Wilson, *Double Act*, 166.

(*Sorcerer's Stone*, 204) makes this novelty item appear more as a branded, marketed novelty item.

Even more than its proclivity for capital letters, Scholastic's use of fonts expresses a greater emphasis on commerce. In Bloomsbury's edition of *Harry Potter and the Prisoner of Azkaban*, the card advertising the Firebolt in Quality Quidditch Supplies does not look markedly different from the text surrounding. The words "THE FIREBOLT" appear centered, italicized, in capitals; below them, the description has been indented and italicized, too—but the font's style and size remain the same (B 43). In contrast, Scholastic's edition not only indents but also gives "THE FIREBOLT" its own logo and prints the advertisement's text in sleek, narrow capital letters that look like they may have been generated by a computer (S 51). It looks exactly like a tag one might see in a store. Without changing anything, we could snip this description from the novel, attach it to a broom, and place it in a display window. In addition to advertising the Firebolt, Scholastic's book jackets all bear Harry Potter's name in a font that, complete with its lightning-bolt "P," can only be described as a logo. Indeed, the font has become the logo, appearing in this format on Warner Brothers' film and even on the British audio cassettes for *Prisoner of Azkaban* and *Goblet of Fire*—notable, because neither the British books nor the first two audio cassettes use Scholastic's "Harry Potter" logo. (They use the more ordinary block capitals that appear on Bloomsbury's books.) In Scholastic's version, "Harry Potter" and "THE FIREBOLT" appear as brand names, corporate logos ready to be transferred onto T-shirts and trading cards.

The fact that marketing motivated Scholastic's translation calls attention to the type of "branding" described above. And yet if Scholastic's books are more commercial, they are also more appealing to hold and to read. In addition to Mary GrandPré's illustrations, David Saylor's art direction has resulted in a much cleaner layout and design than Bloomsbury's: the spacing of the text on the page makes Scholastic's easier on the eyes; its different fonts make news articles look more like actual clippings from the *Daily Prophet* and render personal letters in script intended to suggest the handwriting of the character (Bloomsbury's editions merely indent and italicize). Indeed, Hagrid's letter communicating the failure of Buckbeak's appeal includes smudgy tear-stains to emphasize his grief (*Prisoner of Azkaban*, S 291, B 215). Furthermore, if we are to evaluate these changes in terms of marketing, then it must be noted that Rowling herself agreed to a name change to get the books sold. To appeal to boys who (it was thought) might not want to read a book written by a woman, Bloomsbury encouraged her to use two initials and her surname on *Harry Potter and the Philosopher's Stone* instead of her given name, Joanne Rowling. When Bloomsbury asked for a middle initial, Joanne adopted K for Kathleen, her favorite grandmother's name. As Rowling has said, "I would have let them call me Enid Snodgrass if they published the book."[16]

Just as Rowling's agreement to abbreviate her name makes good business sense, one can certainly understand Levine's desire to protect his investment. As he explains, in 1997 he bid one hundred thousand dollars for a new manuscript by an unknown author. "It's a scary thing when you keep bidding and the stakes keep getting higher and higher," he admits. Though his company supported him, paying that much for the first Potter novel was "a great risk. If people believe in you and you flop, then you walk out on the plank and plunge."[17] Since a lot of capital and potentially his own job was riding on the success of what would be retitled *Harry Potter and the Sorcerer's Stone,* it would be surprising if he did not follow the industry practice of "translating" British works into American English. The fault is not so much with Levine himself, who did what he felt he needed to do; rather, it is with the practice itself and with the effect of such decisions. In essence, the issue of translating British English to American English represents just the latest skirmish in the adversarial relationship between art and commerce.

Though capital motivates its changes, Scholastic tends to frame the issue of translation more in terms of audience than of marketing; the failure to distinguish between the two illustrates the fact that "translation" and "marketing" are indistinguishable from a business perspective, but quite different from a reader's perspective. Levine explains that "A kid should be confused or challenged when the author wants the kid to be confused or challenged and not because of a difference of language." Citing the translation of "jumper" to "sweater," Rowling echoes her editor's explanation. She says, "If I'd left that as it is in the British edition, Harry, Ron and Fred would have all been wearing pinafore dresses as far as the American readers are concerned, and I was more than happy to substitute 'sweater' to avoid that confusion!" Rowling then concludes, "The changes really were minimal."[18] Despite Rowling's and Levine's statements to the contrary, it is difficult to accept the idea that these changes were minimal and that they were made merely to make the books comprehensible to children living in the United States. Certainly, marketing seems a more plausible motive for changing even British spellings to American ones because, really, why would this alteration be necessary? Though an American copy editor might change "pyjamas" to "pajamas," "colour" to "color," "grey" to "gray," "realise" to "realize," "apologise" to "apologize," and "Defence Against the Dark

16. Rowling, reading and question-and-answer session at the National Press Club.
17. Arthur A. Levine with Doreen Carvajal, "Why I Paid So Much," C14.
18. Levine quoted in Radosh, "American Kids," 56; Rowling quoted in Fraser, *Telling Tales,* 31.

Arts" to "Defense Against the Dark Arts," these spellings could have been retained without confusion. The novel is a British novel, written by a native of Great Britain: she ought to be allowed to spell according to the conventions of British English. These are, after all, very British books. The only American characters in all four novels are "a group of middle-aged American witches" who, in *Goblet of Fire,* sit "gossiping happily beneath a spangled banner stretched between their tents which read: *The Salem Witches' Institute*" (B 76, S 82). It seems only fair that novels largely indifferent to the existence of the United States should retain a language that reflects this sensibility.

Spelling aside, many altered words and phrases could be understood without having been changed. Generally speaking, these items fall into three categories: words explained by their context, words that have a similar meaning in the States, and onomatopoetic words. Of those easily explained by the context in which they occur, Scholastic's translators devote a surprising amount of energy to words associated with bodily functions. In *Philosopher's Stone,* Harry pulls his wand out of the unconscious troll's nose, the wand now "covered in what looked like lumpy grey glue." His response is: "Urgh—troll bogies" (130). The phrase "lumpy grey glue" ("lumpy gray glue" in Scholastic's), the wand's recent removal from a nose, and the similarity between "bogies" and "boogers" combine to convey the idea that "bogies" can only be a British word for "snot" or "boogers." Yet Scholastic persuades Harry to say, "Urgh—troll boogers" instead (*Sorcerer's Stone,* 177). Most American children would love to learn a new word for "booger." Indeed, when Rupert Grint (the actor who plays Ron Weasley in the Potter films) explained that Bertie Bott's Every Flavour Beans include the flavors "buttered toast, bogie, [and] vomit," "Today Show" co-host Katie Couric was herself quite pleased to learn that "bogie" was "the British way of saying booger."[19] In any case, the British "bogie" is so close to the American term that it is difficult to imagine any resultant confusion.

Working tirelessly to ensure that young American readers do not grow befuddled by British toilets, Scholastic's editors make the following largely unnecessary changes. Just before Harry and Ron meet Moaning Myrtle, Bloomsbury's Hermione explains that this ghost "haunts the girls' toilet on the first floor." The result, she says, is that the toilet has "been out of order all year because [Myrtle] keeps having tantrums and flooding the place." Generally, Hermione avoids this lavatory because "it's awful trying to go to the loo with her wailing at you" (*Chamber of Secrets,* B 101). In the American edition, Hermione explains that Myrtle "haunts one of the toilets in the girls' bathroom" on that floor and tells us that "it's awful trying to

19. *Behind the Magic of Harry Potter.*

have a pee with her wailing at you" (*Chamber of Secrets*, S 132–33). Though all other text remains the same, any moderately intelligent American child should not need the expressions "go to the loo" and "toilet" translated into "have a pee" and "bathroom." The context makes the meanings adequately clear. Later in *Chamber of Secrets*, the Scholastic editions spend a great deal of time transforming "cubicles" into "stalls" and even the "cistern of the toilet" into the "tank of the toilet" (B 118, 124, 138, 118; S 155, 164, 183, 158). While Professor McGonagall might award Scholastic top marks in transfiguration, such alterations seem rather gratuitous.

If Scholastic's obsessions over "bogies," "toilets," and "the loo" cause a reader to question the editors' sanity, chances are that Britons and Americans will use different words to express this sentiment. Nonetheless, "mad," "barking," and "barking mad" might have remained unchanged in the American editions of the Potter novels because context provides sufficient clues to the words' meanings. After Harry repeats Dumbledore's observation that "to the well-organised mind, death is but the next great adventure," Ron says, "I always said he was off his rocker," while looking "quite impressed at how mad his hero was." Moments later, Ron says "proudly" that "Dumbledore's barking, all right" (*Philosopher's Stone*, 218, 219). Though Scholastic changes "mad" to "crazy" and "barking" to "off his rocker," the original version leaves little confusion about the ideas conveyed (*Sorcerer's Stone*, 302). Throughout the Potter novels, Scholastic seems quite concerned about readers misinterpreting these terms. The U.S. edition of *Prisoner of Azkaban* alone changes "Harry had a mad urge to knock the goblet out of his hands" to "Harry had a crazy urge to knock the goblet out of his hands"; "He's barking mad" to "He's a complete lunatic"; "Are you mad?" to "Are you insane?"; and "I know it sounds mad" to "I know it sounds crazy" (B 118, S 157; B 125, S 167; B 278, S 379; B 298, S 407). Yet, in each case, the context in which the word or phrase occurs leaves no doubt about its intended meaning. Despite Scholastic's claim that it was not trying to "Americanize" the Potter books and Rowling's dismissal of the notion that Scholastic has translated the books into American, it is rather difficult to interpret these changes in any other way.[20]

The novels' slang offers, perhaps, the best arguments for and against Scholastic's methods of translation. As vocabulary very specific to a culture, slang words might be most apt to confuse American children; yet, as eleven-year-old Whitaker Cohen argues, children can figure out "what words mean from their context. There's no need for imitation slang."[21] In *Prisoner of Azkaban*, when Knight Bus conductor Stan Shunpike remarks

20. Fraser, *Telling Tales*, 31.
21. Cohen, "Hands Off Harry!"

that "little 'Arry Potter put paid to You-Know-'Oo," American readers will glean that "put paid" must be near to "routed": the books return to this central incident of Harry's life with such frequency that almost any verb could appear there and we would understand (B 34). However, Scholastic forgoes Stan's colorful colloquialism, giving us instead: "little 'Arry Potter got the better of You-Know-'Oo" (S 39). When debunking the Grim as a foolish superstition, Hermione uses a lively phrase that likewise does not appear in the novel's American edition. Ron tells her, "Grims scare the living daylights out of most wizards," and she wisely replies, "There you are then . . . They see the Grim and die of fright. The Grim's not an omen, it's the cause of death! And Harry's still with us because he's not stupid enough to see one and think, right, well, I'd better pop my clogs then!" (B 85). Given Hermione's argument that gullible wizards would "die of fright," her phrase "pop my clogs" could only mean something close to "die." Not trusting American readers to figure this out for themselves, Scholastic alters the line to "right, well, I'd better kick the bucket then!" (S 110). Even the word "Cracking," which any viewer of Nick Park's popular *Wallace and Gromit* films will recognize instantly, gets replaced. Fred calls Oliver Wood a "Cracking Keeper" in Bloomsbury's edition of *Chamber of Secrets* but a "Spanking Good Keeper" in Scholastic's (B 109, S 144).[22] Though some children might find "Spanking Good" more comprehensible than "Cracking," Scholastic's "imitation slang" seems rather needless. All of these examples feel more like American simulations of British slang than the authentic vernacular, closer to "Americanization" than to "translation."

The most gratuitous translations, however, are those for which the British original is as easily understood as the American "equivalent," regardless of the context in which it appears, such as the changes from "motorbike" to "motorcycle," "holidays" to "vacation" (or "break"), "brilliant" to "excellent" (or "fantastic"), "rubbish" to "lousy" (or "crap" or "bad"). For instance, Scholastic appears to believe that Rowling's use of the word "great" to emphasize size or intensity represents a linguistic difference significant enough to warrant alteration. So, recalling a painful childhood memory in the American edition, Ron remembers his brother transforming his teddy bear into a "great big filthy spider" instead of the "dirty great spider" described in the British version (*Chamber of Secrets*, S 155, B 117). Likewise,

---

22. Another phrase, needlessly translated: Seamus's congratulatory remark, "Good on you, Harry!" becomes "Good for you, Harry!" (Rowling, *Chamber of Secrets*, B 194, S 263). Similarly, near the end of *Chamber of Secrets*, Peeves is "bouncing along the corridor in tearing spirits, laughing his head off," but in Scholastic's he is "bouncing along the corridor in boisterous good spirits, laughing his head off" (Rowling, *Chamber of Secrets*, B 304, S 417). Because each word arrives following "bouncing," "tearing" seems as easily understood as "boisterous good."

Ron calls Hermione's cat a "big stupid furball" in Scholastic's *Prisoner of Azkaban*, but a "stupid great furball" in Bloomsbury's (S 226, B 168). When sandwiched between "dirty" and "spider" or between "stupid" and "furball," the word "great" can only be read as amplifying its peers: Ron clearly does not like the spider, and nor does he admire the "furball." Just as "great" clearly has negative connotations in the preceding phrases, so does "rubbish" in the following ones. There is no need for Harry to worry that he will be "lousy at" his new subjects in Scholastic's edition when he fears that he will be "rubbish at" them in Bloomsbury's edition (*Chamber of Secrets,* S 252, B 187). Similarly, Ron's accusation that Hermione dismisses Divination as "guesswork" only because she does not like being "bad at something" does not have quite the same ring as his claim that she dislikes being "rubbish at something" (*Prisoner of Azkaban,* S 111, B 85). Perhaps tacitly acknowledging that even an American child would understand the meaning of the word "rubbish," Scholastic does not change Hermione's retort that their Divination lesson "was absolute rubbish" (*Prisoner of Azkaban,* B85, S 111). Other similarly needless changes include the following. In *Chamber of Secrets,* "washing-up in the sink" turns into "dishes in the sink" (B 31, S 34). In all of the first three novels, "Brilliant!" becomes "Excellent!" or another substitute word, rendering a line like "You were brilliant, Fawkes" as "You were fantastic, Fawkes" (*Chamber of Secrets,* B 31, S34; B 46, S 53; B 236, S 321). Scholastic also changes "Happy Christmas!" to "Merry Christmas!"; "it looked like it ends up in Hogsmeade" to "it looked like it was heading for Hogsmeade"; and "he'd better skip pudding and escape" to "he'd better skip dessert and escape" (*Prisoner of Azkaban,* B 149, S 201; B 247, S 336; B 25, S 26).

Scholastic may have begun to recognize the superfluity of such alterations, because some words that were translated in earlier books are either not changed or not as consistently changed in later ones. In the first novel, "motorbike" becomes "motorcycle," but the U.S. edition of the third novel retains "motorbike" when Hagrid recalls Sirius Black turning up "on that flyin' motorbike he used to ride" (*Philosopher's Stone,* 16, 17, 19, 24; *Sorcerer's Stone,* 14, 16, 19, 25; *Prisoner of Azkaban,* B 153, S 206). Likewise, though the line "Harry didn't fancy his shepherd's pie" changes to "Harry didn't enjoy his shepherd's pie" in the American *Chamber of Secrets,* the verb "fancy" remains in the line "eat whatever he fancied" from *Prisoner of Azkaban* (*Chamber of Secrets,* B 91, S 119; *Prisoner of Azkaban,* B 42, S 49). And, as has been remarked earlier, *Goblet of Fire* largely abstains from changing British words into American ones.

Of all the unusual alterations to Rowling's British language, the most groundless are changes to onomatopoetic words. The verb "to splutter," for instance, sounds like rapid, confused speech, perhaps punctuated by droplets of spittle; merely saying the word "splutter" could produce the sensation of spluttering. Inexplicably, Scholastic drops the "l," changing the word to "sputter." "Neville's small splutter of terror" becomes "Neville's small sputter of terror" (*Prisoner of Azkaban*, B 101, S 133). After Harry reads the Kwikspell brochure, Mr. Filch "spluttered" a question at Harry, but "sputtered" this same question in Scholastic's edition (*Chamber of Secrets*, B 98, S 128). Emphasizing the baseless nature of these changes, both "splutter" and "sputter" appear in *Webster's Encyclopedic Unabridged Dictionary of the English Language* (1989) as American words with slightly different meanings. The connotations of "sputter" include an angrier tone and the possibility for flying food particles, both of which "splutter" lacks. Should these changes seem needless, then so will dropping the "r" from "urgh." When Harry, Ron, and Hermione are reading "famous cases of marauding beasts" to help prepare Buckbeak's defense, they momentarily appear to have found something useful, "but the Hippogriff was convicted— urgh, look what they did to it" (*Prisoner of Azkaban*, B 164). Bloomsbury generally capitalizes names of magical creatures where Scholastic does not, but beyond the minor change of "H" to "h" in "Hippogriff," the American edition also substitutes the word "ugh" for the word "urgh" (*Prisoner of Azkaban*, S 222). Both words sound guttural—they are grunts, expressing aversion to the treatment of the Hippogriff (or "hippogriff"). For that matter, both recall the sort of sound effect one might find in a comic book. Translating sound effects is a bit much.

The verb "to scarper" aurally recalls the verbs "to skitter," "to scamper," and (arguably) "to clamber," but means "to flee suddenly, especially without having paid one's bills." To my ears, the verb "scarper" sounds a good deal like the act of "scarpering." Scholastic always substitutes a different word—sometimes, "scamper," sometimes "run"—but never uses "scarper." In *Prisoner of Azkaban,* when fleeing Crookshanks, Scabbers "scarpered for the door" in Bloomsbury's version but "scampered for the door" in Scholastic's (B 49, S 60). Later in that same novel, while describing Sirius Black apparently about to attack him, Ron says, "Then I yelled, and he [Black] scarpered," a line which Scholastic changes to "Then I yelled, and he [Black] *scampered*." A moment later, Ron asks Harry, "Why did he scarper?" in the British edition, but "Why did he run?" in the American (B 200, S 270). As well as losing the onomatopoeia of "scarper," "scamper" loses the shadier connotations of the verb ("especially without having paid one's bills"). Given that Scabbers is in fact Wormtail and that Black appears to be a homicidal villain, the verb "scarper" conveys more of these sinister qualities. By contrast, "scamper" sounds more playful, less dark.

Other delightfully British words that transmogrify into less delightful American ones include "wonky," "bobbles," "treacle-thick," and "grass" (as a verb). Some "wonky brass scales" become "lopsided brass scales," and a "revolting old jumper of Dudley's (brown with orange bobbles)" transforms into a "revolting old sweater of Dudley's (brown with orange puff balls)"—though the "jumper" is not onomatopoetic, the "bobbles" are (*Chamber of Secrets*, B 48, S 58; *Philosopher's Stone*, 23, *Sorcerer's Stone*, 24). In his office, Dumbledore sits in a "high-backed chair" which metamorphoses into a "high chair" in America, but the two are not really the same: a "high-backed chair" belongs in an office, but a "high chair" belongs in a kitchen, holding a toddler (*Chamber of Secrets*, B 156, S 208). The Polyjuice Potion is "treacle-thick" in Britain, but "glutinous" in the States, though it is difficult to see how "glutinous" would be easier to understand than "treacle-thick" (*Chamber of Secrets,* B 161, S 215). Suspicious of Tom Riddle's accusation that Hagrid opened the Chamber of Secrets fifty years ago, Ron asks, "Who asked him to grass on Hagrid, anyway?"; Scholastic changes "grass" to "squeal" (*Chamber of Secrets,* B 185, S 250). These changes can only be considered Americanization, because they lose the novels' flavor (or flavour) without providing any appreciable help to an American reader.

Many of these changes result in a concurrent loss of poetry, diminishing the liveliness and vividness of Rowling's original. When Percy's "lumpy jumper" becomes a "lumpy sweater," we lose the rhyme and the phrase becomes more ordinary (*Philosopher's Stone,* 149, *Sorcerer's Stone,* 202). Likewise, the Knight Bus "scattering bushes and bollards, telephone boxes and trees" loses consonance and its poetic rhythms when it becomes a Knight Bus "scattering bushes and wastebaskets, telephone booths and trees" (*Prisoner of Azkaban,* B 35, S 41). The word "bollards" bumps merrily into its neighbor words "bushes" and "boxes," while the combination of this last word's soft "x" and "s" sounds meshes smoothly with "trees." In Scholastic's edition, however, the word "booths" sends the tongue up to the roof of the mouth, and "wastebaskets," without that initial "b" but with an extra syllable, doesn't fit as neatly with its colleagues. Some of the language's color and vitality move away, as in the change from "off they went, crocodile fashion" to "off they marched," banishing the visual metaphor (*Chamber of Secrets,* B 198, S 267). And a "packet of crisps" couples a crunchy, hard "ck" in "packet" with the "cr" in crisps, reminding one of the contents of that packet. In contrast, a "bag of chips" not only lacks the British sound of "packet of crisps" but replaces that crisp phrase with a soggy one (*Philosopher's Stone,* 37, *Sorcerer's Stone,* 44).

Translating words may also result in a loss of puns, as in the changes from "Sellotape" to "Scotch tape" and "dustbins" to "trash cans." Many have noted that with Scotch tape instead of Sellotape, American readers of Scholastic's editions will miss the pun on "Spellotape," which is used to repair wands. "Dustbin," however, has not received any comment. Though *Goblet of Fire* leaves the word "dustbin" as is, the first three Potter novels tend to replace "dustbins" with "trash cans." Hagrid's hands are the "size of dustbin lids" in the U.K., but the "size of trash can lids" in the U.S. (*Philosopher's Stone*, 16, *Sorcerer's Stone*, 14). Similarly, moving a brick in the wall "above the dustbin" opens the way into Diagon Alley in Bloomsbury's editions; this same brick is "above the trash can" in Scholastic's (*Philosopher's Stone*, 55, *Sorcerer's Stone*, 71; *Prisoner of Azkaban*, B 42, S 50). "Dustbins" also appear as the abbreviated "bins" in the British editions, but turn into "trash cans" in the American ones, depriving American readers of the pun in Professor Binns' name (*Prisoner of Azkaban*, B 32, S 36). That is, giving the name "Binns" to the boring ghost who teaches History of Magic seems a humorous way of implying that his classes are "rubbish."

Beyond the loss of poetry are shifts in meaning that appear inconsequential, but turn out to be important. The line-by-line textual comparison necessary for a study such as this one highlights Rowling's careful attention to every nuance of plotting, detail, and language. Sirius Black, the minor character whose motorbike Hagrid rides in the first chapter of the first book, becomes a central character in the third, a fact which may exemplify for most readers Rowling's careful plotting. However, language helps to create this tightly woven narrative, too. Dumbledore's affection for "sherbet lemons," the "Muggle sweet" for which he admits a fondness in *Philosopher's Stone,* turns out to be the password to his office in *Chamber of Secrets;* so, when Harry urgently needs to reach Dumbledore in *Goblet of Fire,* he tries "sherbet lemon" again as a possible password (*Philosopher's Stone*, 13, *Sorcerer's Stone*, 10; *Chamber of Secrets*, B 152, S 204; *Goblet of Fire*, B 483, S 557). Yet, in the Scholastic editions of *Philosopher's Stone* and *Chamber of Secrets,* "sherbet lemon" becomes "lemon drop": Dumbledore claims "lemon drops" as a favored sweet in *Sorcerer's Stone,* and "lemon drop" admits Harry to Dumbledore's office in *Chamber of Secrets* (*Sorcerer's Stone*, 10; *Chamber of Secrets*, S 204). Yet, in Scholastic's *Goblet of Fire,* "sherbet lemon" remains unchanged, which might confuse the careful reader of the American versions of the novels. As Dumbledore says in *Prisoner of Azkaban,* "the consequences of our actions are always so complicated, so diverse, that predicting the future is a very difficult business indeed" (*Prisoner of Azkaban*, B 311, S 426). His comment aptly describes the perils of such transatlantic translating: in novels as intricately plotted as these, every detail counts, and small changes can turn out to have larger, unforeseen consequences in the larger scope of the narrative.

Similar, likely unintended shifts in the meaning can slyly direct the reader's sympathies in directions different from the original, British edition. In chapter 20 of Bloomsbury's *Prisoner of Azkaban,* "Sirius Black" is called "Sirius" instead of "Black," as he had been called during the rest of the novel; using his first name signals his new status as a sympathetic character. However, in chapter 20 of Scholastic's *Prisoner of Azkaban*, "Black" is almost *always* used, placing the character at a greater emotional distance. Although both editions favor "Sirius" over "Black" in chapter 22, the change in Scholastic's earlier chapter suggests that our sympathy toward Sirius Black should develop not after Harry, Ron, and Hermione have learned the truth of his innocence (chapter 20), but instead after he has escaped (chapter 22). Taken individually, these changes may appear insignificant: after all, a small percentage of words were changed and, in this sense, the alterations could be described as relatively minor. However, the cumulative effect is a pervasive if subtle dulling of Rowling's original language. Losing puns, poetry, onomatopoeia, and some of the very "British-ness" of the author's style is a form of transfiguration. Just as the ability to transfigure oneself allows Minerva McGonagall to transform into a cat, so Scholastic's translations transform the original content of the books. As the cat's eyes resemble Professor McGonagall's spectacled eyes, the American books resemble the British ones; however, something of the original disappears in the process.

Despite all of Scholastic's changes to the texts, one suspects that, ultimately, the Potter books may leave a larger imprint on American language and culture than Scholastic's translations have left on Britain's. True, American expressions do emerge in the original versions of Rowling's novels, such as "Potter for President" and "dream team," implying that an unacknowledged American presence has seeped into the books (*Philosopher's Stone*, 136, *Sorcerer's Stone*, 184; *Chamber of Secrets*, B 143, S 191). However, the "Potterisms" cropping up in U.S. media suggest the degree to which Rowling's Potter series has influenced American speech. *New York Times* op-ed columnist Gail Collins, an unabashed fan of Harry Potter, wrote in April of 2000 that "Mrs. Clinton as a candidate is Hermione Granger. She wants to sign up for all the courses, and if there's a scheduling conflict, she'll replicate." On a day when Collins's column began with a reference to Harry Potter ("An Ode to July"), Thomas L. Friedman's piece on the Palestinian-Israeli peace process—which appeared on the same page—bore the title "Lebanon and the Goblet of Fire." Solidifying Rowling's hold on the op-ed page, Maureen Dowd wrote in an October 2000 column, "On the whole, the president has been patient about Al Gore casting him as Lord Voldemort, the Harry Potter villain who inspires such fear that no one dares speak his name." However, she concluded, "Voldemort has not disappeared from the Harry Potter novels simply because no one will say his name." Implying that Harry Potter's influence on American English extends well beyond the *Times,* the *Wall Street Journal* devoted a front-page story to the phenomenon in October of 2000, noting that *Newsday* "called sprinter Michael Johnson a 'muggle' for flaming out of the Olympic 200-meter trials" and that the *Chicago Daily Herald* compared an NBC Olympics commentator to Dementors, presumably because he "suck[ed] the joy out of people." More recently, Simon Ammann, who won two gold medals in the 2002 Winter Olympics, was described as a "20-year-old Swiss jumper who looks and flies like Harry Potter." Of greater interest may be the *Wall Street Journal*'s contention that "Potterisms are moving into the everyday language of work, politics and romance, where they are offering the series' millions of fans a new insiders' short hand for all manner of good and evil." The piece told of a music major who chants "Expecto Patronum" before her piano recitals, an employee of an insurance company referring to an unpleasant executive as "Draco Malfoy," and a person referring to a location she couldn't find as "platform 9 3/4."[23]

As the creative force behind a cultural phenomenon, Rowling may have the last laugh on her American translators, but she would be the exception to the rule. Unless the Potter novels, as a visible example of a pervasive but largely invisible practice, persuade U.S. publishers to end their custom of translating British books into American English, this damaging practice will continue. If readers follow Gleick's example and buy British editions of British books, then perhaps American publishers will get the message: since profit motivates their translations, lost profit may also halt their translations. Certainly, the process of writing this article has persuaded me to buy British versions of British books henceforth. Perhaps others, too, will come to realize that we cannot trust American publishers to deliver a copy of the book that the author wrote. It may cost more to order a book from England, but American readers should have access to the same text of British books that a British reader does. And, more than that, awareness of national and cultural differences expands the reader's knowledge of the world. To know that "trolley"—another word changed by Scholastic—denotes "cart" may be a small addition to a person's linguistic repertoire, but it is worth knowing. Learning different words for the same object enriches our understanding of language; to suggest otherwise is to insult the intelligence of children and young adults. Indeed, learning from our differences is one of the premises upon which multicultural curricula are based.

Translating British English to American English effaces differences, creates distortions, and can introduce meanings unintended by author or translator. Discussing the hazards of translating Rowling's "fantasy milieu,"

23. Gail Collins, "Rudy's Identity Crisis," A31; Gail Collins, "An Ode to July," A31; Thomas Friedman, "Lebanon and the Goblet of Fire," A31; Maureen Dowd, "Dare Speak His Name," 15; Matthew Rose and Emily Nelson, "Potter Cognoscenti All Know a Muggle When They See One," A1; "Swiss Whiz Kid Does It Again: Ammann Wins Second Gold in Ski Jump."

Daniel Radosh calls attention to the varieties of sweets sold at Honeydukes. He writes, "Levine pointed out that when a candy store is stocked with Fizzing Whizzbees, Pepper Imps, and Cockroach Clusters it's supposed to sound exotic, and replacing these sweets with M&M's and Tootsie Rolls would be out of the question." Levine told Radosh that he decided to leave "humbugs" as is because " 'Humbug' is clearly a magical term. . . . It's something that should be imagined." Yet Radosh concludes, "Except it's not. It's a common triangular sucking candy." Considering the amount of work involved in translating such long and intricate novels, Radosh's kicker may seem a bit unfair. However, the decision to translate books that, let's face it, do not need translating causes unforeseen and unnecessary problems. In highlighting these problems, Radosh gets at the heart of the matter: any act of translation bears within it the cultural assumptions of the translator, and these assumptions will distort the original in ways that the translator may not fully realize. As Ann Flowers, a reviewer for *The Horn Book* and a children's librarian for three decades, has said of Americanization: "If it's good enough, it'll come through. If it's not, it's not worth fiddling with."[24] Exactly. Let's call the whole thing off.

24. Radosh, "American Kids," 56; Whitehead, " 'This Is NOT What I Wrote,' " Part 2.

Harry Potter and the Tower of Babel

Translating the Magic

Nancy K. Jentsch

Since their appearance in 1997, the Harry Potter books in English have spread their charms to readers across the globe. It follows that persons not able to understand the original English version make up a large enough market for publishers to consider producing translations. In fact, according to the *Christian Science Monitor* of July 6, 2000, J. K. Rowling's Harry Potter books have been translated into forty languages. The stage and state of Pottermania, though, vary greatly by country. Whereas German readers counted the days until the publication of the fourth book on October 14, 2000, and could already order book five as early as August 2000, readers in the People's Republic of China were not officially introduced to the young sorcerer until October 12, 2000. Thailand welcomed the first Harry Potter book in its native language in July 2000, and the Czech Republic awaited the printing of the second book in Czech in fall 2000.[1]

Each translator involved with these books has been faced with the normal challenges of the occupation, but also with a number of unique situations. For example, the Harry Potter series contains many words newly coined for the books by their author. Though this is not uncommon in children's fantasy literature, translating such words does present unusual difficulties. Elizabeth Devereaux is reported to have said that the Harry Potter books in general are easier to translate than other children's literature that is much more concerned with language, such as Lewis Carroll's *Alice's Adventures in Wonderland*.[2] I would argue, nonetheless, that the translator of the Harry Potter series has a unique challenge in the genre, that is, to portray a setting and its people that are a world apart from ours, and at the same time located due north of London. This prompted Hilal Sezgin of the *Frankfurter*

1. Kim Campbell, "The Whole World Is Wild about *Harry*," 1; "Harry Potter zaubert auch in China"; "Translation of *Harry Potter* Becomes Bestseller in Thailand"; "Harry Potter a Kámen mudrcü" 7.
2. Campbell, "Whole World."

Rundschau to write, "Manche zählen Harry Potter nicht zum Abenteuer-sondern zum Fantasy-Roman. Doch Rowling erzählt nicht von Trollen und Elfen, die in einem fernen Gebirge umherziehen, nicht von Helden, die nie gelebt haben und nie leben werden. Harry Potters Welt ist eine Welt mitten in der unseren, der der Muggel, im Modus des 'Was wäre wenn . . .' " ("Some say Harry Potter is not of the adventure genre, but rather the fantasy genre. But Rowling doesn't tell a tale of trolls and elves that come and go in faraway mountains, or a tale of heroes who have never lived and never will. Harry Potter's world is a world within our own, our Muggle world, in the manner of 'What if . . .' ")[3] This juxtaposition of magical and Muggle worlds is integral to the original text and must be a serious consideration to its translators. The translator thus has to decide not only how to translate, but when to translate and when to leave words in the original. Certainly, names readily understood by the target audience and those that have no further significance can and should be left in the original. After all, English names for people and places can help create the sense of place, integral to a novel whose setting is in large part a boarding school in Britain. Further, it is obvious that J. K. Rowling chooses her characters' names carefully. They often have a meaning, be it in French, the language and literature she studied at the University of Exeter, or otherwise. Malfoy (bad faith), Voldemort (flight from death) and Sirius (the Dog Star) are examples of this. The decision of how much should be left in the original language, and how to translate such significant words (when necessary to promote these meanings) is a subjective one, but also one that will affect the overall success of the translation.

A further challenge to the translator of these works is one that occurs any time an English text is translated into a language that has more than one form for the word "you." The translation should appropriately render the universal "you" of English to specific forms, which in the target language not only denote the relationship of the speakers to each other but also contribute to the readers' sense of characterization. Other more general issues for translators involve the translation of word plays and the age-old dichotomy between faithfulness and freedom in translation.[4]

Publishers in France, Germany, and Spain had come out with the first three books in the series in translation by April 2000, and these volumes are the subject of this study. The French translator of the Harry Potter books is Jean-François Ménard, who was the favorite translator of Roald Dahl. The publisher, Gallimard Jeunesse, changed the title of the first book

3. Hilal Sezgin, "Alle Menschen werden Muggel," 22.
4. For further discussion of theoretical aspects of translation, see Nancy K. Jentsch, "German-English Translation: Theoretical and Practical Aspects," master's thesis, University of Cincinnati, 1982.

to *Harry Potter à l'école des sorciers* (*Harry Potter at the Sorcerers' School*), but the succeeding books retain titles that are translations of the originals. By July 2000, 580,000 copies of the first three books had been sold in France, with the publication date of the fourth book in the series publicized as November 29, 2000. Carlsen Verlag in Hamburg, Germany, publishes Klaus Fritz's translation of the works. The title of the first book in German mirrors the British title, *The Philosopher's Stone*, the German equivalent of which is *Der Stein der Weisen*, but the second book's title, *Harry Potter und die Kammer des Schreckens* (*Harry Potter and the Chamber of Terror*), deviates from the original, though it certainly accurately describes the chamber in question. As of August 10, 2000, *Der Spiegel* reported that 2.3 million copies of the first three books in the Harry Potter series had been sold in Germany. Earlier it had been reported that Harry Potter books had topped *Der Spiegel's* list of bestselling books for most of the year, and, according to the publisher's web site at <http://www.carlsen-harrypotter.de>, those top billings have lasted into 2002. The first edition of book four, which came out on October 14, 2000, was originally set for 350,000 copies, but in September *Der Spiegel* reported that the first printing of that book, which had already been available for sale and in German libraries in English, would be a record one million. Alicia Dellepiano translated the Spanish version of the first book in the series (and the only Spanish translation quoted in this essay) for the Emecé Editores in Barcelona, which maintained direct translations of the first three titles. The first two books in the series had sold 120,000 copies by June 2000, and Emecé's branch in Argentina reported light sales, amounting to fewer than 40,000 copies of the first two books sold by May 2000. (Book three was not published until April 2000, but was in its sixth edition by October 2000.) Despite relatively low numbers, Emecé reported that book four was scheduled to appear in March or April of 2001. In comparison, according to *AP Worldstream,* 30,000 copies of the Thai translation of book one were sold within two weeks of its appearance, bringing it quickly to first place on at least one bestsellers' list.[5]

At more than three million copies, the French, Spanish, and German translations of the Harry Potter books combined represent a good 10 percent of sales of the first three books in the series, which was estimated at

5. Helen M. Jerome, "Welcome Back, Potter," 44; "La magie de Harry Potter"; Christian Fumeron, "Re: Le 4eme tome d'Harry Potter"; "Cover-Wahl im Internet"; "Trubel um des Zauberlehrlings vierten Streich"; "Ansturm auch in Deutschland?"; "Harry Potter für alle"; José María Plaza, "El Éxito de la magia cotidiana"; Loreley Gaffoglio, "Entrevista a Joanne Kathleen Rowling por 'La Revista'"; Susanna Fernandez, "respuesta"; Susana Fernandez, "una respuesta más"; "Translation of *Harry Potter* Becomes Bestseller in Thailand."

thirty million in July 2000.[6] These three translations offer an opportunity to examine the choices translators face and make and the influence their solutions have on such elements as character development, the sense of place, and, in the end, on the relative merit and success of the translation as a whole. While translators of any work face many common challenges and the Harry Potter books present peculiarities such as the presentation of a magical place not far removed from reality and the use of many newly coined but contextually significant terms, it is also unusual to have many translations published soon after the appearance of the original. The situation lends itself well to a comparative study of the translator's art.

The relationships among characters are important aspects of their portrayal and development. One way to determine this relationship is to look at how the characters address one another. French, German, and Spanish share with many other European languages the use of two or more forms for the word "you." Distinctions are thus made between formal and informal relationships as well as between words addressed to either one or more than one person. Since these differentiations are lacking in the original English text, translators must make their own decisions about the use of words such as "du," "Sie," "tú," "tu," "usted," "ustedes," "vosotros," and "vous," and all their related forms.

The pupils at Hogwarts would all very naturally use the informal forms when conversing among themselves, and all three translators have consistently employed these forms in such situations. In none of the books does a student use the informal form of "you" with a teacher, save in the case of Hagrid. In the Spanish version of the book, Harry's special relationship with Hagrid is marked by his use of the informal "tú" with the gigantic gamekeeper beginning in the fifth chapter of book one of the series, after originally addressing the giant Keeper of the Keys with "usted." He is soon joined by his friends Ron and Hermione. In the German books, these four characters also share an unambiguous friendship, marked by their use of the informal form of "you" with one another. Their relationship in the French version is not set so much apart from those of other adults with pupils; while Hagrid uses the informal form with the three central characters, they address him with the formal "vous." Gilderoy Lockhart, for example, as he tries to make Harry his ally, also uses the informal "tu" with him. His motivation for this is obviously quite different from that of Hagrid, a true friend, yet because of the parallel uses of the forms, that difference is masked. Furthermore, elsewhere in the French books this same degree of relationship, where the adult uses the informal "tu" and Harry addresses the

6. Figures on the sale of book three in Spanish are unavailable; Malcolm Jones, "The Return of Harry Potter," 57.

adult with "vous," exists between Harry and Cornelius Fudge and Harry and Mr. Weasley. In the German and Spanish books, on the other hand, the closeness of Hagrid's relationship with the three friends is unique. The subtlety of the difference between formal and informal address and what it has to say about the state of a relationship can be apparent only in a translation to a language with more than one form of address, and the Spanish and German versions have been successful in conveying the specialness of this particular mixed-age clique.

Whenever Harry Potter visits the Leaky Cauldron, he is treated with deference by the bartender/landlord Tom, and with awe by the pub guests. In the original English, this is signaled by Harry's being addressed as Mr. Potter, even at the age of eleven. The French translator takes the cue well and has Tom not only call Harry "Mr. Potter" but also use the formal "vous" with him. This is in contrast to the adults who use the informal "tu" when addressing Harry. In addition, the level of language used by Tom in the French version is one of distinct formality. The German translation is identical in style and mechanics to the French, with "Mr. Potter" being addressed formally as "Sie," despite his age, and the unmistakable formality of Tom's words, "Würden Sie mir bitte folgen" (Would you please follow me) and "Wenn Sie irgendetwas brauchen, Mr Potter, zögern Sie nicht zu fragen" (If you need anything at all, don't hesitate to ask) (*Harry Potter und der Gefangene von Askaban*, 52–53). In contrast, the Spanish translation fails to give its readers an idea of the impression Harry's appearance at the Leaky Cauldron makes on its owner and customers. Here, Harry is addressed by all with the informal "tú" and with all the "Mr. Potters" of the original becoming "Harrys." The French version of Tom's original words of welcome to Harry in book one are, "Soyez le bienvenu, Mr Potter. Bienvenue parmi nous" (Be most welcome, Mr. Potter, welcome in our midst) (*Harry Potter à l'école des sorciers*, 80). In comparison, the Spanish "Bienvenido, Harry, bienvenido" (Welcome, Harry, welcome) (*Harry Potter y la piedra filosofal*, 64) certainly fails to alert the reader to the respect of the magical public for the young boy who has loosed them from the grip of the evil Lord Voldemort.

In the German version of the Harry Potter books, there is unfortunately much inconsistency in the forms of address used by teachers to pupils. This detracts from the translation, as the reader continually wonders if he or she has missed some important relational shift. For example, Professor McGonagall uses the formal form of address with students, while Professor Flitwick uses the informal "du." Common practice in German schools indicates that the informal form is used by teachers with their students until approximately the age of fifteen. In *Harry Potter und der Gefangene von Askaban*, there is a passage where Professor Snape uses the formal form with a female student, the informal form with Harry, and then the formal form with the entire class, all within one page of text (178–79), illustrating well the inconsistencies found throughout the book.

One very poignant moment occurs in book three of the German series, where Harry realizes at last that Sirius Black is his friend and not the arch-enemy he had thought him to be. Black asks Harry if he might want to live with him once he is cleared of charges, and Harry responds, using the familiar form for the first time with the man he had been living in terror of for so long. " 'Are you insane?' said Harry, his voice easily as croaky as Black's. 'Of course I want to leave the Dursleys! Have you got a house? When can I move in?' "(*Prisoner of Azkaban*, 379). In German it appears as " 'Du bist wohl verrückt,' sagte Harry und seine Stimme krächzte längst genauso wie die von Black. 'Natürlich will ich von den Dursleys weg! Hast du ein Haus? Wann kann ich einziehen?' " (*Gefangene von Askaban*, 392). The bond thus formed between Harry and Black remains constant, and the two consistently use "du" with one another from then on.

Voldemort's nickname, "You-Know-Who," was treated as an unchange-able informal form by the German translator, becoming "Du-weißt-schon-wer," the "wer" (who) being declined as necessary by the grammatical context. The "schon" in this translation is an emphatic particle, typical of the German language, which indicates that the speaker does expect the person addressed to be fully aware of who is being talked about. The French and Spanish translators switch from formal to informal forms, as appropriate in the context. For example, Professors McGonagall and Dumbledore discuss "Quien-usted-sabe" at the beginning of the Spanish book one, but in chapter 4 of the same book, Hagrid says, " 'Quien-tú-sabes los mató' " (You-Know-Who killed them) as he explains Harry's parents' death to him (*Piedra filosofal*, 53).

In addition to forms of address, the level of language that is used in dialogue is an important aspect of characterization. In the Harry Potter books, for example, one of the most interesting and well-drawn figures is Hagrid, the gamekeeper and sometimes teacher at Hogwarts. He has a mysterious past that is revealed to the reader in increments, but his rough exterior and softhearted interior are what make him most appealing. An important part of this rough exterior is his manner of speech, which is consistent with his wild clothing and ungroomed appearance. He speaks in an undistin-guishable accent that, by seeming uncouth, belies the emotional and good-hearted man that he is. Unfortunately, none of the translators in this study has chosen to render his speech with anything but normal vocabulary and syntax. Perhaps the translators were concerned that using a particular dialect for the character of Hagrid would be demeaning to the speakers of that dialect, as Hagrid's speech is obviously that of a less-educated and

Table 1.
Words Common to the Harry Potter Books that are Translated in at Least One Language

English	French	German	Spanish
Muggle	Moldu/moldu	Muggel	*muggle*
4 Privet Drive	4, Privet Drive	Ligusterweg 4	Privet Drive, 4
Leaky Cauldron	*Le Chaudron Baveur/* Chaudron baveur	Tropfender Kessel	Caldero Chorreante
Diagon Alley	Chemin de Traverse	Winkelgasse	callejón Diagon
Knut	Noise	Knut	*knut*
Sickle	Mornille	Sickel	*sickle*
Galleon	Gallion	Galleon	galeón
Flourish and Blotts	Fleury et Bott	*Flourish & Blotts*	Flourish y Blotts
Hogwarts	Poudlard	Hogwarts	Hogwarts
Sorting Hat	Choixpeau magique	Sprechender Hut	sombrero seleccionador
Gryffindor	Gryffondor	Gryffindor	Gryffindor
Ravenclaw	Serdaigle	Ravenclaw	Ravenclaw
Hufflepuff	Poufsouffle	Hufflepuff	Hufflepuff
Slytherin	Serpentard	Slytherin	Slytherin
Snape	le professeur Rogue	Professor Snape	el profesor Snape
Madam Hooch	Madame Bibine	Madam Hooch	la señora Hooch
Professor Sprout	le professeur Chourave	Professor Sprout	la profesora Sprout
Madam Pomfrey	Madame Pomfresh	Madam Pomfrey	la señora Pomfrey
Mr. Filch	Mr Rusard	Mr Filch	el señor Filch
You-Know-Who	Tu-Sais-Qui Vous-Savez-Qui	Du-weißt-schon-wer	Quien-tu-sabes Quien-usted-sabe
Quidditch	Quidditch	Quidditch	*quidditch*
Golden Snitch	Vif d'or	Goldener Schnatz	*snitch* dorada
Quaffle	Souafle	Quaffel	*quaffle*
Bludger	Cognard	Klatscher	*bludger*
Beater	Batteur	Treiber	golpeador
Chaser	Poursuiveur	Jäger	cazador
Seeker	Attrapeur	Sucher	buscador
Keeper	Gardien/gardien/Gardien de but	Hüter	guardián
Cleansweep Seven	Astiqueur/Brossdur 7	Sauberwisch Sieben	Cleansweep 7
Scabbers	Croàtard	Krätze	*Scabbers*
Fang	Crockdur	Fang	*Fang*
Mrs. Norris	Miss Teigne	Mrs Norris	*Señora Norris*

uncultured person. In the interest of character development and also of playfulness, though, the translators surely could have come up with an in-offensive solution.[7]

As discussed by Philip Nel in *J. K. Rowling's Harry Potter Novels,* class issues play a significant role in the novels.[8] A skilled translator can portray the

---

7. The Czech translator, for example, renders Hagrid's speech with identifiable colloquial modifications that make for delightful reading.
8. Nel, *J. K. Rowling's Harry Potter Novels,* 43.

important aspect of social class by level of language. The German translator, though hesitant to modify Hagrid's language, demonstrates his ability to do this in book three, where Harry boards the Knight Bus and is greeted by its driver and conductor in very standard and convincing German colloquial speech. Here, "Wen suchst du denn?" (Who are you looking for?) becomes "Wen suchste denn?" and "Und jetzt ist er raus" (Now he's out) is rendered as "Und jetzt isser raus" (*Gefangene von Askaban*, 39, 45). These modifications of standard language do not belong to one dialect area in Germany, but they do imply a certain social milieu. Surely the translator could similarly modify Hagrid's lines to show the gruffness of his speech without offending anyone in Germany.

In the French version, the translator shows an occasional use of colloquial language, but not in the context of Hagrid's speech. The driver and conductor of the Knight Bus let go of an occasional "Ouais" (yeah) and Fred Weasley leaves off an occasional "ne" as in "T'inquiète pas" (Don't worry), which in written French should read "Ne t'inquiète pas." Convincing modifications of speech are Harry's words "Qu'essquiya?" (What's going on?) (*Harry Potter et la Chambre des Secrets*, 117) when woken abruptly by Oliver Wood, which corresponds to "Qu'est-ce qu'il y a?" in written language. Similarly, the translator renders the gnome's scream "Gerroff me! Geroff me!" (*Chamber of Secrets*, 37) in book two as "Fishmoilapaix! Fishmoilapaix!"(Leave me be! Leave me be!) (*Chambre des Secrets*, 44). In written French this should read "Fiche-moi la paix! Fiche-moi la paix!" Similarly, the speech of Hagrid could be written as spoken language, for example using "jensérien" (I don't know anything) for "je ne sais rien" or "tuveupas" (you don't want) for "tu ne veux pas."

The Spanish translator limits Hagrid's colloquial speech to an occasional "buen día" (Hello) instead of "buenos días." Otherwise, his language is rendered without a trace of difference from that of the others. Colloquialisms occur in the book, but always on the level of vocabulary, never syntax or accent. Draco Malfoy, for example, refers to Neville Longbottom as a "gran zoquete" (great fat and ugly little runt) (*Piedra filosofal*, 126) where Rowling uses "great lump" (*Sorcerer's Stone*, 147). The translator shows finesse, though, in her translation of the often recurring references to a "great lump." In the description of Dudley in the opening pages of book one, Rowling has Hagrid refer to him also as a "great lump" (47). This is rendered in Spanish as "bola de grasa" (ball of fat) (*Piedra filosofal*, 46). The translator has captured the difference between these two references to "great lump," and used specific and colorful translations to convey that difference.

One significant aspect of language in the Harry Potter books is J. K. Rowling's sense of playfulness. Who can doubt this important element, when even in the opening pages of book one she wrote these words of Professor McGonagall that describe Harry Potter: "He'll be famous—a legend—I wouldn't be surprised if today was known as Harry Potter day in the future—there will be books written about Harry—every child in our world will know his name!" (*Sorcerer's Stone,* 13). These words and the subsequent references to Harry's celebrity stature throughout book two have, of course, become a prophecy fulfilled, though their original intent was surely a playful one. In names, in the coining of new words, and in Rowling's descriptions of the magical place the reader enters upon opening the covers of her books, she displays a keen sense of language's ability to amuse. Who can leave the world of Harry Potter without fond memories of Diagon Alley, or without a smile for Cornelius Fudge in his pin-striped robes? The playful titles of magical ministries are easily translated, and sound just as comically pompous in any target language. Likewise, the pin-striped robes, the acid green pen, and the tartan dressing gown that make their appearances in the books are easily rendered in other languages.

The word plays are, of course, another matter. While it is impossible to translate most word plays as such, an attempt to capture the tone of the words involved is often feasible. For example, the Spanish translation of Diagon Alley, "callejón Diagon" captures a degree of playfulness, with the shortening of the word "diagonal" to make it match in ending the word "callejón." Similarly, the German translation of the broom called "Cleansweep Seven" mirrors at least some of the author's intent. Though "Cleansweep" has overtones of a winning streak that the German "Sauberwisch Sieben" does not, the German retains not only the allusion to cleaning by broom ("wischen") but also an alliteration, which gives the line of brooms the flashy image inherent not only in the brand name "Cleansweep Seven," but in the names of all the broom models used by Hogwarts pupils. A further example of playfulness expressed in a translation occurs in the first two chapter headings in the Spanish version of book one. "El niño que vivió" (The Boy Who Lived) and "El vidrio que desvaneció" (The Glass That Vanished) are parallel forms grammatically, both using relative pronouns. The second is not a direct translation of the English "The Vanishing Glass," and obviously represents a conscious decision on the part of the translator to show playfulness. The French translation for the "Sorting Hat," which in itself is not a playful term, shows the translator's attention to the role of word play in the books. He chose the brilliant "Choixpeau magique," "Choixpeau" being a play on the words "chapeau" (hat) and "choix" (choice). The French solution to the problem of translating "Tom Marvolo Riddle" so that its letters can be arranged to spell "I am Lord Voldemort" is worth noting. Tom Marvolo Riddle becomes Tom Elvis Jedusor. The French last name has a double meaning, as does the English original: the French is phonetically identical to "jeu du sort" (game of the curse). If this meaning isn't clear to the French reader, it is spelled out in book two when Jedusor explains his identity to Harry in the Chamber of Secrets. Rearranged, the letters spell, of course, "je suis Voldemort" (*Chambre des Secrets*, 331).

Each translator has come up with a different solution for the translation of such newly coined words as Hogwarts, and for the insertion of explanatory material. In the French version, most people's and place names are reinvented in French. Thus, "Squib" becomes "Cracmol" and "Hogwarts" is called "Poudlard." Many of the characters are given French names as well. Longbottom becomes Londubat and Snape is renamed Rogue. These translations are of questionable value, as they do not add to the reader's understanding of the text and they undermine the important sense of place in the novels. They also prove awkward in book four, where Madame Maxime and the pupils from Beauxbatons visit Hogwarts. With the proliferation of French names in the French version of Hogwarts, there is much less of the desired contrast between the visitors and the British pupils and teachers than there would have been had more English names been retained for the Hogwarts contingent. Even in the first three books, the excessive use of translated proper names detracts from the translation's ability to convey a sense of place, particularly the translation of the names of Hogwarts' four houses. With such an abundance of French names used, the reader has much less the sense of being at a British boarding school. For instance, while Professor McGonagall's tartan dressing gown seems incongruous in the halls of Poudlard, its appearance is most natural in the original text. An example of a successful rendering of a name in French is that of Draco Malfoy, which becomes Drago Malefoy. Here the translator is getting across an intended meaning, and unobtrusively aiding the French reader in pronunciation. It could be argued that readers in other countries find words such as "Slytherin" too hard to read and pronounce, and that such words should therefore be translated, even when the translation is not necessary to convey meaning. The flaw in this argument is that many of Rowling's newly coined words are so unusual that even English speakers disagree on their pronunciation. The author even attempts to put an end to the question of how to pronounce "Hermione" in book four of the series, where she renders the name phonetically, ostensibly for the benefit of Hermione's newfound friend, Viktor Krum (*Goblet of Fire*, 419). The questions about pronunciation among English-speaking readers abound to the point that Scholastic even offers its readers a pronunciation guide on its web site. The French translator occasionally finds explanation necessary, as in Justin Finch-Fletchley's mention of Eton in book two, where he explains that Eton is the best private school in England: "Normalement, je devais aller à Eton, le meilleur collège d'Angleterre, mais je préfère être ici" (Normally I should have gone to Eton, the best private school in England, but I'd rather be here) (*Chambre des Secrets,* 106). Rowling says it this way: "My name was down for Eton, you know. I can't tell you how glad I am I came here instead" (*Chamber of Secrets,* 94).

The Spanish translator has approached words that can't easily be translated by using the English word in italics, which is a widely used method of treating foreign words in contemporary Spanish texts. Thus "Mimblewimble" is "*mimblewimble*" and Snitch is "*snitch*." Because of this approach, though, there is no consistency in instances where some magical vocabulary is translated into standard Spanish and other words are left in the original. For example, the names of the magical currency types are "*knuts,*" "*sickles,*" and "galeónes," the last being a standard Spanish word. Proper names and place names tend not to be translated in the Spanish version of the books, which lends to more consistency in the sense of place felt by the reader. There is, however, something disorienting about the fact that the italicization of words occurs without a clear system. Untranslated words are usually italicized, with the exception of people's names and the names of the four houses, which are untranslated but not in italics. Animal names, though, are in italics, even "*Señora Norris,*" which is translated in part! Though the Spanish translator does not translate the name Draco Malfoy, she does add an explanation of it to aid the Spanish reader in seeing the relationship between "Draco" and "dragon." In book one, after Malfoy introduces himself to Ron and Harry, the translator writes, "Draco (dragón) lo miró." (Draco [dragon] looked at him) (*Piedra filosofal,* 94). A further example of an added explanation comes with the first mention of Peeves, the poltergeist. There is no Spanish equivalent for "poltergeist," and Percy explains the phenomenon as "Es un duende, lo que en las películas llaman poltergeist" (It's a ghost—the one that they call a poltergeist in the movies) (111). While the name "Peeves" never appears in italics, in his first appearance, the reader encounters him as "Peeves *el Duende*" (Peeves the ghost) (114), again with the rare occurrence of a Spanish word in italics.

The German translator has the advantage of working with two Germanic languages. "Muggle" is simply rewritten to correspond to German orthography as "Muggel," and "Sickle" easily becomes "Sickel." In book three, Draco Malfoy's taunting "Potty and the Weasel" (*Prisoner of Azkaban,* 80) can be rendered as "Potty und das Wiesel" (*Gefangene von Askaban,* 86), with the expectation that the German reader will make a connection between "Wiesel" and "Weasley." Most people's and place names are not translated into German, except when they have a significance that would otherwise be lost on the German reader. Therefore, Professor Kettleburn becomes "Professor Kesselbrand" (Kettleburn), Crookshanks is "Krummbein" (crooked leg), and Scabbers is called "Krätze" (scabies), but Snape remains Snape and Pomfrey stays Pomfrey. It is curious, therefore, why the translator chose to render "Privet Drive" as "Ligusterweg." Though the words "privet" and "Liguster" denote a shrub commonly used in hedges, the translation of the street name does not seem to be integral to the story. Even the French translator, who translated "Hogwarts," "Hogsmeade," and the names of the school's four houses, didn't touch "Privet Drive." The unnecessary translation of this place designation in the German text detracts from the all-important sense of the story being set in Britain.

Translation requires the use of precise words, lest subtle meanings become blurred. In the German version, for example, the translator renders "cauldron" with the German word "Kessel," which can mean either "cauldron" or "kettle." Although "Kessel" is a word widely used in German fairy tales for a witch's cauldron, "Hexenkessel" (witch's cauldron) would unambiguously represent the English "cauldron" and prevent confusion, especially since the word "Kessel" is used at other times in the books to refer to a tea kettle. Reading the word "Kesselkuchen" (kettle cakes) as it appears in the German translation will not necessarily lead the German reader to the same mental image as would, for example, "Hexenkessel Hörnchen" (cauldron croissants).

Translators can be aided or hampered by specific characteristics of the language they are translating into. The word "Muggle" provides interesting examples in French, German, and Spanish. It is used in the original text both as a noun and as an adjective and is capitalized by Rowling in both instances. The French language does not provide for nouns to be used as adjectives. Though both nouns and adjectives often take appropriate endings (masculine, feminine, and plural), they remain separate parts of speech. Therefore a Muggle can be a "Moldu" or in the case of a woman a "Moldue" and Muggles can be "Moldus" or "Moldues." But as an adjective, as in "côté moldu" (Muggle side) and "parents moldus" (Muggle parents), the word is no longer capitalized, takes the appropriate endings, and follows the noun it modifies, making it without a doubt an adjective. Thus the solution for a newly coined word that doubles as a noun, "Moldu," and an adjective, "moldu," is appropriate for the French language. In German, there is a propensity toward building compounds to accommodate new words, and this technique works also for nouns turned adjectives. Therefore a "Muggel" is a Muggle, and "Muggeleltern" are Muggle parents. Normally, nouns that refer to people have a masculine form and a feminine form. Therefore, one would expect a female Muggle to be a "Muggelin" in German. The translator chose, though, to show gender through the definite article, making "der Muggel" a male and "die Muggel" a female. Spanish, like the other languages, cannot easily make adjectives from nouns. In the Spanish translation, we encounter the noun forms *"muggle"* and "*muggles,*" and also two ways of using "muggle" as an adjective. "Familia de *muggles*" (family of Muggles) and "familias *muggles*" (Muggel families) are examples of the translator's solutions. The use of a foreign word and its italic appearance disturbs the flow of the text more than the French translator's approach, though the Spanish translator retains the placement of adjective following noun and of appropriate singular and plural adjective endings.

In these translations, there are other examples of language-specific solutions, which, when appropriately made, result in a more natural-sounding text. For example, the French translator uses the French verb and its predilection for prefixed forms to his advantage. In book two, he translates "degnome" (*Chamber of Secrets*, 35) simply as "dégnomer" with the noun form "dégnomage" (*Chambre des Secrets*, 43, 45). The result is even more idiomatic than the original, since there is no hyphen in the translation.

In German, nouns are capitalized, but adjectives related to them are not. Therefore the German rendition "undursleyhaft" (J. K. Rowling, *Harry Potter und der Stein der Weisen*, 5) in book one is even more idiomatic than the original "unDursleyish" (*Sorcerer's Stone*, 2), with its internal capital letter. The German translator frequently uses nouns, and often compound nouns, to translate phrases and even clauses of the original. For example, he renders "As you're all in my house" (*Prisoner of Azkaban*, 149) as "Als Ihre Hauslehrerin" (As your house-teacher) (*Gefangene von Askaban*, 157) and "that I am up to no good" (*Prisoner of Azkaban*, 192) as "dass ich ein Tunichtsgut bin" (that I am a do-no-gooder) (*Gefangene von Askaban*, 202). These and other examples of noun substitutions for the original add to the idiomatic nature of the German translation.

The Spanish translator makes good use of the Spanish language's affection for diminutive forms. The endings "-ito," "-ita," "illo," and "-illa" added to a noun make it smaller, dearer, or sweeter than without the ending. The wands that the young magicians carry with them are "varitas, " Draco Malfoy's "little friends" are "amiguitos," and Peeves's "annoying singsong voice" (*Sorcerer's Stone*, 160) is his "molesta vocecita" (annoying little voice) (*Piedra filosofal*, 136). Peeves's words in book one, " 'Naughty, naughty, you'll get caughty" (*Sorcerer's Stone*, 159) become " 'Malitos, malitos, os agarrarán del cuellecito' " (Little bad ones, little bad ones, they'll grab you by your little necks) (*Piedra filosofal*, 135). Also in first book in the series, one of the twins says, " 'Aaah, has ickle Ronnie got somefink on his nose?' " (*Sorcerer's Stone*, 95). The Spanish translation reads, " 'Ah, el pequeñito Ronnie tiene algo en su naricita?' " (Ah, does the little little Ronnie have something on his little nose?) (*Piedra filosofal*, 84). Compound words made up of a verb followed by an object are also characteristic of Spanish. Therefore, Hagrid is a "guardabosque" (one who keeps/guards the forest). In book one, where Neville tries to help Harry by telling Professor McGonagall about Malfoy's threats, Rowling has Harry thinking of him as "Poor, blundering Neville" (*Sorcerer's Stone*, 243). The Spanish translator chooses to use the verb phrase "meter la pata" (to butt in, to upset everything) to form the compound "metepatas," resulting in "Pobre mete-patas Neville" (Poor butter-in Neville) (*Piedra filosofal*, 202). The compound, which so aptly describes Neville, is an accepted word in the Spanish language, making the translator's hyphen unnecessary and awkward.

Each of the translations discussed here demonstrates at least one situation that could have been more accurately or more convincingly portrayed in the target language. The French translator, for example, avoids the use of exact color names that so appeal to the visually oriented reader of the Harry Potter books. On one occasion in book two, Lockhart wears a robe of "deep plum" (*Chamber of Secrets*, 189). The French refers to it as nothing more than "violette" (*Chambre des Secrets*, 202) rather than "prune foncé." He appears later in a robe of "palest mauve" (*Chamber of Secrets*, 113), which in the French is rendered simply as "mauve" (*Chambre des Secrets*, 125). The robes of the Gryffindor Quidditch team are not scarlet, but rather "rouge" (red), which led a French journalist to come to political conclusions not intended in the original.[9] Also in book two, Rowling tells us, "Ron went as brightly pink as Lockhart's valentine flowers" (*Chamber of Secrets*, 331), which the French translation renders as "Le visage de Ron prit une teinte rose vif" (Ron's face took on a bright pink color) (*Chambre des Secrets*, 349), making it impossible for the reader to smell the flowers of the original. The French translator often leaves out other details, both in description and in the portrayal of actions. At the beginning of chapter 10 in book two, for example, Rowling describes how Lockhart has Harry help him reenact scenes from his past, and she mentions the cure of a Babbling Curse, a sick yeti, and a vampire that Lockhart had cured of his bloodthirstiness (*Chamber of Secrets*, 161). The French translator, on the other hand, describes the sketches without details: "Souvent, il demandait à Harry de jouer le rôle d'une créature féroce qu'il avait terrassée, délivrant ainsi tout un village d'une menace mortelle" (Often he asked Harry to play the part of a ferocious creature whom he had brought down, thus delivering an entire village from mortal danger) (*Chambre des Secrets*, 173). In the same book, Professor Binns shows his absentmindedness by calling students by the wrong names, O'Flaherty for Finnigan and Pennyfeather for Patil (*Chamber of Secrets*, 151–52). The French text leaves out any indication of equivocation (*Chambre des Secrets*, 163), and this detracts from the characterization of Professor Binns. Many other examples of the omission of particulars in

---

9. Pierre Bruno, "Moldus, Poufsouffles et stéréotypes."

the French translation occur, weakening the books' ability to transport the reader to Rowling's fantasy world, full of fascinating details, some merely entertaining and others integral to the story. There are also examples of inconsistency in the translation of terms. In book one, the Cleansweep brooms are called "Astiqueurs," (polishers) (*á l'école des sorciers,* 155), but in book two they are "Brossdurs" (stiff brushes) (*Chambre des Secrets,* 123), and in book three their mention is avoided, as the translator has left out the sentences where "Cleansweep" occurred in the original.

In the German translation, two of Hagrid's beasts receive less than perfect treatment. Hagrid's dog Fang is also called "Fang" in the German translation. The word "fang" in German is one of the imperative forms of the verb "to catch." Thus, the German rendition, while it makes sense as the name of a dog, does not at all convey the original ironic intent of the author. Hagrid's hippogriff Buckbeak becomes the German "Hippogreif Seidenschnabel." While "Hippogreif" is an even more exact word than "hippogriff" ("Greif" means "griffin"), "Seidenschnabel" (Silk-Beak) unsatisfactorily represents "Buckbeak." In German, the word "Schnabel" can be either a beak or a bill. Therefore it does not necessarily portray the sharpness of the English "beak," and Buckbeak, no matter how helpful he is in book three, has, as a hippogriff, a sharp side to his personality. Added to the ambiguity of "Schnabel" is the modifier "silk." These two elements combined result in an inaccurate translation.

Another interesting error in the German translation occurs in the naming of the card game Exploding Snap. In Britain, Snap is a common children's card game that comes in numerous variations: Number Snap, Alphabet Snap, etc. The German translator, though, mistakenly renders the name of this game as "Snape explodiert" (Snape exploding). This makes perfect sense to the reader, as who among the Hogwarts pupils (Slytherins excepted) wouldn't have a good time seeing Snape explode? German readers have found this idea so appealing that a fan web site even has an animated demo of "Snape explodiert!"[10]

The Spanish translation is hampered mostly by the appearance of so many words in English (sometimes in italics) whose meanings are important enough that they should be translated in order to convey the author's intent. Examples are "Norberto, el ridgeback noruego," "Fang," "Fluffy," and "Cleansweep 7." A good use of the diminutive would have been with the name "Fluffy," Hagrid's three-headed dog. As "Fluffy," there is no indication of the ironic nature of the name Hagrid has given this ferocious creature. "Fofito" or even "Fluffito" would better relay the author's intent to the Spanish reader. A specific problem with the Spanish translation

10. "Demo von 'Snape explodiert.'"

occurs with the rendition of the name of the Mirror of Erised. "Erised" is, of course, a mirror image of the word "desire." The Spanish translator uses the word "Erised," though a cognate of the word "desire" does not exist in the Spanish language, thus preventing the Spanish reader from knowing the origin of the name and relating it to its mirror image. If the Spanish translator had named the mirror "Oesed" ("deseo"), as the German translator did with "Nerhegeb" ("Begehren") and the French translator with "Riséd" ("désir"), the meaning would become clear to the reader. Further, the "gibberish" inscription above the mirror is rendered in the Spanish translation in its original English form, thereby masking its mirror-image meaning (*Piedra filosofal*, 174).

As to the overall success of the translations, much will depend on the personal reactions of the reader, but there are many areas over which the translators do have control. Their overriding concern is to convey the sense of the original text in the words of the target language. An examination of the French translation, for example, shows that it suffers from the lack of vivid detail that abounds in Rowling's original and enchants young imaginative minds. On the other hand, there are some ingenious translations of both slang and newly coined words that delight the reader with a linguistic bent. Although nouns specific to the magical world are usually capitalized in this translation, thus setting them off in the text, the flow of the text is not disturbed, as the capitalization is consistent. This means that not only the newly coined word "Souafle" (Quaffle) is capitalized but also "Guardien," (Keeper), which is a French word. This mirrors Rowling's capitalizations of words with meanings unique to the magical world, be they accepted English words or not.

The German version of the books, with its almost perfect mix of retained English words and imaginative German translations, reads very smoothly. Fortunately, the translator avoids the current trend of inserting English words into German texts whenever possible, even when a perfectly good German word exists, though he does occasionally use words like "Dad" and "Mum" in his translation. While book sales do not necessarily correspond to the literary merit of a book, it is clear that the German version of the Harry Potter books has sold better than the French and Spanish translations combined. Undoubtedly, the German publisher, Carlsen, has marketed the books much more aggressively than the French and Spanish publishers. Carlsen has a web site dedicated to the Harry Potter series (<http://www.carlsen-harrypotter.de>), complete with excerpts from the books, information about the author, and a chat room. In August 2000, the German publisher announced a "Cover-Wahl" (book cover vote) and gave viewers of the web site the opportunity to choose between two cover designs. More than thirty-eight thousand participants voted, and the overwhelming majority chose a cover similar to the British cover of book four. (*Goblet of Fire* had been available for purchase in Germany in English since July 8, 2000, and was a number one seller in at least one German online bookstore.)[11] The German publisher is also alone among the three in this study to have allowed its customers to order the fourth and fifth Harry Potter books prior to publication.

The Spanish translation suffers mostly from the lack of integration of newly coined words into the text. Many are in italics, disturbing the flow of the text, and often words that should be translated to afford the reader the author's original intent are not. The inconsistency in the use of italics and translations disorients the reader. For example, in the Spanish version of Quidditch, the words "buscador" (Seeker), "cazador" (Chaser), "golpeador" (Beater), and "guardián" (Keeper), which exist in the Spanish language, are used and not set apart by capitalization as in the English original. On the other hand, Rowling's words such as Snitch, Quaffle, etc. are interspersed with them but italicized in the text, serving to disorient the reader, who is seeking to understand the already chaotic rules of Quidditch. There are, however, some very fine translations of descriptions, and the personalities of many characters are well portrayed, mostly by use of very specific adjectives. In coining new words, the translator may have been hampered by the relative rigidity of the Spanish language with respect to new terminology.

The magical world of Harry Potter continues to grow, with readers of the books in all hemispheres, thanks in part to the easy access to merchandise the global marketplace has produced. The sales success of the books in some countries seems to be linked to the success of the books in English, which always arrive before the translations. Despite the shortcomings inherent in these later arrivals, translations continue to be written, published, sold, read, and cherished the world over. For readers with a knowledge of English, the choice will remain whether to read a translation in their native language or the original in a language foreign to them. For others, there is no choice but to enter the magical world through the door opened to them by a translator. Thus translators of the Harry Potter books are faced with numerous unusual situations, and must weigh the options carefully, in order not to compromise J. K. Rowling's characterizations, her novels' sense of place, and her careful use of language, be it in the realm of nomenclature, satire, or playfulness.

11. "Harry Potter für alle"; "German Potter Fans Snap Up English Translation."

Commodity and Culture in the World of Harry Potter

Specters of Thatcherism

Contemporary British Culture in J. K. Rowling's Harry Potter Series

Karin E. Westman

This is not the England of Tony Blair or Princess Di or Martin Amis, but the England we remember from other children's books, an England somehow perpetually Edwardian, notwithstanding certain concessions to modernity like telephones and coeducation.

—*A. O. Scott*

There's always a person who's a ringleader, a trouble-maker [like Draco Malfoy]. . . . We've got one of them, too.

—*Dexter Lateef, age eleven, on the state-run Westminster City School he attends*

While most readers and reviewers of the bestselling Harry Potter series praise J. K. Rowling's ability to create an alternate world, until the publication of *Harry Potter and the Goblet of Fire* few noted the degree of similarity established between the "Muggle" world of humans and the magical world represented by Hogwarts School for Witchcraft and Wizardry. Eleven-year-old Dexter Lateef was in the minority when he acknowledged Rowling's ability to create in her first three books both "a fantasy place that I can get into and escape from reality" and a world "not too far removed from his own world in an inner-city day-school." More typical has been the comment by A. O. Scott that the world of the *Harry Potter* series "is not the England of Tony Blair or Princess Di or Martin Amis, but . . . an England somehow perpetually Edwardian"—and that therefore the series' appeal for child and adult readers alike resides in an ahistorical, ultimately conservative rendering of British childhood experience.[1] Yet the very possibility for the

---

1. All reviewers have not been blind to the realism of Rowling's novels, but most claims for Rowling's realism appear *after* the arrival of *Harry Potter and the Goblet of Fire,* the book touted as introducing Harry and his schoolmates to the more grown-up world of sex and death. With this book, reviewers are more likely to see, as Steven Weisman wrote for the editorial page of the *New York Times,* that "the context of the book is magic, but its subject is society" (Steve Weisman, "A Novel That Is a Midsummer Night's Dream," A30). See also Sarah Johnson, "First Review: New Harry Potter

near global recognition and subsequent embrace of Harry Potter's experiences is only partly the result of Rowling's adept alchemy of the more traditional boarding school and fantasy adventure narratives. Indeed, we must look beyond the gates of Hogwarts and its quill pens and candlelight to the wizarding community that created it and whose political intrigues impinge upon it. If we wish to understand the realism that draws readers such as Dexter Lateef to Rowling's books, we must look to the *materiality* of the parallel world Rowling creates for Harry's adventures in the wizarding world.

Far from Edwardian, the wizarding world struggles to negotiate a very contemporary problem in Britain: the legacy of a racial and class caste system that, though not entirely stable, is still looked upon by a minority of powerful individuals as the means to continued power and control. Rowling's close detail of a late capitalist, global consumer culture marks the wizarding community as an echo of and commentary on both the Muggle world of the novels and the contemporary world of post-Thatcher England—a connection Rowling herself has acknowledged in a Canadian Broadcasting Corporation interview last year.[2]

'a cracker' " for the *Times* (July 8, 2000); Iain Bruce, "Wizard Lives Up to Hype" for the *Sunday Herald* (July 9, 2000); the online exchange at *Slate* between Jodi Kantor and Judith Shulevitz, "The King Lear of the Kid's Section" (July 10–12, 2000); Tim Wynne-Jones, "Harry Potter and the Blaze of Publicity" for the *Ottawa Citizen* (July 16, 2000); Chris Woodhead, "Harry Potter: Can't Do Better" for the *Sunday Telegraph* (July 16, 2000); and Joan Acocella, "Under the Spell: Harry Potter Explained" for the *New Yorker* (July 31, 2000). When reviewers of the first three books do note the realism within Rowling's fantasy, they tend to cite her choice of a conservative British boarding-school setting (see note 26 to follow) and her development of her adolescent characters (see Andrea Behr, "Harry Casts His Spell Everywhere" for the *San Francisco Chronicle*, July 2, 2000). Three notable exceptions are Pico Iyer's "The Playing Fields of Hogwarts," where he reflects on Rowling's pitch-perfect translation of the British boarding school experience for the global ear; the online epistolary exchange between Polly Shulman and A. O. Scott, "Is Harry Potter the New Star Wars" at *Slate;* and Lee Siegel, "Harry Potter and the Spirit of the Age: Fear of Not Flying" (November 22, 1999) in the *New Republic*. Scott and Shulman extended the themes of Rowling's first three novels to the concerns of the late-twentieth-century children and adults who avidly consume them. Siegel coins the term "realistic magicalism" to describe how Rowling "preserves the discontinuity between fantasy and reality," "prov[ing] the strength of her fiction by testing its capacity to assimilate the worldliness."

Dexter Lateef is quoted in Alan Cowell, "Harry Potter Frenzy Continues." In one of the first reviews of *Harry Potter and the Philosopher's Stone* for the *Herald* of Glasgow, Anne Johnstone remarks that "[w]ith renewed concern about bullying in Scottish schools, Harry Potter would make an excellent text for project work for those aged nine to 13" ("Happy Ending, and That's for Beginners," 15). See also Shulman and Scott, "Is Harry Potter the New Star Wars?"

2. My discussion, therefore, argues against claims such as those of Philip Hensher, "Harry Potter, Give Me a Break" in the *Independent* (January 25, 2000) when Hensher writes: "They are written in a way which is designed to be seductively readable;

It is certainly tempting to develop, along with Jesse Cohen of *Slate,* the hypothesis that Voldemort's tenure and reign bear striking resemblance to Margaret Thatcher's rule from 1979 to 1990.[3] Thatcher's rejection of multiculturalism, her isolationist nationalism, her dislike of unions, and her endorsement of strong-arm police tactics would warm Voldemort's heart. But to focus on Voldemort as Thatcher overlooks the specters of Thatcherism that continue to haunt contemporary British society. The world of the novels is set in the same historical time as the government of John Major, Thatcher's "ideological soulmate," and the gradual, often hypocritical rise of New Labor with Tony Blair.[4] The multi-ethnic Hogwarts, with its students such as Cho Chang, Pavarti Patil, Lee Jordan (whose dreadlocks signal his cultural background) and top-notch black Quidditch player Angelina Johnson, hardly offers a rosy-hued return to a child-book Edwardian past, as A. O. Scott and others have claimed, nor does it offer an idyllic version of contemporary late capitalist England where first- and second-generation immigrants are part of British nationhood. The tensions among "Mudbloods," pure bloods, and Muggles, among werewolves, house-elves, giants, and wizards echo the fervent tensions between race and class in the "real" contemporary British body politic of the Dursleys' suburbia and of British readers' own experience. Voldemort, like Thatcher, was ousted from power, but in neither case did their political ideologies leave with them;[5] the world Cornelius Fudge has inherited harbors social inequities and injustices that masquerade behind the draperies of democracy, much as they do in the time of John Major and Tony Blair.

---

they never give way to reflection or those momentary flashbacks of recall that prove so confusing to young readers, but exist in a sort of 'And then, and then, and then' which children find irresistible. But the world of these books is thin and unsatisfactory, their imagery is derivative, their characterisation automatic, and their structure deeply flawed" (1). Anthony Holden, "Why Harry Potter Doesn't Cast a Spell over Me," and Harold Bloom, "Can 25 Million Book Buyers Be Wrong? Yes," continue this vein of criticism in their reviews for the *Guardian* and the *Wall Street Journal,* respectively. Richard Adams goes so far as to call Harry Potter "a Tory" in "Harry Potter and the Closet Conservative." For a refreshing response to Anthony Holden's criticisms of Rowling's series, see Bel Littlejohn's spot-on parody "Harry Potter, What of Him?" For Rowling's comment on Thatcher, see Evan Solomon, "J. K. Rowling Interview."

3. Jesse Cohen, "When Harry Met Maggie."

4. Michael White, "Major to Open Thatcher Wounds." Tony Blair brought Labour to power, but there were compromises for the capitalist-friendly New Labour: the party had to jettison its long-standing Clause 4 of the Labour Manifesto that sought "to secure for the workers by hand or by brain the full fruits of their industry and the most equitable distribution thereof that may be possible upon the basis of the common ownership of the means of production, distribution and exchange, and the best obtainable system of popular administration and control of each industry or service" (quoted in "Major Resigns and Labour Reforms").

5. "Move on from Thatcher."

While the consumer pleasures of Diagon Alley and Hogsmeade's sweet shop humorously illustrate the parallels between the two worlds, the racial, ethnic, and class schisms fracturing the body politic of both realms mark a much more serious continuity between the "real" world of Harry's life on Privet Drive and the "fantasy" wizarding world he experiences during his years at Hogwarts. The materiality of the Muggle and wizarding bodies alike is where Rowling stakes her very "real" moral position on the dangers of a deterministic politics grounded in the body alone. Hardly "conservative tomes for conservative times," as *Guardian* reviewer Claire Armitstead remarked,[6] Rowling's books and their wizarding world offer not simply a fantasy of escape, but a radical way to explore very real issues in contemporary readers' lives.

While some reviewers of *Harry Potter and the Goblet of Fire* expressed surprise to discover evidence of the books' contemporary setting—Rebeken Denn of the *Seattle Post-Intelligencer* regrets how "[t]he previously timeless atmosphere is jarred a bit with mention of Playstations and Aqualungs"—Rowling clearly establishes the series' modernity right from the start.[7] It is true that we are never told *directly* when Harry was born or in what year the novels' narratives take place, but we do learn that the year is 1992 during *Harry Potter and the Chamber of Secrets,* placing the year of Harry's birth as 1980. The Gryffindor ghost, Sir Nicholas de Mimsey-Porpington, celebrates his 500th Death Day in book two, and his cake reads that he died October 31, 1492 (*Chamber of Secrets,* 102). Since Harry turned twelve that summer, he would have been born in 1980. These dates, however, merely confirm our initial impression of the novels' contemporary setting, a time frame established through material possessions at the beginning of *Harry Potter and the Philosopher's Stone:* here, the rampant materialism of Harry's Muggle Aunt and Uncle Dursley, as well as the consuming greed of his cousin Dudley, immediately tips us off to the contemporaneity of the novel's narrative and connects us to the world of the book even as such consumption disgusts. Dudley's ever-growing pile of broken electronic toys—as well as his dusty, unopened books (*Philosopher's Stone,* 32)—signals a technological age familiar to many readers for whom childhood means computer games, televisions, and video cameras.

Our hero Harry Potter, of course, does not own or play with such products, and his privation on Privet Drive emphasizes his exclusion from a materialistic world he desires but resigns himself to live without. To be without, however, is appealing, if access to such toys means being like Dudley:

6. Claire Armitstead, "Wizard, but with a Touch of Tom Brown."
7. Rebeken Denn, " 'Goblet' Darker, but Still Potterific," A4.

"Thirty-six," he said, looking up at his mother and father. "That's two less than last year."

"Darling, you haven't counted Auntie Marge's present, see, it's right here under this big one from Mummy and Daddy."

"All right, thirty-seven then," said Dudley, going red in the face. Harry, who could see a huge Dudley tantrum coming on, began wolfing down his bacon as fast as possible in case Dudley turned the table over.

Aunt Petunia obviously scented danger too, because she said quickly, "And we'll buy you another *two* presents while we're out today. How's that, popkin? *Two* more presents. Is that all right?"

Dudley thought for a moment. It looked like hard work. Finally he said slowly, "So I'll have thirty . . . thirty . . ."

"Thirty-nine, sweetums," said Aunt Petunia.

"Oh." Dudley sat down heavily and grabbed the nearest parcel. "All right then."

Uncle Vernon chuckled.

"Little tyke wants his money's worth, just like his father. Atta boy, Dudley!" He ruffled Dudley's hair. (*Philosopher's Stone*, 21)

Dudley's ruthless extortion of his parents renders the material goods themselves unimportant: the number of presents they give him for his birthday in book one signals not just the Dursleys' middle-class bank account but also the power Dudley exerts over his parents. Dudley does get "his money's worth," as his father jokes, but the "worth" constitutes control of his parents, not a thrifty exchange of the least capital for the most toys. The use value of the toys resides not in play, then, but as a means to an end: power.

Without power himself, Harry's participation in the economy of the Dursley household is therefore limited, in part because he has so little to barter that is of value to the Dursleys. Their world revolves around the fear of appearing different from their middle-class neighbors, and so their desires revolve around the chance to buy the new culturally sanctioned possession, be it a "racing bike" that Dudley will never ride because of his girth (*Philosopher's Stone*, 20) or a "holiday home in Majorca" (*Chamber of Secrets*, 11).[8] Unconscious acts of magic, spurred by emotions of anger and frustration, are at first Harry's only resource—poor coin, indeed, in the Dursley economy, where enduring a kiss and hug from Aunt Marge earns Dudley a "crisp twenty-pound note" (*Prisoner of Azkaban*, 22). Though Harry's threat to perform magic garners him a brief power within the Dursley household at the beginning of book two, this leverage evaporates with the official citation from the Ministry of Magic, reminding Harry—and informing Uncle Vernon—that "under-age wizards are not permitted to perform spells

8. Aunt Petunia and Uncle Vernon's desire for a "holiday home in Majorca" in book two seems to follow from the news in book one that Aunt Petunia's friend Yvonne cannot take care of Harry because, "snapped Aunt Petunia," Yvonne is "[o]n holiday in Majorca" (*Philosopher's Stone*, 22).

outside school" (*Chamber of Secrets*, 21). By the end of book three, Harry can only invoke the indirect power of his escaped convict godfather, Sirius Black, to challenge the Dursleys' consuming desires. Threatening to communicate the details of his penurious life at the Dursleys to his godfather provides the one way Harry might be able to attend the Quidditch World Cup in book four, and Harry uses the news that he is writing to Sirius to persuade Uncle Vernon:

> "You're—you're writing to him, are you?" said Uncle Vernon, in a would-be calm voice—but Harry had seen the pupils of his tiny eyes contract with sudden fear.
> "Well—yeah," said Harry, casually. "It's been a while since he heard from me, and, you know, if he doesn't, he might start thinking something's wrong." (*Goblet of Fire*, 35)

Harry's gambit is successful: Uncle Vernon's desire to be rid of Harry for the rest of the summer and his fear of bodily harm at Black's hands overcome his desire to punish Harry for his wizarding connections. Harry's success, however, relies on a magical power he himself cannot legitimately perform. Harry's own currency of magic is consistently outside the Dursleys' economy, only becoming valuable when Harry enters the wizarding world.

An outsider to the Dursleys' materialism, Harry comes to embody all that his relations are not: he is unselfish, compassionate, and good-hearted. Reading only the Dursley sections of the books, we might expect the focus of Rowling's critique to be the dangers of consumerism and conspicuous consumption, a world Harry would leave behind when he begins his life as a wizard. What are we to make, then, of the rampant consumerism that greets Harry when he enters the wizarding world, a community complete with its own international bank, global trade, and thriving monopolies alongside entrepreneurial ventures? We soon discover that the fantasy of the wizarding world is not its *dis*similarity to the materialism of the Muggle world, but Harry's *access* to the wizarding world's consumer pleasures.

The material excesses of the Dursleys' Muggle world find their comic, and no less prevalent, counterpoint in Harry's first expedition to Diagon Alley for his school supplies. His pockets jingling with bronze Knuts, silver Sickles, and gold Galleons from his newly discovered inheritance stashed at Gringotts' Bank, Harry feels for the first time the thrill of spending money on himself. The temptation to buy—especially to buy luxury items like a "solid gold cauldron" instead of the pewter one indicated on his list of school supplies (*Philosopher's Stone*, 62)—are quashed by Hagrid's sage advice, but the desire to consume conspicuously recurs during Harry's subsequent visits for his second- and third-year supplies. Harry's final response to such material excess, however, is thrift: even in the face of the newest luxury items available, Harry always saves rather than spends. We hear that "he needed to exercise a lot of self-control not to spend the whole lot [of money] at once" (*Prisoner of Azkaban*, 43) when he visits Diagon Alley on his own in book three, but the thought of needing supplies for four more years at Hogwarts tempers his impulse. The alluring advertisement for the Firebolt does test his resolve to the breaking point, but even here Harry reasons to himself, "what was the point in emptying his Gringotts vault for the Firebolt, when he had a very good broom already?" (*Prisoner of Azkaban*, 44).[9]

While the wizarding world offers a fantasy of consumer purchases, Harry remains wary of the conspicuous and selfish consumption embodied by the Dursleys he has left behind. Instead, Harry's greatest pleasure is spending small amounts of money on others, like his friend Ron Weasley, whose family cannot afford indulgences. After buying a selection of treats from the trolley during his first ride on the Hogwarts Express, Harry urges Ron to trade one of the corned beef sandwiches in his "lumpy package" for a newly purchased treat, but then simply encourages Ron to partake: " 'Go on, have a [pumpkin] pasty,' said Harry, who had never had anything to share before or, indeed, anyone to share it with. It was a nice feeling" (*Philosopher's Stone*, 76). And in book two, when "[t]he bag of gold, silver and bronze jangling cheerfully in Harry's pocket was clambouring to be spent, . . . he bought three large strawberry and peanut butter ice-creams which they [Harry, Ron, and Hermione] slurped happily as they wandered up the alley, examining the fascinating shop windows" (*Chamber of Secrets*, 48). The barrage of consumer pleasures they experience at the Quidditch World Cup yields a parallel scene in book four, when Harry purchases three pairs of Omnioculars—each gift costing, at ten Galleons each, as much as Ron's other purchases put together (*Goblet of Fire*, 86). Harry's gifts of pasties, ice-creams, and Omnioculars are, unlike the coerced exchanges at the Dursleys, actual gifts, with no expectation of a gift in return, and they give Harry pleasure. Rowling's narrative, then, acknowledges the overwhelming desire to enter a system of capitalist exchange. Although Harry and the reader both spend much time admiring those "fascinating shop windows," the narrative also suggests that *consuming* that system's goods only pays off emotionally when items are needed or are given to others as gifts.

Harry's access to capital may therefore be a fantasy come true, but he cannot act upon that fantasy and stay true to other values he holds. His

---

9. The existence of "second-hand robe shop[s]" (*Chamber of Secrets*, 47), visited by the poorer Weasley family, suggests that other wizards and witches exercise similar economy from need more than firm resolve.

unearned but wisely managed wizard wealth challenges not only a Dursley-esque bourgeois form of material exchange but also the economic system he and his inheritance *could* rightfully follow in the wizarding world: the "old money" aristocracy exemplified by Draco Malfoy, whose family, as his French name "Mal Foi" or "Bad Faith" suggests, aligned themselves with the evil forces of Lord Voldemort before the balance of power shifted once again to the more democratic forces of the Ministry of Magic. The Malfoys' manor house (*Chamber of Secrets*, 44), complete with a house-elf enslaved to them for life (unless freed by the family) (*Chamber of Secrets*, 27–28), illustrates one way of life for those with wizard money and stands in marked contrast to the Weasleys' genteel wizard poverty, which prevents new purchases of much-needed robes, wands, and school books, or even sufficient supplies of Floo powder in the flower pot (*Chamber of Secrets*, 40). For Harry to engage in such established economic exchanges would mean buying (into) the ideologies of nationhood that underwrite the materialist morality of both the Muggle and wizard worlds. Harry and the reader quickly discover that ideologies of difference, marked through the body, run beneath the democratic appearances of both the Muggle and wizarding worlds, forging a material bond between the two realms that extends beyond mere economic materialism to racism and class prejudice. What reviewers have generally seen as the series' new turn toward realism in *Goblet of Fire*—a new narrative interest in issues of racism, prejudice, and nationalism—is really the further development of materialist ideologies introduced in the earlier books.[10]

In *Philosopher's Stone, Chamber of Secrets,* and *Prisoner of Azkaban,* Rowling offers a sustained critique of ideologies based upon material difference, establishing a realistic narrative frame for the action of subsequent books like *Goblet of Fire*. In the first three books, fears of miscegenation threaten the Hogwarts student body, just as they threaten the larger body politic of the wizarding world and of the Muggle world of Harry's Uncle and Aunt. The Dursleys' failed attempts to suppress Harry's wizarding past—by refusing to speak of it and by keeping Harry out of sight whenever possible—frustrate their bourgeois goal to be the same as everyone else on Privet Drive. Difference, whether in appearance, birth, or belief, will not be tolerated by Uncle Vernon, or by Aunt Petunia, who always keeps a sharp eye on "Mrs. Next Door's problems" (*Philosopher's Stone*, 10).[11] Uncle Vernon's

10. For instance, David Kipen of the *San Francisco Chronicle* is relieved to discover in book four that "[f]or a change, Rowling's on about some things besides the trials of growing up," like "class," "racism," and, "believe it or not, the European union" ("The Trouble with Harry").

11. In book four, we hear further examples of the Dursleys' fear of difference: Uncle Vernon's fear of the mailman's laugh when the mailman delivers Mrs. Weasley's

sister, Marge, roots this fear of difference in the body at the opening to book three. A breeder of dogs, she thinks of Harry's low character in terms of pedigree: "It's one of the basic rules of breeding. . . . You see it all the time with dogs. If there's something wrong with the bitch, there'll be something wrong with the pup . . . All comes down to blood . . . Bad blood will out" (*Prisoner of Azkaban*, 24–26). Aligning poor blood with low social class, Uncle Vernon tells Marge that Harry's father "didn't work," prompting Marge to elaborate her view of Harry's parentage: "As I expected! . . . A no-account, good-for-nothing, lazy scrounger who—" (*Prisoner of Azkaban*, 26–27). But she is cut off by Harry, whose anger at such lies prompts him to perform an unconscious act of magic, blowing her already large body up to dangerously larger proportions. Significantly, this scene occurs *after* Harry's first two years at Hogwarts, where he (and the reader) have already begun to learn the service Harry's parents performed for the good of the wizarding world against Lord Voldemort. Marge's comments are therefore all the more horrifying given the reader's knowledge of Harry's history. Perhaps more important, this scene's presence at the opening to book three provides continuity between the Muggle world of the Dursleys and the beliefs that ignite Harry's adventures in the wizarding world of book two: the fear of mixed blood.

At Hogwarts, the fear of miscegenation finds expression through those like Malfoy who sling taunts of "Mudblood," segregating Muggle-born witches and wizards such as Harry's friend Hermione from "pure bloods" like himself. Harry is introduced to the racial politics of the wizarding world when he meets Malfoy at Madam Malkin's Robes for All Occasions in book one and must respond to Malfoy's question about his parents: "But they were *our* kind, weren't they? . . . I really don't think they should let the other sort in, do you? . . . I think they should keep it in the old wizarding families" (*Philosopher's Stone*, 60–61). Malfoy's opinion may be a minority one, but it is powerful and long-standing: as we learn in book two from Professor Binns, the great split between Salazar Slytherin and the other three founders of Hogwarts occurred because Slytherin "wished to be more *selective* about the students admitted to Hogwarts" (*Chamber of Secrets*, 114). The fact that Malfoy has inherited his pure-blood views from his father, Lucius Malfoy, is also significant. If Lucius Malfoy, who remains faithful to the dethroned Dark Lord and who sits on the school's Board of Governors

---

excessively stamped letter (33), Uncle Vernon's view that Harry and his wizard life represent "unnaturalness" (35), and Harry's memory of the Dursleys' response to an "old tramp" talking to himself, someone who has failed to be "normal" in terms of social behavior and class: "Aunt Petunia had seized Dudley's hand and pulled him across the road to avoid him; Uncle Vernon had then treated the family to a long rant about what he would like to do with beggars and vagrants" (481).

until the end of book two, upholds such beliefs, we know that such opinions are held not just by schoolboys but also by men with power. When Malfoy calls Hermione "You filthy little Mudblood" (*Chamber of Secrets*, 86), he is then tapping into a deep vein of cultural division and emotion. His taunt has the cultural shock of the word "nigger" in contemporary America, as seen by the response his "Mudblood" comment elicits:

> Harry knew at once that Malfoy had said something really bad because there was an instant uproar at his words. Flint had to dive in front of Malfoy to stop Fred and George [Weasley] jumping on him, Alicia shrieked *"How dare you!"* and Ron plunged his hand into his robes, pulled out his wand, yelling, "You'll pay for that one, Malfoy!" and pointed it furiously under Flint's arm at Malfoy's face. (*Chamber of Secrets*, 87)

Ron later explains, "It's about the most insulting thing he could think of. . . . Mudblood's a really foul name for someone who was Muggle-born . . . Dirty blood, see. Common blood" (*Chamber of Secrets*, 89). For those like the Malfoys, the legacy of a wizard's blood trumps all other categories of identity—a lesson Malfoy has learned all too well from his father's example earlier in the novel at Flourish and Blotts, when Mr. Malfoy more subtly levels the same taunt at Hermione's parents and Mr. Weasley lunges for him (*Chamber of Secrets*, 51).

Of course, as Ron points out to Harry, in the reality of the wizarding world, "[i]t's mad" to make such a distinction between "dirty blood" and "pure blood": "Most wizards these days are half-blood anyway. If we hadn't married Muggles we'd've died out" (*Chamber of Secrets*, 89).[12] Indeed, two little-known facts emerge in book two about Voldemort (the heir of Slytherin) and his ideology of race: that he had a Muggle father and a witch mother (*Chamber of Secrets*, 182) and that he grew up in the Muggle world, as his school-boy diary bought in "Vauxhall Road" indicates (*Chamber of Secrets*, 173). Further, the adjective frequently used by those who uphold Voldemort's ideology of difference is the word "common," a word with strong class connotations in British culture. The choice of adjective indicates the role class plays within this old wizarding concern for "purity": since claims of "pure blood" are illusory in a wizarding culture that has married Muggles to survive, class difference stands in for a whole set of ideological beliefs based on difference. "Pure blood," then, is a construction of identity based upon the body, but upon a body that reveals the fissures

---

12. For some of the history behind contemporary wizard-Muggle relations, see Rowling's *Quidditch through the Ages, by Kennilworthy Whisp,* where we learn that the International Statute of Wizarding Secrecy, passed in 1692, gave all wizards the right to carry a wand for self-protection, as the wizarding community planned "their retreat into hiding" (16, 28).

such an ideology strives to occlude. To be "pure blood" means not to be of pure blood, per se, but to subscribe to a particular set of ideological beliefs based on differences in social class and its concomitant power.

In the first three books, the old wizarding fear of mixed blood and its accompanying materialist ideologies appear as secondary, if significant, narrative issues. Indeed, we learn at the end of book two that the main plot of the book—the brief return of Voldemort through Ginny Weasley and Tom Riddle's diary—was initiated by Lucius Malfoy as political subterfuge against the passage of Arthur Weasley's Muggle Protection Act (*Chamber of Secrets,* 247). In *Goblet of Fire,* however, Rowling leaves little doubt in her readers' minds that prejudice based on differences in class, race, and nation occurs in the wizarding world, just as it does in the world of her readers. In book four, Rowling heightens the existing realism of the previous books to make her clearest statement against a politics based on the body, advocating instead the power of informed choices rather than "natural" differences. The more explicit cultural parallels Rowling draws between the two worlds in book four further highlight the role a politics of "purity" will play in the coming battle for political control of the wizarding world. What might have appeared to the casual reader in *Chamber of Secrets* to be a schoolboy taunt from Malfoy becomes Voldemort's political manifesto by the end of *Goblet of Fire.*

Significantly, Rowling represents a greater spectrum of positions on these cultural issues in book four than in the previous three books, from the blatant and almost caricatured racism and snobbery of Voldemort to the humanism of Arthur Weasley and Albus Dumbledore. While these more extreme viewpoints define the boundaries of political choice within the wizarding world, Rowling focuses a good portion of her narrative upon positions between these two extremes, particularly the persistence of Voldemort's ideological beliefs within the wizarding culture at large. Her decision to sketch a morally complex, sometimes ambivalent world heightens the realism of the series: wizards' contradictory opinions on wizard-Muggle relations, for instance, illustrate how subscribing to a set of cultural beliefs can be a deliberate political choice, but may also be the result of ignorance, of a moment's emotional turmoil, or the belief that it is simply "natural" for cultural differences to persist. Making her target the formation and replication of ideology rather than prejudice per se provides Rowling with the opportunity to show how contemporary cultural opinion becomes naturalized as truth, as well as how that "truth" can change.

The chapters set at the Quidditch World Cup are often cited by reviewers as the mere prelude to the action of the Triwizard Tournament and the section most easily cut from the heft of book four by a more ruthless editorial pen. David Kipen of the *San Francisco Chronicle* feels the book "takes a meandering 150-page detour" with the Quidditch World Cup; for Robert McCrum of the *Observer*, these chapters are "an entertaining set piece which is merely the curtain-raiser to Harry's return to another term at Hogwarts."[13] Harry's and the readers' experiences at the Quidditch World Cup are hardly expendable. The events Harry witnesses there reinforce the existing link between the magical world of the series and contemporary British culture's involvement with international politics and global capitalism. Rowling's heightened realism in book four encourages her readers to see the fractured wizarding body politic as commenting on, rather than being removed from, Britain's struggles to find its footing in this new European Union millennium.

Although Harry and his readers may not have known about Harry's global circumstances, the visit to the Quidditch World Cup indicates that this international wizarding world has always been there, should Harry have cared to ask. Born to and raised by Muggles, Hermione knows from her reading about the communities of wizards in other countries as well as rival international schools, while Ron has always been vaguely aware of the international context for his British wizarding life (*Goblet of Fire*, 78, 111). By contrast, "[i]t was only just dawning on Harry how many witches and wizards there must be in the world; he had never really thought much about those in other countries" (*Goblet of Fire*, 75). Harry's sudden consciousness of this larger international context speaks not to a shift in Rowling's narrative style, then, but marks our consistent narrative alignment with Harry's more naive point of view and our subsequent education, along with his, about the wizarding world. Education and a growing contextual awareness for one's own actions supercede innate intelligence and "natural" knowledge within the pages of Rowling's books—a theme we recognize from the earlier books' emphasis on making informed choices within one's cultural circumstances as opposed to following a destiny determined by biological difference. As Dumbledore says to Harry at the end of book two, "It is our choices, Harry, that show what we truly are, far more than our abilities" (*Chamber of Secrets*, 245). Harry now has the choice to be part of a global community.

13. Kipen, "The Trouble with Harry"; Robert McCrum, "Plot, Plot, Plot That's Worth the Weight." While Kipen and McCrum are critical of the opening section, Tim Wynne-Jones of the *Ottawa Citizen* (July 16, 2000) offers mixed praise: "It's dodgy, perhaps, but interesting" ("Blaze of Publicity," C16). By contrast, twelve-year-old Megan Stanley from East London explains for Sarah Johnson of the *Times* that she "liked the fact that the Quidditch World Cup scene 'isn't just written purely to describe the game—it is a convenient time for Voldemort's sign to appear,'" concluding, "It is probably a taster of Harry's final, dramatic adventure with Voldemort." As Sarah Johnson notes in her report, "Children notice structure and technique more than adults realise" ("So Quiet, It Was Magic").

Rowling's inclusion of international wizarding communities continues the series' aim to present difference as the result of learned behavior rather than of nature alone:

> Three African wizards sat in serious conversation, all of them wearing long white robes and roasting what looked like a rabbit on a bright purple fire, while a group of middle-aged American witches sat gossiping happily beneath a spangled banner stretched between their tents which read: The Salem Witches' Institute. Harry caught snatches of conversation in strange languages from the inside of tents they passed, and though he couldn't understand a single word, the tone of every single voice was excited. (*Goblet of Fire,* 76)

The news that each wizarding community is more like its Muggle neighbors than like fellow wizards speaks to the power of acculturation: the wizards and witches Harry observes differ because their cultural circumstances have shaped their habits of dress and preferred foods. In turn, those differences in appearance, name, language, and food seem less important than the similarity between the various representatives of the international community. Rowling's description of Harry's response to his new global perspective ends not with difference, but commonality: the emotional excitement Harry hears in "every single voice" forms the link between the diverse groups.

Events such as the Quidditch World Cup and the subsequent Triwizard Tournament (*Goblet of Fire,* 165–66) exist to build upon these emotional similarities, creating shared experiences across "[d]ifferences of habit and language" (*Goblet of Fire,* 627). Such events also intersect with the global wizarding economy at official and unofficial levels, illustrating a striking moment of realism between the wizarding world and the international sporting events of readers' lives. Reviewer Mark Lawson noted for *Guardian* readers how timely Rowling's plot must appear to her British and international reading public, even getting in a passing reference to the recent arrest of Prime Minister Tony Blair's young son in Leicester Square for intoxication:

> While the newspapers report the failure of England's bid to stage the football World Cup, *Harry Potter and the Goblet of Fire* begins with great excitement in the wizard homes of Britain over the staging in this country of the World Cup of Quidditch, Rowling's ingenious invented game. It's such a happy coincidence that you read on half-expecting Harry to be arrested in Leicester Square after taking too many magical potions.
>
> In fact, though the closeness to the FIFA announcement is an accident, the book feels thematically shaped to fit the summer of Euro 2000 and the Sydney Olympics.[14]

As Lawson notes, some of the realism of Rowling's narrative is the result of "happy coincidence," but her choice of setting—a major international

14. Mark Lawson, "Rowling Survives the Hype."

sporting event—provides a recognizable venue through which to address the commercialization of sports, the increasing interdependence of national economies, and the frequent pairing of nationalism and violence that has marred many sporting events for England, particularly in soccer.[15]

Legal and illegal money constantly changes hands at the Quidditch World Cup: Ministry ticket sales boom as entrepreneurial enterprises and gambling flourish. Vendors hawk Irish and Bulgarian merchandise in green and red, while wizards such as Ludo Bagman engage in suspect betting, much as one might expect at a sporting event of international scope. The Quidditch World Cup also gathers together top officials from various levels of the national and international political world, offering Ministry members such as Barty Crouch and Arthur Weasley the chance to discuss informally the controls on international trade:

> "Ali Bashir's on the warpath. He wants a word with you about your embargo on flying carpets."
> Mr. Weasley heaved a deep sigh. "I sent him an owl about that just last week. If I've told him once I've told him a hundred times: carpets are defined as a Muggle Artefact by our Registry of Proscribed Charmable Objects, but will he listen?"
> "I doubt it," said Mr. Crouch, accepting a cup from Percy. "He's desperate to export here."
> "Well, they'll never replace brooms in Britain, will they?" said Bagman.
> "Ali thinks there's a niche in the market for a family vehicle," said Mr Crouch. "I remember my grandfather had an Axminster that could seat twelve—but that was before carpets were banned, of course." (*Goblet of Fire*, 83–84)

To hear Crouch, Weasley, and Bagman discussing brand-name carpets like cars certainly illustrates the humorous side of Rowling's realism, but the frustrations of international and EU trade sanctions provide another layer of realism for the British reader in the year 2000. International wizarding trade, like recent regulations on the British import and export of beef, cheese, and other products, is hardly stable, as Crouch's comments about flying carpets illustrate. Trade policy in both worlds also depends as much on negotiations and lobbying as established rules: Ali Bashir's persistent

---

15. In his best-selling memoir *Fever Pitch* (1992), novelist Nick Hornby describes the racist and anti-Semitic outbursts that accompany British football, as well as the fatal accidents that have resulted from a combination of old venues, crowded stands and retaining fences, failures in safety and crowd control, and the high emotions of fans themselves (156–57, 188–91, 218, 220). Rowling's description of the stadium built for the Quidditch World Cup may likely draw upon her time in Portugal: with its "immense gold walls," everything "suffused with a mysterious golden light that seemed to come from the stadium itself" (*Goblet of Fire*, 87–88), the Quidditch stadium echoes the location to which Hornby traveled to watch his beloved Arsenal earn "a credible 1–1 draw in front of eighty-thousand Portuguese in the intimidating Stadium of Light" (246).

attempts to sway Arthur Weasley and Barty Crouch indicate a global economy dependent on behind-the-scenes networking as well as official policy.

The need for trade regulations also occupies the newly employed Percy Weasley during the opening of book four—and perhaps with good reason, according to Rowling's narrative. Rowling alludes to the tiring bureaucracy of trade regulations not so much to offer "a thinly disguised attack" on the EU, as reviewer Tom Kemp notes,[16] but for reasons that contribute to the series' concern with the relationship between the personal and the political. Responding to Harry's polite inquiry about his work at the beginning of book four, Percy explains that he is hard at work on the question of cauldron thickness: " 'A report for the Department of International Magical Co-operation,' said Percy smugly. 'We're trying to standardise cauldron thickness. Some of these foreign imports are just a shade too thin—leakages have been increasing at a rate of almost three per cent a year—' " After a snide comment from Ron, Percy resumes: " 'You might sneer, Ron, . . . but unless some sort of international law is imposed we might well find the market flooded with flimsy, shallow-bottomed products which seriously endanger—' " (53), only to be cut off yet again as Ron responds to Percy's arrogance. Even though we may sympathize with Ron's frustration at Percy's pride in his new middle-management position, Percy's work on standardizing cauldron thickness for international trade is timely, given what we learn at the opening to chapter 14: "The next two days passed without great incident, unless you count Neville melting his sixth cauldron in Potions" (*Goblet of Fire*, 185). Though Neville's melted cauldrons earn him detention from Snape and therefore suggest that the damage results from Neville's personal failings as a wizard, the fault may lie not simply with Neville but, as Percy predicts, in a "market flooded with flimsy, shallow-bottomed products." Rowling offers an "attack," but not aimed merely at "EU bureaucracy," as Kemp claims. Her narrative asks the reader to question Percy's smug pride, Ron's quick judgment of Percy's statements on the basis of their tone alone, and Snape's narrow focus on individual action rather than its context.

The economic materialism of the Quidditch World Cup chapters certainly underscores the role international sporting events play within both

16. Tom Kemp, "Wonderful—but It's a Whopper," 14. In his review of *Goblet of Fire* for the *Daily Telegraph*, Kemp writes, "Perhaps Rowling has her eye a little more on her adult readership in this fourth book. It contains, for instance, a thinly disguised attack on EU bureaucracy. Percy Weasley, the boring, pompous former head boy of Hogwarts, is now a junior official at the Ministry of International Magical Co-Operation, preparing a paper on the standardisation of cauldron thickness." David Kipen in his *San Francisco Chronicle* review hears reference to the EU, too, but offers an equally reductive reading, only seeing "Hogwarts' jockeying for advantage against its obviously French and German rivals" ("The Trouble," D1).

the wizard and contemporary global economies, encouraging readers to think of the wizarding world as similar to, rather than different from, their own. There are, of course, wizarding bodies engaging in these economic exchanges, the bodies of fans and players, whose own materiality takes quite a beating both on and off the Quidditch pitch. Rowling's choice of an international sporting event therefore not only allows her to connect the economic materialism of the wizarding world to the contemporary experiences of her readers but also to highlight the parallel critique of materialism introduced in the earlier books: a materialist morality and politics based in bodily difference and the resulting prejudice against anyone not of "pure" wizard blood and class.

Mr. Weasley's observation to Harry—" 'Always the same, . . . we can't resist showing off when we get together' " (*Goblet of Fire*, 73, 213)— emphasizes the role national pride plays in wizarding lives, regardless of any goals outlined by the Department for International Magical Co-Operation. This pride is clearly in evidence at the Quidditch World Cup, according to Rowling's descriptions of the Irish and Bulgarian teams and their fans:

> "Er—is it my eyes, or has everything gone green?" said Ron.
> It wasn't just Ron's eyes. They had walked into a patch of tents that were all covered with a thick growth of shamrocks, so that it looked as though small, oddly shaped hillocks had sprouted out of the earth. . . .
> "Like the decorations?" said Seamus, grinning, when Harry, Ron, and Hermione had gone over to say hello. "The Ministry's not too happy."
> "Ah, why shouldn't we show our colours?" said Mrs. Finnegan. "You should see what the Bulgarians have got dangling all over *their* tents. You'll be supporting Ireland, of course?" she added, eyeing Harry, Ron, and Hermione beadily.
> When they had assured her that they were indeed supporting Ireland, they set off again, though, as Ron said, "Like we'd say anything else surrounded by that lot." (*Goblet of Fire*, 76)

The rivalry between the Irish and Bulgarian teams only intensifies as the day progresses and the game itself approaches, and it culminates in a bloody and brutal match punctuated by the rival teams' mascots attacking each other on the field without the referees' intervention. Like the Ministry officials at the campsite, the referees cannot contain the surges of emotion channeled through nationalist pride and, increasingly, into violent behavior.

As the evening proceeds, such life-threatening "showing off" becomes not only a way to express nationalist pride but also "proper wizarding pride" (*Goblet of Fire*, 617), both of which are at odds with the Ministry's official policy. Indeed, nationalist differences are put aside in light of a shared bond against a common (in both senses of the word) group: Muggles. The riot following the Irish victory develops in part from the nationalist high spirits already flowing and in part from crowd dynamics that have put so many wizards together in one place. But regardless of the initial catalyst, the form the wizards' "high spirits" ultimately assume—the torture of a Muggle family—creates one of the most disturbing and frightening scenes for Harry and his friends during the book. This scene underscores the degree to which Voldemort's extreme racism and his hatred of Muggles and mixed races remain a part of wizarding culture as a whole, emerging when wizards feel free from Ministry control and their everyday obligations to Ministry policies on wizard-Muggle relations.

Harry, Ron, and Hermione watch a group of Voldemort's former supporters, "their heads hooded and faces masked," using the Imperius curse (which, they will later learn, is one of the three illegal curses), to humiliate and violate the rights of the Muggle family who manages the campsite (*Goblet of Fire,* 108, 187–90). Perhaps most disturbingly, the Death Eaters are quickly joined by a "marching crowd" of Quidditch Cup fans who cheer them on rather than stopping them (*Goblet of Fire,* 108). While the hooded figures have resonance for American readers familiar with Ku Klux Klan marches, the British reader may hear echoes of the British National Party and the National Front, both of whom share some of the KKK's concerns. More than an echo of the "hooliganism" that has plagued large European sporting events,[17] the "marching group" suggests an organized political demonstration that nonetheless leaves terror, destruction, and confusion in its wake. That Muggles are the target of the crowd's "fun" is evident not just from the image of the Roberts family suspended in the sky, but also Malfoy's comments to Ron, Hermione, and Harry: "Granger, they're after *Muggles,*" Malfoy says. "D'you want to be showing off your knickers in mid-air? Because if you do, hang around . . . they're moving this way, and it would give us all a laugh" (*Goblet of Fire,* 110). As Malfoy's comments suggest, Muggles and Mudbloods alike are the target of the crowd's pleasure, a desire that Malfoy sees continuing beyond the Roberts family.

Rowling has created a realistic riot scene that is frightening not just for the Muggle family in the air but also for those people—Muggle, Mudblood, or even wizard—on the ground. The careless disregard the Death Eaters and their fellow marchers show for Mrs. Roberts' privacy or the child's safety extends to anyone in the path of the "marching" and "laughing" crowd, increasing the danger and horror of a scene the official governing body is helpless to contain:

> Ministry wizards were dashing from every direction towards the source of the trouble. . . . The coloured lanterns that had lit the path to the stadium had been extinguished. Dark figures were blundering through the trees; children were crying; anxious shouts and panicked voices reverberated around them in

17. Lawson, "Rowling Survives."

the cold night air. Harry felt himself being pushed hither and thither by people whose faces he could not see. (*Goblet of Fire*, 109)

Buffeted by the crowd, unaided by those who should provide protection, Harry and his friends subsequently witness the failure of the Ministry to contain, control, and punish those who performed the curse and who terrorized the Roberts family and others attending the World Cup. Seeking to understand what he has experienced, Harry later questions Mr. Weasley about the Death Eaters' actions, asking, "What's the point?" " 'The point?' said Mr. Weasley, with a hollow laugh. 'Harry, that's their idea of fun. Half of the Muggle killings back when You-Know-Who was in power were done for fun. I suppose they had a few drinks tonight and couldn't resist reminding us all that lots of them are still at large. A nice little reunion for them,' he finished disgustedly" (*Goblet of Fire*, 127–28). While Mr. Weasley has correctly identified the "spot of Muggle-torture" Death Eaters like Lucius Malfoy have enjoyed (*Goblet of Fire*, 564), Mr. Weasley's analysis falls short of the scene Harry has witnessed: the scene describing the Muggles' levitation indicates that many other wizards believe this activity to be "their idea of fun." Such prejudiced opinions about wizard-Muggle relations therefore exist not only in the minds of Voldemort and his remaining thirty-odd Death Eaters but also within a large crowd of wizard sports fans—a much more disturbing and complicated picture of the racial politics in the wizarding world than Mr. Weasley's assessment indicates, and one that mirrors the conflict between racial equality and prejudice in contemporary British culture.[18]

Prejudice based on claims of material differences between bodies, then, exists at several levels of cultural experience in Rowling's novels: in the definitive stance of Voldemort who cannot abide "that champion of commoners, of Mudbloods and Muggles, Albus Dumbledore" (*Goblet of Fire*, 562); in the preferred but secret stance of Death Eaters like Lucius Malfoy; and perhaps most extensively in the lingering belief system valued by an older wizarding culture. This last level of prejudice appears when the social dynamics are favorable for its recurrence, but it may otherwise silently coexist with the illusion of equality. The residual traces of anti-Muggle prejudice that emerge during the Quidditch World Cup illustrate how deep and broad

18. Large-scale racial conflicts have emerged many times in recent British history: not only were there race riots in Brixton (1981) and Tottenham (1985) during Margaret Thatcher's tenure, but also in Bradford (1995) when John Major was prime minister. The summer of 2001, under Tony Blair, saw a resurgence of ethnic conflict in Bradford once again (April), Oldham (May), Leeds (June), Burnley (June), and Accrington (June) ("A Long Hot Summer"). See Sarah Lyall's "Why Are You Here?: Britain's Race Problem" (June 3, 2001) in the *New York Times* for an international news analysis of the recent riots and the government's response.

such sentiments run in the wizarding culture, how they persist as an organizing principle of that world. Try as Dumbledore might to offer another kind of cultural environment for his students, the multiethnic Hogwarts is hardly immune from similar tendencies, constructed as it is by the wizarding culture. Shot through as the wizarding world is with racial prejudice, Hogwarts registers the prejudices based on class and racial difference that inform the world outside its gates.

Given the history and culture of the wizarding world, we may be prepared for Professor Lupin's treatment as a werewolf in book three and Hagrid's experiences as a half-giant in book four. The range of prejudiced responses, however, may shock: Rowling's sharpest critique of racial prejudice and materialist politics appears through Hogwarts student Ron Weasley, first in book three and then more prominently in book four. Lupin is scorned by Malfoy for his shabby robes and by contemporary Severus Snape for past schoolboy exploits; his presence at Hogwarts reveals the degree of latent prejudice lingering in even Ron Weasley's otherwise well-meaning and Muggle-loving heart: the news (late into book three) that Lupin suffers the effects of a werewolf bite received as a child prompts Ron's immediate, bitter, highly italicized response: *"Get away from me, werewolf!"* (*Prisoner of Azkaban,* 253), a response not echoed by Muggle-raised Harry and Hermione. Lupin's status as werewolf—an existence that had no cure when he was a boy and still leaves him unemployed because of prejudice like Ron's (*Prisoner of Azkaban,* 258, 261)—could represent contemporary prejudice against homosexuals or those infected with HIV, as Polly Shulman and A. O. Scott suggest, but a direct referent may not be necessary. More important, the tensions between werewolves and wizards, like the tensions between Mudbloods, pure bloods, and Muggles, echo the fervent tensions between race and class in the "real" contemporary British body politic of the Dursleys' suburbia and of British readers' own experiences.

Rowling's decision to reveal Ron Weasley harboring prejudice for werewolves in book three is telling in retrospect, since we learn in book four that his prejudice against werewolves is not isolated but of a piece with other cultural fears against nonwizard species. What might have seemed merely an odd quirk in his character in book three represents a cultural legacy by book four, linking Ron to the very materialist ideologies he otherwise condemns in Voldemort and the Malfoys. Ron's reaction to the news that Hagrid is half-giant is less emotional than his reaction to news that Lupin is werewolf, but it shares the same cultural logic: "Ron looked around at Harry, his expression very serious indeed," as he explains, "they're just vicious, giants. It's like Hagrid said, it's in their natures, they're like trolls . . . they just like killing, everyone knows that" (*Goblet of Fire,* 373–74). Passing on to Harry the cultural belief ("everyone knows that") that character adheres in the body ("it's in their natures"), Ron reveals his link to a materialist morality he repudiates in another context.

As one not brought up by wizarding parents or within wizarding culture, Hermione easily voices opposition to Ron's claim, not "find[ing] the news that Hagrid was a half-giant nearly as shocking as Ron did":

> "Well, I thought he must be," she said, shrugging. "I knew he couldn't be pure giant, because they're about twenty feet tall. But honestly, all this hysteria about giants. They can't *all* be horrible . . . it's the same sort of prejudice that people have towards werewolves . . . it's just bigotry, isn't it?"
> Ron looked as though he would have liked to reply scathingly, but perhaps he didn't want another row, because he contented himself with shaking his head disbelievingly while Hermione wasn't looking. (*Goblet of Fire*, 377)

Significantly, Rowling leaves this argument unresolved, giving Ron rather than Hermione the last "word" in the narrative of the scene. For Ron's response isn't "just bigotry," as Hermione claims: Harry learns from Ron that no giants remain in Britain, and hardly any remain abroad, since many were killed by Aurors for their service to Voldemort (*Goblet of Fire*, 374, 381–82). The cultural logic of Ron's and the wizarding world's prejudice against giants rests upon generalization, in conjunction with a materialist ideology of difference: If some giants acted for Voldemort, it follows that all giants have or may have such tendencies; Hagrid, now revealed to be part giant because of his mother Fridwulfa, should be seen as having such tendencies, too, regardless of the character and actions he has presented thus far. The result of such cultural logic is prejudice, as Rowling makes clear from others' responses to Hagrid's mother,[19] but the explanation for that prejudice is more complicated than Hermione's response allows, touching as it does on the multiple levels of individual experience, cultural belief, and history. Whereas Ron's experiences with Muggles prevent him from generalizing on their characters, he easily participates in perpetuating the beliefs of his wizarding culture in the case of other species.

---

19. Journalist Rita Skeeter emphasizes Hagrid's half-breed status in her *Daily Prophet* article, as well as the scandal that he's been crossing breeds of creatures in his creation of the Skrewts; she closes by writing, "Albus Dumbledore surely has a duty to ensure that Harry Potter, along with his fellow students, is warned about the dangers of associating with part-giants" (*Goblet of Fire*, 382). Malfoy's taunt to Harry about Hagrid's absence from classes also emphasizes the danger of mixed blood as much as a wizarding fear of giant blood alone: "Missing your half-breed pal? . . . Missing the elephant man?" (*Goblet of Fire*, 385). Hagrid himself consoles Hermione about the hate mail she receives after Rita Skeeter's column revealing her Muggle birth by telling her some of his own: " 'Yeh're a monster an' yeh should be put down.' 'Yer mother killed innocent people an' if you had any decency you'd jump in a lake' " (*Goblet of Fire*, 473). Even though they are "jus' nutters," as Hagrid tells Hermione, these views represent one end of a spectrum of opinion in the wizarding world about other magical species.

Rowling's most complex exploration of residual prejudice based on material difference is the Hogwarts community's response to Hermione's political organization, the Society for the Promotion of Elfish Welfare. Humorously abbreviated as S.P.E.W., Hermione's well-meaning campaign provides, on the one hand, a satirical look at the numerous left-wing fringe movements more prominent in British than American culture and at the nineteenth-century tradition of well-to-do liberals speaking for the lower classes whom they have never met.[20] Hermione does indeed have, as author and reviewer Penelope Lively remarks, "Fabian tendencies," tendencies that are tempered by the discovery that one of her constituents, the house-elf Winky, may not want to be liberated from her work, and that most of the Hogwarts house-elves look askance at one of their kind who would choose paid labor over servitude. Yet Rowling's choice of house-elves for Hermione's burgeoning political activism is more than a source of humor. The subplot on house-elf rights coincides with the series' more explicit critique of residual prejudice against Muggles, Mudbloods, werewolves, and giants, offering further evidence for Rowling's investigation of how cultural beliefs are naturalized as truth. For in choosing to raise others' consciousness about the rights of house-elves, Hermione has selected a group whose place within the wizarding world is determined by the intersection of racial and class categories, the two categories concurrently explored in the main plotline between Harry and Voldemort. In this subplot, then, Rowling creates one of her most indicting, if most subtle, criticisms of the materialist ideologies of difference, as she reveals the institutionalized snobbery of British boarding school and university life.

Who works for whom, within an increasingly capitalist society? Hermione pursues this extremely contemporary concern when she discovers that Hogwarts runs smoothly thanks to the nearly invisible presence of unpaid house-elves in the kitchens and around the castle. For the British reader, the "slavery" of the house-elves would suggest not only a history of race relations, as for the American reader, but class relations in British schools.[21] Like the "scouts" or cleaning staff for British public schools and Oxbridge universities who clean rooms and prepare meals with as little evidence of their presence as possible, the house-elves occupy a world connected to,

---

20. Monty Python's take on such political groups in *The Life of Brian* offers another example of such satire, when they present multiple fringe groups and political factions in response to Jesus, such as "The People's Front of Judea."

21. The house-elves' position as workers of a minority race caught within a lower socioeconomic class may also be an analog for Britain's immigrant labor force, an integral part of British culture since the beginning of the Welfare State after World War II. Rowling's social critique would then extend to the ramifications of welfare capitalism as well as snobbery in the British public schools and universities.

but in class terms completely separate from, the students they serve.[22] The house-elves are therefore not only a different species within the wizarding world, but, unlike wizards of mixed blood, goblins, or other species of magical creatures, are born into a servant class, one that suffered acutely under Voldemort, as Dobby explains to Harry in book two: "But mostly, sir, life has improved for my kind since you triumphed over He-Who-Must-Not-Be-Named" (*Chamber of Secrets*, 133–34). House-elves cannot participate, then, in the global culture of the magical world, unless they pursue the difficult and disgraceful path of seeking employment, as Dobby has done (*Goblet of Fire*, 330–31). Their race determining their class, the house-elves illustrate how one material difference (race) can naturalize another (class) within a society that marks difference and accords power though material signs.

While the responses Hermione receives to her political organization do not explicitly condone the servitude placed upon the house-elves, they speak to the persistent beliefs in a "natural" difference that we have seen in other areas of wizarding culture. Ron sees no need to help them: " 'Well, the elves are happy, aren't they?' Ron said. 'You heard old Winky back at the match . . . "House-elves is not supposed to have fun" . . . that's what she likes, being bossed around . . .' " (*Goblet of Fire*, 112). Ron's brother George echoes his comments (*Goblet of Fire*, 210–11), also basing his opinion on the house-elves' current happiness, while Hagrid looks both to the house-elves' "nature" and their successful assimilation into wizarding culture: " 'It'd be doin' 'em an unkindness, Hermione,' he said gravely, . . . 'It's in their nature ter look after humans, that's what they like, see? Yeh'd be makin' 'em unhappy ter take away their work, an' insultin' 'em if yeh tried ter pay 'em.' " He concludes, "I'm not saying there isnt' the odd elf who'd take freedom, but yeh'll never persuade most of 'em ter do it—no, nothin' doin', Hermione" (*Goblet of Fire*, 233). Ron, George, and Hagrid all see the house-elves' role within wizarding society as "natural," to use Hagrid's term, a condition of being not subject to alteration and one that is rightfully maintained because of the house-elves' willingness to serve. Hermione's objections to their views emphasize the role many wizards play in maintaining the status quo: " 'It's people like *you*, Ron,' Hermione began hotly, 'who prop up rotten and unjust systems, just because they're too lazy to—' " (*Goblet of Fire*, 112), and, in responding to George's claim that the house-elves "think they've got the best job in the world," Hermione exclaims, "That's because they're uneducated and brainwashed!" (*Goblet*

---

22. I am indebted to my former colleague Simon Lewis at the College of Charleston for this cultural reference. My discussion here about the role of house-elves in Rowling's series is informed by his knowledge of British culture and our discussions on the topic.

of Fire, 211). Even if she fails to consider her own class presumptions in knowing what is best for the house-elves, Hermione's criticisms highlight for the reader how a belief in house-elves' servitude may appear "natural" to those brought up in the wizarding culture, how that belief may be absorbed unwittingly as truth. Her task is difficult in a culture where Ron's remark "We've been working like house-elves" (*Goblet of Fire,* 197)— a version of the British idiom "working like a black" or "working like a nigger"—reinforces an ideology he has elsewhere fought against. Though Ron quickly excuses his statement (" 'It's just an expression,' said Ron hastily"), language has the ability to carry and convey ideological meaning, as Ron's own response to the word "Mudblood" in book two indicates.

Their discussions about house-elves constantly interrupted during book four, Rowling's young characters are not able to resolve the issues Hermione raises about house-elf rights. Yet Rowling's narrative also illustrates how participation in ideological systems is hardly ever seamless. Within those fissures lies, perhaps, the possibility for change, through awareness and education. After Ron exclaims he and Harry have been "working like house-elves," Hermione's presence and her new political awareness prompt him to *account* for his speech, even if he still turns to the ideologically freighted phrase without thinking. Rowling's series offers the reader a realistic frame for the house-elf debate and for change, ranging from Harry's success in freeing Dobby from the Malfoys' power to the characters' increasing awareness of the culture's recurring prejudices based on supposedly "natural" differences. Hermione may not be successful in her activism thus far, but Rowling's series suggests that Hermione's efforts may not be in vain. At least one house-elf, Dobby, did wish to leave the service of a master who abused his rights. Dobby also tells Harry in book two that "Harry Potter shone like a beacon of hope for those of us who thought the Dark days would never end, sir" (*Chamber of Secrets,* 134). Dobby was not alone, then, in his misery, suggesting that the house-elves' "happiness" may be due more to a benevolent "master" like Dumbledore than to the "natural" position they hold within the wizarding world. A change of working conditions appears to promote happiness more than fulfilling one's duty to a master.

Rowling's subplot on house-elves illustrates most acutely the complexity of prejudice within the supposed "fantasy" world of the series, a world that frequently bears much more resemblance to the ambiguities of contemporary British culture than any supposedly idyllic realm of fifty years before. Those reviewers who persist in reading Rowling's series as a throwback to some other culturally stable time see only the fact of her boarding school setting and not the close detail that creates it, detail that indicates a world patterned on the tensions of Britain as it enters the new millennium. If we must look back fifty years for a historical parallel, we must recognize that period as the turbulent times preceding World War II, when the political fate of Britain was poised between Liberalism and fascism, between Churchill and Hitler.[23] Such tensions, though, have hardly been put to rest by Welfare Capitalism, Thatcherism, or New Labour. Contemporary events equally resonate with the series' concerns about how power is gained, exercised, and maintained within society.

Claiming to dislike fantasies herself, Rowling stated in a recent interview with Anne Johnstone: "For me one of the big challenges [in my books] was to make sure I knew the laws, both physical laws and the legal system within the wizarding world because until you know the boundaries, there's no tension" (10). The worlds of Muggles and wizards are not separate realms of reality and fantasy—or even quite separate, as reviewer Polly Shulman notes; she is "impressed with [Rowling's] technique for interweaving her magical world with Muggle life," so that "[h]er wizard world exists in the interstices of everyday Britain." Yet even Shulman's metaphor may be slightly off-base, for "interweaving" suggests two separate entities, or parallel worlds, placed side by side, whereas we are slowly learning the degree to which the worlds not only overlap but consciously meet, merge, and interact.[24] Given the material connections between Muggle and wizard worlds and Rowling's insistent questioning of those who subscribe, consciously or not, to materialist ideologies of difference, the series partakes in a tradition of narrative realism as much as fantasy. The body can bear marks of difference that confer authority—remember Albus Dumbledore's comment to Professor McGonagall that "scars can come in useful" (*Philosopher's Stone*, 17)—but the series' emphasis on choice (*Chamber of Secrets*, 245) continues to argue against the determinism of materialist ideologies found within the wizarding world of Rowling's novels and within the everyday lives of readers like Dexter Lateef.

23. Several reviewers make the argument that Rowling's books are either "nostalgic" (Hattenstone, "Harry, Jesse and Me") or "innately conservative" (Natasha Walter, "Wizard Tales of Good and Evil") or both as a result of their setting; see also Holden, "Why Harry Potter Doesn't Cast a Spell over Me"; "Thank Heavens for Harry"; Richard Adams, "Harry Potter and the Closet Conservative," and Bloom, "Can 35 Million Book Buyers Be Wrong? Yes." Judging by prepublication reviews posted on Amazon.co.uk, Andrew Blake's *The Irresistible Rise of Harry Potter: Kid-Lit in a Globalized World* (2002) may also continue this argument. Rowling has several times refuted this reading of her series, including in her responses to the Hattenstone article.

24. his review of book four for the *Ottawa Citizen*, Wynne-Jones also hears such echoes of the pre–World War II era: "In fact, *The Goblet of Fire* ends with the wizard world in the same brooding uncertainty as Europe found itself about the time Hitler goose-stepped into Sudetanland."

Harry Potter and the Technology of Magic

Elizabeth Teare

The July/August 2001 issue of *Book* lists J. K. Rowling as one of the ten most influential people in publishing.[1] She shares space on this list with John Grisham and Oprah Winfrey, along with less famous but equally powerful insiders in the book industry. What these industry leaders have in common is an almost magical power to make books succeed in the marketplace, and this magic, in addition to that performed with wands, Rowling's novels appear to practice. Opening weekend sales charted like those of a blockbuster movie (not to mention the blockbuster movie itself), the reconstruction of the venerable *New York Times* bestseller lists, the creation of a new nation's worth of web sites in the territory of cyberspace, and of course the legendary inspiration of tens of millions of child readers—the Harry Potter books have transformed both the technologies of reading and the way we understand those technologies. What is it that makes these books—about a lonely boy whose first act on learning he is a wizard is to go shopping for a wand—not only an international phenomenon among children and parents and teachers but also a topic of compelling interest to literary, social, and cultural critics? I will argue that the stories the books tell, as well as the stories we're telling about them, enact both our fantasies and our fears of children's literature and publishing in the context of twenty-first-century commercial and technological culture.

The classics of children's fantasy literature are Luddite, or at best ambivalent, in their attitudes toward modern commodity culture. The great example is Tolkien, whose hobbits destroy the One Ring and Sauron's industrial hell to restore Middle Earth to pastoral, precapitalist serenity (though, Tolkien acknowledges, that serenity is ultimately doomed). In C. S. Lewis's Narnia, too, the arrival of industry heralds the Fall. The same principles hold true in fantasies set in more contemporary worlds. Magic in Diana Wynne Jones and Susan Cooper and Elizabeth Goudge is natural and inborn or, if man-made, is antique, given as a gift or found. Magic cannot be

1. Abramson et al., "People Who Decide What America Reads," 39.

329

bought or sold: anyone who tries to commodify it is doomed to the kind of horrible fate best portrayed by Roald Dahl. The acquisitive children who accompany Charlie through the chocolate factory all get their appropriate comeuppance; James's aunts are crushed by the giant peach when they try to exhibit it for profit.

Philip Pullman's recent *His Dark Materials* trilogy comes closest to celebrating the complicated technologies of its alternate universes. Each volume of the trilogy is named for the marvelous instrument its heroes receive or construct: *The Golden Compass, The Subtle Knife, The Amber Spyglass.* All three novels celebrate the inventive technologies Pullman's parallel universes have developed, particularly the aeronautic devices: balloons, witches' broomsticks (actually pine branches), zeppelins, "gyropters," and the extraordinary "intention craft" directed by its pilot's desires.[2] As the story develops, however, all these inventions are used for, and often destroyed in, a vividly described and bloody universal war. The Subtle Knife turns out to be draining consciousness from the universe and letting in soul-sucking specters. And paradise is a world inhabited by gentle and civilized quadrupeds whose most elaborate technologies are fishing nets and the wheel.

Ursula Le Guin has recently made explicit the opposition of children's fantasy literature to commodity culture. In her new collection of stories, she not only adds to her chronicle of what she carefully notes is the "nonindustrial society" of her Earthsea archipelago but also includes, in her Foreword, a powerful critique of what she calls "commodified fantasy." According to Le Guin, the "mills of capitalism" take advantage of modern "long[ing] for the unalterable . . . stability, ancient truths, immutable simplicities" of fantasy by providing readers with empty imitations. Le Guin writes, "Commodified fantasy takes no risks: it invents nothing, but imitates and trivializes. It proceeds by depriving the old stories of their intellectual and ethical complexity, turning their action to violence, their actors to dolls, and their truth-telling to sentimental platitude. Heroes brandish their swords, lasers, [and] wands, as mechanically as combine harvesters, reaping profits. . . . The passionately conceived ideas of the great story-tellers are copied, stereotyped, reduced to toys, molded in bright-colored plastic, advertised, sold, broken, junked, replaceable, interchangeable."[3] The metaphor in Le Guin's last sentence is particularly powerful, evoking the world of tie-in marketing campaigns and the "bright-colored plastic" toys in McDonald's Happy Meals. In returning to Earthsea in *Tales of Earthsea* and the new novel *The*

---

2. Philip Pullman, *The Golden Compass*, 218.
3. Ursula Le Guin, *Tales of Earthsea*, 267, xiii–xiv.

Other Wind, Le Guin argues by example for a return to the "nonindustral" practice of fantasy writing. And by implication she raises questions about the Harry Potter books, with their burgeoning industry of bright plastic tie-in merchandise. Are Rowling's novels too, as they have been published and marketed, only "commodified fantasy"?

As with the plots of the fantasy genre, so with the stories we tell ourselves about their place in children's culture. The producers and consumers of children's literature have traditionally constructed their cultural position in opposition to capitalist enterprise. Books last. They are reread. It doesn't matter that their covers get torn. Child readers, according to advocates of book culture, are better children than those who clamor for the newest video games. And publishers are better, more wholesome, than the manufacturers who flood the children's market with toys like Pokémon and participate in an interlocking system of cartoons and video games and movies and plastic toys and clothing and accessories and trading cards, all designed to encourage continued consumption in search of the rare missing card, like the golden ticket to Willy Wonka's factory.

In the last twenty years, however, this pastoral vision of children's book culture has become as endangered as Tolkien's Shire. Books have lost children's attention, and therefore market share, to other media that present narrative fantasies: movies, video, and video games. Pokémon is only one of the most visible examples. But it is not only the competition. Children's publishing is itself increasingly tainted. The rise of the franchise series—Animorphs, Goosebumps, the Baby Sitters Club, even the educationally "historical" American Girl—works to create the same kind of desire for mass-produced similarity and for serial acquisition that Pokémon does. (And even Pokémon has a franchised series of books.) Increasingly, too, successful children's books are part of their own systems of tie-ins. Read the American Girls and buy the dolls, their outfits and furniture (displayed behind glass in the Chicago flagship store as if they are valuable museum artifacts), the matching doll-and-owner American Girl jackets, tickets to the American Girl revue. Nancy Drew never carried all this baggage. Disney, of course, is the merchandising master of this game.

Then Harry Potter appeared on the scene, initially offering a strong counternarrative to the Disney story and allowing its publishers, particularly Bloomsbury in the United Kingdom and Scholastic in the United States, to retake the high ground and redirect the story they tell about themselves. Much of the power of the Harry Potter story is in the way it seems to resist the pressures of children's commodity culture. Account after account in the press features a parent describing the change in her child (most often it is a mother and son), who has learned to love reading by reading these books: "they took my non-reader and turned him into a reader."[4] Such stories also feature children who loudly resist Harry Potter tie-in products that might trammel their imaginations. In October 1999, when Rowling's book tour took her to Washington, D.C., the *Washington Post* featured an article about the challenges faced by parents who couldn't buy ready-made Albus Dumbledore and Hermione Granger Halloween costumes and were forced, joyfully, to help their children make their own. The same article, published well before Rowling's film and product-licensing deal with Warner Brothers, quotes a boy who perfectly embodies adult fantasies of children's contented innocence and resistance to commercial exploitation of the book. " 'I don't think they should make TV shows because then when you imagine stuff from the book, then it will be much different,' says Sam Piazza, 10, of Silver Spring."[5]

Rowling's authorial biography has been pressed into service to support this noncommercial narrative. According to legend, Rowling was a single mother on the dole when she developed the Harry Potter stories, writing in cafés while her daughter napped. She has protested this account of herself as an unworldly and suffering romantic genius, but she is also quoted, on the Scholastic web site as well as in numerous articles, as saying that all she wants to do is write, whether or not she is paid: "I have always written and I know that I always will; I would be writing even if I hadn't been published."[6] The publishers have matched this story of commercial innocence with one of technological innocence. They have hardly advertised, they claim; the books are a grassroots phenomenon, built on the innocent desire and pleasure of children. Rowling has endorsed this idea, claiming "she was hard-pressed to answer the question she often asked as a child. Why? 'I suppose it's mainly word of mouth,' she offered of the books' success in the London *Guardian.* 'I think children just tell one another about it.' "[7]

Supporters of the innocence myth point to experiences like that of Politics and Prose, an independent bookstore in Washington, D.C., which cited "unprecedented interest" as the reason for a special "crowd control strategy" put in place when Rowling appeared there to sign *Harry Potter and the Prisoner of Azkaban.* Elements of the strategy include the following: "2) We will give out 500 tickets, no more than 4 per person standing in line. We are sure that Ms. Rowling will be able to sign 500 books. . . . 3) Ms. Rowling will start to sign at 4 P.M. and she will sign NO MORE THAN ONE BOOK FOR EACH PERSON. She will sign until 6 P.M."[8] In fact, Rowling signed

4. Linton Weeks, "Sheer Sorcery."
5. Libby Copeland, "Sew-cery: Young Fans Conjure Some Wizardly Costumes."
6. "Meet J. K. Rowling," Scholastic Press Harry Potter Web Site.
7. Marc Shapiro, *J. K. Rowling: The Wizard behind Harry Potter,* 83.
8. Politics and Prose bookstore, e-mail to subscribers.

nine hundred books in two hours, for admirers who had lined up as early as 8 A.M. and who "clapped and cheered as though [Rowling] were Literate Spice."[9]

Linton Weeks of the *Washington Post,* who coined this Spice Girls simile, aptly captures the conflicts that lie behind the narrative of Harry Potter's innocence and suggest the fundamental question. Are the Harry Potter books a real alternative to children's commodity culture, or are they just the most cleverly packaged part of it? Rowling's celebrity is more like that of Oprah Winfrey herself than that of Oprah's Book Club authors—it is Winfrey, after all, with whom Rowling shares space on the *Book* list. And with the flood of Harry Potter products released into the marketplace since the Warner licensing agreement, it is much more difficult to differentiate between Harry Potter and the Powerpuff girls. The release of the movie, with its ubiquitous advertising, has blurred the distinction further.

Children's literature critic Jack Zipes has argued that "it is exactly because the success of the Harry Potter novels is so great and reflects certain troubling sociocultural trends that we must try to evaluate the phenomenon." Zipes argues that the Harry Potter books are so successful because they are so "formulaic," that they could not succeed unless they were. There is something wonderfully paradoxical about the phenomena surrounding the phenomenon of the Harry Potter books. For anything to become a phenomenon in Western society, it must become *conventional;* it must be recognized and categorized as unusual, popularly accepted, praised, or condemned, worthy of everyone's attention; it must conform to the standards of exception set by the mass media and promoted by the culture industry in general. To be phenomenal means that a person or commodity must conform to the tastes of hegemonic groups that determine what makes up a phenomenon. It is impossible to be phenomenal without conforming to conventionality.[10] Zipes admits with pleasure Rowling's wit and humor, but he resists the argument that her books are something special. Their much-touted exceptionality is in fact a sign of their entanglement in the commodified culture industry they are believed to transcend. Zipes points out that the Harry Potter books, especially in hardback, are too expensive for children to buy for themselves, so they must be purchased by reasonably well-off adults; he doubts that as many children have actually read the books as have been exposed to them. The seeming success among children of the conventional Harry Potter books is for Zipes another sign that middle-class parents are "turning [their children] into commodities" by providing

9. Linton Weeks, "Charmed, I'm Sure."
10. Jack Zipes, *Sticks and Stones: The Troublesome Success of Children's Literature from Slovenly Peter to Harry Potter,* 172, 171, 175.

them with the cultural signs, like books, that adults think signal parenting success (xi).

Zipes's skepticism about the "Harry Potter phenomenon" is justified on several counts. The publishers and marketers of Harry Potter are of course steeped in the commercial technologies they affect to despise. They couldn't buy publicity like their celebrated lack of publicity, which has garnered them everything from Rowling's 1999 "Woman of the Year" honors from *Glamour* to raves on air and in print from George Will.[11] And the novels' publishers, especially Scholastic, have made ample use of the nonprint technologies the books are said to resist. The elaborate Scholastic web site encourages young visitors to play Harry Potter trivia games and to post entries identifying the character they most admire. To play some games, they must register their "personally identifiable information," which Scholastic in a lengthy privacy notice acknowledges the company may use "to provide parents, via e-mail or other means, with information about materials, activities, or other things that may be of interest to parents or their children, including products or services of third parties."[12] There is a page for teachers and parents, too, suggesting topics of discussion for class reading groups and home discussion. It is worth pointing out that, despite the elegant interactive design of the web page, the questions it actually poses are as inane and moralizing as those in any old-fashioned junior-high literature anthology: "In *The Prisoner of Azkaban,* when Harry has the opportunity to kill the character responsible for his parents' death, he chooses not to do it. How does that separate him once and for all from his archenemy, Voldemort?"[13] A question like this could as easily appear on a dittoed handout from the 1970s as on a flickering screen in the 2000s. Such familiarity might reconcile parents who worry about the hours their children spend at the computer—if it doesn't induce despair about the unimaginative, coercive questions children now face not only at school but in the broad "cultural pedagogy" sponsored by corporations.[14]

More problematic is the relation in which the Harry Potter books find themselves to Internet commerce. In late spring 1999, as the first U.S. volume gained popularity, eager American consumers discovered that they could order copies of the second and third volumes directly from Britain over the Internet, from Amazon.com's U.K. affiliate. Scholastic immediately moved up the publication dates of its own second and third volumes

---

11. "1999 Women of the Year"; George Will, "Harry Potter: A Wizard's Return."
12. "Privacy Notice," Scholastic Web Site.
13. In "Conflict," "Harry Potter Discussion Guides," Scholastic Web Site.
14. Shirley R. Steinberg and Joe L. Kincheloe, eds., *Kinderculture: The Corporate Construction of Childhood,* 4.

and made sure the fourth and subsequent books would be published simultaneously in the United Kingdom and the United States. Scholastic also challenged Amazon.com for violating international territorial publishing rights. Amazon has argued in return that buying a book from a British web site is legally just like Americans buying it in a British bookstore when they are visiting the country. Web sites based in Britain display, though not prominently, a warning that they can ship only one copy to a customer overseas. The Association of American Publishers is now involved, and Rowling's books are providing a test case for the role of traditional territorial rights in the age of e-commerce. In this context, it is impossible to understand the Harry Potter books solely as texts, apart from their status as commodities.

It is possible, however, to take a more optimistic point of view than Zipes's on the way the books as commodities function in children's culture. In *Sold Separately: Children and Parents in Consumer Culture,* Ellen Seiter argues that "[c]hildren are creative in their appropriation of consumer goods and media, and the meanings they make with these materials are not necessarily and not completely in line with a materialist ethos."[15] In the second half of this essay, I will argue that the Harry Potter books themselves attempt to make their own "creative . . . appropriation" of the problem of "consumer goods and media" in both book culture and children's culture. When Zipes concedes that "[p]erhaps it is because the novels are a hodgepodge of . . . popular entertainments that [Rowling's] novels are so appealing," he glimpses an important part of Rowling's method. Unlike Ursula Le Guin, who turns away from "commodified fantasy," Rowling works such fantasy into her fiction. The Harry Potter books offer instructions on how to live in commodity culture, with Rowling advocating, though not always consistently or successfully, resistance to the consumerist pressures both children and adults face. Their engagement with these issues is indeed one reason the novels are "so appealing."

Rowling wittily addresses questions of contemporary book culture in the books themselves, particularly in *Harry Potter and the Chamber of Secrets.* This second novel in the series features celebrity author Gilderoy Lockhart, whom we first meet at a book-signing in wizard London's largest bookstore, Flourish and Blotts. Lockhart's appearance prefigures the crowds that have grown around Rowling's. Lockhart's appeal is sexual, not innocent—most of the crowd is middle-aged witches—but the long line, newspaper

---

15. Ellen Seiter, *Sold Separately: Children and Parents in Consumer Culture,* 10. Zipes cites this passage from Seiter but counters that children's "creative . . . appropriation," like that of adults, is ultimately only "a false freedom of choice, for all our choices are prescribed and dictated by market systems" (Zipes, *Sticks and Stones,* 4).

photographer, and cheering crowd are recognizable from any collection of articles about Rowling or, indeed, any media celebrity.

Lockhart embodies empty celebrity. He views anything that happens around him as "all publicity." Like many another dim celebrity with a rudimentary sense of his own market power, Lockhart spends hours answering fan mail and signing pictures. Rowling strikes a satiric blow against the book culture into which she has been swept as Lockhart is gradually revealed as a fraud, detested by Hogwarts faculty and students alike. His spells usually fail. His franchise of autobiographical adventures, from *Gadding with Ghouls* to *Travels with Trolls* to *A Year with the Yeti,* is faked, its heroic stories stolen from less photogenic witches and wizards. Explaining this literary theft to Harry, Lockhart invokes a doctrine of "common sense" for understanding and manipulating book culture. Lockhart's cynical sense of what makes a book valuable takes on a darker tone when he decides that Harry and Ron's knowledge of his fraud is too great a threat to his success. He attacks them magically, trying to wipe out their memories rather than help them rescue Ron's sister, Ginny, from the Chamber of Secrets. To save his reputation, Lockhart is prepared not only to destroy the boys' minds but also to abandon Ginny to certain death. Here, celebrity is villainy (*Chamber of Secrets,* 63, 297).

When Lockhart's spell backfires and he loses his own identity, the pleased reader echoes the dismissive comment of Professor Minerva McGonagall: "that's got *him* out from under our feet" (*Chamber of Secrets,* 295). The pleasure of unmasking Lockhart aligns Rowling's readers with Harry himself, one of the first characters to see through Lockhart's façade. Harry's resistance to Lockhart's media obsession highlights an important theme running through all the books. His distaste for the trappings of fame thrust upon him—photo ops, groupies, journalistic puff pieces—constantly reminds the reader of his boyish modesty and good taste. Through Harry, Rowling builds into her novels the possibility of resistance to celebrity book culture, as Harry models the kind of "creative appropriation" possible for children faced with such cultures in the real world.

Another sign of Rowling's knowing use of the commodification of books is the 2001 publication of two of "Harry's favorite books" in support of the U.K. charity Comic Relief, to create "a fund set up in Harry Potter's name . . . specifically to help children in need throughout the world." Both *Fantastic Beasts and Where to Find Them* and *Quidditch through the Ages* are carefully and imaginatively designed to use and comment on the conventions of twenty-first-century publishing. Both books claim to be published by wizard presses (Obscurus and Whizz Hard) "in association with" Scholastic and to be sold in both wizard and Muggle bookstores. On the back covers, below the ISBN number and UPC bar code, the price appears in both Muggle and wizard money: "$3.99 US (14 Sickles 3 Knuts)." Each "special edition" features a foreword by wizard Albus Dumbledore, famous headmaster of Hogwarts; *Quidditch through the Ages* also offers a page of endorsements by several authors the devoted Harry Potter reader will recognize. The most wittily self-referential of these blurbs comes from "Gilderoy Lockhart, author *Magical Me,*" who remarks that "Mr. Whisp shows a lot of promise. If he keeps up the good work, he may well find himself sharing a photoshoot with me one of these days!" Rowling's resurrection of Lockhart gives added bite to her parody of both the form and the content of publishing's promotional ephemera.

Quidditch through the Ages claims to be a Hogwarts library book, with a list of borrowers, including Harry, Ron, Hermione, and the heroic Cedric Diggory, noted in the front. *Fantastic Beasts and Where to Find Them* offers a more significant conceit: it is presented as a facsimile of Harry's own book. According to Dumbledore's foreword, "You hold in your hands a duplicate of Harry Potter's own copy of *Fantastic Beasts,* complete with his and his friends' informative notes in the margins. Although Harry seemed a trifle reluctant to allow this book to be reprinted in its present form, our friends at Comic Relief feel that his small additions will add to the entertaining tone of the book" (viii). The "small additions" include games of hangman and tic-tac-toe, Quidditch graffiti, and annotations that allude to Harry's adventures with giant spiders, dragons, merpeople, werewolves, and others. The additions are indeed "entertaining," making the reader who gets the jokes feel especially clever. They also allude again to the role of celebrity in book culture: the fact that *Fantastic Beasts* bears "Harry's signature," even as a joke, does make it more appealing (and hence valuable) to its readers, as does Rowling's signature on individual volumes of the novels themselves. The market for signed copies of the Harry Potter books is strong enough that a Virginia man was able to bilk twenty eBay auction-site buyers out of hundreds of dollars for fraudulent signed first editions. Such fraud is possible because "legitimate first-edition, first-print Harry Potter books go for more than $3,000 on the open market," according to Matt Duffy of *Auction Watch.*[16] Rowling parodies her fans' interest in books as collectible commodities when she attaches Harry's signature to the charity books at the same time as she uses that interest to generate more money for the Comic Relief fund to which she has also attached his signature and her own.

Most critics who have weighed in on the Harry Potter phenomenon to date have placed the books firmly in the Luddite tradition of children's fantasy. The September 20, 1999, cover article in *Time* concludes with a

16. Matt Duffy, "Alleged Harry Potter Fraud on eBay."

celebratory contrast between Warner Brothers' plans for "fantastical" special effects for the then upcoming movie—"Technology is now incredible," says the producer—and the "interesting" fact that the wizard world of the books "contains no technology at all. Light is provided by torches and heat by massive fireplaces. Who needs electricity when you have plenty of wizards and magic wands? . . . Technology is for Muggles, who rely on contraptions because they cannot imagine the conveniences of magic. Who wouldn't choose a wizard's life?"[17] The train to Hogwarts, powered by a "scarlet steam engine," serves as a transition from the crowds at Kings Cross to what Alison Lurie calls the "pre-industrial" world of Hogwarts, where students write on rolls of parchment with quills.[18] And full-blooded wizards who have no day-to-day contact with the nonmagical Muggle world can hardly understand—though they are often fascinated by the ingenuity of—telephones or cars or the "escapators" they've heard of in the tube stations they don't need to use.

Certainly the contrast between Harry and his Muggle relatives reinforces the distance between their commercial, technological world and his purer one. His stupid cousin Dudley Dursley, in particular, who receives stacks of video games one birthday, represents all children obsessed with acquiring and discarding the electronic toys with which his playroom is littered: "Nearly everything . . . was broken. . . . Other shelves were full of books. They were the only things in the room that looked as though they'd never been touched" (*Sorcerer's Stone*, 37–38). Dudley is clearly a nonreader, the figure against whom all children who side with Harry Potter—particularly the formerly nonreading boys to whom the series famously appeals—will set themselves. (Dudley, besides being thuggish, is fat. He clearly descends from Dahl's Augustus Gloop, whose gluttony Rowling can make even more contemptible by implicitly calling on current concern about obesity and inactivity among couch-potato kids.) The Dursleys, Dudley's parents and Harry's guardians, are the kind of materialistic adults who would riot at Toys R Us for the latest Pokémon figure for their darling boy, while giving Harry old socks or fifty-pence pieces as Christmas presents.

Harry's idol, headmaster Albus Dumbledore, stakes out the anti-Dursley position most clearly when he explains to Harry his reasons for destroying the Sorcerer's Stone of the first novel's title: "As much money and life as you could want! The two things most human beings would choose above all—the trouble is, humans do have a knack of choosing precisely those things that are worst for them" (*Sorcerer's Stone*, 297). Readers who see

17. Paul Gray, "Wild about Harry: The Exploits of a Young Wizard Have Enchanted Kids," 72.
18. Alison Lurie, "Not for Muggles."

Rowling's fantasy world as more pure than our reality can turn to such Dumbledorean paradoxes, worthy of Tolkien's Gandalf or Susan Cooper's Merriman, for evidence. The problem with such a reading, however, is that Dumbledore does not represent the majority of Rowling's wizard world. In fact, he resists its desires, turning down a nomination to be Minister of Magic. Dumbledore is considered, even by admiring students, to be "a bit mad" and "off his rocker" (*Sorcerer's Stone,* 123, 302).

The virtuous Dumbledore apart, the wizard world more generally is much like ours: highly commercialized and obsessed with its technologies. Gringott's, the wizard bank, is fully international (Bill Weasley works for its branch in Egypt); it also seems to have no competition. This monopoly troubles no one in the world of the novels, perhaps because Rowling takes care to make the bank a model of integrity and capitalist morality. Over its doors is engraved a poem warning patrons (and potential thieves) that they will "pay dearly" for "the sin of greed" (*Sorcerer's Stone,* 72).

In *Harry Potter and the Goblet of Fire,* the reader learns about international wizard commerce as well. The Ministry of Magic, which in the earlier books has been concerned with domestic British issues, is revealed to have important international responsibilities. Percy Weasley begins working for the Department of International Cooperation, whose concerns include an effort "to standardize cauldron thickness" (for safety reasons) and to prevent the illegal import of flying carpets (56).

The first set piece of *Goblet of Fire* is also a scene of international magical commerce, when the Weasley family, Hermione, and Harry attend the World Cup of Quidditch. This international sporting event, like the Triwizard Tournament that follows it, not to mention the Olympics, is in theory intended to create wholesome "ties between young witches and wizards of different nationalities." In practice, the World Cup, again like the Olympics or World Cup soccer, is a richly productive site for commercial enterprise. As they approach the stadium, Harry and his friends are besieged by commodity culture: "Salesmen were Apparating every few feet, carrying trays and pushing carts full of extraordinary merchandise." The schlocky souvenirs they "push" are irresistible to the children, who arrive at the game with "their moneybags considerably lighter." The Quidditch stadium, too, is a commercial vehicle, with a "gigantic blackboard . . . flashing advertisements across the field" (*Goblet of Fire,* 187, 93, 94). Rowling is at her most playful in creating the excesses of wizardly mass production, but the humor loses some of its force when the reader remembers that "collectible figures" like those the children buy are part of the vast array of Harry Potter merchandise now available. Though these figures, easily found in bookstore children's sections and on the same Internet sites that sell the books, do not fly or stroll, some of them cost more than one hundred dollars.

Money is always a concern and often a worry in Rowling's world, as we might expect, since expensive accessories of magic—spellbooks, cauldrons, potion ingredients, wands—must be purchased before any magic can be performed. The commercial mystique of wands is especially great. Although, as A. O. Scott points out, Rowling's wands appear to be "artisanal handcrafts,"[19] that fact is used primarily to enhance their market value. Venerable wand merchant and authority Mr. Ollivander himself tells Harry that "no two Ollivander wands are alike" and that "of course, you will never get such good results with another wizard's wand" (*Sorcerer's Stone*, 82–84). Magic wands, like Muggle cars or computers, are marketed to match their buyer's personality, and settling for second-hand will make you a lesser wizard. While wizardly technologies may not look like the commodities we are used to, they are nonetheless marketed and consumed as ours are.

Rowling builds her strongest critique of the importance of money to children on the story of Ron Weasley and his wand, a saga that extends through the first three volumes of the series. The Weasleys, supporting seven children on a Ministry of Magic salary, are not only poorer than most wizards but also famous for their poverty, as the wealthy and sneering Draco Malfoy constantly points out. Because of his poverty, Ron faces a series of what he perceives as humiliations—hand-me-down textbooks, hideous second-hand dress robes, the constant awareness of Harry's comparative wealth—that remind the reader how sensitive children are to the pressures of consumerism. The most important of Ron's humiliations by far is his wand.

Although Mr. Ollivander has made it clear that successful wizards must have custom-fitted wands, Ron begins his Hogwarts career with his brother Charlie's worn-out wand. Worse, when that wand is damaged at the beginning of the second novel, Ron doesn't dare ask his parents for a new one. Through *Chamber of Secrets*, Ron struggles in his classes as his wand, though "patched up . . . with some borrowed Spellotape . . . seem[s] to be damaged beyond repair. It [keeps] crackling and sparking at odd moments" and causes him disaster after disaster both in class and out (95). This wand turns out to have some value, when its tendency to backfire is what foils Lockhart's memory charm on the way to the Chamber of Secrets, but Ron cannot see or recognize that value. He gets his own wand only by luck, when his father wins the lottery at the beginning of *Prisoner of Azkaban*.

Ron's sufferings, along with the more serious anxieties of his loving, courageous parents and older brothers, Fred and George, talented inventors and budding entrepreneurs with no capital, allow Rowling to comment on the difficulties faced by people who don't have enough money to provide

19. A. O. Scott, "A Dialogue on Harry Potter."

their children with the commodities that trigger self-esteem in capitalist culture. Here, she is making a serious critique. She undermines that critique, however, when she cannot bear to deprive the Weasleys of the commodities and capital that according to Harry their niceness "deserve[s]" (*Prisoner of Azkaban*, 9). In the third novel, Mr. Weasley wins the lottery; in the fourth, Harry himself gives Fred and George his Triwizard tournament prize money, on the condition that they also replace Ron's embarrassing dress robes (*Goblet of Fire*, 733). Harry as hero is generous and superior to the lure of gold, in part because he has plenty already, but he is also a means for Rowling to sidestep the most painful consequences, for both adults and children, of her magical world's commodity culture.

Rowling's children are fully exposed to the temptations of commerce in the magic world. They love to buy, and a visit to the local village is an occasion to stock up on nose-biting teacups, dungbombs, and "shelves upon shelves of the most succulent-looking sweets imaginable" (*Prisoner of Azkaban*, 197). (What Dudley Dursley is despised for desiring, Harry and his friends eat constantly.) One particular brand of candy, Chocolate Frogs, increases its appeal by including Famous Witch and Wizard trading cards. Although Ron has about five hundred cards, he continues constantly to consume Chocolate Frogs in his search for the rare Agrippa and Ptolemy. Though they most closely resemble baseball cards, Rowling's Witches and Wizards cannot help recalling Pokémon and the more wizardly Magic: The Gathering, as well as the Harry Potter game cards now available at bookstore checkout counters.

And the most important accoutrement of wizard childhood, the broomstick, is the most like Muggle toys. The brand of broomstick one rides is a status symbol, and the best model of one year, Harry's Nimbus 2000, can be made obsolete by the next year's Nimbus 2001, acquired by arch-rival Draco Malfoy. The best broomstick, the "state-of-the-art . . . streamlined, superfine" Firebolt (this is the broom's advertising copy, provided by Rowling), is an object of awed desire, too expensive and exclusive to have a price tag. Naturally responding to this tempting display, Harry realizes he has "never wanted anything as much in his whole life" (*Prisoner of Azkaban*, 51–52). Harry disciplines this desire because "he had a very good broom already," and of course he is rewarded by receiving a Firebolt from the mysterious benefactor later revealed to be the adult who cares the most about Harry—his godfather, Sirius Black. The value of this loving gift only increases in the fourth book, when Harry uses his prized Firebolt to win the first challenge of the Triwizard Tournament. In the case of broomsticks, at least, the novels endorse the value of (high-quality, expensive) consumer goods and of the purchase of those goods as a sign of adult nurturing of children.

Like her account of celebrity book culture, Rowling's depiction of her consuming children is gently satiric. Unlike the adults, however, the children in her world are not punished when they succumb to the lure of commodities. Neither, in our world, are either the children or the adults whose commodities of choice are the Harry Potter books. The adult readers, critics, and publishers concerned with the definition of culture, in particular, have found in Rowling's narratives a story that allows them both to participate in the messy world of millennial commerce and technology and to hold themselves apart from it. The novels' uneven, interesting, and compromised depiction of children and commodity culture offers a useful arena in which such concerns can be thought about, though not satisfactorily resolved.

Apprentice Wizards Welcome

Fan Communities and the Culture of Harry Potter

Rebecca Sutherland Borah

As I made my way to the back of the line at 11:32 P.M., I couldn't help but think I should have gotten there earlier, not because I was going to be at the end of a long queue, but because this was the largest group of persons with this particular interest I'd ever seen assembled in one place. Roughly 150 people ranging in age from five to well over fifty-five waited patiently for the doors of our local bookstore to open. Many of them looked like parents with youngsters in grade school or junior high, but quite a few people looked to be of college age or well out of school like myself. What would bring all of us together to wait in line at a time of night when most of us would normally have been at home and in bed? If you don't know the answer, you obviously did not watch the national news nor read a newspaper nor cruise the Internet during that first week of July 2000.

With a rustle of homemade robes, squeals of excitement, and just a few muffled yawns, the doors were soon thrown open and "HP4" made its way into the hands of eager Harry Potter fans. The massive $3.5 million media hype leading up to the publication of *The Goblet of Fire* exposed the viewing public to something a loyal and expanding fan base has known since the publication of J.K. Rowling's first novel in 1997: not only are the Harry Potter books a delight to read, but they define a complete, magical world that is rich enough to enjoy either in solitude or, better yet, in the company of one's fellow readers. I admit to being something of a latecomer to the hero of Hogwarts. I've enjoyed fantasy narratives for three decades (from comic books and *Star Trek* to Tolkien and role-playing games) and followed fan culture both formally and informally for almost two-thirds of that time. When I first heard about the British boy wizard, I mentally put Harry on a "to buy and read over the summer" list, but it took me several more months to fall completely under his spell. What I have come to know about Harry's fans since then has surprised me. More so than the majority of popular narratives found in print and other media formats, Rowling's series of novels has inspired an unusually large variety of readers—of both sexes, from different ages, races, and cultures—to participate in activities related to or inspired by her fiction. From Internet web pages to classrooms to reading circles to corporate-sponsored chat sessions, her readers share their experiences by discussing plots, writing fan fiction, throwing theme parties, devising games, asking and answering questions, passing rumors, and creating artwork. But I'm getting ahead of myself. Although Harry Potter fandom is currently one of the fastest growing, most visible, and most publicly discussed of followings, Rowling's works are by no means the first popular narrative to inspire such activities.

In his book, *Textual Poachers: Television Fans and Participatory Culture,* Henry Jenkins describes activities that involve people enjoying, discussing, and reimagining a specific text as "participatory culture." Jenkins explains in his book's introduction that the study looks at "a social group struggling to define its own culture and to construct its own community within the context of . . . a postmodern era" as they insist "on making meaning from materials others have characterized as trivial and worthless."[1] In his study Jenkins examines the fan communities connected to fantasy and science fiction series found primarily on television and experienced as fan culture from the mid-1980s through the early 1990s. These series include British imports *Blake's 7, Doctor Who,* and *The Avengers,* as well as American shows such as *Beauty and the Beast* (with Linda Hamilton and Ron Perlman), *Alien Nation, Dark Shadows, Twin Peaks,* and, most notably, *Star Trek* and *Star Trek: The Next Generation.* Jenkins takes care to contextualize his position as both a participant in and researcher of fan culture by noting "[a]nthropology and sociology have entered a period of experimentation as ethnographers seek new methods ranging from autobiographical accounts of fieldwork to various forms of dialogic writing. Central to this move has been the recognition that there is no privileged position from which to survey a culture. Rather, each vantage point brings with it both advantages and limitations, facilitating some types of understanding while blinding us to others."[2] Thus, Jenkins is able to access and use information from both the academic sphere and fandom in order to bring about a better understanding of participatory culture.

Jenkins sets up his research by discussing the process of becoming a fan and forming a community around a "text." He then goes on to describe how fans translate and discuss texts together, develop an aesthetic or "rules" for interpreting a text, and often produce texts (including written stories and criticism, artwork, and videos) inspired by the original product. He uses the story of the velveteen rabbit to illustrate how a consumable product (a toy/text) can be made "real" through the process of breaking down its

1. Henry Jenkins, *Textual Poachers: Television Fans and Participatory Culture,* 3.
2. Ibid., 4.

integrity (loving the toy to pieces/reading, studying, discussing, and revising a text) and reimagining/reinventing it to suit one's needs. Rather than being passive receivers of consumable texts, fans are active participants who share their experiences and rework texts. As Jenkins concludes: "The text becomes something more than what it was before, not something less."[3]

During the mid-1980s, and especially in the years since Jenkins conducted his research, academic interest in various types of fan communities has increased. These studies focus on, but are not limited to, romance readers (Modleski, 1990; Radway, 1984), film viewers (Austin, 1989, 1997; Fuller, 1997), comics and comic book readers (Inge, 1990; Pearson and Uricchio, 1991; Tankel and Murphy, 1998), television viewers (Bacon-Smith, 1992; Tulloch and Jenkins, 1995; Fiske, 1989; Ang, 1985, 1991; Brown, 1990); and role-playing "gamers" (Fine, 1983).[4] Perhaps the primary cause of this increased scholarly interest is the growing proliferation of narratives and narrative forms that inspire fan activities. Fan communities have spontaneously sprung up around new texts and forms of media such as those based on collector cards, video games, and the Internet, and these groups exhibit characteristics different from yet similar to, and sometimes overlapping, previously established fan communities. Likewise, fans of particular narrative genres, such as science fiction or fantasy or action-adventure, readily consume texts across a wide variety of media. For example, fans of *Star Trek: Voyager* may have watched *Babylon 5,* read novels by Orson Scott Card, played Magic: The Gathering, helped Lara Croft raid a tomb, or attended the opening of *Star Wars, Episode One: The Phantom Menace.*

While Jenkins limits most of his study to television-inspired examples (with an emphasis on *Star Trek* fan culture) whose fan communities are overwhelmingly made up of adult female viewers, his theories are certainly applicable to readers of Rowling's books. This study examines Harry Potter fans and their activities in public, in private, and on the Internet. Because

3. Ibid., 52.
4. Tania Modleski, *Loving with a Vengeance: Mass-Produced Fantasies for Women;* Janice A. Radway, *Reading the Romance;* Bruce Austin, *Immediate Seating: A Look at Movie Audiences;* Bruce Austin, "Researching Film and Television Audiences"; Katherine H. Fuller, "*Motion Picture Story Magazine* and the Gendered Construction of the Movie Fan"; Thomas M. Inge, *Comics as Culture;* Roberta Pearson and William Uricchio, eds., *The Many Lives of Batman: Critical Approaches to a Superhero and His Media;* Jonathan David Tankel and Keith Murphy, "Collecting Comic Books: A Study of the Fan and Curatorial Consumption"; Camille Bacon-Smith, *Enterprising Women: Television Fandom and the Creation of Popular Myth;* John Tulloch and Harvey Jenkins, *Science Fiction Audiences: Watching* Doctor Who *and* Star Trek; John Fiske, *Understanding the Popular;* Ien Ang, *Desperately Seeking the Audience;* Ien Ang, *Watching* Dallas; Mary E. Brown, *Television and Women's Culture*; Gary Alan Fine, *Shared Fantasy: Role-Playing Games as Social Worlds.*

many of those studied are underage, I have changed their names and with-held some personal details to protect their anonymity. Like Jenkins, I po-sition myself as a researcher within the fan community. Despite the risks and fears of "going native" and compromising a so-called *objective* stance, I believe that no research can be devoid of subjectivity and hierarchies; therefore, it is better to acknowledge my critical stance and my privileged position as a researcher and fan among my fellows. I have collected data through interviews and during formal and informal discussions. I have also observed and participated with fans through numerous web sites and mes-sage boards.

The first question any researcher of fan culture needs to ask is, "Just whom am I studying?" In the case of Rowling's fans, the answer seems quite apparent. Surely, her audience must be made up of the legions of eight- to twelve-year-old fans, mostly boys, who have set aside their electronic toys to read about Harry Potter? Newspapers, magazines, talk shows, television news programs, and magazine shows on all the major American networks covered the publication of *Harry Potter and the Goblet of Fire.* Both lo-cal and national reports featured photogenic children—mostly cherubic, middle-class, and white—dressed in homemade robes and pointed hats, at-tending parties and waiting to get their hands on "HP4." Thanks to this heavy media coverage, a casual observer might think that a series of books marketed to children has an audience limited to that demographic; however, this is far from the complete picture.

The majority of the 37 million–plus copies of Rowling's books in print most probably did make their way into the hands of children; however, the story certainly does not end there. Older readers have made up a substan-tial portion of Rowling's audience from the start. Older siblings, parents, grandparents, teachers, and readers of fantasy and science fiction immedi-ately took to the first book. In Britain, the first three novels were published with a second more "mature" set of covers with photolike images in black and white for adults who want to read about their favorite boy wizard in public without being stigmatized. As the books gained more attention in the media, adult celebrities as diverse as Steven Spielberg, Drew Barrymore, Dave Barry, Rosie O'Donnell, and Stephen King proclaimed their fandom and helped make Harry Potter books a "must read" for trend-conscious adults. Recently, Matthew Rose and Emily Nelson reported in their *Wall Street Journal* article, "Potter Cognoscenti All Know a Muggle When They See One," on the growing phenomena of "Potterisms" used by adults at home and in corporate and academic settings.[5] On a similar note, in "Why

5. Matthew Rose and Emily Nelson, "Potter Cognoscenti All Know a Muggle When They See One."

'Harry Potter' Did a Harry Houdini," Richard Corliss argues that Rowling's books should stay on the regular *New York Times* list for bestselling fiction and not be relegated to its new children's category specifically because of the number of adults reading the books. Corliss postulates:

> Is a children's book a work written for kids? Or read mostly by them? If it's the second, then Harry Potter should be on both lists, adult and fiction. According to the NPD Group, a leading market research firm that tracks book-buying in 12,000 households, nearly 30 percent of Harry Potter purchases were made for a reader 35 or older. And we know one middle-aged, childless movie critic (all right, we *are* that critic) who last summer read the first three books aloud to his enthralled wife, also an adult. The Potter series is one of those cultural events that [spill] out of narrow categories and into the Zeitgeist. Reading the books, kids feel more mature, adults feel younger. And all become part of a community where age doesn't matter.[6]

Clearly, Rowling's novels, especially since the publication of *Goblet of Fire* with its increasingly more mature themes and darker tone, have crossed over from "just children's fare" to a broader, more adult audience.

Although determining the exact numbers of different types of readers is nearly impossible, observing postings on popular Internet message boards such as "The Unofficial Harry Potter Fan Club" and "The Unofficial Harry Potter Website" reveals that "boarders" (people who frequent electronic message boards) often request head counts and role calls during which "posters" (those who post messages) reveal their age, gender, and other personal information. Certainly, not all Harry Potter fans are active on or even connected to the Internet; nevertheless, the information posted there does give a fair sampling of this growing segment of Rowling's audience.

By reading numerous topics on several message boards and starting "threads" (posted topics) of my own, I was able to arrive at the following conclusions. Roughly two thirds of the posters on mainstream Harry Potter fan message boards are under the age of eighteen, with most falling between the ages of twelve and sixteen and America Online catering to a slightly younger audience. As much as two-thirds of this subgroup is female, while among older posters this gender split is even higher. These demographics do of course vary a bit by message board, with the age going steeply upward on professional movie-related sites, such as "Count Down to Harry Potter" and "Coming Attractions," which added boards dedicated to the (at that time) forthcoming movie. Generally, these sites' posters are between the ages of sixteen and twenty-four years of age and up to 70 percent of them are male; therefore, it is not surprising that these figures hold true for the Harry Potter–dedicated message boards on these sites. (As I suspected,

6. Richard Corliss, "Why 'Harry Potter' Did a Harry Houdini."

when the movie neared its release date, these demographics shifted slightly toward younger female posters. However, by and large, fans tended to stick to the boards where they were already a part of the established local fan community.) At thirty-six I was often, though not always, the oldest participant who would divulge his or her age on the message boards. Posters over twenty-five were in the minority on all the mainstream message boards I observed—the only exceptions being message boards dedicated specifically to parents or educators—yet adults participated just as enthusiastically as younger fans on every message board I observed.

Determining a given group's ethnic or cultural makeup is an even tougher task than investigating age or gender, especially over the Internet, so this study does not attempt to separate out fans of different nationalities. However, thanks to what information people did volunteer, it is apparent that Rowling's books appeal to an international and multicultural audience that includes American fans of African, Asian, and Latino/a descent. All of the teachers and librarians I spoke with confirmed that young readers from across cultural, social, and economic spectrums read Rowling's books, so I believe I'm correct in asserting that Harry Potter appeals to a much more divergent group of readers than one might initially assume. Indeed, I found that despite the cost of the hardback books and the expense of being connected to the Internet, many children with limited economic means still managed to participate in fandom through library resources or by sharing books and computer access with friends.

Because of the Harry Potter fan community's diversity, rapid growth, and visibility, it is imperative to note its differences from, as well as similarities to, other established groups. Since fan communities often overlap and converge, a good place to start is with the well-established community of fantasy and science fiction fandom. Rowling's novels can best be described as belonging to the fantasy genre since her characters inhabit a world where magic is real and the fantastic is an everyday occurrence. Media fandom, such as that which focuses its attention on science fiction and fantasy narratives, has its roots in the followers of pulp magazines from the 1930s and 1940s. As Jenkins describes it,

> science fiction fandom may be traced back to the letter columns of Hugo Gernsback's *Amazing Stories,* which provided a public forum by which fans could communicate with each other and with the writers their reactions to published stories. . . . Since Gersbeck and other editors also included addresses for all correspondents, the pulps provided a means by which fans could contact each other, enabling a small but dedicated community of loyal science fiction readers to emerge. Fans, under the approving eye of Gernsback and the other pulp editors, organized local clubs and later, regional science fiction conventions to provide an arena where they could exchange their ideas about their favorite genre. By 1939, fandom had grown to such a scale that it could

ambitiously host a world science fiction convention, a tradition which has continued to the present day.[7]

However, as female readers tried to participate in science fiction fandom, they often found themselves and their opinions marginalized by the well-established male fans and writers. By the 1960s, the growing number of television programs that focused on science fiction and fantasy themes attracted many female fans who were soon able to claim the new media as their own. By doing so, they were able to "feminize" their forms of participation. Jenkins describes their activities as typically including the viewing (and often reviewing) of their favorite television shows or movies, discussing and critiquing story lines with other fans, and creating their own texts inspired by the original products.

Unlike more mature fan communities that have been the focus of some critical study, the culture of younger fans has received very little academic scrutiny. In fact, the popular media and the business community, not the academy, have paid the most attention to youth fan culture. This is hardly surprising for a couple of reasons. The Mighty Morphin' Power Rangers, Pokémon, Goosebumps, the Babysitters' Club, Animorphs, and the latest Disney production are just a few of the narrative texts aimed at youngsters between the ages of six and fourteen that have inspired fan activity over the past decade; however, these "franchises" are highly commercialized and solely meant to incite youthful consumers to buy and collect the merchandise attached to them. Especially notable is the Walt Disney Corporation, which under the leadership of Michael Isner has produced and marketed an enviable string of more than a dozen heavily merchandised hits since *The Little Mermaid* in 1987. From discount chains to Disney stores, goods of every description emblazoned with new and "classic" characters can all be purchased and collected.

It can be a big mistake, however, to assume mass marketing equates to fan-friendliness. According to the corporations, young fans should consume as much as possible, but woe to fans of any age who would like to make any corporate-owned property their own. Even more so than adult fans, younger fans are discouraged from creating their own texts and making their own objects in favor of buying "genuine" goods and joining "official" fan clubs. Rather than being encouraged to connect with other readers/viewers and to participate in shared communal activities (which don't directly benefit a company), youngsters are often treated as passive consumers, ready to accept whatever is hailed as the newest fad to be viewed and collected. Generally, as young audiences age, many fans lose interest in

7. Jenkins, *Textual Poachers*, 46.

their initial pursuits, due in part to being over-targeted with mass-produced consumables that quickly become obsolete memorabilia. As they move into adolescence, these fans often shift their attentions to different pastimes such as sports, video games, or social activities, which may lead them into other types of fan communities.

Into this complex mix of competing and overlapping communities of consumers and fans comes Harry Potter. Part of the answer to why Harry Potter appeals to such a diverse range of fans lies in the story of his creator. The origins of J. K. Rowling are by now so well publicized in the media that they have reached almost mythological proportions. Joanne Kathleen Rowling was born in Chipping Sodbury General Hospital in Gloucestershire, England, on July 31, 1965. The future author was a good student who enjoyed writing from an early age. She entertained her sister and later her friends with imaginative stories that involved them in adventurous tales.

As Rowling grew older, her parents pushed her to study French so that she could become a secretary, but she turned out to be unsuited for this profession because she was an admittedly poor organizer and liked to day-dream. Rowling came up with the idea for Harry while waiting on a stalled train between Manchester and London in 1990. Later that year she took a job in Oporto, Portugal, as an English teacher. There in 1991 she met and later married the journalist Jorge Arantes. Their daughter, Jessica, was born in July 1993, but by the end of the year Rowling's marriage had ended and she moved with her infant daughter to Edinburgh, Scotland, to be near her sister Diana.

Unable to find a job that would pay enough to cover day-care expenses for Jessica, Rowling went on public assistance for a short period of time so she could finish her novel. As Elizabeth D. Schafer remarks in her book, *Exploring Harry Potter,* "Rowling originally created the story to entertain herself and did not intentionally pen a children's book. She considered her imaginary world as a personal escape from despair, and she praises the book for providing a challenging project that boosted her morale."[8] The story of how Rowling would pack up her daughter and visit local coffeehouses in order to find a pleasant place to work is now legendary. During her October 16, 2000, Scholastic.com interview, Rowling was asked if she still had the napkins on which she wrote the first book. Obviously a bit chagrined, she responded, "I'm giggling . . . where did you read that? I didn't write on napkins; I wrote in notepads. We really need to squash this myth before people ask to see the used tea bags on which I drafted the first book!"[9]

8. Elizabeth D. Schafer, *Exploring Harry Potter: Beacham's Sourcebooks for Teaching Young Adult Fiction,* 29.
9. J. K. Rowling, "Live Interview on Scholastic.com, October 16, 2000."

Once the novel was completed in 1995, Rowling was able to secure the services of literary agent Christopher Little, who then submitted the book to a number of publishers. After nine rejections, Bloomsbury Publishing offered Rowling an advance of thirty-three hundred dollars (a fair amount for a first-time children's author) and accepted the book in 1996. At that point the book was titled *Harry Potter and the Philosopher's Stone,* and Rowling was asked to use her initials rather than her full name because of the belief common among children's publishers that boys will not believe that a female writer can understand a young male protagonist (à la S. E. Hinton). When the American publishing rights came up for auction in 1997, Scholastic, Inc., bid an unheard of sum and paid Rowling an advance of $105,000.

One of the main reasons Scholastic was willing to go out on a limb to get the rights to Rowling's book has to do with the overwhelming response of fan communities on the Internet. Because the British edition came out months before the American rights were auctioned, the book's first readers were able to start building positive word of mouth over the Internet. Thanks to online booksellers with British divisions, potential American readers could easily buy British editions and not have to wait for the American ones. As Jesse Kornbluth describes the situation,

> [Readers] began expressing their enthusiasm on America Online long before the Harry Potter craze really caught on in America. That's because the 9-year-old son of an AOL executive was one of the first book's earliest American readers. And after he polished it off, he declared it just about the greatest thing he'd ever read. His father then told friends in the editorial department, and they promptly built a special feature in the Families Channel about Harry (Keyword: Harry Potter). This special [site] is a compendium of all things Harry. . . . As a general rule, members go to specials in large numbers when they are promoted on the welcome screen or the main screen of a channel. When the promotion withers, so does the traffic. But Harry Potter was the exception. The link to this area was passed around like a chain letter, and the young readers posted in droves. "This area has been steadily popular all year long whether it's heavily promoted or not," notes Bonnie Weinstein, senior programming manager of the Families Channel. "That tells me that this is something that caught on just because of the members."[10]

Thanks to these initial fan activities and a little good luck, Scholastic's calculated risk on a new "unknown" author does not look quite so harebrained in retrospect. Rowling managed to tap into the imagination of her readers, and they responded to each new book with mounting enthusiasm. Soon the awards and accolades came as well. For *Harry Potter and the Sorcerer's (Philosopher's) Stone* she was awarded the Smarties Prize, the British Book

---

10. Jesse Kornbluth, "@ Harry Potter Online and in Print."

Awards Children's Book of the Year, *Publishers Weekly* Best Book of 1998, *School Library Journal* Best Book of 1998, and the *Parenting* Book of the Year Award 1998. For *Harry Potter and the Chamber of Secrets*, she received her second Smarties Prize (a first) and the Children's Book Awards for both long novel and overall novel for 1999. Rowling was named Author of the Year at the 2000 British Book Awards as well, and the Jim Dale–voiced recording of *Harry Potter and the Goblet of Fire* won the Audie Award and a Grammy in 2001. The list of awards and honors continues to grow with each book (and act of charity) for which Rowling is responsible.

Most literary reviewers and social critics had positive comments about the books, citing Rowling's abilities both to entertain and to convey valuable life lessons. One religious critic, Douglas Todd, described the series as "a fantasy that, not so ironically, is about real life, particularly about loss, powerlessness and solitude. And right and wrong."[11] Lee Siegel's essay in the *New Republic* went even further:

> [The] rapturous reception of the Harry Potter books is heartening, because J. K. Rowling is a literary artist, and these three books possess more imaginative life than the majority of novels that are published in this country in any given year. They are full of marvelous invention and humor and fun, but they have more than that. They are not fantasy-escapes from mundane existence, as they are being hailed; they are escapes from a general condition of hyper-rationality that, because it ignores the element of incalculability in life, has become unreasonable to the point of seeming receptive to fantasy and the occult as escapes from life. With Harry Potter, Rowling has brought reality back into the literature of escape, and back into our fantasy-culture. What a rarity, a literary imagination that is not self-conscious, and studied, and uptight.[12]

Some critics in Britain and the United States held less favorable opinions about Rowling and some of her readers. Both William Safire and Daniel Mendelsohn complained about adult readers indulging in juvenile literature. Even well-known academic curmudgeon Harold Bloom felt the necessity to offer his opinion. His *Wall Street Journal* essay begins, "Taking up arms against Harry Potter, at this moment, is to emulate Hamlet taking arms against a sea of troubles. By opposing the sea, you won't end it. The Harry Potter epiphenomenon will go on, doubtless for some time, as J. R. R. Tolkien did, and then wane."[13] For all his self-absorbed posturing, it was painfully obvious to anyone who had read the first novel that Bloom had not bothered to read the whole tome before he penned his sour critique.

11. Douglas Todd, "The Spiritual World of Harry Potter."
12. Lee Siegel, "Fear of Not Flying: Harry Potter and the Spirit of the Age," 40.
13. William Safire, "Besotted with Potter"; Daniel Mendelsohn, "Troubled Harry"; Harold Bloom, "Can 35 Million Book Buyers Be Wrong? Yes."

The unease of some academics and cultural critics who accuse adult Harry Potter readers of "growing down" or lowering intellectual standards implies that there is something unnatural or deficient about those who engage in fandom. No matter what age a fan is, he or she often faces some form of ridicule or censure from either so-called intellectual superiors on one side or a text's producer/manufacturer on the other. Fan activities represent a challenge to both the academy, which mandates taste, and the producers of the texts, who own the commercial rights to characters and concepts. Up until December of 2000, Harry Potter fans, at least the younger ones, had not felt the full ire of critics nor the harassment of producers as other fan communities have experienced in the past (witness lampoons such as *Saturday Night Live*'s infamous "Get a Life" sketch or writer Anne Rice's pleas on her web site to discourage fan fiction involving her characters). Even editorial cartoons dealing with Harry Potter have been extremely mild, focusing mainly on the positive perception that the books promote literacy and discourage children from playing video games and watching television. In large part this is due to the perceived age of most readers and the trendiness of the books. As Norah Myers, a twelve-year-old reader from an inner-city public school, put it, "It's way cool to read Harry Potter. Everyone in my class thinks so." Aside from a few critics and members of the religious right, the vast majority of those who express an opinion are still wild about Harry Potter. Whether society will continue to feel this way as readers mature and popularity ebbs a bit is a different matter; however, some ugliness has started to taint the magic relationship between the creator and her producers on one side and some enterprising fans on the other.

Despite Rowling's initial queasiness about seeing her creations reduced to cheesy toys in fast-food lunch bags, the author finally sold Warner Brothers the rights to develop and market products based on her works as well as the film development rights. On December 21, 2000, the United Nations World Intellectual Property Organization, based in Geneva, ruled in favor of Time Warner, which immediately gained ownership of more than one hundred Potter-related domain names. That same month, as the company proceeded with its plans to fully merchandize its new property, Time Warner/Warner Brothers began to take notice of the thousands of unofficial fan web sites populating the Internet. One such case attracted international attention. Claire Field, the fifteen-year-old British creator of a Harry Potter fan web page (harrypotterguide.co.uk), received a letter from Warner Brothers' London legal department in early December of 2000 asking her to explain her "intent." According to one fan page, the letter states:

> J. K. Rowling and Warner Bros. are the owners of the intellectual property rights in the "Harry Potter" books. Ms. Rowling and Warner Bros. are

concerned that your domain name registration is likely to cause consumer confusion or dilution of the intellectual property rights described herein. Your registration of the above domain name, in our opinion, is likely to infringe the right described above and we would ask therefore that you please, within 14 days of today's date provide written confirmation that you will as soon as practicable (and in any event within 28 days of today's date) transfer to Warner Bros. the above domain name. We are prepared to reimburse the registration fee incurred in your registering the above-mentioned domain name. If we do not hear from you by 15 December 2000 we shall put this matter into the hand of our solicitors.[14]

Feeling intimidated and frightened, Field went public and contacted the *Mirror,* a British tabloid, and the story was picked up by other online media sources and printed in newspapers. Soon other teenage web site owners across the globe reported receiving similar letters demanding they state their intentions, give up their domain addresses, and quit using any officially licensed images. Stephanie Grunier and John Lippman in their *Wall Street Journal* article, "Warner Bros. Claims Harry Potter Sites," quote Warner Brothers' senior intellectual-property lawyer Nils Montan as saying that he is sorry if fans misunderstand the company's intentions, but the company has no way of knowing who is just a well-meaning fan and who is not among the hundreds of people they contacted regarding copyright violations. Montan comments that some of those contacted are "cybersquatters" out to make a buck, including one individual who has registered nearly sixty domain names using trademarked names from Rowling's books.[15] In some cases this has certainly proved true. According to Steven Bonisteel in his *Washington Post* article, "WIPO Rules in Harry Potter Case,"

> In the Warner case, an unknown individual or business with a post office box address in Agoura Hills, Calif., registered a stockpile of addresses such as "HarryPotterFilms.net," "HarryPotterDVD.com," and "HarryPotterMusic.com."
> The WIPO arbitrators noted that, while some of the domains were registered as long ago as November 1999, "the vast majority" of them were registered after news broke in March 2000 about plans to release a Harry Potter movie.
> The current holder of the domains did not respond to the allegations.
> "It is difficult to discern any motive other than that of preventing the owner of the (Harry Potter trademark) from reflecting the mark in a corresponding domain name," the panel said, adding: "The panel believes that the registration of over one hundred such domain names is sufficient to constitute a pattern of conduct."[16]

14. Alastair Alexander, *Potterwar.org* home page.
15. Stephanie Grunier and John Lippman, "Warner Bros. Claims Harry Potter Sites."
16. Steven Bonisteel, "WIPO Rules in Harry Potter Case."

Unfortunately, many fans with legitimate nonprofit web sites are still not free of harassment. Field and other fan site creators are fighting Warner Brothers online and in the press, so more legal cases are likely to follow. However, many other fans, especially younger ones, have quietly given over their domain names. Alistair Alexander and Heather Lawver, cofounders of Defense Against the Dark Arts (DADA), launched a campaign to make the public aware of Warner Brothers' actions. They called for a boycott of the feature film and related products (potterwar.uk.org) until Warner Brothers quit harassing fans.[17] Warner Brothers took this group's threats seriously and managed to smooth over the most serious problems in the press. However, their heavy-handed legal tactics did have some negative consequences such as creating an adversarial relationship with parts of the fan community. Thinly veiled attempts to control fans by asking them to register their Harry Potter Internet sites with Warner Brothers through the official movie sites were not overly successful. Furthermore, the official site did not succeed at siphoning off fans from established online communities other than their own captive audience within the AOL community.

Now that we have some concept of who reads Harry Potter, it is time to examine what makes many of these people fans as opposed to just readers or members of an audience. In her study of *Quantum Leap* fans interacting over the Internet, "Uncertain Utopia: Science Fiction Media Fandom and Computer Mediated Communication," Andrea MacDonald explains some of the differences:

> Fans are people who attend to a text more closely than other types of audience members. Texts provide a focal point through which fans can identify to which community they belong. They might even adopt ideals, beliefs, and values (or ideology depending on how you look at it) that they feel the text valorizes. . . . Some fans choose to congregate and share their interests either by talking, writing, painting, or singing about them. Others are "lurkers," either unable or unwilling to actively participate in a community of fans.[18]

Fans are people who read, reread, and interpret texts. They seek out other fans to discuss these texts (or read these discussions, as is the case with "lurkers" on the Internet) and reshape their readings. Some of the fans I encountered first experienced Harry Potter books as part of their school curriculum. Educators from grade school through the college level have used Rowling's books to teach their students subjects as diverse as science, marketing, English as a second language, and of course literature. When a

17. Alexander, *Potterwar.org.*
18. Andrea MacDonald, "Uncertain Utopia: Science Fiction Media Fandom and Computer-Mediated Communication," 136.

teacher uses a text that has an established fandom, especially among his or her students, that teacher may harness the natural impulse of fans to reread, critique, and reshape a text to teach students any number of subjects. In fact, Jenkins holds that the recursiveness of fan activity changes the reading process:

> Fan reading . . . is a social process through which individual interpretations are shaped and reinforced through ongoing discussions with other readers. Such discussions expand the experience of the text beyond its initial consumption. The produced meanings are thus more fully integrated into the readers' lives and are of a fundamentally different character from meanings generated through a casual and fleeting encounter with an otherwise unremarkable (and unremarked upon) text. For the fan, these previously "poached" meanings provide a foundation for future encounters with the fiction, shaping how it will be perceived, defining how it will be used.[19]

Many educators will recognize the connections between this type of fan reading behavior and developing critical thinking skills. When educators harness these behaviors, the individual and group accomplishments can be dramatic.

Jesse Nash, a teacher of English as a second language, notes in his article "Using Harry Potter in the Adult ESL Classroom" that his adult students wanted him to read Rowling's first book to them when they found Nash was reading it himself. He was able to harness their enthusiasm and teach them vocabulary and language skills by using scenes from the novel: "I had always suspected that learning English would be easier if teachers could find a way to make the experience enjoyable. Harry Potter has helped make learning English an enjoyable enterprise for my students. But I was certain something very good was going on when the students began to use the time after the Harry Potter reading to talk about their own fears, worries, and hopes. Teaching them English is going to be much easier, I'm convinced, if they wish to talk about themselves and their most intimate thoughts in English."[20] Most of Nash's students initially wanted him to read them *Harry Potter and the Sorcerer's Stone* because their own children or relatives were fans and loved Rowling's books. Clearly there is a connection between fan behavior that reexamines, evaluates, and interprets a text and the activities Nash's students continued even beyond the classroom.

Of course, not every student is a Harry Potter fan; as a matter of fact, dealing with works as famous as Rowling's novels creates its own set of complications. Michelle Gibson said she chose to use *Sorcerer's Stone* in her college literature class because the book seemed tailor-made for her "Best-Sellers" course, as it dealt with the fleeting nature of fame and the impact of

19. Jenkins, *Textual Poachers*, 45.
20. Jesse Nash, "Using Harry Potter in the Adult ESL Classroom."

mass popularity—two aspects she wanted her students to critically examine throughout the course. Unfortunately, a number of her students assumed Rowling's book to be simplistic because it was marketed to children; thus, they read uncritically and initially missed some of the issues Gibson hoped they would recognize and connect to the themes of the course. Once Gibson pointed out the novel's complexities, these students were better able to appreciate what they had missed. Students familiar with the book did not make the same mistake of judging it by its reputation or its cover.[21]

Fanlike reading may start in a classroom—and some teachers may be able to exploit it to suit their academic goals—but fan activity usually goes beyond an educational setting. Although some of the younger fans with whom I have communicated have studied one of Rowling's books as part of a class—generally, English, reading, or foreign languages—the majority of younger fans were introduced to Harry Potter by friends or family members rather than through academic instruction. All of the school-age children I interviewed (twenty) were aware that they could get information about Harry Potter over the Internet, but only a few had participated in any fan activities on the web (mostly viewing the official movie site). All had learned about Harry Potter from friends and had in turn initiated others into *the club*. A typical response was: "I loaned my first book to two of my friends, so that way they'd know what the rest of us are talking about. It's really hard not to let a secret slip, so we can't talk about certain parts with everyone." None of them restricted their discussions to just Harry Potter. They talked about other fan interests such as Pokémon, music and music videos, television, movies, sports, school, and social activities. Several had participated in school, bookstore, or public library activities with a Harry Potter theme. Half had made an object such as a wand, picture, or costume inspired by the books (making baby mandrakes was a favorite activity at one library party). Most looked forward to purchasing "official" Warner Brothers' products, but several were skeptical about merchandising what they felt was too personal to be mass marketed: "I want to see what they'll sell, but I don't think it will be special if everyone has it."

The adults I interviewed (ten) shared many of the same opinions, but their fan activities were much more subdued. Only two participated in public fan activities unless a child accompanied them. The five parents often read with their children, and most took part in organized activities. One mother reported, "We've read each book more than once aloud to each other, and we'll probably do them all again when the next book comes out." Some had helped with "costumes and props" for parties, and one had helped to stage a themed birthday party. None of the ten adults had participated in Internet

---

21. Michelle Gibson, personal interview.

fan activities, but two had ordered books and read reviews on bookseller's sites. All but two had been introduced to Harry Potter through friends or their children. All enjoyed talking to other adult readers about Harry Potter, but none of them made it a regular, ongoing activity. One remarked, "It's great fun when you meet someone who's read the books, but I feel a little silly trying to explain them to outsiders." Another mother confided, "I have more fun talking about them [the characters] with my son's friends than anyone else." Some regarded reading the books as guilty pleasures, while others defended the books' merits: "These are the most moral and imaginative books I've read in a long time. I think some adults would smile more if they'd read them." Two adults reported reading passages aloud to their spouses, and seven said they had recommended the books to family members and friends who were reading or had read them. Three said they had refrained from discussing them with friends or family members they thought would be offended by the books' contents. Four had given the books as presents to other adults while six had bought them for children. All of the adults I spoke with had mixed feelings about the merchandising campaign surrounding the movie. One said, "I really want a T-shirt, but I don't want to see everyone wearing one. It's just not cool." Another lamented: "I was really disappointed when I read she [Rowling] had sold the movie and copyrights because everything has required readers to use their imaginations up till now. I want Hermione to look like my image of Hermione, not Hollywood's."

All of the people I interviewed participated in some type of fan activity—mainly rereading the texts or repeatedly listening to the tapes and discussing topics related to the books with other readers. Younger readers participated in more activities more often than older readers, but all those questioned said they considered themselves fans or enthusiasts. None of them reported being offended by the books, though several worried about censorship issues. However, no one who had read at least the first three books, including younger readers, felt anyone under ten years of age should read past the second book unsupervised. All but one planned to see the Warner Brothers' movie when it arrived in theaters, and all plan to continue reading the series, " . . . as long as it stays good." Not surprisingly, these fans congregated in very small groups, usually made up of friends and family members, or they were individuals who communicated with other fans by chance or circumstance. Some predicted trouble ahead if Rowling and Warner Brothers chose to strictly enforce copyrights: "I don't think they realize what a mess being heavy-handed with these children will cause." Another joked, "I wouldn't want millions of kids toting heavy books after me. But seriously, it's like that old cliché, they'll be cutting off their nose to spite their face."

The growth of the Internet as a means for fans to communicate and participate in fan activities has had a profound effect on Harry Potter fan culture. From the initial "buzz" on AOL, which boosted Rowling's earning potential, to the growing uneasiness between fan web sites and Warner Brothers, Harry Potter fans are an increasingly web-connected population. These Harry Potter fans exhibit behaviors that are fairly typical of Internet fan communities. They have web sites devoted to "all things Potter," which include discussion boards and forums, news posts, contests, games, art, creative writing, newsletters, chat rooms, and links to other fan sites and official pages. Most sites are also typically filled with advertisements that direct viewers to products that may or may not have anything to do with Harry Potter.

In the past, fans had to rely on conventions to get together in person; however, the Internet has greatly enhanced many fans' abilities to communicate with one another. Perhaps the most useful and dynamic means of electronic communications happens through discussion boards. Although chat rooms perform similar functions, studying conversations held in them is difficult due to their ethereal nature. Therefore, for this study, I concentrated my attention on discussion boards because they contain information that is not only convenient to study but also arguably more thoughtful and detailed than chat conversations, since participants may take their time and respond at their leisure. Sometimes called forums or message boards, these devices give fans of all ages, cultures, and backgrounds (or at least those who have access to the Internet) a chance to interact with other fans and participate in fan culture more fully than was possible a few decades ago. Very similar to their low-tech counterparts, electronic message and discussion boards allow fans or "posters" to submit messages and respond to other fans' "posts." Most sites that cater to younger fans, such as *The Unofficial Harry Potter Fan Club,* have moderators who read through electronic submissions before posting them to be read on the web site. Sites intended for older fans typically work on the honor system, and their owners reserve the right to banish any participants who do not abide by the rules. The number of fans who communicate through message boards is staggering. Warner Brothers opened the official *Harry Potter and the Sorcerer's Stone Movie Site* on February 15, 2001, and within four days fans posted roughly ten thousand messages on its discussion boards.

Using these electronic forums, fans may interact much as they would in person. They ask questions, exchange information, debate, gossip, tell jokes, critique various aspects of the books, share fan fiction, and form relationships with other fans. Once message posters feel comfortable with each other, they often exchange personal information and divulge details about their day-to-day lives. Sometimes they communicate using other venues besides the Internet as well. I found that older fans are more likely to carry conversations and relationships beyond message boards; however, younger fans also reported having phone conversations and chat sessions with online friends. A new poster often posts an initial greeting with an introduction like, "Hi, I'm new to the board. I love Harry Potter and can't wait for the next book." Other posters interested in engaging the new person typically answer with welcome messages that offer information about themselves and the site and sometimes ask questions. The new poster usually then responds and can feel he or she is part of the conversation. With a little effort and some thoughtful or witty responses, a new poster can quickly become accepted as a member of the board's local fan community.

During discussion board exchanges, fans often express their opinions by posting topics that challenge the status quo. Those whose only interest is to bait or taunt the other posters ("Gary Snotter Sucks!!") and cause uproar among the legitimate fans are known as "trolls." However, most posters, especially regular participants, get much of their entertainment from serious conversations that negotiate the meaning of a text within that particular community of fans. One such serious topic posted by a thirteen-year-old female I will call Cherie drew a thread of thoughtful responses. Cherie initially wrote:

> *Subject: Do you ever get the feeling that the HP books are SEXIST?*
> Hi, well I was just wondering about the sexism in the series. Do you think it exists, even when J. K. Rowling is a woman? I was just thinking about this and it occurred to me that the most developed and interesting characters are all males, and the major roles in the book are male roles. Harry's the hero, Voldemort's the most powerful villain in the world, Dumbledore's one of the best, Moody's the most interesting Auror, nearly the whole Ministry is male, the Weasley twins are the comic relief, Sirius is the wild, fatherly figure . . . and so on. As for the female characters, we have Parvati and Lavendar. They are written as giggling (and ditzy?) girls. And Hermione? Well, I'll take a poll. Who has the larger part in the story, Hermione or Ron? I'm not saying that I resent the books for being more masculine than feminine, but I was just wondering if anybody else felt there was some sexism. The story's very enjoyable with all the guy characters, but I personally don't like the way the female characters are written. And plus, wouldn't it still have been acceptable if Voldemort had been a woman? A cold, murderous woman that is able to lead evil men? Where's the harm in having a commanding female presence? Oh yes, and the Triwizard Tournament was also something. 3/4 of them were guys and Fleur was given last place. Any comments on that?

Within six hours of Cherie's first posting, twelve different posters had responded at least once. Several fans, most likely younger ones, replied with rather indignant denials of the presence of sexism in the series. One "Community Moderator" responded at length with messages of 482 and 569 words, roughly twice as long as Cherie's initial question and counter-response. Several other responses were detailed, point-by-point refutations, which opened up the conversation to further layers of exchange and debate. One older poster, whom I will call Prof. Darius, encouraged the participants to define their terms:

> In a discussion like this one, it is important that we understand what we mean by "sexist." Perhaps we could agree to define it as "disrespectful to women"; but then we'd have the question of "what exactly constitutes disrespect to women?"
>
> Really, there are two separate issues here. The first is the "nature vs. nurture" question: Is it part of the nature of humanity that males and females exhibit personality differences resulting in men taking more visible roles in society (both heroic and villainous)? Or is the observed prominence of men, along with the observed personality differences that underlie it, the result of a corrupt society's efforts to keep females in submission?
>
> The second issue is: If indeed females are not fundamentally different in personality from males, except that society has conditioned them to be that way, is it wrong (sexist, demeaning, disrespectful, etc.) to portray it as it is in literature without that literature expressing a clear-cut disapproval? (In other words, "if you aren't part of the solution, are you part of the problem?")
>
> I do not expect to reach a conclusion on this discussion board that will satisfy everyone; certainly there are intelligent and thoughtful people in the world who hold differing views on both of the above questions. But I will say that to conclude that the HP books are "sexist," you would have to hold the views that (1) the observed differences between men and women are due to a corrupt society, and that (2) it is irresponsible for a writer to portray it as it is and let the reader think that things are OK.

Prof. Darius went on to compare Rowling's worldview with that of C. S. Lewis. Rather than shutting the debate down, which sometimes happens when more mature posters step into the conversation, the exchange continued with Cherie replying to earlier posts and other board members stepping up to support her position and offering more evidence from the texts, interviews with J. K. Rowling, and past personal experiences. Most posters cited evidence from the novels and from their own lives to support their positions, but more sophisticated posters, such as Prof. Darius, introduced evidence from other literary works and applied different types of academic criticism. The thread continued to receive posts for more than a month. Most threads or topics do not attain this degree of complexity or sophistication—topics such as speculation about the next book and "who's your favorite . . ." usually predominate. However, I found weightier conversations that showed a high level of intellectual engagement and creative thinking on all the fan message boards I visited.

Communications scholars such as Nancy K. Baym point out that fan interactions over the Internet go beyond what could be perceived as idle chatter to encompass an array of activities aimed at meeting fans' objectives:

"[Fans'] goals include the enhancement of interpretive resources, the creation of a performance space with the potential status and recognition that entails, and, perhaps most provocatively, the opportunity to engage in public discussions of normally private socioemotional issues. These findings raise questions about the functions implicitly served by the frequently overlooked mundane interactions between fans."[22] Though the academy clearly values "serious" and "intellectual" conversations over so-called gossip, even the most commonplace conversations serve the purpose of supporting or building up a community. In the case of Harry Potter fans, their communications do support Baym's identified purposes. On message boards, trivia-related threads and agonistic exchanges do exist alongside confessional narratives. There is, however, an arguably more civil, nurturing, and supportive atmosphere within the Harry Potter online community, even on the adult fan pages, than one usually finds at fan sites in general. For example, one look at the message boards on *Ain't It Cool News* would make Miss Grundy's hair curl. There are certainly hierarchies among Harry Potter fans, but the initiation process for new fans is usually quick, supportive, and painless. For example, because some fans have not read all the books or kept up with the latest rumors about the movie, other fans and sometimes moderators post "spoiler warnings" to protect the less knowledgeable. Privileging the reading experience and respecting others' points of view is almost a given on Potter sites. Taunting and verbal jousting among posters does happen (witness the jabs posted on the Slytherins' board by other houses on the official movie site), but most fans on Harry Potter pages show a remarkable degree of discretion on line. Even when fans are prodded by religious conservatives or angered by Warner Brothers' legal maneuverings, their discussions are still generally congenial and inclusive, whereas similar topics on other fan sites usually spark a "flame war" of angry responses with little thought given to verbal restraint. The unusually egalitarian atmosphere on Harry Potter message boards may be due to the type of readers attracted to Rowling's texts; the unusually broad mix of ages, cultures, and backgrounds among fans; or the presence of many parents, educators, and web supervisors within the electronic fan community.

To go against this unwritten code of conduct seems to violate the spirit of the novels themselves. When Warner Brothers demanded that fan site creators state their intentions, it shocked many of these devotees to think that anyone would want to make a dishonest buck off Harry, but not because they were naive. They regarded the accusation as a grave insult to their own character as fans and to that of Rowling's works as well. This strangely

22. Nancy K. Baym, "Talking about Soaps: Communicative Practices in a Computer-Mediated Fan Culture."

noble worldview goes completely against the chaotic and commercial nature of the Internet, which has more of the feel of the wild, wild West about it than a British boarding school. Although other fan sites geared toward younger users can no doubt claim similar amounts of enforced civility, no other fan community exhibits such a quaint combination of behaviors and so remarkable a potential for growth.

Harry Potter fans are first and foremost a diverse group of individuals who have come to read Rowling's books and participate in fan activities in numerous and creative ways, both in person and at a distance. Although Rowling's fans tend to exhibit behaviors typical of most fan communities, their diversity and privileging of Rowling's worldview make them unique because members communicate inclusively, not by dumbing-down their ideas, but by exhibiting a hypersensitivity to their perceived audience. This is especially true of, but not limited to, their communication over the Internet. Clever educators at all levels and in many subjects can obviously take advantage of fan behaviors to create effective learning opportunities. However, other entities with less benign objectives also want to take advantage of fan behaviors.

Since the record-breaking debut of the first motion picture in theaters (as of February 1, 2002, the film had grossed $844.5 million worldwide), the ranks of Rowling's fans have grown even larger. Although most fans are still looking forward to both the next book and now the next movie, clearly some fans are troubled by the exploitative nature of the entertainment industry and its commodification of all things Harry. Whether or not Warner Brothers will be able to sell fans on its continued commercializing of the object of their affection remains to be seen. Coca-Cola had to make concessions to both Rowling and fans over its movie-affiliated ad campaign. Consequently, the first movie was free of product placement, and Coca-Cola will donate $18 million over three years to the Reading Is Fundamental campaign. (Coca-Cola sales are rumored not to have grown since the ad campaign, so the fans appear to have voiced their disapproval after all.) Whether fans remain steadfast and enthusiastic as the marketing of Harry Potter merchandise continues for several more years remains to be seen. Thus far, the merchandise appears to have sold well, but not to the degree that clearance aisles have remained free of mountain troll glue bottles, golden snitch key chains, and potions class perfume kits. (Believe it or not, Rowling herself vetoed some objects she did not feel were appropriate or of high enough quality.) To complicate matters, Warner Brothers has yet to settle their Internet domain name dispute but appears to have backed down from prosecuting "legitimate" fans. Nevertheless, for some, the magic of creating their own Harry Potter–inspired texts on the Internet vanished when they surrendered their web addresses. In more established fan communities, as Jenkins explains, "Fans recognize that their relationship to the text remains a tentative one, that their pleasures often exist on the margins of the original text and in the face of the producer's own efforts to regulate its meanings. While fans display a particularly strong attachment to popular narratives, acting upon them in ways which make them their own property in some senses, they are also acutely and painfully aware that those fictions do not belong to them and that someone else has the power to do things to those characters that are in direct contradiction to the fans' own cultural interests."[23] As the Harry Potter fan community continues to develop and mature, their awareness of just how tenuous their relationship to the text is will no doubt also increase. On the other hand, since today's fans often have more experience and better resources to communicate and organize, perhaps their situation is more hopeful and empowered than that of other groups connected to films and television series such as *Star Wars* or *Buffy the Vampire Slayer*. As long as Rowling continues to craft her stories with the same integrity, magic, and knowledge of her audience, the author and her texts will no doubt continue to enjoy loyal fan support. As for Warner Brothers and Hollywood, the movie franchise is clearly a financial success, but fans will likely continue to have a far less harmonious relationship with entities that clearly plan to exploit them and the world they love.

23. Jenkins, *Textual Poachers*, 24.

About the Contributors

Rebecca Sutherland Borah is assistant professor of English at the University of Cincinnati's University College, where she teaches written composition and Censorship in Literature and the Arts. Dr. Borah has a long-standing interest in popular culture and has presented numerous papers at national conferences on topics as varied as vampires, comic books, science fiction, fantasy, gender issues, mentoring, service learning, and composition studies.

Amanda Cockrell is director of Hollins University's graduate program in children's literature and managing editor of *The Hollins Critic*. She teaches creative writing in the university's master of arts in liberal studies program, has received a National Endowment for the Arts fellowship in fiction, and is the author of several novels, the latest of which is *Pomegranate Seed*.

Terri Doughty teaches English and children's literature at Malaspina University-College in Nanaimo, British Columbia. She is currently working on an edition of prose from the *Girl's Own Paper*.

Eliza T. Dresang holds the rank of professor at the Florida State University School of Information Studies. Her recent scholarly publications include *Radical Change: Books for Youth in a Digital Age* (H. W. Wilson, 1999), as well as numerous articles and book chapters applying the theoretical framework in *Radical Change* to the analysis of children's literature. Dr. Dresang is a frequent speaker at national and international conferences, three of which have focused on her own work, and she has served on and chaired numerous juries for children's literature awards including the Newberry, the Caldecott, the Batchelder, the Pura Belpré, and the Jane Addams Book Award.

M. Katherine Grimes directs the First-Year Experience program and teaches English at Ferrum College in Virginia. Her scholarship and teaching frequently focus on psychology and young people, especially in works by

Southern U.S. writers. Dr. Grimes is a contributor to the *Companion to Southern Literature* (Louisiana State University Press, 2001) and *AppLit*, an award-winning web site for teachers and readers of Appalachian literature.

Nancy Jentsch teaches German and Spanish at Northern Kentucky University in Highland Heights. Her paper on the translations of the Harry Potter novels, presented for the Kentucky Philological Association in 2001, was the editor's choice essay for the 2001 *Kentucky Philological Review*. Ms. Jentsch has also published poem translations and edited an anthology of poetry written in German by women living in the United States (*In Her Mother's Tongue*, Emerson Press, 1983).

Jann Lacoss holds a Ph.D. in Slavic folklore from the University of Virginia. She specializes in gross, scary, and taboo childlore. After serving several years as a faculty consultant for the Teaching Resource Center and teaching Russian folklore at the University of Virginia, she now works as an independent consultant. She is currently editing a collection of Russian children's folklore.

Farah Mendlesohn is editor of *Foundation: The International Review of Science Fiction* and has published a number of articles on science fiction and fantasy television, including "Surpassing the Love of Vampires: Why a Queer Reading of Buffy and Willow Doesn't Work," in David Lavery and Rhonda Wilcox, ed., *Fighting the Forces: Essays on the Meaning of Buffy the Vampire Slayer* (Rowman and Littlefield, 2001). Dr. Mendlesohn is currently writing on Diana Wynne Jones and is senior lecturer in American studies at Middlesex University, London.

Roni Natov is professor of English at Brooklyn College, CUNY, where she teaches classes in children's studies. With Geraldine DeLuca she cofounded *The Lion and the Unicorn* and has coedited it for seventeen years. She has published widely in children's literature, including articles, interviews, and a book, *Leon Garfield* (Twayne, 1994). Her book *The Poetics of Childhood* will be published by Routledge.

Philip Nel is assistant professor of English at Kansas State University, where he teaches courses in children's literature and in contemporary American literature. He is the author of *J. K. Rowling's Harry Potter Novels: A Reader's Guide* (Continuum Publishing, 2001) and *The Avant-Garde and American Postmodernity: Small Incisive Shocks* (University Press of Mississippi, November 2002).

Mary Pharr is professor of English at Florida Southern College. Coeditor of *The Blood Is the Life: Vampires in Literature* (Bowling Green State University Popular Press, 1999), she has also written and presented extensively on fantasy and horror in film and fiction.

Pat Pinsent is senior research fellow at University of Surrey Roehampton, where she was a principal lecturer in English for many years. Her books on children's literature include *Children's Literature and the Politics of Equality* (1997) and *The Power of the Page: Children's Books and their Readers* (1993). She has also contributed widely to books and journals, both on children's literature and her original research specialty, seventeenth-century poetry. Currently she is a tutor on the Roehampton M.A. in children's literature, particularly the Distance Learning mode, for which she produced the course material.

David K. Steege is associate dean of the college and associate professor of English at Carthage College in Wisconsin. As an Americanist, he has presented and published on Edgar Allan Poe and humorist Samuel Hoffenstein. More recently, he has turned to British children's fantasy; his essay on Hugh Lofting and the British Empire will be published in a forthcoming volume on history in children's literature.

Elizabeth Teare is assistant professor of English at the University of Dayton, where she teaches nineteenth-century British literature. She writes about the history of the novel and has recently published articles on Matthew Arnold and on smuggling. She presented an early version of her essay in this volume at the 1999 MLA convention in Chicago.

Karin E. Westman is assistant professor of English at Kansas State University. She has published *Pat Barker's Regeneration: A Reader's Guide* (Continuum, 2001) and articles on A. S. Byatt and Virginia Woolf.

Lana A. Whited is professor of English at Ferrum College in Virginia. Her essay on fact-based homicide novels of the 1930s, '40s, and '50s will appear in *Twisted from the Ordinary: Critical Essays on American Literary Naturalism* (University of Tennessee Press, 2003). She also teaches journalism at Ferrum and writes a weekly column on media issues for roanoke.com.

Bibliography

Abanes, Richard. *Harry Potter and the Bible: The Menace behind the Magick.* Camp Hill, Pa.: Horizon Books, 2001.

Abramson, Marla, Jennifer Clarson, Matthew Flamm, and Kristin Cloberdanz. "Ten People Who Decide What America Reads." *Book Magazine,* July/August 2001, 36–41.

Acocella, Joan. "Under the Spell: Harry Potter Explained." *New Yorker,* July 31, 2000, 74–78.

Adams, Richard. "Harry Potter and the Closet Conservative." *Voice of the Turtle,* January 8, 2002. <http://www.voiceoftheturtle.org/reviews/books/richard_potter.shtml>. Accessed April 18, 2002.

Adler, Bill. *Kids' Letters to Harry Potter: An Unauthorized Collection.* New York: Carroll and Graf, 2001.

Alexander, Alastair. "A Brief History of PotterWar." *Potterwar.org.* February 10, 2001. <http://potterwar.org.uk>.

Altick, Richard D., and John J. Fenstermaker. *The Art of Literary Research.* 4th ed. New York: W. W. Norton, 1993.

American Booksellers Foundation for Free Expression. *KidSPEAK* (formerly *Muggles for Harry Potter*) 2001. <http://www.mugglesforharrypotter.com/>. Accessed October 15, 2000.

Ang, Ien. *Desperately Seeking the Audience.* New York: Routledge, 1991.

———. *Watching Dallas.* New York: Methuen, 1985.

Anshen, Ruth Nanda. "World Perspectives." Preface to *Myth and Reality,* by Mircea Eliade. Translated by Willard R. Trask. World Perspectives Series, vol. 31. Edited by Ruth Nanda Anshen. New York: Harper and Row, 1963.

"Ansturm auch in Deutschland?" *Spiegel Online,* July 7, 2000. <http://www.spiegel.de/kultur/literatur/0,1518,84071,00.html>. Accessed July 31, 2000.

Appleyard, J. A. *Becoming a Reader.* Cambridge: Cambridge University Press, 1990.

Armitstead, Claire. "Wizard, but with a Touch of Tom Brown." *The Guardian,* July 8, 1999. <http://www.guardianunlimited.co.uk>. Accessed August 8, 1999.

Associated Press. "Couple Seeks Harry Potter Ban." *Portland Oregonian,* January 27, 2000. Dow-Jones Interactive. Stanley Library of Ferrum College, Ferrum, Va. <http://nrstg2s.djnr.com>. Accessed June 10, 2001.

Associated Press. "Harry Potter Banned." September 26, 2000. Dow-Jones Interactive. Stanley Library of Ferrum College, Ferrum, Va. <http://nrstg2s.djnr.com>. Accessed June 10, 2001.

Attebery, Brian. *Strategies of Fantasy.* Bloomington: Indiana University Press, 1992.

Austin, Bruce. *Immediate Seating: A Look at Movie Audiences.* Belmont, Calif.: Wadsworth, 1983.

———. "Researching Film and Television Audiences." In *In the Eye of the Beholder: Critical Perspectives in Popular Film and Television,* edited by Gary R. Edgerton, Michael T. Marsden, and Jack Nachbar, 85–96. Bowling Green, Ohio: Bowling Green State University Popular Press, 1997.

Bacon-Smith, Camille. *Enterprising Women: Television Fandom and the Creation of Popular Myth.* Philadelphia: University of Pennsylvania Press, 1992.

Barlow, Dudley. "AAUW Gender Equity Research: Scholarship or Partisanship?" *School Digest* 64 (March 1999): 46–50.

Baumrind, Diana. "Sex Differences in Moral Reasoning: Response to Walker's Conclusion That There Are None." *Child Development* 57 (1986): 511–21.

Baym, Nancy K. "Talking about Soaps: Communicative Practices in a Computer-Mediated Fan Culture." In *Theorizing Fandom: Fans, Subculture and Identity,* edited by Cheryl Harris and Alison Alexander, 111–29. Cresskill, N.J.: Hampton Press, 1998.

Bedford, Martha. Letter to the Editor. *New York Times,* July 11, 2000, A30.

Beech, Linda Ward. *Scholastic Literature Guide: Harry Potter and the Chamber of Secrets by J. K. Rowling.* New York: Scholastic, 2000.

———. *Scholastic Literature Guide: Harry Potter and the Goblet of Fire by J. K. Rowling.* New York: Scholastic, 2000.

———. *Scholastic Literature Guide: Harry Potter and the Prisoner of Azkaban by J. K. Rowling.* New York: Scholastic, 2000.

———. *Scholastic Literature Guide: Harry Potter and the Sorcerer's Stone by J. K. Rowling.* New York: Scholastic, 2000.

Behind the Magic of Harry Potter. Host: Katie Couric. NBC. November 11, 2001.

Behr, Andrea. "Harry Casts His Spell Everywhere." *San Francisco Chronicle,* July 2, 2000, 28.

Belenky, Mary Field et al. *Women's Ways of Knowing: The Development of Self, Voice, and Mind.* New York: HarperCollins, 1986.

Belsey, Catherine. "Constructing the Subject: Deconstructing the Text." In *Feminist Literary Criticism and Social Change,* edited by J. Newton and D. Rosenfelt. New York: Routledge, 1986.

Berendt, Thomas J. *Child Development.* Fort Worth, Texas: Harcourt Brace Jovanovich, 1991.

Berger, Kathleen Stassen. *The Developing Person Through the Life Span.* 2d ed. New York: Worth, 1988.

Best, Michael. "Shakespeare's 'The Winter's Tale.'" *Internet Shakespeare Editions.* February 6, 2000. <http://castle.uvic.ca/shakespeare/Annex/DraftTxt/WT/>. Accessed February 8, 2002.

"Bestsellers: Hardcover Fiction." *New York Times Book Review,* February 14, 1999. <http://www.nytimes.com/books/98/12/27/bsp/besthardfiction.html>. Accessed December 6, 1999.

"Bestsellers: Hardcover Fiction." *New York Times Book Review,* December 27, 1998. <http://www.nytimes.com/books/99/02/14/bsp/besthardfiction.html>. Accessed December 6, 1999.

Bettelheim, Bruno. *The Uses of Enchantment: The Meaning and Importance of Fairy Tales.* 1975. New York: Vintage, 1989.

Blair, Neil. E-mail to Lana A. Whited. March 6, 2002.

Bloch, Ernst. *The Utopian Function of Art and Literature.* Translated by Jack Zipes and Frank Mecklenberg. Cambridge, Mass.: MIT Press, 1988.

Bloom, Harold. "Can 35 Million Book Buyers Be Wrong? Yes." *Wall Street Journal,* July 11, 2000, A26.

Bloor, Edward. *Tangerine.* 1997. New York: Scholastic, 1998.

Bonisteel, Steven. "WIPO Rules in Harry Potter Case." *WashTech,* December 22, 2000. <http://www.washtech.com/news/regulation/6181-1.html>. Accessed February 12, 2001.

"Books: Best of 2001." *Time,* December 24, 2001, 85.

Bronner, Simon. *American Children's Folklore.* Little Rock, Ark.: August House, 1988.

Brontë, Charlotte. *Jane Eyre.* 1842. New York: Penguin, 1985.

Brown, Lynn Mikle, and Carol Gilligan. *Meeting at the Crossroads: Women's Psychology and Girls' Development.* Cambridge, Mass.: Harvard University Press, 1992.

Brown, Mary E., ed. *Television and Women's Culture: The Politics of the Popular.* Beverly Hills, Calif.: Sage, 1990.

Bruce, Iain. "Wizard Lives up to Hype." *Sunday Herald,* July 9, 2000, 3.

Brumberg, Joan Jacobs. *The Body Project: An Intimate History of American Girls.* New York: Random House, 1997.

———. "When Girls Talk." *Chronicle of Higher Education,* November 24, 2000, B7-B10.

Bruno, Pierre. "Moldus, Poufsouffles et Stéréotypes." *Libération.com.* February 2, 2001. <http://www.liberation.fr/quotidien/debats/janvier01/20010120a.html>.

Brunvand, Jan Harold. *The Study of American Folklore.* New York: W. W. Norton, 1986.

Buchanan, Ben. *My Year with Harry Potter: How I Discovered My Own Magical World.* New York: Lantern Books, 2001.

Buck, William. "Introduction." *Mahabharata,* February 8, 2002. <http://www.geocities.com/Tokyo/Bridge/1771/Desh/Mb/mb.html>.

Bulfinch, Thomas. *Bulfinch's Mythology.* New York: Gramercy, 1979.

Cagle, Darryl. "Darryl Cagle's Professional Cartoonist Index." *Slate,* February 1, 2002. <http://www.cagle.slate.msn.com/news/harrypotter/main.asp>.

Campbell, Joseph. *The Hero with a Thousand Faces.* New York: Pantheon, 1949.

———. *The Hero with a Thousand Faces,* 2d ed. Bollingen Series, no. 17. Princeton: Princeton University Press, 1968.

———. *The Power of Myth.* New York: Doubleday, 1988.

Campbell, Kim. "The Whole World Is Wild about Harry." *Christian Science Monitor,* July 6, 2000, 1.

Carpenter, Humphrey, and Mari Prichard. *The Oxford Companion to Children's Literature.* Oxford, U.K.: Oxford University Press, 1985.

Cart, Michael. *From Romance to Realism: Fifty Years of Growth and Change in Young Adult Literature.* New York: HarperCollins, 1996.

Casey, Kevin R. "Case Summary: Perseverance Pays?" *Muggles.com,* February 21, 2001. <http://www.muggles.com>. Accessed March 16, 2002.

Caughey, Bruce H. Letter to the Editor. *Denver Post,* November 19, 1999, final edition. Dow-Jones Interactive. Stanley Library of Ferrum College, Ferrum, Va. <http://nrstg2s.djnr.com>. Accessed June 10, 2001.

Chaudhuri, Sukanta. "Harry Potter and the Transfiguration of Language." *New Straits Times* (Malaysia), August 9, 2000, Literature and Books, 5.

Churchill, Winston Spencer. Speech before the British House of Commons, June 18, 1940. Quoted in John Bartlett, *Familiar Quotations,* edited by Emily Morison Beck, 14th ed.

Clark, Laura. "Potter Patter Is Children's New Lingo." *Daily Telegraph* (Sydney), October 13, 2001, 23.

Clifford, Matthew. "Harry Potter Ban." Letter to the Editor. *The Times* (London), April 4, 2000. Dow-Jones Interactive. Stanley Library of Ferrum College, Ferrum, Va. <http://nrstg2s.djnr.com>. Accessed June 10, 2001.

Clute, John. "Grail, Groundhog, God Game: or, Doing Fantasy." *Journal of the Fantastic in the Arts* 10, no. 4 (2000): 330–37.

Clute, John, and John Grant, eds. *The Encyclopedia of Fantasy.* London: Orbit, 1997.

Cohen, Jesse. "When Harry Met Maggie." *Slate,* November 16, 2001. <http://www.slate.com>.

Cohen, Whitaker E. "Hands Off Harry!" Letter to the editor. *New Yorker,* October 18 and 25, 1999, 16.

Colbert, David. *The Magical Worlds of Harry Potter.* Wrightsville Beach, N.C.: Lumina Press, 2001.

Colby, A., and Lawrence Kohlberg. *Theoretical Foundations and Research Validation. Standard Issue Scoring Manual.* Cambridge, U.K.: Cambridge University Press, 1987.

Coleridge, Samuel Taylor, and William Wordsworth. *Biographia Literaria.* In *The Longman Anthology of British Literature.* New York: Addison-Wesley, 1999. Vol. 2.

Collins, Gail. "Moby Dick on a Broom." *New York Times,* July 7, 2000, A19.

———. "An Ode to July." *New York Times,* July 11, 2000, A31.

———. "Rudy's Identity Crisis." *New York Times,* April 14, 2000, A31.

———. "What Hillary Said." *New York Times,* July 18, 2000, A25.

Copeland, Libby. "Sew-cery: Young Fans Conjure Some Wizardly Costumes." *Washington Post,* October 20, 1999, Style.

Corliss, Richard. "Why 'Harry Potter' Did a Harry Houdini." *Time,* July 21, 2000. *CNN.com Book News.* <http://www.cnn.com/2000/books/news/07/21/potter7_21.a.tm/>. Accessed November 3, 2000.

"Cover-Wahl im Internet." *Spiegel Online,* August 10, 2000. <http://www.spiegel.de/druckversion/0,1588,88499,00.html>. Accessed September 11, 2000.

Cowell, Alan. "Harry Potter Frenzy Continues." *New York Times,* July 8, 2000. <http://www.nytimes.com>.

Crago, Hugh. "Can Stories Heal?" In *Understanding Children's Literature,* edited by Peter Hunt, 163–73. London: Routledge, 1999.

Cross, Gillian. *The Demon Headmaster.* Oxford, U.K.: Oxford University Press, 1982.

Dahl, Roald. *James and the Giant Peach*. London: Allen and Unwin, 1967.

"Darryl Cagle's Professional Cartoonist Index." *Slate* <http://www.cagle.slate.msn.com/news/harrypotter/main.asp.> Accessed February 1, 2002.

Davis, Cath Filmer. "What Is a Who and What Does It Do? Identity in Lloyd Alexander's Prydain Series." In *The Fantastic Self: Essays on the Subject of the Self*, edited by Janeen Webb and Andrew Enstice, 152–58. North Perth, W. Australia: Eidolon Publications, 1999.

De Beauvoir, Simone. *The Second Sex*. New York: Knopf, 1993.

"Demo von 'Snape explodiert.'" February 1, 2002. <http://www.hp-fc.de/anim_gif/snapeexp.swf>.

Dening, Penelope. "Wiz Kid." *Irish Times on the Web*, September 12, 1998. <http://www.irish-times.com/irish-times/paper/19980912/fea27.html>. Accessed March 8, 1999.

Denn, Rebeken. "'Goblet' Darker, but Still Potterific." *Denver Post*, July 9, 2000, A4.

Devereaux, Elizabeth, et al. "Flying Starts." *Publishers Weekly.com*, December 21, 1998. <http://www.publishersweekly.com/articles/19981221_70662.asp>. Accessed June 8, 2001.

Dickens, Charles. *David Copperfield*. 1850. Oxford, U.K.: Oxford University Press, 1994.

"Do You Ever Get the Feeling the HP Books Are Sexist?" Web forum. *The Un-official Harry Potter Fan Club Web Site*. September 26–October 16, 2000.

Donahue, Deirdre. "Some Want Harry to Vanish till Kids Are Older." *USA Today*, June 15, 2000, D1.

Doniger, Wendy. "Can You Spot the Source?" *London Review of Books*, February 17, 2000, 26–27.

Doolittle, Hilda (H. D.). *HERmione*. New York: New Directions, 1981.

Dowd, Maureen. "Dare Speak His Name." *New York Times*, October 22, 2000, 15.

Dresang, Eliza T. *Radical Change: Books for Youth in a Digital Age*. New York: H. W. Wilson, 1999.

Duffy, Matt. "Alleged Harry Potter Fraud on eBay." *Auction Watch Daily*, April 9, 2001. <http://www.auctionwatch.com/awdaily/dailynews/april01/1-040901.html>.

Dundes, Alan. "The Dead Baby Joke Cycle." *Western Folklore* 38 (July 1979): 145–57.

Eddings, David. *The Seeress of Kell*. London: Bantam, 1991.

"Enchanting Chapters in the Life of a 'Modern-Day C. S. Lewis.'" *Sunday Times* (London), August 9, 1998. <http://www.suntimes.co.za/1998/08/09/arts/arts03.htm>. Accessed March 8, 1999.

Erikson, Erik H. *Childhood and Society.* 2d ed. New York: Norton, 1963.

Evans, Ivor H., ed. *Brewer's Dictionary of Phrase and Fable.* Centenary ed. New York: Harper and Row, 1981.

Fernandez, Susana. "Re: Respuesta." E-mail to Nancy K. Jentsch. October 2, 2000.

———. "Re: Una Respuesta Más." E-mail to Nancy K. Jentsch. September 28, 2000.

Fine, Gary Alan. *Shared Fantasy: Role-Playing Games as Social Worlds.* Chicago: University of Chicago Press, 1983.

Fisher, Bob. *Bulfinch's Mythology: The Age of Fable.* 1996–2000. February 8, 2002. <http://www.bulfinch.org/>.

Fiske, John. *Understanding the Popular.* London: Unwin Hyman Press, 1989.

"*Forbes* Celebrity 100." *Forbes.com,* March 9, 2001. <http://www.forbes.com/lists/results.ihtml?passListid=53>.

Fort, Matthew. "Harry's Game." *The Guardian Weekend,* June 26, 1999, 34–36.

Fraser, Lindsey. *Conversations with J. K. Rowling.* New York: Scholastic, 2001. (U.S. version of *Telling Tales.*)

———. *Telling Tales: An Interview with J. K. Rowling.* London: Mammoth, 2000.

Freud, Sigmund. *The Basic Writings of Sigmund Freud.* Translated and edited by A. A. Brill. New York: Modern Library–Random House, 1938.

———. *The Fantastic: A Structural Approach to a Literary Genre.* Edited by Tzvetan Todorov. Translated by Richard Howard. Cleveland: Case Western Reserve University, 1973.

Friedman, Thomas L. "Lebanon and the Goblet of Fire." *New York Times,* July 11, 2000, A31.

Fuller, Katherine H. "*Motion Picture Story Magazine* and the Gendered Construction of the Movie Fan." In *In the Eye of the Beholder: Critical Perspectives in Popular Film and Television,* edited by Gary R. Edgerton, Michael T. Marsden, and Jack Nachbar, 97–112. Bowling Green, Ohio: Bowling Green State University Popular Press, 1997.

Fumeron, Christian. "Re: Le 4eme Tome d'Harry Potter." E-mail to Nancy K. Jentsch. October 6, 2000.

Furlong, Monica. *Wise Child.* Gollancz, 1987. London: Transworld, 1990.

Gaffoglio, Loreley. "Entrevista a Joanne Kathleen Rowling por 'La Revista.'" *Diario La Nación,* May 14, 2000. <http://www.emece.com.ar/Shop/entrepott.htm>. Accessed August 30, 2000.

Gathorne-Hardy, Jonathan. *The Old School Tie: The Phenomenon of the English Public School.* New York: Viking Press, 1977.

"German Potter Fans Snap Up English Translation." September 22, 2000. <http://uk.news.yahoo.com/000909/4/aiq10.html>.

Gershwin, Ira. "Let's Call the Whole Thing Off." Music by George Gershwin. 1937.

Gibson, Michelle. Personal interview by Rebecca Sutherland Borah. October 17, 2000.

Gilligan, Carol. *In a Different Voice: Psychological Theory and Women's Development.* Cambridge, Mass.: Harvard University Press, 1982.

Gish, Kimbra Wilder. "Hunting Down Harry Potter: An Exploration of Religious Concerns about Children's Literature." *Horn Book,* May/June 2000, 262–71.

Gleick, Peter H. "Harry Potter, Minus a Certain Flavour." *New York Times,* July 10, 2000, A25.

Gosling, Ju. "The History of Girls' School Stories." *The Virtual World of Girls,* 1998. <http://users.netmatters.co.uk/ju90/his.htm>. Accessed May 15, 2001.

Grant, John. "Gulliver Unravels: Generic Fantasy and the Loss of Subversion." *Extrapolation* 41, no. 1 (2000): 21–27.

Gray, Paul. "Wild about Harry: The Exploits of a Young Wizard Have Enchanted Kids." *Time,* September 20, 1999, 66+.

Greene, Thomas. *The Descent from Heaven: A Study in Epic Continuity.* New Haven, Conn.: Yale University Press, 1963.

Grinder, Robert E. *Adolescence.* 2d ed. New York: Wiley, 1978.

Grunier, Stephanie, and John Lippman. "Warner Bros. Claims Harry Potter Sites." *Wall Street Journal Interactive,* December 21, 2000. <http://www.zdnet.com/zdnn/stories/news/0,4586,2667273,00.html>. Accessed January 10, 2001.

Guest, Barbara. *Herself Defined: The Poet H. D. and Her World.* Garden City, N.Y: Doubleday, 1984.

Halliday, M. A .K. *Language as a Social Semiotic: The Social Interpretation of Language and Meaning.* London: Edward Arnold, 1978.

Hamilton, Edith. *Mythology: Timeless Tales of Gods and Heroes.* Boston: Mentor/Little, Brown, 1942.

Harding, D. W. "Psychological Processes in the Reading of Fiction." In *The Cool Web: The Pattern of Children's Reading,* edited by Margaret Meek, Aidan Warlow, and Griselda Barton, 58–72. London: Bodley Head, 1977. Reprint from *British Journal of Aesthetics* 2, no. 2 (1962).

Harrington-Lueker, Donna. " 'Harry Potter' Lacks for True Heroines." *USA Today,* July 11, 2000, 17A.

"Harry and the Web Wars." Editorial. *Boston Globe,* March 25, 2001, E6. Lexis-Nexis Academic Universe. Lexis-Nexis. <http://www.lexis-nexis.com>. Accessed March 7, 2002.

"Harry Potter a Kámen mudrc." *Dnes,* July 15, 2000, Prázdniny, 7.

Harry Potter and the Sorcerer's Stone, Warner Brothers. October 29, 2000. <http://movies.warnerbros.com/ harrypotter/index.html>.

" 'Harry Potter': Arthur Levine." Transcript of online chat. *USA Today,* June 28, 2000. <http://www.usatoday.com/community/chat/0628levine.htm>. Accessed July 6, 2000.

"Harry Potter für Alle." *Spiegel Online,* September 5, 2000. <http://www.spiegel.de/kultur/literatur/0,1518,91975,00.html>. Accessed September 11, 2000.

"Harry Potter zaubert auch in China." *Spiegel Online,* September 11, 2000. <http://www.spiegel.de/kultur/literatur/0,1518,92832,00.html>. Accessed September 11, 2000.

Hattenstone, Simon. "Harry, Jesse and Me." *The Guardian,* July 8, 2000, Weekend, 32+. <http://www.guardianunlimited.co.uk>.

Hein, Rudolf. "Harry Potter Glossary." *Rudi Hein's Language Page.* September 3, 1997. <http://www.rudihein.de/>. Accessed February 8, 2002.

Hendricks, Rhoda A., ed. *Classical Gods and Heroes: Myths as Told by the Ancient Authors.* New York: Morrow, 1972.

Hensher, Philip. "Harry Potter, Give Me a Break." *The Independent,* January 25, 2000, 1.

"Hermione." *Encyclopedia Mythica.* www.pantheon.org/mythica/articles/h/hermione.html.

Hernandez, H. *A Brief Biography of H. D.* February 8, 2002. <http://www.imagists.org/hd/bio.html>.

Hogarth, Grace Allen. "Transatlantic Editing." *Horn Book,* October 1965, 520–23.

Holden, Anthony. "Why Harry Potter Doesn't Cast a Spell over Me." *The Observer,* June 25, 2000. <http://www.observer.co.uk/review/story/0,6903,335923,00.html>. Accessed June 26, 2000.

———. "Why Harry Potter Doesn't Cast a Spell over Me." *The Guardian,* June 25, 2000. <http://www.guardianunlimited.co.uk>.

Hollindale, Peter. *Signs of Childness in Children's Literature.* Stroud: Thimble Press, 1997.

Hornby, Nick. *Fever Pitch.* London: Gollanz, 1992.

Horowitz, Anthony. *Groosham Grange.* London: Walker Books, 1995.

Hubert, Jennifer. "Boy Meets Book: Best Boy Reads." *Reading Rants,* October 13, 2000. <http://tln.lib/mi.us/~amutch/jen/boys.htm>.

Hughes, Thomas. *Tom Brown's School Days*. 6th English ed. New York: John Wurtele Lovell, n.d.

Ibbotson, Eva. *The Secret of Platform 13*. London: Pan Macmillan, 1994.

Inge, Thomas M. *Comics as Culture*. Jackson: University Press of Mississippi, 1990.

"International Release Dates." *The Official Harry Potter Website*, February 8, 2002. <http://www.jkrowling.com>.

Ironside, Virginia. *Vampire Master of Burlap Hall*. 1987. London: Walker Books, 1997.

Ivanits, Linda. *Russian Folk Belief*. Armonk, N.Y.: M. E. Sharpe, Inc., 1989.

Iyer, Pico. "The Playing Fields of Hogwarts." *New York Times Book Review*, October 10, 1999, 39.

Jacobs, Alan. "Harry Potter's Magic." *First Things* 99 (January 2000): 21 pars. <http://www.firstthings.com/ftissues/ft0001/reviews/jacobs.html>. Accessed October 1, 2000.

Jenkins, Henry. *Textual Poachers: Television Fans and Participatory Culture*. New York: Routledge, 1992.

Jentsch, Nancy K. "German-English Translation: Theoretical and Practical Aspects." Master's thesis, University of Cincinnati, 1982.

Jerome, Helen M. "Welcome Back, Potter." *Book*, May/June 2000, 40–45.

Johnson, Sarah. "First Review: New Harry Potter 'A Cracker.'" *The Times*, July 8, 2000.

———. "So Quiet, It Was Magic." *The Times*, July 10, 2000.

Johnstone, Anne. "Happy Ending, and That's for Beginners." *The Herald* (Glasgow), June 24, 1997, 15.

———. "A Kind of Magic." *The Herald Saturday Magazine* (Glasgow), July 8, 2000, 8–12.

Jones, Diana Wynne. *Charmed Life*. 1977. London: HarperCollins, 2000.

———. *The Lives of Christopher Chant*. 1988. London: HarperCollins, 2000.

———. *Witch Week*. 1982. London: HarperCollins, 2000.

Jones, Malcolm. "The Return of Harry Potter." *Newsweek*, July 10, 2000, 57.

———. "Why Harry's Hot." *Newsweek*, July 17, 2000, 55.

Jung, Carl Gustav. *The Basic Writings of C. G. Jung*. Edited by Violet Staub de Laszlo. New York: Modern Library–Random House, 1959.

———. *Psychology of the Unconscious*. Translated by Beatrice M. Hinkle. New York: Dodd, Mead, 1916.

Kantor, Jodi, and Judith Shulevitz. "The King Lear of the Kid's Section." *Slate*, July 10–12, 2000. <http://www.slate.com>.

Kaul, Donald. "Take That, You Little Wizard." *Kansas City Star,* November 6, 1999. Dow-Jones Interactive. Stanley Library of Ferrum College, Ferrum, Va. <http://nrstg2s.djnr.com>. Accessed June 10, 2001.

Kemp, Gene. *The Turbulent Term of Tyke Tiler.* 1977. Harmondsworth: Penguin, 1979.

Kemp, Tom. "Wonderful—But It's a Whopper." *The Daily Telegraph,* July 10, 2000, 14.

Kidd, Kenneth. "Boyology in the Twentieth Century." *Children's Literature* 28 (2000): 44–72.

Kilday, Gregg. "Potter Training." *Premiere,* August 2000, 47–48.

King, Martin Luther, Jr. "Letter from Birmingham Jail." April 16, 1963. *Nobel Prize Winners 2000–1901, The Nobel Prize Internet Archive,* <http://www.almaz.com/nobel/peace/mlk-jail.htm>. Accessed June 26, 2001.

King, Stephen. "Wild about Harry." Review of *Harry Potter and the Goblet of Fire,* by J. K. Rowling. *New York Times Book Review,* July 23, 2000, 13–14.

Kipen, David. "The Trouble with Harry." *San Francisco Chronicle,* July 10, 2000, D1.

Kipling, Rudyard. *Stalky and Co.* London: Macmillan, 1899.

Kirkpatrick, Robert J. *The Encyclopaedia of Boys' School Stories.* Aldershot: Ashgate, 2000.

Knapp, Mary, and Herbert Knapp. *One Potato, Two Potato.* New York: W. W. Norton, 1976.

Knight, India. "The Trouble with Harry." *Sunday Times* (London), April 2, 2000. Dow-Jones Interactive. Stanley Library of Ferrum College, Ferrum, Va. <http://nrstg2s.djnr.com>. Accessed June 10, 2001.

Kohlberg, Lawrence. *The Philosophy of Moral Development: Moral Stages and the Idea of Justice. Essays on Moral Development.* Vol. 1. San Francisco: Harper and Row, 1981.

Kohlberg, Lawrence. *The Psychology of Moral Development: The Nature and Validity of Moral Stages. Essays on Moral Development.* Vol. 2. San Francisco: Harper and Row, 1984.

Kornbluth, Jesse. "@ Harry Potter Online and in Print." *Time Digital Magazine,* August 2, 2000. <http://www.time.com/time/digital/magazine/articles/0,4753,50909-2,00.html>. Accessed November 24, 2000.

Kronzek, Allan Zola, and Elizabeth Kronzek. *The Sorcerer's Companion: A Guide to the Magical World of Harry Potter.* New York: Broadway Books, 2001.

Kuitenbrouwer, Peter and Shannon Black. "School Board Puts Limits on

Harry Potter Books Due to 'Magic': Ontario Board Not Banning Series, but Requiring Parental Consent for Class Use." *National Post* (Canada), National edition. Dow-Jones Interactive. Stanley Library of Ferrum College, Ferrum, Va. <http://nrstg2s.djnr.com>. Accessed June 10, 2001.

"La magie de Harry Potter." *L'Express.fr,* July 13, 2000. <http://www.lexpress.fr/express/for . . . rs/ Dossier/harrypotter/dossier.asp>. Accessed September 28, 2000.

Lacoss, Jann. "Contemporary Russian Childlore." Ph.D. diss., University of Virginia, 1997.

Langley, Lis. "Charmed, I'm Sure." *Orlando Weekly* (Florida), February 3, 2000. <http://www.orlandoweekly.com/juice/index.asp?j=2294>. Accessed February 8, 2002.

Lawson, Mark. "Rowling Survives the Hype." *The Guardian,* July 8, 2000. <http://www.guardianunlimited.co.uk>.

Lawver, Heather, and Alastair Alexander, *Defense against the Dark Arts.* March 7, 2002. <http://www.dprophet.com/dada.>

Le Guin, Ursula K. *Earthsea Revisioned.* Cambridge, U.K.: Green Bay Publications, 1993.

———. *The Farthest Shore.* 1973. Harmondsworth, U.K.: Penguin, 1974.

———. *The Language of the Night.* New York: HarperCollins, 1989.

———. *Tales of Earthsea.* New York: Harcourt, 2001.

———. *Tehanu: The Last Book of Earthsea.* New York: Atheneum, 1990.

———. *The Tombs of Atuan.* 1972. Harmondsworth, U.K.: Penguin, 1974.

———. *The Tombs of Atuan.* New York: Atheneum, 1970.

———. *A Wizard of Earthsea.* New York: Parnassus, 1968.

———. *The Wizard of Earthsea.* 1968. Harmondsworth, U.K.: Penguin, 1971.

Lemann, Nicholas. "The Battle over Boys." *New Yorker,* July 10, 2000, 79–83.

L'Engle, Madeline. *A Swiftly Tilting Planet.* New York: Farrar, Straus, 1978.

———. *A Wind in the Door.* New York: Farrar, Straus, 1973.

———. *A Wrinkle in Time.* New York: Farrar, Straus, 1962.

"Letters." *Atlantic Monthly,* August 2000, 6–13. <http://www.theatlantic.com/issues/2000/08/letters.htm>. Accessed February 8, 2002.

Levine, Arthur A., with Doreen Carvajal. "Why I Paid So Much." *New York Times,* October 13, 1999, C14.

Lewis, C. S. *The Lion, the Witch, and the Wardrobe.* New York: Macmillan, 1950.

———. *The Magician's Nephew.* London: Bodley Head, 1955.

Lipson, Eden Ross. "Book's Quirky Hero and Fantasy Win the Young." *New York Times,* July 12, 1999. <http://www.nytimes.com/library/books/071299potter-sales.html>. Accessed October 25, 2000.

Littlejohn, Bel. "Harry Potter, What of Him?" *The Guardian* (Manchester, U.K.), June 30, 2000. <http://www.guardianunlimited.co.uk>.

Lively, Penelope. "Harry's in Robust Form, Although I'm Left Bugg-Eyed." *The Independent,* July 13, 2000, 5.

"A Long Hot Summer: How Violence Has Swept the North." *The Observer* (London), July 8, 2001. <http://www.guardian.co.uk>.

Lucking, David. " 'The Price of One Fair Word': Negotiating Names in Coriolanus." *Early Modern Literary Studies* 2, no. 1 (1996): 1–22. <http://purl.oclc.org/emls/02–1/luckshak.html>. Accessed February 8, 2002.

Lurie, Alison. "Not for Muggles." *New York Review of Books,* December 16, 1999. <http://www.nybooks.com/nyrev/WWWarchdisplay.cgi?19991216006R>.

Lyall, Sarah. "Why Are You Here?: Britain's Race Problem" *New York Times,* June 3, 2001, 1, 4.

Mabillard, Amanda. "Shakespeare's Sources: The Winter's Tale." *Shakespeare Online,* February 8, 2002. <http://www.shakespeare-online.com>.

McCrum, Robert. "Plot, Plot, Plot That's Worth the Weight." *The Guardian* (Manchester, U.K.), July 9, 2000. <http://www.guardianunlimited.co.uk>.

MacDonald, Andrea. "Uncertain Utopia: Science Fiction Media Fandom and Computer-Mediated Communication." In *Theorizing Fandom: Fans, Subculture and Identity,* edited by Cheryl Harris and Alison Alexander, 131–52. Cresskill, N.J.: Hampton Press, 1998.

McGavran, James Holt, ed. *Romanticism and Children's Literature in Nineteenth-Century England.* Athens: University of Georgia Press, 1991.

McGillis, Roderick. *The Nimble Reader: Literary Theory and Children's Literature.* New York: Twayne, 1996.

McGrath, Barbara. *Newfoundland's Genealogical and Historical Data.* June 2000. <http://www.chebucto.ns.ca/Heritage/NGB/Hr_Main/topsail.html#GRANGER>. Accessed February 8, 2002.

McKinley, Robin. *The Blue Sword.* New York: Morrow, 1983.

McLean, Gareth. "Hogwarts and All." *The Guardian* (Manchester), October 19, 2001. <http://film.guardian.co.uk/harrypotter/news/0,10608,577192,00.html>.

Maguire, Gregory. "Lord of the Golden Snitch." Review of *Harry Potter and the Prisoner of Azkaban*, by J. K. Rowling. *New York Times Book Review*, September 5, 1999, 12. <http://www.nytimes.com/books/yr/mo/day/reviews/990905.05maguire.html>. Accessed September 7, 1999.

"Major Resigns and Labour Reforms." *This Sceptred Isle*. BBC History. December 14, 2001. <http://www.bbc.co.uk/radio4/sceptred_isle/>.

Makinen, Merja. E-mail to Farah Mendlesohn. October 26, 2002.

Mandelbaum, Allen, and Marialuisa De Romans. *The Odyssey of Homer: A New Verse Translation*. Berkeley: University of California Press, 1990.

Marlowe, Jonathan. "Harry Potter's Magic Less Dangerous than Ours." *Charlotte Observer*, August 21, 2000, 9A.

Mendelsohn, Daniel. "Troubled Harry." *New York Magazine*, July 24, 2000. *Newyorkmetro.com*. <http://www.nymag.com/page.cfm?page id=3533>. Accessed March 11, 2002.

Messe, Elizabeth A. *Crossing the Double-Cross: The Practice of Feminist Criticism*. Chapel Hill: University of North Carolina Press, 1986.

Miéville, China. "The Conspiracy of Architecture: Notes on a Modern Anxiety." *Historical Materialism* 2 (1998): 13.

———. E-mail to Farah Mendelsohn. October 22, 2000.

Millett, Kate. *Sexual Politics*. London: Sphere Books, 1971.

Mitchell, Sally. *The New Girl*. New York: Columbia University Press, 1995.

Modleski, Tania. *Loving with a Vengeance: Mass-Produced Fantasies for Women*. 2d ed. New York: Routledge, 1990.

Moorcock, Michael. *Wizardry and Wild Romance: A Study of Epic Fantasy*. London: Gollancz, 1987.

Moore, Sharon, ed. *Harry Potter, You're the Best: A Tribute from Fans the World Over*. New York: St. Martin's–Griffin, 2001.

———. *We Love Harry Potter!* New York: St. Martin's–Griffin, 1999.

"Move On from Thatcher." *UK Politics*. BBC News. September 6, 2001. <http://www.bbc.co.uk/hi/english/uk_politics/newsid_1528000/1528372.stm>.

"Muggle Court to Decide: Who Conjured the Boy Wizard?" *Calgary Herald*," June 18, 2002. Lexis-Nexis Academic Universe, Lexis-Nexis. Stanley Library of Ferrum College, September 7, 2002. <http://www.lexis-nexis.com/universe/>.

Murphy, Jill. *Adventures of the Worst Witch*. St. Helens: Book People, 1998. (First published in three volumes: *The Worst Witch*, 1974; *The Worst Witch Strikes Again*, 1980; *A Bad Spell for the Worst Witch*, 1982).

Myers, Walter Dean. *Monster*. New York: HarperCollins, 1999.

Nash, Jesse. "Using Harry Potter in the Adult ESL Classroom." *TESOL Matters,* February/March 2000. *TESOL On-Line.* <http://www.tesol. org/isaffil/intsec/columns/200002-ae.html>. Accessed December 5, 2000.

Nazarro, Joe. "Scripting Spells." *Starlog: Fantasy Worlds,* February 2002, 20–25.

Nel, Philip. E-mail to Lana A. Whited. March 7, 2002.

———. *J. K. Rowling's Harry Potter Novels: A Reader's Guide.* New York: Continuum International Publishing Group, 2001.

Nesbit, E. *The Story of the Treasure Seekers.* 1899. London: Penguin, 1994.

"1999 Women of the Year." *Glamour,* December 1999, 168.

Nodelman, Perry. "Some Presumptuous Generalizations about Fantasy." In *Only Connect.* 3d ed., edited by Sheila Egoff et al., 175–78. Oxford: Oxford University Press, 1996.

Oliande, Sylvia L. "Harry Potter Books OK'd for Simi Schools." *Los Angeles Daily News,* November 18, 1999. Dow-Jones Interactive. Stanley Library of Ferrum College, Ferrum, Va. <http://nrstg2s. djnr.com>. Accessed June 10, 2001.

Pearson, Roberta, and William Uricchio, eds. *The Many Lives of Batman: Critical Approaches to a Superhero and His Media.* New York: Routledge, 1991.

Pennington, John. "From Elfland to Hogwarts, or the Aesthetic Trouble with Harry Potter." *The Lion and the Unicorn* 26 (January 2002): 78–97. http://muse.jhu.edu/journals/lion_and_the_unicorn/.

Pierce, Tamora. "Fantasy: Why Kids Read It, Why Kids Need It." 1993. Reprinted in *Only Connect,* 3d ed., edited by Sheila Egoff et al., 179–83. Oxford: Oxford University Press, 1996.

Pipher, Mary. *Reviving Ophelia: Saving the Selves of Adolescent Girls.* New York: Putnam, 1994.

Plaza, Jose María. "El Éxito de la Magia Cotidiana." *El Mundo,* June 17, 2000. <http://www.el-mundo.es/2000/06/17/opinion/17N0038. html>. Accessed September 21, 2000.

Politics and Prose Bookstore. Washington, D.C. E-mail to subscribers. October 18, 1999.

Pollock, William. *Real Boys.* New York: Random House, 1998.

Price, Tom. Letter to the Editor. *Columbian,* November 11, 1999. Dow-Jones Interactive. Stanley Library of Ferrum College, Ferrum, Va. <http://nrstg2s.djnr.com>. Accessed June 11, 2001.

Pringle, David. *Modern Fantasy: The Hundred Best Novels.* London: Grafton Books, 1988.

Pritzker, Olivia Batker. Letter to the Editor. *New Yorker,* August 21 and 28, 2000, 14.

Propp, Vladimir. *Morphology of the Folktale.* Austin: University of Texas Press, 1968.

Pullman, Philip. *The Golden Compass.* New York: Random House, 2000.

Radosh, Daniel. "Why American Kids Don't Consider Harry Potter an Insufferable Prig." *New Yorker,* September 20, 1999, 54, 56.

Radway, Janice A. *Reading the Romance.* Chapel Hill: University of North Carolina Press, 1984.

Ragland, Lord. "The Hero: A Study in Tradition, Myth, and Drama, Part II." Reprinted in Robert Segal, ed., *In Quest of the Hero* (Princeton, N.J.: Princeton University Press, 1990), 87–175.

Rahn, Suzanne. *Rediscoveries in Children's Literature.* New York: Garland, 1995.

Rank, Otto. *The Myth of the Birth of the Hero.* 1909. Translated by F. Robbins and Smith Ely Jelliffe. Reprinted in Robert Segal, ed., *In Quest of the Hero* (Princeton, N.J.: Princeton University Press, 1990), 1–86.

Reed, John R. *Old School Ties: The Public School in British Literature.* Syracuse, N.Y.: Syracuse University Press, 1964.

Reynolds, Kimberley. *Young People's Reading at the End of the Century.* Roehampton, London: National Centre for Research in Children's Literature, 1996.

Richardson, Alan. "Romanticism and the End of Childhood." In *Literature and the Child,* edited by James Holt McGavran (Iowa City: University of Iowa Press, 1999), 23–43.

Robertson, Andy. "Fictionmags." ListServ posting. July 16, 2000.

Rose, Matthew, and Emily Nelson. "Potter Cognoscenti All Know a Muggle When They See One." *Wall Street Journal,* October 18, 2000, A1, A10. CESNUR. <http://www.cesnur.org/recens/potter_068.htm>. Accessed November 3, 2000.

Rowling, J. K. "Barnes and Noble Chat with J. K. Rowling." October 20, 2000. <http://www.hpnetwork.f2s.com/jkrowling/jkrbnchat.html>.

———. "Chat with J. K. Rowling" Yahoo! October 20, 2000. <http://chat.yahoo.com/c/yahooligans/>. Accessed October 20, 2000.

———. *Fantastic Beasts and Where to Find Them, by Newt Scamander.* New York: Scholastic, 2001.

———. "A Good Scare." *Time,* October 30, 2000, 108.

———. "Harry and Me." *The Times* (London), June 30, 2000. <http://www.the-times.co.uk/onlinespecials/features/harrypotter/story28.html>.

———. *Harry Potter à L'école des Sorciers.* Translated by Jean-François Ménard. Paris: Éditions Gallimard Jeunesse, 1998.

———. *Harry Potter and the Chamber of Secrets.* London: Bloomsbury, 1998.

———. *Harry Potter and the Chamber of Secrets.* New York: Scholastic, 1999.

———. *Harry Potter and the Goblet of Fire.* London: Bloomsbury, 2000.

———. *Harry Potter and the Goblet of Fire.* New York: Scholastic, 2000.

———. *Harry Potter and the Philosopher's Stone.* London: Bloomsbury, 1997.

———. *Harry Potter and the Prisoner of Azkaban.* London: Bloomsbury, 1999.

———. *Harry Potter and the Prisoner of Azkaban.* New York: Scholastic, 1999.

———. *Harry Potter and the Prisoner of Azkaban.* Read by Stephen Fry. Audiocassette. London: Cover to Cover Cassettes, 2000.

———. *Harry Potter and the Sorcerer's Stone.* New York: Scholastic, 1998.

———. *Harry Potter et la Chambre des Secrets.* Translated by Jean-François Ménard. Paris: Éditions Gallimard Jeunesse, 1999.

———. *Harry Potter und der Gefangene von Askaban.* Translated by Klaus Fritz. Hamburg: Carlsen Verlag, 1999.

———. *Harry Potter und der Stein der Weisen.* Translated by Klaus Fritz. Hamburg: Carlsen Verlag, 1998.

———. *Harry Potter y la Piedra Filosofal.* Translated by Alicia Dellepiane. Barcelona: Emecé Editores España, 1999.

———. Interview by Christopher Ludden. *The Connection,* WBRU. October 15, 1999.

———. Interview by Malcolm Jones. "The Return of Harry Potter!" *Newsweek,* July 10, 2000, 56–60.

———. "Live Interview on Scholastic.com, Oct. 16, 2000." Internet chat transcript. October 18, 2000. <http://www.scholastic.com/harrypotter/author/transcript2.htm>.

———. *Quidditch through the Ages, by Kennilworthy Whisp.* New York: Scholastic, 2001.

———. Radio interview. National Public Radio. December 28, 1998.

———. Reading and Question-and-Answer Session at National Press Club. October 20, 1999. *Book-TV,* C-SPAN2. Broadcast November 6, 1999.

———. "The Surprising Success of Harry Potter." Interview by Larry King. *Larry King Live!* Cable News Network. October 20, 2000.

———. "A Talk with J. K. Rowling." *Kansas City Star,* November 13, 2001, E1-E2.

Safire, William. "Besotted with Potter." *New York Times,* January 27, 2000, A27. (Syndicated in many newspapers; reprinted in the *Roanoke Times* as "Adult Fare Harry Potter Is Not.")

Salmon, Edward. "What Girls Read." *Nineteenth Century* 20 (1886): 524.

Savill, Richard. "Harry Potter and the Mystery of J K's Lost Initial." *Daily Telegraph* (London), July 19, 2000, 3.

Schafer, Elizabeth D. *Exploring Harry Potter.* Beacham's Sourcebooks for Teaching Young Adult Fiction. Osprey, Fla.: Beacham Publishing Corp., 2000.

Schoefer, Christine. "Harry Potter's Girl Trouble." *Salon,* January 12, 2000. <http://www.salon.com/books/feature/2000/01/13/potter/index.html>. Accessed May 28, 2001.

Scholastic, Inc. v. Nancy Stouffer. 124 F.Supp.2d 836, 2000 U.S. Dist. LEXIS 17474 (S.D.N.Y. 2000).

———. 2000 U.S. Dist. LEXIS 11516 (S.D.N.Y. 2000).

Scholastic Press Harry Potter Web Site. <http://www.scholastic.com/harrypotter/jkinterview.htm>.

Scott, A. O. "A Dialogue on Harry Potter." *Slate.* <http://slate.msn.com//code/BookClub.asp>.

Searsmith, Kelly. "News from Somewhere: A Case for Romance-Tradition Fantasy's Reformist Poetic." *Journal of the Fantastic in the Arts* 11, no. a (2000): 62–76.

Segal, Robert A. "Introduction: In Quest of the Hero." In Segal, *In Quest of the Hero* (Princeton, N.J.: Princeton University Press, 1990), vii–xli.

Seiter, Ellen. *Sold Separately: Children and Parents in Consumer Culture.* New Brunswick, N.J.: Rutgers University Press, 1993.

Sendak, Maurice. Personal interview by Geraldine DeLuca and Roni Natov. 1977.

———. *Where the Wild Things Are.* New York: Harper, 1963.

Senior, W. A. "One Ring to Rule Them All." *Journal of the Fantastic in the Arts* 11, no. 1 (2000): 5–7.

Sezgin, Hilal. "Alle Menschen werden Muggel." *Frankfurter Rundschau,* July 8, 2000, 22.

Shandler, Sara. *Ophelia Speaks: Adolescent Girls Write about Their Search for Self.* New York: HarperCollins, 1999.

Shapiro, Marc. *J. K. Rowling: The Wizard behind Harry Potter.* New York: St. Martin's Griffin, 2000.

Sherwin, Adam, and Grace Bradberry. "Harry Potter Gets the Hollywood Treatment." *The Times* (London), September 23, 1999, 1.

Shulman, Polly, and A. O. Scott. "Is Harry Potter the New Star Wars?" *Slate,* August 23, 1999. <http://www.slate.com>. Accessed August 26, 1999.

Siegel, Lee. "Harry Potter and the Spirit of the Age: Fear of Not Flying." *New Republic*, November 22, 1999, 40. <http://www.thenewrepublic. com>.

Smith, Sean. *J. K. Rowling: A Biography*. London: Michael O'Mara Books, 2001.

Solomon, Evan. "J. K. Rowling Interview." *Hot Type*. CBC. July 2000. <http://cbc.ca/programs/sites/hottype_rowlingcomplete.html>.

Sommers, Christina Hoff. "The War against Boys." *Atlantic Monthly*, May 2000, 59–74. <http://www.theatlantic.com/issues/2000/05/ sommers.htm>. Accessed February 8, 2000.

———. *The War against Boys*. New York: Simon and Schuster, 2000.

"Spielberg Plans to Put Harry on the Big Screen." *Evening News* (Edinburgh), September 23, 1999, 3+.

Steinberg, Shirley R., and Joe L. Kincheloe, eds. *Kinderculture: The Corporate Construction of Childhood*. Boulder, Colo.: HarperCollins/Westview Press, 1997.

Stephens, John. *Language and Ideology in Children's Fiction*. Harlow: Longman, 1992.

Stouffer, Nancy Kathleen. Telephone interview with Lana A. Whited. March 17, 2002.

"Swiss Whiz Kid Does It Again: Ammann Wins Second Gold in Ski Jump." *Kansas City Star*, February 14, 2002, Games 3.

Tankel, Jonathan David, and Keith Murphy. "Collecting Comic Books: A Study of the Fan and Curatorial Consumption." In *Theorizing Fandom: Fans, Subculture and Identity*, edited by Cheryl Harris and Alison Alexander, 55–68. Cresskill, N.J.: Hampton Press, 1998.

"Thank Heavens for Harry." *Daily Telegraph*, July 11, 2000, 19.

Thurber, James. *The Thirteen Clocks*. New York: Simon and Schuster, 1950.

Todd, Douglas. "The Spiritual World of Harry Potter." *Kansas City Star*, October 6, 2000.

Toelken, Barre. *The Dynamics of Folklore*. Boston: Houghton Mifflin Company, 1979.

Tolkien, J. R. R. *The Hobbit; or There and Back Again*. Boston: Houghton Mifflin, 1966.

———. *The Lord of the Rings*. Boston: Houghton Mifflin, 1954–1956.

Tong, Rosemarie Putnam. *Feminist Thought: A More Comprehensive Introduction*. 2d ed. New York: HarperCollins, 1998.

"Translation of *Harry Potter* Becomes Bestseller in Thailand." *AP Worldstream*, August 31, 2000. <http://search.epnet.com>. Accessed August 31, 2000.

Trites, Roberta Seelinger. *Waking Sleeping Beauty: Feminist Voices in Children's Novels*. Iowa City: University of Iowa Press, 1997.

"The Trouble with Muggles." *Book,* May/June 2000, 43.

"Trubel um des Zauberlehrlings Vierten Streich." *Spiegel Online,* June 28, 2000. <http://www.spiegel.de/kultur/literatur/nf/0,1518,82942,00.html>. Accessed July 31, 2000.

Tucker, Nicholas. "The Rise and Rise of Harry Potter." *Children's Literature in Education* 30, no. 4 (1999): 221–34.

Tulloch, John, and Harvey Jenkins. *Science Fiction Audiences: Watching Doctor Who and Star Trek*. New York: Routledge, 1995.

Turner, Victor. *The Ritual Process*. Ithaca, N.Y.: Cornell University Press, 1989.

Usborne, David, "U.S. Parents Want 'Evil' Harry Potter Banned." *The Independent* (London), October 14, 1999. Dow-Jones Interactive. Stanley Library of Ferrum College, Ferrum, Va. <http://nrstg2s.djnr.com>. Accessed June 10, 2001.

van Gennep, Arnold. *The Rites of Passage*. Chicago: University of Chicago Press, 1960.

Vandergrift, Kay E. *Mosaics of Meaning: Enhancing the Intellectual Life of Young Adults through Story*. Lanham, Mass.: Scarecrow Press, 1996.

Veldman, Meredith. *Fantasy, the Bomb, and the Greening of Britain: Romantic Protest, 1945–1980*. Cambridge, U.K.: Cambridge University Press, 1994.

Vukovic, Danica. "Bonding and Separating of Female Characters in *Women in Love*." November 30, 2001. <http.//web.ukonline.co.uk/rananim/lawrence/women.thml>.

Waggoner, Diana. *The Hills of Faraway: A Guide to Fantasy*. New York: Atheneum, 1978.

Walker, Lawrence. "Sex Differences in the Development of Moral Reasoning: A Rejoinder to Baumrind." *Child Development* 55 (1984): 677–91.

Walter, Natasha. "Wizard Tales of Good and Evil." *The Independent* (London), August 7, 2000, 5.

Walter, Virginia. *Making Up Megaboy*. Illustrated by Katrina Roeckelein. Dorling Kindersley, 1998.

Watson, Jeanie. "Coleridge and the Fairy Tale Controversy." In *Literature and the Child,* edited by James Holt McGavran. Iowa City: University of Iowa Press, 1999.

Weedon, Chris. *Feminist Practice and Poststructuralist Theory*. 2d ed. Maiden, Mass.: Blackwell, 1996.

Weeks, Linton. "Charmed, I'm Sure." *Washington Post,* October 20, 1999, Style.

———. "Sheer Sorcery." *Washington Post,* September 9, 1999, Style.

Weisman, Steven. "A Novel That Is a Midsummer Night's Dream." *New York Times,* July 11, 2000, A30.

White, E. B. *Charlotte's Web.* New York: Harper, 1952.

White, Michael. "Major to Open Thatcher Wounds." *The Guardian* (Manchester), August 11, 1999.

Whitehead, Jane. " 'This Is NOT What I Wrote!': The Americanization of British Children's Books." Part 1. *Horn Book,* November–December 1996, 687+. Expanded Academic ASAP. Hale Library, Kansas State University. <http://infotrac.galegroup.com/menu>. Accessed October 23, 2000.

———. " 'This Is NOT What I Wrote!': The Americanization of British Children's Books." Part 2. *Horn Book,* January–February 1997, 27+. Expanded Academic ASAP. Hale Library, Kansas State University. <http://infotrac.galegroup.com/menu>. Accessed October 23, 2000.

Will, George. "Harry Potter: A Wizard's Return." *Washington Post,* July 4, 2000, Op-ed.

Wilson, Jacqueline. *Double Act.* Illustrated by Nick Sharratt and Sue Heap. New York: Delacorte, 1998.

The Witches Voice Inc. *Witchvox.com. 1995–2002.* <http://www. witchvox.com/>. Accessed February 8, 2002.

Wollstonecraft, Mary. *A Vindication of the Rights of Woman.* 1792. New York: Knopf, 1992.

Woodhead, Chris. "Harry Potter: Can't Do Better." *Sunday Telegraph,* July 16, 2000, 13.

Wynne-Jones, Tim. "Harry Potter and the Blaze of Publicity." *Ottawa Citizen,* July 16, 2000, C16.

Yolen, Jane. "Aesthetics of Harry." Online posting. March 9, 2002. Child Lit Discussion List. <http://www.rci.rutgers.edu/~mjoseph/childlit/about.html>.

———. "Turtles All the Way Down." 1991. Reprinted in *Only Connect,* 3d ed., edited by Sheila Egoff et al., 164–74. Oxford, U.K.: Oxford University Press, 1996.

Zipes, Jack. "The Phenomenon of Harry Potter, or Why All the Talk?" In *Sticks and Stones: The Troublesome Success of Children's Literature from Slovenly Peter to Harry Potter,* 170–89. New York: Routledge, 2000.

———. *The Trials and Tribulations of Little Red Riding Hood: Versions of the Tale in Sociocultural Context.* South Hadley, Mass.: Bergen and Garvey, 1983.

Index